Real Functions

P W S

THE PRINDLE, WEBER AND SCHMIDT
COMPLEMENTARY SERIES IN MATHEMATICS

Under the consulting editorship of

HOWARD W. EVES

The University of Maine

TITLES IN THE SERIES

Howard W. Eves, Functions of a Complex Variable, Volume One
Howard W. Eves, Functions of a Complex Variable, Volume Two
Edward H. Barry, Introduction to Geometrical Transformations, Volume Three
Richard E. Johnson, Vector Algebra, Volume Four
Margaret F. Willerding, Mathematical Concepts, A Historical Approach, Volume Five
Lyle E. Mehlenbacher, Foundations of Modern Mathematics, Volume Six
Maurice Frechet and Ky Fan, Initiation to Combinatorial Topology, Volume Seven
Casper Goffman, Real Functions, Volume Eight
C. Stanley Ogilvy, A Calculus Notebook, Volume Nine
Howard Levi, Topics in Geometry, Volume Eleven
Paige, Willcutt, and Wagenblast, Mathematics Methods for Junior High School Teachers, Volume Twelve
John G. Hocking, Conference on the Topology of Manifolds, Volume Thirteen
Marvin Marcus and Henry Minc, A Survey of Matrix Theory and Matrix Inequalities, Volume Fourteen
Nicholas D. Kazarinoff, Ruler and the Round, Volume Fifteen

Real Functions

CASPER GOFFMAN

PRINDLE, WEBER & SCHMIDT, INCORPORATED

Boston, Massachusetts London Sydney

In memory of
Henry Blumberg

53 State Street, Boston, Massachusetts

Printed in the United States of America

SECOND PRINTING: AUGUST 1970

Preface

The material in this book has been used by the author for many years in beginning real variables courses. It can be covered in a year's course, in a class meeting three times a week.

This book is written as a textbook. Accordingly, there are many exercises. Some of them, the simpler exercises, are included to help fix certain concepts in the minds of the students. The exercises at the end of each chapter are numbered according to the section to which they refer. For example, Exercise 3 of Section 4 is numbered 4.3.

I am grateful to Professor L. W. Cohen of Queens College, Professor C. J. Pipes of Southern Methodist University, and Dr. C. V. Newsom. I am especially grateful to Professor Howard W. Eves for his considerable assistance and editorial help in the preparation of this edition.

CASPER GOFFMAN
June, 1967

Contents

1

Sets and Operations

1. *Sets*

Mathematics deals with special kinds of sets. In arithmetic we are concerned with the set of positive integers, the set of even positive integers, the set of all integers, the set of rational numbers, etc. The elements of these sets are numbers. In elementary geometry we are concerned with the set of all triangles, the set of equilateral triangles, the set of all circles, the set of all polygons, etc. The elements of these sets are figures.

In matters concerning functions of a real variable, interest is centered on certain kinds of sets of real numbers. The investigation of the properties of these sets depends upon a rigorous definition of the real numbers. This will be given in Chapter 3. Although this book will be concerned mainly with special sets, certain relations between sets which will be used consistently hold for general sets. It is the purpose of this chapter to present these relations.

2. *Subsets*

We use the notation $x \in A$ to denote that x is an element of the set A. This notation has become standard. Sometimes, instead of using the words "x is an element of A," we shall say that x is a member of A or that x belongs to A. That x does not belong to A is denoted by $x \notin A$. For example:

1. If A is the set of integers and $x = 2$, then $x \in A$.
2. If A is the set of integers and $x = 1/2$, then $x \notin A$.
3. If A is the set of isosceles triangles and x is a triangle the lengths of whose sides are 3, 4, and 5, then $x \notin A$.
4. If A is the set of right triangles and x is the triangle of example 3, then $x \in A$.

5. If A is the set of polynomials and x is the function $f(t) = t^2$, then $x \in A$.
6. If A is the set of polynomials and x is the function $f(t) = \sin t$, then $x \notin A$.

DEFINITION 1. A is said to be a *subset* of B if every member of A is a member of B.

$A \subset B$ is the notation used for "A is a subset of B."

Evidently $A \subset B$ if and only if for every $x \in A$ it is true that $x \in B$.

If $A \subset B$ and $B \subset A$, the sets A and B are identical; i.e., they are composed of the same elements.

DEFINITION 2. If $A \subset B$ and it is not true that $B \subset A$ then A is said to be a *proper subset* of B.

Evidently, A is a proper subset of B if and only if (1) for every $x \in A$ it is true that $x \in B$ and (2) there is an $x \in B$ such that $x \notin A$.

The notation $A \supset B$ is often used, as a convenience, to denote that B is a subset of A.

We give several examples of these concepts:

1. If A is the set of even positive integers and B is the set of all positive integers, then $A \subset B$, but it is not true that $B \subset A$, so that A is a proper subset of B.
2. If A is the set of even positive integers and B is the set of odd positive integers, then neither $A \subset B$ nor $B \subset A$ so that neither A nor B is a subset of the other.
3. If A is the set of positive integers and B is the set of even integers, then neither $A \subset B$ nor $B \subset A$ so that neither A nor B is a subset of the other.
4. If A is the set of equilateral triangles and B is the set of isosceles triangles, then A is a proper subset of B.

3. *The positive integers*

Since we shall use the set of positive integers consistently in this book, it is appropriate that we introduce it now.

The positive integers form a set P which is an order; i.e., there is a relation "$<$" which holds between pairs of elements of P such that

1. if $a \in P$, $b \in P$, and $a \neq b$, then either $a < b$ or $b < a$,
2. if $a < b$, then it is not true that $b < a$,
3. if $a < b$ and $b < c$, then $a < c$.

The statement "$a < b$" is read "a is less than b." If $a < b$ it is sometimes convenient to say $b > a$ and to read this as "b is greater than a."

The order P of positive integers satisfies three additional conditions:

1. For every non-empty $S \subset P$, S has a first element; i.e., there is an element $a \in S$ such that $b \geq a$ for every $b \in S$.

An immediate consequence of this condition is that P itself has a first element which we denote by "1."

Another consequence of (1) is that every element $a \in P$ has an immediate successor: i.e., there is an element $a' \in P$ such that $a' > a$ and a' is the first element greater than a.

2. If $a \in P$ and $a \neq 1$, then a has an immediate predecessor; i.e., there is an element $b \in P$ such that $a = b'$.
3. P has no last element.

We can now prove that the so-called principle of finite induction holds for the system P of positive integers.

THEOREM 1. (Principle of Finite Induction.) If $S \subset P$, $1 \in S$, and if for every $a \in S$ it follows that $a' \in S$, then $S = P$.

Proof. Let $\bar{S}$ consist of all elements in P which are not in S. Suppose that S is a proper subset of P. Then there are elements in $\bar{S}$. By condition 1, $\bar{S}$ has a first element a. Since, by hypothesis, $1 \in S$, $a \neq 1$. Hence, by condition 2, a has an immediate predecessor b. Since a is the first element in $\bar{S}$ it follows that $b \in S$. But $b' = a$. Accordingly, by hypothesis, $a = b' \in S$. The assumption that S is a proper subset of P has thus led to a contradiction, so $S = P$.

We shall use the standard notation $1' = 2$, $2' = 3$, $\cdots$ and shall write $1, 2, 3, \cdots, n, \cdots$ for the set of all positive integers.

DEFINITION 3. A set S of positive integers is called *finite* if there is a positive integer n such that $n > a$ for every $a \in S$.

S will be called infinite if it is not finite; i.e., for every positive integer n there is an $a \in S$ such that $a > n$.

4. *The union of sets*

We now define the basic operations for sets. It will be convenient to illustrate these operations by means of intervals in the "real-number continuum." The intuitive idea of real numbers as being represented by the points on a line is adequate for our present purpose. A rigorous definition of the real numbers will be given in Chapter 3 and a full treatment of the operations on intervals will be given in Chapter 4. By an open interval (a, b). where $a < b$, we mean all numbers x such that $a < x < b$; by a closed interval $[a, b]$ we mean all x such that $a \leqq x \leqq b$. The notations $[a, b)$ and $(a, b]$ designate the sets for which $a \leqq x < b$ and $a < x \leqq b$, respectively.

As a first operation on sets we consider the *union*. The union of two sets A and B is the set whose elements are all the members of A together with all the members of B. The union of A and B is denoted by $A \cup B$. For example, if

$A = [0, 2]$ and $B = [1, 3]$ then $A \cup B = [0, 3]$. It is evident that for any two sets A and B

$$A \cup B = B \cup A.$$

We may just as well define the union for any finite number of sets, or for an infinite sequence of sets, or for that matter, for an arbitrary system of sets. We shall give the definition for all three cases. The student will observe, however, that the third case includes the other two as special cases.

DEFINITION 4a. If $A_1, A_2, \cdots, A_n$ is a finite number of sets (i.e., a set A_k associated with every positive integer $k \leq n$), their union

$$A = \bigcup_{k=1}^{n} A_k = A_1 \cup A_2 \cup \cdots \cup A_n$$

is the set consisting of all elements belonging to at least one of the sets A_1, $A_2, \cdots, A_n$.

Thus

$$A = \bigcup_{k=1}^{n} A_k$$

is the set consisting of all $x \in A_k$ for some k, where $1 \leq k \leq n$.

We have already given one example of this concept. Further examples:

1. If $A = [0, 1]$ and $B = [2, 3]$ the set $A \cup B$ consists of all points in $[0, 1]$ and all points in $[2, 3]$.
2. If A_1 is the set of integers which are not multiples of 2 and A_2 is the set of integers which are not multiples of 3, then $A_1 \cup A_2$ is the set of integers which are not multiples of 6.

DEFINITION 4b. If $A_1, A_2, \cdots, A_n, \cdots$ is an infinite sequence of sets (i.e., a set A_k associated with every positive integer k), their union

$$A = \bigcup_{k=1}^{\infty} A_k$$

is the set consisting of all elements belonging to at least one of the sets A_k, $k = 1, 2, \cdots, n \cdots$.

We now give the definition of union for an arbitrary system of sets A_α, $\alpha \in \mathsf{A}$. The first case above is that for which A is a finite set of positive integers $1, 2, \cdots, n$, and the second case is that for which A is the set of all positive integers $1, 2, \cdots, n, \cdots$. In the general case, A can be any set, and there is associated with every element $\alpha \in \mathsf{A}$ a set A_α. For example, A could be the set of all real numbers.

DEFINITION 4c. If A_α, $\alpha \in \mathsf{A}$, is a system of sets, their union

$$A = \bigcup_{\alpha \in \mathsf{A}} A_\alpha$$

is the set consisting of all elements belonging to at least one A_α, where $\alpha \in \mathsf{A}$.

In order to make Definition 4c more meaningful at this time, we consider the case where A is the set of real numbers. Suppose that for every $\alpha \in \mathsf{A}$ there is a set A_α of real numbers. We may give a simple interpretation to the set

$$A = \bigcup_{\alpha \in \mathsf{A}} A_\alpha$$

as follows. Let S be any set in the cartesian plane. For each $\alpha \in \mathsf{A}$, let A_α be the set of β such that $(\alpha, \beta) \in S$. The set

$$A = \bigcup_{\alpha \in \mathsf{A}} A_\alpha$$

is the projection of S on the β-axis.

5. *The intersection of sets*

The second basic operation on sets is the *intersection*. The intersection of two sets A and B is the set consisting of all elements belonging to both A and B. The intersection of A and B is denoted by $A \cap B$. It is evident that for any two sets A and B

$$A \cap B = B \cap A.$$

We now define the intersection of an arbitrary system A_α, $\alpha \in \mathsf{A}$, of sets.

DEFINITION 5. If A_α, $\alpha \in \mathsf{A}$, is a system of sets, their intersection

$$A = \bigcap_{\alpha \in \mathsf{A}} A_\alpha$$

is the set consisting of those elements belonging to all the sets A_α, $\alpha \in \mathsf{A}$.

Thus

$$x \in A = \bigcap_{\alpha \in \mathsf{A}} A_\alpha$$

if and only if $x \in A_\alpha$ for every $\alpha \in \mathsf{A}$.

For the special case where A is the finite set of positive integers $1, 2, \cdots, n$, the definition states that the intersection

$$A = \bigcap_{k=1}^{n} A_k$$

of the sets $A_1, A_2, \cdots, A_n$ is the set consisting of all elements belonging to all the sets $A_1, A_2, \cdots, A_n$. For the case where A is the infinite sequence $1, 2, \cdots, n, \cdots$,

$$A = \bigcap_{k=1}^{\infty} A_k$$

is the set of elements belonging to all the sets $A_1, A_2, \cdots, A_n \cdots$.

Some examples of set intersections are

1. If $A_1 = [0, 2]$ and $A_2 = [1, 3]$, then $A_1 \cap A_2 = [1, 2]$.
2. If A_1 is the set of all integers which are multiples of 2 and A_2 is the set of all integers which are multiples of 3, then $A_1 \cap A_2$ is the set of all integers which are multiples of 6.
3. If $A_1 = [0, 1]$ and $A_2 = [2, 3]$, then $A_1 \cap A_2$ is the empty set; i.e., it has no members. More will be said regarding the empty set later.
4. Let S be a set of points in the cartesian plane, let A be the set of real numbers, and let A_α be the set of β such that $(\alpha, \beta) \in S$. The set $A = \bigcap_{\alpha \in \mathsf{A}} A_\alpha$ is the projection on the β-axis of that subset of S composed of lines parallel to the α-axis which belong to S. In other words, $\beta \in A$ if and only if $(\alpha, \beta) \in S$ for every α.

A third useful operation, meaningful only for pairs of sets, is the *difference.*

DEFINITION 6. For two sets A and B, the difference $C = A - B$ is the set consisting of all elements in A which are not in B.

Thus C is the set consisting of all $x \in A$ such that $x \notin B$.

While the union and intersection of two sets are commutative operations, the difference is not; indeed, $A - B = B - A$ only if $A = B$. If $A = B$, then $A - B$ and $B - A$ are the empty set, so that, of course, $A - B = B - A$. Suppose $A \neq B$. Suppose, first, that there is an $x \in A$ such that $x \notin B$. Then $x \in A - B$ and $x \notin B - A$ so that $A - B \neq B - A$. However, if every $x \in A$ is such that $x \in B$ then since $A \neq B$ there is an $x \in B$ such that $x \notin A$. But, then, $x \in B - A$ and $x \notin A - B$, so that, again, $A - B \neq B - A$.

If $B \subset A$, the difference $C = A - B$ is usually called the *complement of B relative to A.*

In nearly all the considerations of this book, all sets which arise are subsets of some given set U. In such a case, the difference $C = U - A$, $A \subset U$, is simply called the *complement* of A and is denoted by $C(A)$.

In order that every subset of U should have a complement, the *empty set* ϕ, which contains no elements, must be admitted as a subset of U. Then ϕ is the complement of U.

DEFINITION 7. A and B are *disjoint* if $A \cap B = \phi$.

Our first proposition gives a relation between all the operations which have been introduced thus far.

PROPOSITION 1. For every system A_α, $\alpha \in \mathsf{A}$, of subsets of U, we have

1. $\bigcup_{\alpha \in \mathsf{A}} A_\alpha = C(\bigcap_{\alpha \in \mathsf{A}} C(A_\alpha))$,
2. $\bigcap_{\alpha \in \mathsf{A}} A_\alpha = C(\bigcup_{\alpha \in \mathsf{A}} C(A_\alpha))$.

Proof. We prove only (1). The proof of (2) is quite similar and is left to the student.

Our method consists of showing that $\bigcup_{\alpha\in A} A_\alpha \subset C(\bigcap_{\alpha\in A} C(A_\alpha))$ and that $C(\bigcap_{\alpha\in A} C(A_\alpha)) \subset \bigcup_{\alpha\in A} A_\alpha$, so that $\bigcup_{\alpha\in A} A_\alpha = C(\bigcap_{\alpha\in A} C(A_\alpha))$.

For every $x \in \bigcup_{\alpha\in A} A_\alpha$ there is an $\alpha \in A$ such that $x \in A_\alpha$. Hence $x \notin C(A_\alpha)$ so that $x \notin \bigcap_{\alpha\in A} C(A_\alpha)$. Accordingly, $x \in C(\bigcap_{\alpha\in A} C(A_\alpha))$. We thus have shown that $\bigcup_{\alpha\in A} A_\alpha \subset C(\bigcap_{\alpha\in A} C(A_\alpha))$.

For every $x \in C(\bigcap_{\alpha\in A} C(A_\alpha))$, $x \notin \bigcap_{\alpha\in A} C(A_\alpha)$. Hence there is an $\alpha \in A$ such that $x \notin C(A_\alpha)$. But then $x \in A_\alpha$. Accordingly, $x \in \bigcup_{\alpha\in A} A_\alpha$. It follows that $C(\bigcap_{\alpha\in A} C(A_\alpha)) \subset \bigcup_{\alpha\in A} A_\alpha$.

The two inclusions show that $\bigcup_{\alpha\in A} A_\alpha = C(\bigcap_{\alpha\in A} C(A_\alpha))$.

Examples 2, §4, and 2, §5, furnish an illustration of this proposition. For let A be the set of integers which are multiples of 2, B the set of integers which are multiples of 3, and U the set of all integers. Then $C(A)$ and $C(B)$ are the sets of integers which are not multiples of 2 and of 3, respectively. Now, $A \cap B$ is the set of integers which are multiples of 6, and $C(A) \cup C(B)$, the set of integers which are not multiples of 6, so that $A \cap B = C(C(A) \cup C(B))$, which is in accordance with Proposition 1.

6. *Limits of sequences of sets*

If $A_1, A_2, \cdots, A_n, \cdots$ is any sequence of sets, the set of all elements which belong to any infinite number of sets in the sequence is called its *limit superior*, and the set of all elements which belong to all but a finite number of sets in the sequence is called its *limit inferior*. The limit inferior is always a subset of the limit superior. If the limit inferior is the same set as the limit superior, the limit of the sequence of sets is said to exist. In other words, the limit of $A_1, A_2, \cdots, A_n, \cdots$ exists if every element which belongs to an infinite number of the sets belongs to all but a finite number of them.

DEFINITION 8. If $A_1, A_2, \cdots, A_n, \cdots$ is a sequence of sets, its limit superior, $\overline{\lim}\, A_n$, is the set consisting of all elements belonging to an infinite number of the sets. Its limit inferior, $\underline{\lim}\, A_n$, consists of all elements belonging to all but a finite number of the sets.

Now if $x \in \overline{\lim}\, A_n$, then x is in an infinite number of sets in the sequence $A_1, A_2, \cdots, A_n, \cdots$. Hence $x \in \bigcup_{k=n}^{\infty} A_k$ for every positive integer n. For if there were an m such that $x \notin \bigcup_{k=m}^{\infty} A_k$, then x would belong to only a finite number of the sets in the sequence. It follows that

$$x \in \bigcap_{n=1}^{\infty} \left(\bigcup_{k=n}^{\infty} A_k \right).$$

Conversely, suppose $x \in \bigcap_{n=1}^{\infty} \left(\bigcup_{k=n}^{\infty} A_k \right)$. Then for every positive integer n, $x \in \bigcup_{k=n}^{\infty} A_k$. In other words, for every positive integer n there is an integer $m(n) \geqq n$ such that $x \in A_{m(n)}$. Accordingly, x is in an infinite number of the sets $A_1, A_2, \cdots, A_n, \cdots$ so that $x \in \overline{\lim}\, A_n$.

We have now shown that $\overline{\lim}\, A_n \subset \bigcap_{n=1}^{\infty} \left(\bigcup_{k=n}^{\infty} A_k \right)$ and that $\bigcap_{n=1}^{\infty} \left(\bigcup_{k=n}^{\infty} A_k \right) \subset \overline{\lim}\, A_n$. Hence $\overline{\lim}\, A_n = \bigcap_{n=1}^{\infty} \left(\bigcup_{k=n}^{\infty} A_k \right)$. Henceforth, we shall write $\bigcap_{n=1}^{\infty} \left(\bigcup_{k=n}^{\infty} A_k \right)$ simply as $\bigcap_{n=1}^{\infty} \bigcup_{k=n}^{\infty} A_k$.

The above remarks constitute a proof of the first part of the following proposition.

PROPOSITION 2. If $A_1, A_2, \cdots, A_n, \cdots$ is a sequence of sets, $\overline{\lim}\, A_n = \bigcap_{n=1}^{\infty} \bigcup_{k=n}^{\infty} A_k$ and $\underline{\lim}\, A_n = \bigcup_{n=1}^{\infty} \bigcap_{k=n}^{\infty} A_k$.

The proof of the second part is left for the student.

DEFINITION 9. If $A_1, A_2, \cdots, A_n, \cdots$ is a sequence of sets and $\overline{\lim}\, A_n = \underline{\lim}\, A_n$ then the limit, $\lim A_n$, of $A_1, A_2, \cdots, A_n, \cdots$ is said to exist and $\lim A_n = \overline{\lim}\, A_n = \underline{\lim}\, A_n$.

Accordingly, $\lim A_n$ exists if every element which belongs to an infinite number of sets in the sequence $A_1, A_2, \cdots, A_n, \cdots$ belongs to all but a finite number of them. Or, if one prefers, $\lim A_n$ exists if $\bigcap_{n=1}^{\infty} \bigcup_{k=n}^{\infty} A_k = \bigcup_{n=1}^{\infty} \bigcap_{k=n}^{\infty} A_k$. We leave it for the student to show that $\bigcup_{n=1}^{\infty} \bigcap_{k=n}^{\infty} A_k \subset \bigcap_{n=1}^{\infty} \bigcup_{k=n}^{\infty} A_k$ always, so that to prove that $\lim A_n$ exists one needs only to show that $\bigcap_{n=1}^{\infty} \bigcup_{k=n}^{\infty} A_k \subset \bigcup_{n=1}^{\infty} \bigcap_{k=n}^{\infty} A_k$.

Examples:

1. If $A_n = [0, n/(n+1)]$, $n = 1, 2, \cdots$, then $\bigcap_{k=n}^{\infty} A_k = [0, n/(n+1)]$ and $\bigcup_{k=n}^{\infty} A_k = [0, 1)$, where the interval $[0, 1)$ is the set of all numbers

x such that $0 \leqq x < 1$. Then $\bigcup_{n=1}^{\infty} \bigcap_{k=n}^{\infty} A_k = [0, 1)$ and $\bigcap_{n=1}^{\infty} \bigcup_{k=n}^{\infty} A_k = [0, 1)$ so that $\overline{\lim}\, A_n = \underline{\lim}\, A_n$.

We have accordingly shown that the limit of the sequence exists and is the interval $[0, 1)$.

2. If $A_n = [-1/n, (2n-1)/n]$, $n = 1, 2, \cdots$, then $\bigcap_{k=n}^{\infty} A_k = [0, (2n-1)/n]$ and $\bigcup_{k=n}^{\infty} A_k = [-1/n, 2)$. Then $\bigcup_{n=1}^{\infty} \bigcap_{k=n}^{\infty} A_k = [0, 2)$ and $\bigcap_{n=1}^{\infty} \bigcup_{k=n}^{\infty} A_k = [0, 2)$ so that $\overline{\lim}\, A_n = \underline{\lim}\, A_n$ and $\lim A_n$ exists and is the interval $[0, 2)$.
3. If $A_n = [0, 1]$ for odd values of n and $A_n = [-1, 0]$ for even values of n, then $\bigcap_{k=n}^{\infty} A_k$ consists of the single point 0 for all values of n, while $\bigcup_{k=n}^{\infty} A_k = [-1, 1]$ for all n. Hence $\overline{\lim}\, A_n = \bigcap_{n=1}^{\infty} \bigcup_{k=n}^{\infty} A_k = [-1, 1]$ and $\underline{\lim}\, A_n = \bigcup_{n=1}^{\infty} \bigcap_{k=n}^{\infty} A_k = [0]$, the set consisting of the single element 0. In this case, the limit of the sequence $A_1, A_2, \cdots, A_n, \cdots$ does not exist.

There is an important class of sequences of sets, the (monotonically) nonincreasing and (monotonically) nondecreasing sequences for which the limit exists.

DEFINITION 10. A sequence $A_1, A_2, \cdots, A_n, \cdots$ of sets is called (monotonically) nondecreasing if $A_1 \subset A_2 \subset \cdots \subset A_n \subset \cdots$, i.e., if A_n is a subset of A_{n+1} for every positive integer n. It is called (monotonically) nonincreasing if $A_1 \supset A_2 \supset \cdots \supset A_n \supset \cdots$, i.e., if A_{n+1} is a subset of A_n for every positive integer n. A sequence $\{A_n\}$ is called monotonic if it is either nondecreasing or nonincreasing. (Hereafter, the adjective *monotonically* may be deleted.)

In example (1) above, the sequence is monotonically nondecreasing. In (2), the sequence is not monotonic, which shows that there are other sequences, besides the monotonic ones, whose limits exist. Example (3) shows that there are sequences of sets whose limits do not exist.

Another example is the following:

1. If $A_n = [0, 1/n]$, $n = 1, 2, \cdots$, the sequence $A_1, A_2, \cdots, A_n, \cdots$ is nonincreasing, and $\lim A_n$ exists and consists of the single point 0.

PROPOSITION 3. If $A_1, A_2, \cdots, A_n, \cdots$ is nondecreasing, then $\lim A_n$ exists and $\lim A_n = \bigcup_{n=1}^{\infty} A_n$.

Proof. We first show that $\bigcup_{n=1}^{\infty} A_n = \underline{\lim}\, A_n$. Suppose $x \in \bigcup_{n=1}^{\infty} A_n$. Then there is an n such that $x \in A_n$. But since the sequence $A_1, A_2, \cdots, A_n, \cdots$ is nondecreasing, $x \in A_{n+1}, x \in A_{n+2}, \cdots$. Hence $x \in \bigcap_{k=n}^{\infty} A_k$ so that $x \in \bigcup_{n=1}^{\infty} \bigcap_{k=n}^{\infty} A_k$ $= \underline{\lim}\, A_n$. Therefore, $\bigcup_{n=1}^{\infty} A_n \subset \underline{\lim}\, A_n$.

Suppose $x \in \underline{\lim}\, A_n$. Then $x \in \bigcup_{n=1}^{\infty} \bigcap_{k=n}^{\infty} A_k$ and there is an n such that $x \in \bigcap_{k=n}^{\infty} A_k$. Hence $x \in A_n$, so that $x \in \bigcup_{n=1}^{\infty} A_n$. Therefore, $\underline{\lim}\, A_n \subset \bigcup_{n=1}^{\infty} A_n$. The two inclusions show that $\bigcup_{n=1}^{\infty} A_n = \underline{\lim}\, A_n$.

We now show that $\bigcup_{n=1}^{\infty} A_n = \overline{\lim}\, A_n$. Suppose $x \in \bigcup_{n=1}^{\infty} A_n$. Then there is an m such that $x \in A_m$. But, since $A_1, A_2, \cdots, A_n, \cdots$ is nondecreasing, $x \in A_{m+1}, x \in A_{m+2}, \cdots$. It follows that $x \in \bigcup_{k=n}^{\infty} A_k$ for every n. Hence $x \in \bigcap_{n=1}^{\infty} \bigcup_{k=n}^{\infty} A_k = \overline{\lim}\, A_n$. Therefore, $\bigcup_{n=1}^{\infty} A_n \subset \overline{\lim}\, A_n$.

Suppose $x \in \overline{\lim}\, A_n$. Then $x \in \bigcap_{n=1}^{\infty} \bigcup_{k=n}^{\infty} A_k$ so that $x \in \bigcup_{k=1}^{\infty} A_k$. Therefore, $\overline{\lim}\, A_n \subset \bigcup_{n=1}^{\infty} A_n$. The two inclusions show that $\bigcup_{n=1}^{\infty} A_n = \overline{\lim}\, A_n$.

We have thus shown that the limit of $A_1, A_2, \cdots, A_n, \cdots$ exists and is the set $\bigcup_{n=1}^{\infty} A_n$.

PROPOSITION 4. If $A_1, A_2, \cdots, A_n, \cdots$ is monotonically nonincreasing, then $\lim A_n$ exists and $\lim A_n = \bigcap_{n=1}^{\infty} A_n$.

The proof, which is very similar to that of Proposition 3, is left to the student.

Examples:

1. If $A_n = [1/(n+1), (n+1)/(n+2)]$, $n = 1, 2, \cdots$, then $\lim A_n = (0, 1)$.
2. If $A_n = [0, 1/n]$, $n = 1, 2, \cdots$, then $\lim A_n = [0]$, the set consisting of the single point 0.
3. If $A_n = [0, (n+1)/n]$, $n = 1, 2, \cdots$, then $\lim A_n = [0, 1]$.

7. *A connection with algebra*

A set S together with two operations for pairs of elements of S is called a *ring* if the operations satisfy certain conditions. In a ring, the operations called *sum* and *product*, and written $a + b$ and ab, are such that for every $a \in S$, $b \in S$, both $a + b$ and ab are elements of S, and satisfy the following conditions:

1. $a + (b + c) = (a + b) + c$,
2. $a + b = b + a$,
3. for every $a \in S$, $b \in S$, there is an $x \in S$ such that $a + x = b$,
4. $a(bc) = (ab)c$, and
5. $a(b + c) = ab + ac$, $(b + c)a = ba + ca$.

Examples of rings are

1. The set of integers with the usual operations of addition and multiplication.
2. The set of square matrices of order n with real elements and the usual addition and multiplication of matrices as operations.

We now return to the set of subsets of a given set U. One may ask whether this system forms a ring if the two basic operations *union* and *intersection* are taken as the sum and product operations.

Let U be the set of subsets of U. If $A \in \mathsf{U}$, $B \in \mathsf{U}$, then evidently $A \cup B$ and $A \cap B$ are both subsets of U and so belong to U. Moreover, (1) $A \cup (B \cup C) = (A \cup B) \cup C$; (2) $A \cup B = B \cup A$; (4) $A \cap (B \cap C) = (A \cap B) \cap C$; and (5) $A \cap (B \cup C) = (A \cap B) \cup (A \cap C)$, $(B \cup C) \cap A = (B \cap A) \cup (C \cap A)$. But it is not always true that (3) if $A \in \mathsf{U}$, $B \in \mathsf{U}$, then there is an $X \in \mathsf{U}$ such that $A \cup X = B$. For there is no such X if $A - B$ is not empty. Hence the set of subsets of U does not form a ring if the operations are union and intersection. If, however, the addition operation is taken to be the operation $(A \cup B) - (A \cap B)$ and the multiplication is still $A \cap B$, the system does form a ring. Notice that the addition operation results in the set of all elements which belong to A or to B but not to both A and B.

The proof that the set of subsets of U now constitutes a ring is left to the student. In addition, this ring satisfies the condition:

6. $aa = a$.

Rings which satisfy this latter condition are called *Boolean rings.*

8. *Equivalence relations*

One of the most important concepts in all of mathematics is that of *equivalence relation.* Since equivalence relations arise in a variety of places in real-variable theory, it is appropriate to discuss equivalence relations, in general, at the outset.

An equivalence relation is simply a subdivision of a given set U into disjoint subsets, i.e., into a system S_α, $\alpha \in \mathsf{A}$, of subsets of U such that every

$x \in U$ is in one and only one set S_α. Two elements $a \in U$, $b \in U$, are said to be equivalent,

$$a \sim b,$$

if and only if they belong to the same S_α.

THEOREM 2. A relation "$\sim$" is an equivalence relation for a set U if and only if for every $a \in U$, $b \in U$, $c \in U$,

1. $a \sim a$,
2. if $a \sim b$, then $b \sim a$,
3. if $a \sim b$ and $b \sim c$, then $a \sim c$.

Proof. Suppose the relation "$\sim$" is an equivalence relation. Then U is subdivided by the relation into disjoint subsets S_α, $\alpha \in \mathsf{A}$, such that every $a \in U$ is in S_α for one and only one α, and $a \sim b$ if and only if $a \in S_\alpha$, $b \in S_\alpha$, for the same $\alpha \in \mathsf{A}$. Now $a \sim a$. If $a \sim b$ then $a \in S_\alpha$, $b \in S_\alpha$, for the same α, so that $b \sim a$. If $a \sim b$ and $b \sim c$ then $a \in S_\alpha$ and $b \in S_\alpha$ for the same $\alpha \in \mathsf{A}$, while $b \in S_\alpha$ and $c \in S_\alpha$ for the same $\alpha \in \mathsf{A}$, whence a and c belong to the same S_α, so that $a \sim c$.

Conversely, a relation which satisfies (1), (2), and (3) above is an equivalence relation, but we leave the proof to the student.

We give some examples of equivalence relations.

1. Congruence modulo m is an equivalence relation. Let U be the set of integers and m a fixed integer. Then, by definition, $a \equiv b$ modulo m if and only if $a - b$ is a multiple of m. This relation is an equivalence relation. For $a \equiv a$ modulo m; if $a \equiv b$ modulo m, then $b \equiv a$ modulo m; and, if $a \equiv b$ modulo m and $b \equiv c$ modulo m, then $a \equiv c$ modulo m.
2. The extension from the system of positive integers to the system of all integers can be accomplished by defining a certain equivalence relation in the set U whose elements are the pairs of positive integers (a, b). The relation we have in mind is that

$$(a, b) \sim (c, d)$$

if and only if $a + d = b + c$. This is an equivalence relation; for conditions (1) and (2) are obviously satisfied. To show that (3) is satisfied, suppose $(a, b) \sim (c, d)$ and $(c, d) \sim (e, f)$. Then $a + d = b + c$ and $c + f = d + e$. It follows that $a + d + c + f = b + c + d + e$ so that $a + f = b + e$ and $(a, b) \sim (e, f)$. Equivalence classes of pairs of positive integers may be considered as elements. If addition, multiplication, etc., are defined appropriately for these elements, and the elements are then designated in the conventional manner, the system obtained is the system of all integers.

Exercises

1.1 (a) Give five examples of sets of numbers, at least four of which are infinite, different from those given in the text.
(b) Give five examples of other kinds of mathematical sets.

2.1 Show that if $A \subset B$ and $B \subset C$ then $A \subset C$.

2.2 If $A \subset B$ and $C \subset B$, what can be said about A in relation to C? Illustrate.

3.1 Show that every non-empty finite set of positive integers has a largest element.

3.2 Prove by the principle of finite induction that for every positive integer n,

$$1 + 2 + \cdots + n = \frac{n(n+1)}{2}.$$

3.3 Prove the binomial theorem by using the principle of finite induction.

5.1 If A is the set of all rational numbers which can be written as fractions whose denominator is 6 and B is the set of all rational numbers which can be written as fractions whose denominator is 8, what is the set $A \cup B$? $A \cap B$?

5.2 If A_α, $\alpha \in \mathsf{A}$, is a set of sets, show that $\bigcap_{\alpha \in \mathsf{A}} A_\alpha \subset \bigcup_{\alpha \in \mathsf{A}} A_\alpha$.

5.3 If $A_1, A_2, \cdots$ is a sequence of subsets of U, show that $\bigcap_{n=1}^{\infty} A_n = C(\bigcup_{n=1}^{\infty} C(A_n))$, where complementation is relative to U.

5.4 If $\mathsf{B} \subset \mathsf{A}$ and A_α is given for every $\alpha \in \mathsf{A}$, show that $\bigcup_{\alpha \in \mathsf{B}} A_\alpha \subset \bigcup_{\alpha \in \mathsf{A}} A_\alpha$ and $\bigcap_{\alpha \in \mathsf{A}} A_\alpha \subset \bigcap_{\alpha \in \mathsf{B}} A_\alpha$.

5.5 If $A_\alpha \subset B_\alpha$ for every $\alpha \in \mathsf{A}$ show that $\bigcup_{\alpha \in \mathsf{A}} A_\alpha \subset \bigcup_{\alpha \in \mathsf{A}} B_\alpha$ and $\bigcap_{\alpha \in \mathsf{A}} A_\alpha \subset \bigcap_{\alpha \in \mathsf{A}} B_\alpha$.

5.6 If A and B are subsets of U, express $A - B$ in terms of their union, intersection, and complements relative to U.

5.7 Show that if A is the complement of B relative to U then B is the complement of A relative to U.

5.8 Show that A and B are disjoint if and only if $A - B = A$ and $B - A = B$.

6.1 If $A_1, A_2, \cdots$ is a sequence of sets, $B_n = \bigcup_{k=n}^{\infty} A_k$ and $C_n = \bigcap_{k=n}^{\infty} A_k$, show that $B_1, B_2, \cdots$ is nonincreasing and $C_1, C_2, \cdots$ is nondecreasing

6.2 Show that $\bigcup_{n=1}^{\infty} A_n = \bigcup_{n=1}^{\infty} B_n$ and $\bigcap_{n=1}^{\infty} A_n = \bigcap_{n=1}^{\infty} C_n$, where the B_n and C_n are defined as in Exercise 6.1.

6.3 If for every positive integer n, A_n is the set of real numbers greater than n, find $\lim A_n$.

6.4 Show, for a sequence of disjoint sets, that the limit exists and is empty.
6.5 Show that if $A_1, A_2, \cdots$ is a nonincreasing sequence of sets, then $\overline{\lim}\, A_n = \underline{\lim}\, A_n = \lim A_n$.
6.6 Prove the second part of Proposition 2.
6.7 Show that if $A_1, A_2, \cdots$ is any sequence of sets then $\underline{\lim}\, A_n \subset \overline{\lim}\, A_n$.
7.1 Show that if $A - B$ is not empty there is no set X such that $A \cup X = B$.
7.2 If for the set of all subsets of a given set U the operations of addition and multiplication of sets A and B are taken to be $(A \cup B) - (A \cap B)$ and $A \cap B$, respectively, show that the system obtained is a Boolean ring.
7.3 Consider all sets which are unions of finite numbers of open intervals, together with the empty set. Is this system a ring? Take operations as in Exercise 7.2.
7.4 Consider all finite sets together with the empty set. Is this system a ring? Take operations as in Exercise 7.2; as union and intersection.
8.1 Show that a relation which satisfies conditions (1), (2), and (3) of Theorem 2 is an equivalence relation.
8.2 Which of the following relations are equivalence relations?

(a) The set is *all triangles in the plane* and the relation is *congruence*.
(b) The set is *all triangles in the plane* and the relation is *similarity*.
(c) The set is *all positive integers* and the relation is *being relatively prime*.
(d) The set is *all lines in the plane* and the relation is *parallelism*.
(e) The set is *all lines in the plane* and the relation is *perpendicularity*.

8.3 Give three further equivalence relations, and two relations which are not equivalence relations.
8.4 If we have the equivalence relation

$$(a, b) \sim (c, d) \quad \text{if} \quad a + d = b + c$$

for pairs of positive integers, show that if addition for pairs is defined by

$$(a, b) + (c, d) = (a + c, b + d),$$

then $(a, b) \sim (a', b')$ and $(c, d) \sim (c', d')$ implies $(a, b) + (c, d) \sim (a', b') + (c', d')$ so that we have, in effect, defined addition between equivalence classes.
8.5 Define multiplication between the equivalence classes of Exercise 8.4 so that the definition is appropriate for the interpretation of equivalence classes of pairs of positive integers as integers.
8.6 Show that the system given by Exercises 8.4 and 8.5 is a ring, the elements being equivalence classes of pairs of positive integers.

References

BIRKHOFF and S. MACLANE, *A Survey of Modern Algebra*, New York, 1941.
H. HAHN, *Reelle Funktionen*, New York, 1948, Chap. 1.
P. R. HALMOS, *Measure Theory*, New York, 1950, Chap. 1.
F. HAUSDORFF, *Mengenlehre*, New York, 1944, Chap. 1.
E. LANDAU, *Grundlagen der Analysis*, New York, 1946.
N. H. MCCOY, *Rings and Ideals*, New York, 1948, Chap. 1.

2

Equivalence of Sets. Cardinal Numbers

1. *Equivalence between sets*

Two sets are called *equivalent* if their elements may be put into one-to-one correspondence with each other. Thus the set of fingers and the set of toes of a normal human are equivalent sets.

The concept of equivalence for sets is formulated in terms of mappings, which we discuss in some detail. A set A is mapped *into* a set B by a *mapping* f if there is associated with each $a \in A$ a single element $f(a)$ in B. Such a mapping f has the property:

1. If $a \in A$, there is one and only one $b = f(a) \in B$.
   For example, the set A of all integers is mapped into the set B of non-negative integers by the mapping $f(n) = n^2$. A set A is mapped *onto* a set B if A is mapped *into* B by a mapping f such that each $b \in B$ is the associate of some $a \in A$. Such a mapping has property (1) and also property
2. If $b \in B$, there is an $a \in A$ such that $f(a) = b$.
   In the above example, A is mapped onto the set C of all squares of nonnegative integers. A set A is in one-to-one correspondence with a set B if A is mapped onto B by a mapping f such that each $b \in B$ is the associate of a single $a \in A$. Such a mapping has properties (1), (2), and property
3. If $a_1, a_2 \in A$ and $a_1 \neq a_2$, then $b_1 = f(a_1)$, $b_2 = f(a_2) \in B$, and $b_1 \neq b_2$.

We remark that if A is in one-to-one correspondence with B, then B is in one-to-one correspondence with A. Let $f(a) = b$ be a mapping of A onto B with properties (1), (2), (3). We define the (inverse) mapping f^{-1} by

$f^{-1}(b) = a$ whenever $f(a) = b$. Then property (1) for f^{-1} follows from properties (2), (3), for f, and properties (2), (3), for f^{-1}, follow from property (1) for f.

DEFINITION 1. If A is in one-to-one correspondence with B, we shall write $A \sim B$ and say that A is equivalent to B.

In order to avoid possible misunderstanding, we mention that it is only necessary to obtain one example of a mapping of A onto B with properties (1), (2), (3), in order to establish the equivalence of A and B. An example of a mapping which lacks one or more of these properties does not show that A and B are not equivalent. In order to have a proof that A and B are not equivalent, we must show that no mapping of A into B has properties (1), (2), (3). This point will be illustrated, but first we should like to show that the equivalence concept of Definition 1 has the general properties of an equivalence relation as given by Theorem 2, Chapter 1.

THEOREM 1. If A is any class whose members are sets $A, B, \cdots$, the relation "$\sim$" is an equivalence relation for the sets in A.

Proof. If $A \in \mathsf{A}$, the mapping $a = f(a)$ of A into itself has properties (1), (2), (3), so that $A \sim A$. If A, $B \in \mathsf{A}$ and the mapping f of A into B has properties (1), (2), (3), then by the above remark, the mapping f^{-1} of B into A also has properties (1), (2), (3), so that $A \sim B$ implies $B \sim A$. If $A, B, C \in \mathsf{A}$, and the mappings f and g of A into B and B into C, respectively, have properties (1), (2), (3), then the mapping h, where $h(a) = g(f(a))$, of A into C also has properties (1), (2), (3). Hence $A \sim B$ and $B \sim C$ imply $A \sim C$. Accordingly, the relation "$\sim$" is by Theorem 2, Chapter 1, an equivalence relation and it decomposes A into disjoint classes of sets.

2. *Examples of equivalent sets*

The nontrivial nature of the above ideas is indicated by the following examples.

1. Let A be the set of even positive integers and B the set of all positive integers. The mapping $y = x$ of A into B does not have property (2), for the number 1 in B has not been given a mate by this particular mapping. However, this does not prove that A and B are not equivalent. Indeed, consider the mapping $y = x/2$ of A into B. This mapping has properties (1), (2), (3), as the student may readily verify. In accordance with our previous remarks, it follows that A and B are equivalent.

   Incidentally, we have here an example of a set which is equivalent to one of its proper subsets. A set S is *finite* if it is either empty or is equivalent to a finite set of positive integers; otherwise it is *infinite*. We shall show later that every infinite set is equivalent to one of its proper subsets. We leave it as an exercise for the student to show that no finite set has this property.

2. Let A be the set of positive integers and B the set of all integers. The mapping $y = [x/2](-1)^x$, where $[x/2]$ denotes the largest integer not greater than $x/2$, establishes a one-to-one correspondence between A and B. Hence the set of positive integers and the set of all integers are equivalent sets.
3. Let A be the set of real numbers in the closed interval $[a_1, a_2]$ and B the set of real numbers in the closed interval $[b_1, b_2]$. The mapping

$$y = \frac{b_2 - b_1}{a_2 - a_1} x - a_1 \frac{b_2 - b_1}{a_2 - a_1} + b_1$$

establishes a one-to-one correspondence between A and B.
4. The same mapping function as in (3) establishes a one-to-one correspondence between the open intervals (a_1, a_2) and (b_1, b_2).

Thus all closed intervals belong to the same equivalence class and all open intervals belong to the same equivalence class. We ask now whether these equivalence classes are the same class.

5. Let A be the open interval (a_1, a_2) and B the closed interval $[b_1, b_2]$. Since A contains a closed subinterval, say $[a_1 + \frac{1}{4}(a_2 - a_1),\ a_2 - \frac{1}{4}(a_2 - a_1)]$, and B contains an open subinterval, say (b_1, b_2), it follows from examples (3) and (4) that A is equivalent to a subset of B and B is equivalent to a subset of A. It is not an immediate consequence of these observations that A is equivalent to B. However, it would follow that A is equivalent to B if we knew in general that whenever each of two sets is equivalent to a subset of the other then the two sets are equivalent. This is a valid result which is known as Bernstein's Theorem.

The brunt of the proof of Bernstein's Theorem, which is quite subtle, is absorbed by the following lemma.

LEMMA 1. If A is a set, A_1 a subset of A, and A_2 a subset of A_1, and if $A \sim A_2$, then $A \sim A_1$.

Proof. Since $A \sim A_2$ there is a one-to-one correspondence between A and A_2. This correspondence establishes a one-to-one correspondence between the subset A_1 of A and a subset A_3 of A_2, which in turn establishes a one-to-one correspondence between the subset A_2 of A_1 and a subset A_4 of A_3, and so on. We obtain in this way by finite induction a monotonically nonincreasing sequence of sets

$$A \supset A_1 \supset A_2 \supset \cdots \supset A_n \supset \cdots$$

such that

$$A \sim A_2 \sim \cdots \sim A_{2n} \sim \cdots$$

and

$$A_1 \sim A_3 \sim \cdots \sim A_{2n+1} \sim \cdots .$$

Moreover,

$$A = (A - A_1) \cup (A_1 - A_2) \cup \cdots \cup (A_{n-1} - A_n) \cup \cdots \\ \cup (A \cap A_1 \cap A_2 \cap \cdots),$$

and

$$A_1 = (A_1 - A_2) \cup (A_2 - A_3) \cup \cdots \cup (A_{n-1} - A_n) \cup \cdots \\ \cup (A_1 \cap A_2 \cap \cdots).$$

For if $x \in A$ and $x \notin (A - A_1)$, $x \notin (A_1 - A_2)$, $\cdots$, then $x \in A_1$, $x \in A_2$, $\cdots$, so that $x \in A \cap A_1 \cap A_2 \cap \cdots$; and if $x \in A_1$ and $x \notin (A_1 - A_2)$, $x \notin (A_2 - A_3)$, $\cdots$, then $x \in A_2$, $x \in A_3$, $\cdots$, so that $x \in A_1 \cap A_2 \cap \cdots$.

Now the one-to-one correspondence between A and A_2 which establishes a one-to-one correspondence between A_1 and A_3 also establishes a one-to-one correspondence between $A - A_1$ and $A_2 - A_3$. Hence $(A - A_1) \sim (A_2 - A_3)$. Similarly $(A_2 - A_3) \sim (A_4 - A_5)$, $(A_4 - A_5) \sim (A_6 - A_7)$, $\cdots$. Also, obviously $(A_1 - A_2) \sim (A_1 - A_2)$, $(A_3 - A_4) \sim (A_3 - A_4)$, $\cdots$, and $A \cap A_1 \cap \cdots \cap A_n \cap \cdots \sim A_1 \cap A_2 \cap \cdots \cap A_n \cap \cdots$.

The one-to-one correspondences between the disjoint subsets of A of the above decomposition and the corresponding disjoint subsets of A_1 determine a one-to-one correspondence between A and A_1. Hence $A \sim A_1$.

THEOREM 2. (Bernstein's Theorem). If $A \sim B_1$, $B_1 \subset B$, and $B \sim A_1$, $A_1 \subset A$, then $A \sim B$.

Proof. Since $A \sim B_1$ there is a one-to-one correspondence between A and B_1. This establishes a one-to-one correspondence between the subset $A_1 \subset A$ and a subset $B_2 \subset B_1$. Now, since $B \sim A_1$ and $B_2 \sim A_1$, it follows that $B \sim B_2$. But $B \supset B_1 \supset B_2$ so that, by Lemma 1, $B \sim B_1$. But $A \sim B_1$. Therefore $A \sim B$.

Bernstein's Theorem may now be used to complete the proof that open intervals and closed intervals are equivalent.

We shall find numerous other applications of this theorem.

3. *Denumerable sets*

The above considerations make it possible to distinguish between denumerable and nondenumerable infinite sets.

DEFINITION 2. A set S is *denumerable* if it is equivalent to the set of all positive integers.

An infinite set S which is not denumerable will be called *nondenumerable*.

Thus far, we have not shown the existence of nondenumerable sets; this will be done later in the chapter.

A denumerable set S, in view of its one-to-one correspondence with the positive integers, can be arranged as a sequence $a_1, a_2, \cdots, a_n, \cdots$, where a_n is the mate of the positive integer n as given by the correspondence.

PROPOSITION 1. The union of two denumerable sets is a denumerable set.

Proof. We first prove the theorem for disjoint sets. Let A and B be disjoint denumerable sets. We have shown that the set of even positive integers is denumerable. It is similarly true that the set of odd positive integers is denumerable. There exist, accordingly, one-to-one correspondences between A and the set of even positive integers and between B and the set of odd positive integers. If the element of A, mated with the even integer $2n$, is labeled a_{2n}, and the element of B, mated with the odd integer $2n - 1$, is labeled a_{2n-1}, the set $A \cup B$ has as its elements $a_1, a_2, \cdots, a_n, \cdots$. This establishes a one-to-one correspondence between $A \cup B$ and the set of positive integers. Hence $A \cup B$ is denumerable.

The case where A and B are not disjoint follows by Bernstein's Theorem.

COROLLARY 1. The union of a denumerable set and a finite set is a denumerable set.

The proof is left to the student.

The following stronger proposition holds.

PROPOSITION 2. If each set of a denumerable set of sets is denumerable, their union is a denumerable set.

Proof. We again prove the theorem for disjoint sets. The case for which sets are not disjoint then follows by Bernstein's Theorem. The set of sets may be set up in one-to-one correspondence with the positive integers; then the sets are labeled $A_1, A_2, \cdots, A_n, \cdots$. For every n, the set A_n may be set up in one-to-one correspondence with the positive integers so that its elements are labeled $a_{n1}, a_{n2}, \cdots, a_{nm}, \cdots$. To prove the theorem we have only to establish a one-to-one correspondence between the double sequence of elements a_{nm}, $n, m = 1, 2, \cdots$, and the positive integers.

This may be done in the following way: for every pair n, m, the number of distinct pairs of positive integers k, l for which $k + l < n + m$ is given by

$$s = \tfrac{1}{2}(m + n - 2)(m + n - 1),$$

and the number of distinct pairs of positive integers k, l for which $k + l = n + m$ and $k \leqq n$ is n. The mapping

$$u = \tfrac{1}{2}(m + n - 2)(m + n - 1) + n$$

accordingly establishes a one-to-one correspondence between the elements a_{nm}, $n, m = 1, 2, \cdots$, and the positive integers u.

We now prove two propositions of a different sort pertaining to denumerable sets.

PROPOSITION 3. Every infinite set S has a denumerable subset.

Proof. Let $a_1 \in S$. Suppose we have, for any positive integer n, distinct elements $a_1, a_2, \cdots, a_n$ in S. Since S is infinite there is an element $a_{n+1} \in S$ distinct from all the elements $a_1, a_2, \cdots, a_n$. By the principle of finite induction, S has a subset $\{a_1, a_2, \cdots, a_n, \cdots\}$ in one-to-one correspondence with the set of positive integers. Accordingly, S has a denumerable subset.

PROPOSITION 4. Every infinite set is equivalent to one of its proper subsets.

Proof. First, every denumerable set $D = \{a_1, a_2, \cdots\}$ is equivalent to a proper subset. For the set $E = \{a_2, a_3, \cdots\}$ is a proper subset of D. The function $a_{n+1} = f(a_n)$ establishes a one-to-one correspondence between D and E.

Now let A be any infinite set. Then, by Proposition 3, A has a denumerable subset. Let $A = C \cup \{a_1, a_2, \cdots\}$, where C and $\{a_1, a_2, \cdots\}$ are disjoint sets and where C could possibly be empty. Then $B = C \cup \{a_2, a_3, \cdots\}$ is a proper subset of A. But A and B are evidently equivalent.

4. *Nondenumerable sets*

Not all infinite sets are denumerable. For example, the set of real numbers in the closed interval $I = [0, 1]$ is nondenumerable. A full development of the real-number system will be given in Chapter 3. We take the liberty at this time to borrow a property of the real numbers. It is the following property:

If $I_1 \supset I_2 \supset \cdots \supset I_n \supset \cdots$ is a monotonically nonincreasing sequence of closed intervals then the set $\bigcap_{n=1}^{\infty} I_n$ is a nonempty set.

We now show that the closed interval $[0, 1]$ of real numbers is nondenumerable. Let there be a mapping of the positive integers into $[0, 1]$. Label the mates of the positive integers $1, 2, \cdots, n, \cdots$ by this mapping as $a_1, a_2, \cdots, a_n, \cdots$. We shall show that there is a point in $[0, 1]$ which has not been labeled so that the mapping does not have property (2).

Let $I_1 \subset I$ be a closed interval such that $a_1 \notin I_1$. This is possible since a_1 is just a single point. Then let $I_2 \subset I_1$ be a closed interval such that $a_2 \notin I_2$. If we have closed intervals $I_1 \supset I_2 \supset \cdots \supset I_n$ such that $a_1 \notin I_1, a_2 \notin I_2, \cdots, a_n \notin I_n$, then there is a closed interval $I_{n+1} \subset I_n$ such that $a_{n+1} \notin I_{n+1}$. By finite induction we have a nonincreasing sequence of closed intervals

$$I_1 \supset I_2 \supset \cdots \supset I_n \supset \cdots$$

such that $a_1 \notin I_1, a_2 \notin I_2, \cdots, a_n \notin I_n, \cdots$. Since $\bigcap_{n=1}^{\infty} I_n$ is nonempty, there is an $a \in \bigcap_{n=1}^{\infty} I_n$. Now $a \in I$. But $a \neq a_n$, for every positive integer n, since

$a \in I_n$ but $a_n \notin I_n$. Hence our mapping does not have property (2) and, since it was arbitrary, the set of positive integers and the closed interval [0, 1] are not equivalent, so that [0, 1] is nondenumerable.

5. *Cardinal number*

Of course, two finite sets which are equivalent have the "same number of elements," and conversely, if they have the same number of elements there is a one-to-one correspondence between them.

This leads us to give the following definition pertaining to cardinal number for arbitrary sets.

DEFINITION 3. Two sets have the same cardinal number if and only if they are equivalent.

The denumerable sets all have the same cardinal number, that of the set of positive integers. The symbol $\aleph_0$ (aleph zero, aleph being the first letter of the Hebrew alphabet) designates this cardinal number.

We have already shown that the set of all integers has cardinal number $\aleph_0$. The rational numbers form a set of cardinal number $\aleph_0$ also. The proof of this, which follows from Proposition 2, is left to the student.

The closed interval [0, 1] of real numbers does not have cardinal $\aleph_0$. The letter c is often used to designate this cardinal number. Since, as we have shown, all intervals, open or closed, are equivalent, it follows that every interval has cardinal number c.

It is desirable to order the cardinal numbers according to "size." The following remarks are pertinent in this connection.

For any two sets A and B, there are four possibilities:

1. A is equivalent to a subset of B and B is equivalent to a subset of A,
2. A is equivalent to a subset of B but B is not equivalent to any subset of A,
3. B is equivalent to a subset of A but A is not equivalent to any subset of B,
4. A is not equivalent to any subset of B and B is not equivalent to any subset of A.

Case (4) can never arise. We shall assume this without proof for the present. The proof is a rather delicate matter which depends on the theory of ordinal numbers. It will be given in Chapter 10.

PROPOSITION 5. If $A' \sim A$ and $B' \sim B$, the same relation [(1), (2), or (3)] holds between A' and B' as between A and B.

The proof is left to the student.

If (1) holds for two sets A and B then, by Bernstein's Theorem, $A \sim B$.

Now, if a is the cardinal number of A and b is the cardinal number of B, we may, in view of Proposition 5, say without fear of confusion:

$a = b$, if (1) holds,
$a < b$, if (2) holds,
$a > b$, if (3) holds.

This orders the cardinal numbers. As a consequence of Proposition 3, the cardinal number $\aleph_0$ is the smallest infinite cardinal number. For suppose A has cardinal number $\aleph_0$ and B is any infinite set. By Proposition 3, B has a denumerable subset so that A is equivalent to a subset of B. Hence the sets A and B satisfy either condition (1) or (2). Accordingly, if b is the cardinal number of B then $\aleph_0 \leqq b$.

6. *Arithmetic of cardinal numbers*

The usual operations between finite cardinal numbers may be defined for arbitrary cardinal numbers. In these definitions, the cue is taken from the finite case. The problem is to find that characterization of the operation in the finite case which does not depend on "finiteness" but is meaningful in the general case.

DEFINITION 4a. If a and b are any cardinal numbers, the sum, $a + b$, is the cardinal number of $A \cup B$, where A and B are any two disjoint sets whose cardinal numbers are, respectively, a and b.

One must show, in order for the definition to have meaning, that the sum $a + b$ does not depend upon the choice of the sets A and B. To show this let A and A' be any two sets whose cardinal number is a, and B and B' be any two sets whose cardinal number is b, such that A and B are disjoint and A' and B' are disjoint. Then since $A \sim A'$ and $B \sim B'$, it follows that $A \cup B \sim A' \cup B'$ so that they have the same cardinal number.

More generally, the sum may be defined for any set of cardinal numbers.

DEFINITION 4b. The sum of a set of cardinal numbers a_α, $\alpha \in \mathsf{A}$, is the cardinal number of a set $\bigcup_{\alpha \in \mathsf{A}} A_\alpha$, where the sets A_α are any mutually disjoint sets (i.e., if $\alpha \neq \beta$, then $A_\alpha \cap A_\beta = \phi$) such that, for every $\alpha \in \mathsf{A}$, the cardinal number of the set A_α is a_α.

Some of the properties of finite cardinal numbers are not valid for infinite cardinal numbers. A first example pertains to the sum of cardinal numbers. For every finite cardinal number a (a different from the cardinal number of the empty set) we have $a + a \neq a$. But, for every infinite cardinal number a, we have $a + a = a$.

We shall prove this for the two infinite cardinal numbers we have met, $\aleph_0$ and c.

1. $\aleph_0 + \aleph_0 = \aleph_0$.

For let A be the set of even positive integers, B the set of odd positive integers, and C the set of all positive integers. Since all of these sets are of cardinal number $\aleph_0$ it follows, by Definition 4a, that $\aleph_0 + \aleph_0 = \aleph_0$.

2. $c + c = c$.

For c is the cardinal of any interval, open, closed, or closed on one end. The sets $(1/2, 1]$, $[0, 1/2]$, and $[0, 1]$ are all of cardinal number c. But $(1/2, 1] \cup [0, 1/2] = [0, 1]$.

We now give another property of the cardinal number c.

3. $c + c + \cdots + c + \cdots = c$.

For the sets $(1/2, 1]$, $(1/3, 1/2]$, $\cdots$ and $(0, 1]$ all have cardinal number c.

A consequence of (3) is that the set of all real numbers has cardinal number c. To show this consider the intervals

$$[0, 1), [1, 2), [-1, 0), [2, 3), [-2, -1), \cdots.$$

Each of these sets has cardinal number c and their union is the set of all real numbers. It follows from this that the set of real numbers has cardinal number c.

DEFINITION 5. The product ab of two cardinal numbers a and b is the cardinal number of the set of all pairs (x, y), $x \in A$, $y \in B$, where A is a set whose cardinal number is a and B is a set whose cardinal number is b.

Again, this definition is independent of the choice of sets A and B whose cardinal numbers are a and b respectively. For if A' and B' are two such sets then $A \sim A'$ and $B \sim B'$, so that there are mappings $x' = f(x)$ and $y' = g(y)$ of A into A' and B into B', respectively, with properties (1), (2), (3). It is clear that $(x', y') = (f(x), g(y))$ is a mapping of the set of all pairs (x, y) into the set of all pairs (x', y') with properties (1), (2), (3), so that the two sets of pairs have the same cardinal number.

The product may also be defined for any set of cardinal numbers. We leave this definition for the student to make.

As with the sum operation, multiplication of infinite cardinal numbers is different from that of finite cardinal numbers. For example:

1. $\aleph_0 \cdot \aleph_0 = \aleph_0$.

Let A and B each be the set of positive integers. The set of all pairs (m, n) of positive integers has cardinal number $\aleph_0 \cdot \aleph_0$. But this set is mapped onto the set of positive integers by

$$u = \tfrac{1}{2}(m + n - 2)(m + n - 1) + n,$$

as was shown in the proof of Proposition 2. Hence its cardinal number is $\aleph_0$, so that $\aleph_0 \cdot \aleph_0 = \aleph_0$.

2. $c \cdot c = c$.

Let A and B each be the set of real numbers in the half-open interval

(0, 1]. Then the cardinal number of the set of points in the square $0 < x \leqq 1$, $0 < y \leqq 1$ is $c \cdot c$. We will show that there is a one-to-one correspondence between this square and a subset of the interval (0, 1]. Write every (x, y) as a pair of nonterminating decimals $(.a_1a_2 \cdots a_n \cdots, .b_1b_2 \cdots b_n \cdots)$. This may be done in one and only one way. Mate with this point the number $.a_1b_1\, a_2b_2 \cdots a_nb_n \cdots$. This is the desired mapping. The proof that this mapping establishes a one-to-one correspondence between the square and a subset of the interval (0, 1] is left to the student. Bernstein's Theorem may then be invoked to complete the proof that $c \cdot c = c$.

DEFINITION 6. If a and b are two cardinal numbers, a^b is the cardinal number of all functions on B with values in A, where A and B have cardinal numbers a and b, respectively.

For example, consider 2^3. Here A is a set of cardinal number 2 and B a set of cardinal number 3. Let $B = \{a, b, c\}$ and $A = \{0, 1\}$. The set of functions on B with values in A has the following members: $\{0, 0, 0\}$, $\{0, 0, 1\}$, $\{0, 1, 0\}$, $\{1, 0, 0\}$, $\{0, 1, 1\}$, $\{1, 0, 1\}$, $\{1, 1, 0\}$, $\{1, 1, 1\}$. Hence $2^3 = 8$.

7. *The set* 2^A

We associate with every set A the set 2^A of all functions on A with values 0 or 1. If a is the cardinal number of A, then, by Definition 6, the cardinal number of 2^A is 2^a.

A one-to-one correspondence between the set 2^A and the set of subsets of A, including the empty set ϕ, is obtained by mating with each function on A with values 0 or 1 the subset of A on which the function is 1. This remark is helpful in proving the following theorem. Indeed, we shall also refer to the set of subsets of A as 2^A.

THEOREM 3. For every cardinal number a, $2^a > a$.

Proof. Let A be a set whose cardinal number is a. Let there be a mapping $A_\alpha = f(\alpha)$ of A into a class of subsets A_α of A. We show that this is not a one-to-one correspondence between A and the class 2^A of all subsets of A. For we show that there is a subset B of A such that $B \neq A_\alpha$ for every $\alpha \in A$. For every $\alpha \in A$ we decide whether $\alpha \in B$ as follows: if $\alpha \in A_\alpha$, then $\alpha \notin B$, and if $\alpha \notin A_\alpha$, then $\alpha \in B$. This set B has the asserted property since for every $\alpha \in A$, $A_\alpha \neq B$, since α is in exactly one of the sets A_α and B. It follows that there is no one-to-one correspondence between A and 2^A.

It is easy, however, to establish a one-to-one correspondence between A and a subset of 2^A. Such a correspondence is given by the mapping which associates with every $\alpha \in A$ the function which is 1 at α and 0 everywhere else.

Therefore, $2^a > a$.

In particular, $2^{\aleph_0} > \aleph_0$. We show that $2^{\aleph_0} = c$, the cardinal number of the interval [0, 1]. In order to show this we use the binary expansions of the numbers in [0, 1]. Every $x \in [0, 1]$ may be expressed in the form

$$\sum_{n=1}^{\infty} \frac{a_n}{2^n}$$

where $a_n = 0$ or 1 for every n. The number may accordingly be represented by the expression $.a_1a_2 \cdots a_n \cdots$, which is called its *binary expansion*. The set of binary expansions is in obvious one-to-one correspondence with the set of all functions on the positive integers with values 0 or 1. Hence the set of binary expansions is of cardinal number $2^{\aleph_0}$. But every number in [0, 1] has either one or two binary expansions. For those numbers which have two binary expansions, one of them is terminating. It is easy to show that the terminating expansions are $\aleph_0$ in number. All of this means that $c + \aleph_0 = 2^{\aleph_0}$. But, since $c + c = c$, by Bernstein's Theorem, $c + \aleph_0 = c$. We have thus shown that $c = 2^{\aleph_0}$.

Since $2^{\aleph_0} > \aleph_0$, we have a second proof that $c > \aleph_0$.

Exercises

1.1 Prove that a finite set is not equivalent to any of its proper subsets.

2.1 Show that the set of points interior to any ellipse and the set of points interior to any circle are equivalent.

2.2 Show that if the sets A_α, $\alpha \in \mathsf{A}$, are disjoint and the sets B_α, $\alpha \in \mathsf{A}$, are disjoint and if $A_\alpha \sim B_\alpha$ for every $\alpha \in \mathsf{A}$, then

$$\bigcup_{\alpha \in \mathsf{A}} A_\alpha \sim \bigcup_{\alpha \in \mathsf{A}} B_\alpha.$$

2.3 Prove, without using Bernstein's Theorem, that an open interval and a closed interval are equivalent.

2.4 Prove, without using Bernstein's Theorem, that the interior of a circle is equivalent to the union of the interior and the boundary.

2.5 Give a proof that the set of all real numbers and an open interval are equivalent by establishing a one-to-one correspondence between the two sets.

2.6 If $y = f(x) = [x/2](-1)^x$ on the positive integers, what is $f^{-1}(y)$?

3.1 Complete the proof of Proposition 1.

3.2 Prove, without using Bernstein's Theorem, that the union of a finite set and a denumerable set is denumerable.

3.3 Give details of the proof that the diophantine equation

$$k = \tfrac{1}{2}(m + n - 2)(m + n - 1) + n$$

has a unique solution in positive integers m and n for every positive integer k.

3.4 Generalize Exercise 3.3.
3.5 Show that the set of all algebraic numbers is denumerable.
3.6 Show that the union of a finite or denumerable number of denumerable sets is denumerable whether the sets are disjoint or not.
3.7 Show that every infinite set can be decomposed into a denumerable number of disjoint sets each of which is infinite.
4.1 Show that the set of irrational numbers is nondenumerable.
5.1 Prove Proposition 5.
6.1 Show that $c + \aleph_0 = c$, without using Bernstein's Theorem.
6.2 Complete the proof started in the text that $c \cdot c = c$.
6.3 For any cardinal numbers a, b, and c, show that $a^b a^c = a^{b+c}$.
6.4 Show that $(a^b)^c = a^{bc}$.
6.5 Generalize the definition of product of cardinal numbers to an arbitrary set a_α, $\alpha \in \mathsf{A}$, of cardinal numbers.
6.6 Show that the definition of *power* is a special case of the one for *product* given in Exercise 6.4.
6.7 Using the definition of Exercise 6.4, find

$$\aleph_0! = 1 \cdot 2 \cdot 3 \cdots n \cdots .$$

6.8 Given cardinal numbers $b_\alpha < a_\alpha$, $\alpha \in \mathsf{A}$, show that

$$\sum_{\alpha \in \mathsf{A}} b_\alpha < \prod_{\alpha \in \mathsf{A}} a_\alpha .$$

This is known as König's Theorem.

7.1 Show that $c^{\aleph_0} = c$.

7.2 Show that the terminating binary expansions are $\aleph_0$ in number.

References

H. Hahn, *Reelle Funktionen*, New York, 1948, Chap. 2.
F. Hausdorff, *Mengenlehre*, New York, 1944, Chap. 2.
E. W. Hobson, *The Theory of Functions of a Real Variable*, Cambridge, 1927, Chap. 4.
E. Kamke, *Theory of Sets*, translated by F. Bagemihl, New York, 1950.
W. Sierpinski, *Leçons sur les nombres transfinis*, Paris, 1928.

3

The Real Numbers

1. *The rational numbers*

New number systems are introduced in mathematics mainly in order to remedy certain defects in existing systems.

For example, a defect in the system of positive integers is that subtraction is sometimes impossible; the removal of this defect yields the system of all integers.

On the other hand, the system of all integers is defective when one wishes to divide, and the removal of this defect leads to the rational numbers.

We shall assume that the rational number system R is given at the start. We list some properties of R:

(a) *R is a field.* That is, R is a set such that for every $a \in R$, $b \in R$, there are two unique elements $a + b$ and ab in R, called respectively the *sum* and *product* of a and b, such that

1. $a + (b + c) = (a + b) + c$,
2. $a + b = b + a$,
3. for every a and b in R there is an $x \in R$ such that $a + x = b$,
4. $a(bc) = (ab)c$,
5. $a(b + c) = ab + ac$, $(b + c)a = ba + ca$.

These, as we have noted in Chapter 1, are the axioms for a ring. It is an easy matter to show that every ring has a unique element θ such that, for every a in the ring, $a + \theta = \theta + a = a$. θ is called the *identity with respect to addition*. It is then easy to show that $a \cdot \theta = \theta$ for every a. In the rational number system R, the number 0 is the identity with respect to addition.

That the ring R of rational numbers is a field is expressed by the following additional conditions which it satisfies:

6. if $a \in R$, $a \neq 0$, and $b \in R$, there is an $x \in R$ such that $ax \neq b$,

7. $ab = ba$,
8. R has at least two elements.

Every field F has a unique element e such that for every $a \in F$, $ae = ea = a$. The proof of this is left for the student. The element e is called the *identity* (in F) *with respect to multiplication*. For the rational numbers R the identity with respect to multiplication is the number 1.

(b) *R is an order*. This means that there is a relation called "greater than" and written ">" in R such that

1. for every $a \in R$, $b \in R$, $a \neq b$, either $a > b$ or $b > a$.
2. if $a > b$, then it is not true that $b > a$,
3. if $a > b$ and $b > c$, then $a > c$.

(c) *R is an ordered field.* This connects the field operations with the order relations as follows:

1. If $a > 0$ and $b > 0$, then $a + b > 0$ and $ab > 0$.
2. $a > b$ if and only if $a - b > 0$.

(d) *R has no proper ordered subfield.*

Two ordered fields F_1 and F_2 are said to be *isomorphic* if there is a one-to-one correspondence $x_2 = f(x_1)$ between them such that

1. for every $x_1 \in F_1, y_1 \in F_1$,

$$f(x_1 + y_1) = f(x_1) + f(y_1), \text{ and}$$
$$f(x_1 y_1) \quad = f(x_1) f(y_1),$$

2. for every $x_1 \in F_1, y_1 \in F_1$, if $x_1 > y_1$, then $f(x_1) > f(y_1)$.

We show that the above properties which the rational numbers have are *categorical*. This means that if F_1 and F_2 are both ordered fields having no proper ordered subfields, then F_1 and F_2 are isomorphic. In other words, the rational numbers are effectively the only system with the above properties.

We first prove the following proposition. (Since our main interest is in the real-number system, certain routine portions of the proof will be left for the student to complete.)

PROPOSITION 1. Every ordered field F contains a subfield isomorphic with the orderea field of rational numbers.

Proof. F has identities θ and e with respect to addition and multiplication, respectively. Since F has at least two elements, there is an $x \in F$ such that $x \neq \theta$. But $xe = x$ and $x\theta = \theta$ so that $e \neq \theta$.

We note without proof that for every $x \neq \theta$, $xx > \theta$. In particular, $ee > \theta$. But $ee = e$. Hence $e > \theta$.

For every positive integer n, we use the notation ne to designate that member of F obtained by adding e to itself n times, and by $-ne$ the solution to the equation $ne + x = \theta$. Then, for all integers n, m, $m \neq 0$, we designate by ne/me the solution to the equation $(me)x = ne$. The following facts are easy to establish:

1. For any integers k, n, m where $k \neq 0$ and $m \neq 0$, $kne/kme = ne/me$.
2. If m_1, m_2, n_1, n_2 are integers, where $m_1 \neq 0$ and $m_2 \neq 0$, then

$$\frac{n_1e}{m_1e} + \frac{n_2e}{m_2e} = \frac{(n_1m_2 + m_1n_2)e}{m_1m_2e} \text{ and } \frac{n_1e}{m_1e}\frac{n_2e}{m_2e} = \frac{n_1n_2e}{m_1m_2e}.$$

3. If m_1, m_2, n_1, n_2 are integers, where $m_1 \neq 0$ and $m_2 \neq 0$, then

$$\frac{n_1e}{m_1e} > \frac{n_2e}{m_2e} \quad \text{if and only if} \quad \frac{n_1}{m_1} > \frac{n_2}{m_2}.$$

It is clear that the mapping $f(n/m) = ne/me$ produces an isomorphism between the rationals R and a subfield of the ordered field F.

PROPOSITION 2. If an ordered field F has no ordered proper subfield it is isomorphic with the field of rational numbers.

Proof. By Proposition 1, F has a subfield F' which is isomorphic with the rational numbers. Since F has no proper subfield of this kind, $F' = F$.

One further property of the rational numbers that we wish to mention at this time is that they form an archimedean system. By this we mean that if $a > 0$ and $b > 0$ there is a positive integer n such that $na > b$ and $nb > a$.

We proceed now to a discussion of the main defect in the rational number system. The defect is that there are infinite sequences of rational numbers which converge but which have no limits. Another defect which the rational number system has is that not all quadratic equations with rational coefficients have solutions, but this is not within our present line of interest.

The decimal expansions of the rational numbers between 0 and 1 have the following property: after a finite number of terms, the expansion becomes a repeating one, i.e., it has the form

$$.a \cdots a_n b_1 \cdots b_m b_1 \cdots b_m b_1 \cdots b_m \cdots.$$

For example:

$$\frac{37}{175} = .21 \quad 142857 \quad 142857 \quad 142857 \quad 142857 \quad \cdots,$$

where the sequence 142857 repeats ad infinitum.

This property of the rational numbers permits us to give an example of a sequence of rational numbers which converges but whose limit does not exist among the rational numbers. Let

$r_1 = .01$

$r_2 = .01001$

$\cdots\cdots\cdots\cdots$

$r_n = .01001 \cdots 010 \underbrace{\cdots}_{n} 01$

$\cdots\cdots\cdots\cdots$

This sequence $\{r_n\}$ converges, since for every $\epsilon > 0$, if N is large enough so that $(.1)^N < \epsilon$, then for every $n, m > N$, we have $|r_n - r_m| < \epsilon$. We notice, however, that there is no rational number r such that $r = \lim_{n \to \infty} r_n$. For if r is a rational number, the decimal expansion of r has the form

$$r = .a_1 \cdots a_n b_1 \cdots b_m b_1 \cdots b_m b_1 \cdots b_m \cdots .$$

But it is obvious that no such decimal expansion can be the limit of the sequence $\{r_n\}$.

For the theory of real functions, this is a serious defect which we shall remedy by making an appropriate extension of the rational number system. It is convenient to consider a new system whose elements are themselves certain classes of sequences of rational numbers. With addition, multiplication, and order defined for the new entities, they will be shown to be an ordered field which does not have the above-mentioned defect. They are the real numbers.

2. *Equivalence classes of fundamental sequences of rational numbers*

Our treatment will be essentially self-sufficient. We define fundamental sequences of rational numbers and prove all the facts regarding them which are needed. We also say a few words about convergent series.

A sequence $\{r_n\}$ of rational numbers is a mapping which mates a rational number r_n with every positive integer n. The terms in the sequence need not all be different from each other. For example, $\{0, 0, \cdots, 0, \cdots\}$ and $\{1, 1/2, \cdots, 1/n, \cdots\}$ are sequences. A sequence is not a set but every sequence has associated with it a set, the set of values assumed by its terms. In the above examples, the value sets are $\{0\}$ and $\{1, 1/2, \cdots, 1/n, \cdots\}$, respectively.

The main idea in our discussion is that of fundamental sequence of rational numbers.

DEFINITION 1. For every rational number r, $|r| = \max\,[r, -r]$. $|r|$ is called the *absolute value* of r.

PROPOSITION 3. For every pair r_1, r_2 of rational numbers, $|r_1 + r_2| \leq |r_1| + |r_2|$, $|r_1 r_2| = |r_1||r_2|$, and $|r_1| - |r_2| \leqq |r_1 - r_2|$.

The proof is left for the student.

DEFINITION 2. A sequence $\{r_n\}$ of rational numbers is *fundamental* if, for every rational number $\epsilon > 0$, there is a positive integer N such that if $n, m > N$ then $|r_n - r_m| < \epsilon$.

A fundamental sequence is also called a *convergent sequence*, a *regular sequence*, or a *Cauchy sequence*.

The theory of convergent series is closely related to that of convergent sequences.

DEFINITION 3. A series $r_1 + r_2 + \cdots + r_n + \cdots$ of rational numbers is said to converge if the associated sequence $\{s_n\}$ is fundamental, where $s_k = r_1 + r_2 + \cdots + r_k$, $k = 1, 2, \cdots$.

For example, the series

$$\frac{1}{2} + \left(\frac{1}{2}\right)^2 + \cdots + \left(\frac{1}{2}\right)^n + \cdots$$

is convergent since the associated sequence $\{1 - 1/2^n\}$ is fundamental. The series

$$1 + \frac{1}{2} + \cdots + \frac{1}{n} + \cdots$$

is not convergent.

PROPOSITION 4. A series $r_1 + r_2 + \cdots + r_n + \cdots$ of positive rational numbers converges if and only if, for every rational number $\epsilon > 0$, there is a positive integer n such that, for every positive integer p,

$$r_n + r_{n+1} + \cdots + r_{n+p} < \epsilon.$$

The proof is left for the student.

DEFINITION 4. In the rational number system, r is said to be a limit of a fundamental sequence $\{r_n\}$ if, for every rational number $\epsilon > 0$, there is an N such that if $n > N$ then $|r - r_n| < \epsilon$.

If r is a limit of $\{r_n\}$, we write $r = \lim_{n\to\infty} r_n$.

PROPOSITION 5. In the rational number system, every fundamental sequence $\{r_n\}$ has at most one limit.

Proof. Suppose r is a limit of $\{r_n\}$. Let $s \neq r$. There is an N such that for every $n > N$,

$$|r - r_n| < \frac{|s - r|}{2}.$$

But then, for every $n > N$,

$$|s - r_n| > \frac{|s - r|}{2},$$

so that s is not a limit.

We have already seen that there are fundamental sequences which have no limits in the set of rational numbers. Hence a fundamental sequence of rational numbers has either one limit or no limit.

We shall define an equivalence relation for the set of fundamental sequences of rational numbers.

DEFINITION 5. Two fundamental sequences of rational numbers, $\{r_n\}$ and $\{s_n\}$, are equivalent if for every rational number $\epsilon > 0$ there is an integer N such that if $n > N$, then $|r_n - s_n| < \epsilon$; i.e. if $\lim_{n \to \infty} (r_n - s_n) = 0$.

We shall designate this relation by $\{r_n\} \sim \{s_n\}$.

For the case where a fundamental sequence $\{r_n\}$ has a limit, the following proposition holds.

PROPOSITION 6. If $\{r_n\}$ is a fundamental sequence whose limit r exists and if $\{s_n\}$ is equivalent to $\{r_n\}$, then r is also the limit of $\{s_n\}$.

Proof. Let $\epsilon > 0$. There is an N_1 such that if $n > N_1$, then $|r - r_n| < \epsilon/2$. There is an N_2 such that if $n > N_2$, then $|r_n - s_n| < \epsilon/2$. Let $N = \max(N_1, N_2)$. For every $n > N$,

$$|r - s_n| \leqq |r - r_n| + |r_n - s_n| < \frac{\epsilon}{2} + \frac{\epsilon}{2} = \epsilon .$$

Hence r is the limit of $\{s_n\}$.

Proposition 6 is the motivation for the above definition of equivalence. We now prove:

PROPOSITION 7. The equivalence relation of Definition 5 satisfies:

1. $\{r_n\} \sim \{r_n\}$.
2. If $\{r_n\} \sim \{s_n\}$, then $\{s_n\} \sim \{r_n\}$.
3. If $\{r_n\} \sim \{s_n\}$ and $\{s_n\} \sim \{t_n\}$, then $\{r_n\} \sim \{t_n\}$.

The proof is left to the student.

By Theorem 2, Chapter 1, it follows that our equivalence relation separates the set of all fundamental sequences into disjoint classes. We shall use Greek letters $\rho, \sigma, \tau, \cdots$ to denote classes of equivalent fundamental sequences. $\rho, \sigma, \tau, \cdots$ will be the elements which we consider. We define sum and product of these elements.

3. *Sum of equivalence classes*

In order to be able to define the sum of two equivalence classes of fundamental sequences of rational numbers, we need the following two propositions.

PROPOSITION 8. If $\{r_n\}$ and $\{s_n\}$ are fundamental sequences of rational numbers, then $\{r_n + s_n\}$ is a fundamental sequence.

Proof. Let $\epsilon > 0$. Since $\{r_n\}$ is a fundamental sequence, there is an N_1 such that if $n, m > N_1$ then $|r_n - r_m| < \epsilon/2$. Likewise, there is an N_2 such that if $n, m > N_2$ then $|s_n - s_m| < \epsilon/2$. Let $N = \max(N_1, N_2)$, i.e., the larger of the two integers N_1 and N_2. If $n, m > N$, then

$$|(r_n + s_n) - (r_m + s_m)| \leqq |r_n - r_m| + |s_n - s_m| < \frac{\epsilon}{2} + \frac{\epsilon}{2} = \epsilon .$$

Hence, for every $\epsilon > 0$, there is an N such that if $n, m > N$ then $|(r_n + s_n) - (r_m + s_m)| < \epsilon$, so that $\{r_n + s_n\}$ is a fundamental sequence.

PROPOSITION 9. If $\{r_n\} \sim \{r_n'\}$ and $\{s_n\} \sim \{s_n'\}$, where $\{r_n\}$, $\{r_n'\}$, $\{s_n\}$, $\{s_n'\}$, are fundamental sequences of rational numbers, then $\{r_n + s_n\} \sim \{r_n' + s_n'\}$.

Proof. Let $\epsilon > 0$. Since $\{r_n\} \sim \{r_n'\}$ there is an N_1 such that if $n > N_1$ then $|r_n - r_n'| < \epsilon/2$. Likewise, there is an N_2 such that if $n > N_2$ then $|s_n - s_n'| < \epsilon/2$. Let $N = \max (N_1, N_2)$. If $n > N$, then

$$|(r_n + s_n) - (r_n' + s_n')| \leqq |r_n - r_n'| + |s_n - s_n'| < \frac{\epsilon}{2} + \frac{\epsilon}{2} = \epsilon .$$

Hence, for every $\epsilon > 0$, there is an N such that if $n > N$ then

$$|(r_n + s_n) - (r_n' + s_n')| < \epsilon, \text{ so that } \{r_n + s_n\} \sim \{r_n' + s_n'\}.$$

Propositions 8 and 9 allow us to define the sum of two equivalence classes of fundamental sequences of rational numbers.

DEFINITION 6. If ρ and σ are equivalence classes of fundamental sequences of rational numbers, $\rho + \sigma$ is the equivalence class to which $\{r_n + s_n\}$ belongs, where $\{r_n\}$ is any element of ρ and $\{s_n\}$ is any element of σ.

Proposition 8 assures that $\{r_n + s_n\}$ is a fundamental sequence and Proposition 9 assures that all $\{r_n + s_n\}$ for all permissible choices of $\{r_n\}$ and $\{s_n\}$ belong to the same equivalence class.

4. *Product of equivalence classes*

We again need certain simple facts about fundamental sequences.

PROPOSITION 10. If $\{r_n\}$ is a fundamental sequence of rational numbers, there is a rational number $M > 0$ such that $|r_n| < M$ for every positive integer n.

Proof. Since $\{r_n\}$ is a fundamental sequence, there is an N such that for every $n > N$, $|r_N - r_n| < 1$. Let $M = \max (|r_1|, |r_2|, \cdots, |r_N|) + 1$. For every $n \leqq N$, $|r_n| < M$. Suppose $n > N$. Since $|r_N - r_n| < 1$, $|r_n| < |r_N| + 1 \leqq M$ so that $|r_n| < M$ in this case also.

PROPOSITION 11. If $\{r_n\}$ and $\{s_n\}$ are fundamental sequences of rational numbers, then $\{r_n s_n\}$ is a fundamental sequence.

Proof. Let $\epsilon > 0$. By Proposition 10, there are rational numbers $M_1 > 0$, $M_2 > 0$, such that $|r_n| < M_1$ and $|s_n| < M_2$ for every positive integer n.

Since $\{r_n\}$ is a fundamental sequence, there is an N_1 such that if $n, m > N_1$ then $|r_n - r_m| < \epsilon/2M_2$. Similarly, there is an N_2 such that if $n, m > N_2$ then $|s_n - s_m| < \epsilon/2M_1$. Let $N = \max(N_1, N_2)$. If $n, m > N$, then

$$|r_n s_n - r_m s_m| = |r_n s_n - r_n s_m + r_n s_m - r_m s_m|$$

$$\leqq |r_n||s_n - s_m| + |s_m||r_n - r_m| < M_1 \cdot \frac{\epsilon}{2M_1} + M_2 \cdot \frac{\epsilon}{2M_2} = \epsilon.$$

Hence for every $\epsilon > 0$ there is an N such that if $n, m > N$ then $|r_n s_n - r_m s_m| < \epsilon$. Therefore, $\{r_n s_n\}$ is a fundamental sequence.

PROPOSITION 12. If $\{r_n\} \sim \{r_n'\}$ and $\{s_n\} \sim \{s_n'\}$, where $\{r_n\}$, $\{r_n'\}$, $\{s_n\}$, $\{s_n'\}$, are fundamental sequences of rational numbers, then $\{r_n s_n\} \sim \{r_n' s_n'\}$.

Proof. Let $\epsilon > 0$. By Proposition 10, there are rational numbers $M_1 > 0$, $M_2 > 0$, $M_3 > 0$, and $M_4 > 0$ such that $|r_n| < M_1$, $|r_n'| < M_2$, $|s_n| < M_3$, and $|s_n'| < M_4$ for every positive integer n. Let $M = \max(M_1, M_2, M_3, M_4)$. Since $\{r_n\} \sim \{r_n'\}$ and $\{s_n\} \sim \{s_n'\}$, there are positive integers N_1 and N_2 such that if $n > N_1$ then $|r_n - r_n'| < \epsilon/2M$ and if $n > N_2$ then $|s_n - s_n'| < \epsilon/2M$. Let $N = \max(N_1, N_2)$. For every $n > N$,

$$|r_n s_n - r_n' s_n'| = |r_n s_n - r_n' s_n + r_n' s_n - r_n' s_n'|$$

$$\leqq |s_n||r_n - r_n'| + |r_n'||s_n - s_n'| < M \cdot \frac{\epsilon}{2M} + M \cdot \frac{\epsilon}{2M} = \epsilon.$$

Hence for every $\epsilon > 0$ there is an N such that if $n > N$ then $|r_n s_n - r_n' s_n'| < \epsilon$. Therefore, $\{r_n s_n\} \sim \{r_n' s_n'\}$.

Propositions 11 and 12 allow us to define the product of equivalence classes of fundamental sequences of rational numbers.

DEFINITION 7. If ρ and σ are equivalence classes of fundamental sequences of rational numbers, $\rho\sigma$ is the equivalence class to which $\{r_n s_n\}$ belongs, where $\{r_n\}$ is any element of ρ and $\{s_n\}$ is any element of σ.

Proposition 11 assures that $\{r_n s_n\}$ is a fundamental sequence and Proposition 12 assures that all $\{r_n s_n\}$ for all permissible choices of $\{r_n\}$ and $\{s_n\}$ belong to the same equivalence class.

We now come to an important proposition.

PROPOSITION 13. The set of equivalence classes of fundamental sequences of rational numbers is a field.

Proof. We have already shown that for every ρ and σ in the system there are elements $\rho + \sigma$ and $\rho \cdot \sigma$ in the system. We now prove that the field properties are satisfied. That

1. $\rho + (\sigma + \tau) = (\rho + \sigma) + \tau$,
2. $\rho + \sigma = \sigma + \rho$,

3. $\rho + \xi = \sigma$ has a solution for every ρ and σ,
4. $\rho(\sigma\tau) = (\rho\sigma)\tau$, and
5. $\rho(\sigma + \tau) = \rho\sigma + \rho\tau$, $(\sigma + \tau)\rho = \sigma\rho + \tau\rho$,

follows immediately from the fact that these rules hold for the rational numbers. For example, consider (3): a solution to $\rho + \xi = \sigma$ is the equivalence class of fundamental sequences which has the sequence $\{s_n - r_n\}$ as a member, where $\{r_n\}$ and $\{s_n\}$ are any sequences in ρ and σ, respectively. The identity θ with respect to addition is the class which has the sequence $\{0, 0, \cdots, 0, \cdots\}$ as a member. The field property

7. $\rho\sigma = \sigma\rho$

is obviously satisfied so that it remains only to prove

6. $\rho\xi = \sigma$

has a solution for every ρ and σ provided that $\rho \neq \theta$.

Let $\{r_n\} \in \rho$ be such that $r_n \neq 0$ for every n, and let $\{s_n\} \in \sigma$. The sequence $\{s_n/r_n\}$ has the property $\{r_n(s_n/r_n)\} = \{s_n\}$. We must show that this sequence is a fundamental sequence. To show this, let $\epsilon > 0$. Since $\rho \neq \theta$, $\{r_n\}$ does not have 0 as limit. Hence, there is a $K > 0$ and an N_1 such that for every $n > N_1$, $|r_n| > K$. There are rational numbers $M_1 > 0$, $M_2 > 0$, such that $|r_n| < M_1$ and $|s_n| < M_2$ for every positive integer n. Let $M = \max(M_1, M_2)$. There are positive integers N_2 and N_3 such that for every $n, m > N_2$, $|r_n - r_m| < K^2\epsilon/2M$ and for every $n, m > N_3$, $|s_n - s_m| < K^2\epsilon/2M$. Let $N = \max(N_1, N_2, N_3)$. For every $n, m > N$,

$$\left|\frac{s_n}{r_n} - \frac{s_m}{r_m}\right| = \left|\frac{s_n r_m - s_m r_n}{r_n r_m}\right| = \left|\frac{s_n r_m - s_n r_n + s_n r_n - s_m r_n}{r_n r_m}\right|$$

$$\leq \left|\frac{s_n}{r_n r_m}\right| |r_m - r_n| + \left|\frac{r_n}{r_n r_m}\right| |s_n - s_m| < \frac{M}{K^2} \cdot \frac{K^2\epsilon}{2M} + \frac{M}{K^2} \cdot \frac{K^2\epsilon}{2M} = \epsilon.$$

Hence $\{s_n/r_n\}$ is a fundamental sequence. We must still show that if $\{r_n'\} \in \rho$ and $r_n' \neq 0$ for every n, $\{s_n'\} \in \sigma$, $\{s_n'/r_n'\} \sim \{s_n/r_n\}$. The proof of this, which involves the technique we have been using repeatedly, is left to the student.

This completes the proof that our system is a field.

5. *Order between equivalence classes*

The real-number system is an order as well as a field. In this section, we define an order relation for equivalence classes of fundamental sequences of rational numbers.

PROPOSITION 14. If $\{r_n\}$ and $\{s_n\}$ are fundamental sequences of rational numbers, then either

1. $\{r_n\} \sim \{s_n\}$, or
2. there is a $k > 0$ and an N such that if $n > N$ then $r_n > s_n + k$, or
3. there is a $k > 0$ and an N such that if $n > N$ then $s_n > r_n + k$.

Proof. Suppose that $\{r_n\}$ is not equivalent to $\{s_n\}$. Then there is a $k > 0$ such that for every positive integer μ there is a $\nu > \mu$ such that $|r_\nu - s_\nu| > 2k$. On the other hand, since $\{r_n\}$ and $\{s_n\}$ are fundamental sequences, there is an N_1 such that if $n, m > N_1$ then $|r_n - r_m| < k/2$ and there is an N_2 such that if $n, m > N_2$ then $|s_n - s_m| < k/2$. Let $N \geqq \max(N_1, N_2)$ be such that $|r_N - s_N| > 2k$. There are two possibilities: $r_N > s_N$ or $s_N > r_N$.

Suppose $r_N > s_N$. Then $r_N > s_N + 2k$. For every $n > N$, $|r_N - r_n| < k/2$ and $|s_N - s_n| < k/2$, so that

$$r_n > r_N - \frac{k}{2} > s_N + 2k - \frac{k}{2} = s_N + \frac{3k}{2}.$$

But $s_N > s_n - k/2$, so that $r_n > s_N + 3k/2 > s_n + k$.

If $s_N > r_N$ it follows, in the same way, that for every $n > N$, $s_n > r_n + k$.

PROPOSITION 15. If $\{r_n\} \sim \{r_n'\}$ and $\{s_n\} \sim \{s_n'\}$ are fundamental sequences of rational numbers, the same relation in Proposition 14 holds between $\{r_n'\}$ and $\{s_n'\}$ as between $\{r_n\}$ and $\{s_n\}$.

Proof. Suppose $\{r_n\} \sim \{s_n\}$. Then $\{r_n'\} \sim \{r_n\} \sim \{s_n\} \sim \{s_n'\}$ so that $\{r_n'\} \sim \{s_n'\}$.

Suppose there is a $k > 0$ and an N_1 such that if $n > N_1$ then $r_n > s_n + k$. Since $\{r_n\} \sim \{r_n'\}$ and $\{s_n\} \sim \{s_n'\}$, there are integers N_2 and N_3 such that if $n > N_2$ then $|r_n - r_n'| < k/3$ and if $n > N_3$ then $|s_n - s_n'| < k/3$. Hence, for every $n > N_2$, $r_n' > r_n - k/3$ and for every $n > N_3$, $s_n > s_n' - k/3$. Let $N = \max(N_1, N_2, N_3)$.

For every $n > N$,

$$r_n' > r_n - \frac{k}{3} > s_n + k - \frac{k}{3} > s_n' + k - \frac{k}{3} - \frac{k}{3} = s_n' + \frac{k}{3}.$$

Hence there is an $l = k/3 > 0$ and an N such that for every $n > N$, $r_n' > s_n' + l$.

The proof for the third case is the same as that for the second.

Propositions 14 and 15 allow us to define an order relation between our elements.

DEFINITION 8. If ρ and σ are equivalence classes of fundamental sequences of rational numbers, then $\rho > \sigma$ if for $\{r_n\} \in \rho$ and $\{s_n\} \in \sigma$ there is a $k > 0$ and an N such that if $n > N$ then $r_n > s_n + k$.

We show that this relation has the properties of an order relation.

PROPOSITION 16. (1) For every ρ and σ, $\rho \neq \sigma$, either $\rho > \sigma$ or $\sigma > \rho$; (2) if $\rho > \sigma$, then it is not true that $\sigma > \rho$; (3) if $\rho > \sigma$ and $\sigma > \tau$, then $\rho > \tau$.

The proof is left to the student.

Moreover, we now have the following proposition.

PROPOSITION 17. The equivalence classes of fundamental sequences of rational numbers form an ordered field.

Proof. Suppose $\rho > \theta$ and $\sigma > \theta$. Let $\{r_n\} \in \rho$ and $\{s_n\} \in \sigma$. There are numbers $k_1 > 0$ and $k_2 > 0$ and N_1 and N_2 such that if $n > N_1$ then $r_n > k_1$ and if $n > N_2$ then $s_n > k_2$. Let $N = \max(N_1, N_2)$. For every $n > N$, $r_n + s_n > k_1 + k_2$ and $r_n s_n > k_1 k_2$. Hence $\rho + \sigma > \theta$ and $\rho\sigma > \theta$.

6. *Convergence and limit*

We now show that the number system developed in the last few sections is free from the defect which the rational numbers have. This requires definitions of fundamental sequence and of limit for this system.

DEFINITION 9. A sequence $\{r_{1n}\}$, $\{r_{2n}\}$, $\cdots$, $\{r_{mn}\}$, $\cdots$ of fundamental sequences is called a *fundamental sequence of fundamental sequences* if, for every $\epsilon > 0$, there is an N such that if $k, l > N$ then there is a $\nu(k, l)$ such that if $\mu > \nu(k, l)$ then

$$|r_{k\mu} - r_{l\mu}| < \epsilon.$$

This definition says that for every $\epsilon > 0$ there is an N such that for every $k, l > N$ the sequences $r_{k1}, r_{k2}, \cdots, r_{kn}, \cdots$ and $r_{l1}, r_{l2}, \cdots, r_{ln}, \cdots$ are in the following relationship to each other: there is a positive integer $\nu(k, l)$, which may be different for other choices of k and l, such that for every $\mu > \nu(k, l)$,

$$|r_{k\mu} - r_{l\mu}| < \epsilon.$$

PROPOSITION 18. If $\{r_{1n}\} \sim \{s_{1n}\}$, $\{r_{2n}\} \sim \{s_{2n}\}$, $\cdots$ are two sequences of fundamental sequences of rational numbers and if $\{r_{1n}\}$, $\{r_{2n}\}$, $\cdots$ is a fundamental sequence of fundamental sequences of rational numbers, then $\{s_{1n}\}$, $\{s_{2n}\}$, $\cdots$ is also a fundamental sequence of fundamental sequences of rational numbers.

Proof. Let $\epsilon > 0$. There is an N such that if $k, l > N$ then there is a $\nu(k, l)$ such that if $\mu > \nu(k, l)$ then $|r_{k\mu} - r_{l\mu}| < \epsilon/3$. But, for every m, there is a $\nu(m)$ such that if $\mu > \nu(m)$ then $|r_{m\mu} - s_{m\mu}| < \epsilon/3$. For every pair k, l of positive integers, let

$$\mu(k, l) = \max(\nu(k, l), \nu(k), \nu(l)).$$

For every $\mu > \mu(k, l)$, where $k, l > N$, we have

$$|s_{k\mu} - s_{l\mu}| \leqq |s_{k\mu} - r_{k\mu}| + |r_{k\mu} - r_{l\mu}| + |r_{l\mu} - s_{l\mu}| < \frac{\epsilon}{3} + \frac{\epsilon}{3} + \frac{\epsilon}{3} = \epsilon.$$

Hence, for every $\epsilon > 0$, there is an N such that if $k, l > N$ then there is a $\mu(k, l)$ such that if $\mu > \mu(k, l)$ then $|s_{k\mu} - s_{l\mu}| < \epsilon$, so that $\{s_{1n}\}, \{s_{2n}\}, \cdots$ is a fundamental sequence of fundamental sequences of rational numbers.

This proposition allows us to define fundamental sequence of equivalence classes.

DEFINITION 10. The sequence $\rho_1, \rho_2, \cdots$ of equivalence classes of fundamental sequences of rational numbers is fundamental if every sequence $\{r_{1n}\}, \{r_{2n}\}, \cdots$ is fundamental, where

$$\{r_{mn}\} \in \rho_m, m = 1, 2, \cdots.$$

We now introduce the definition of limit of a fundamental sequence for the entities we are considering. First, we define the limit of a fundamental sequence of fundamental sequences.

DEFINITION 11. If $\{r_{1n}\}, \{r_{2n}\}, \cdots$ is a fundamental sequence of fundamental sequences of rational numbers, a fundamental sequence $\{r_n\}$ is its limit if, for every $\epsilon > 0$, there is an N such that for every $k > N$ there is a $\nu(k)$ such that if $n > \nu(k)$ then $|r_n - r_{kn}| < \epsilon$.

We are now ready to prove the basic proposition.

PROPOSITION 19. Every fundamental sequence of fundamental sequences of rational numbers has a limit.

Proof. Let $\{r_{1n}\}, \{r_{2n}\}, \cdots, \{r_{mn}\}, \cdots$ be a fundamental sequence of fundamental sequences of rational numbers. Let $\epsilon_1 + \epsilon_2 + \cdots + \epsilon_p + \cdots$ be a convergent series of positive rational terms. There is an $r_{m_1n_1}$ such that if $n > n_1$ then $|r_{m_1n_1} - r_{m_1n}| < \epsilon_1$ and if $m > m_1$ then there is a $\nu(m, m_1)$ such that if $\nu > \nu(m, m_1)$ then $|r_{m_1\nu} - r_{m\nu}| < \epsilon_1$. There is an $r_{m_2n_2}$ such that $|r_{m_2n_2} - r_{m_1n_1}| < 2\epsilon_1$, such that if $n > n_2$ then $|r_{m_2n_2} - r_{m_2n}| < \epsilon_2$ and if $m > m_2$ then there is a $\nu(m, m_2)$ such that if $\nu > \nu(m, m_2)$ then $|r_{m_2\nu} - r_{m\nu}| < \epsilon_2$. For every positive integer p, suppose we already have $r_{m_1n_1}, r_{m_2n_2}, \cdots, r_{m_pn_p}$. There is an $r_{m_{p+1}n_{p+1}}$ such that $|r_{m_pn_p} - r_{m_{p+1}n_{p+1}}| < 2\epsilon_p$, such that if $n > n_{p+1}$ then $|r_{m_{p+1}n_{p+1}} - r_{m_{p+1}n}| < \epsilon_{p+1}$, and if $m > m_{p+1}$ there is a $\nu(m, m_{p+1})$ such that if $\nu > \nu(m, m_{p+1})$ then $|r_{m_{p+1}\nu} - r_{m\nu}| < \epsilon_{p+1}$.

We consider the sequence $r_{m_1n_1}, r_{m_2n_2}, \cdots, r_{m_pn_p}, \cdots$. We prove (1) that it is a fundamental sequence, and (2) that it is a limit of the sequence $\{r_{1n}\}, \{r_{2n}\}, \cdots, \{r_{mn}\}, \cdots$ of fundamental sequences.

Proof of (1). Let $\epsilon > 0$. There is a positive integer p such that if $k > p$, $l > 0$ then $\epsilon_k + \epsilon_{k+1} + \cdots + \epsilon_{k+l-1} < \epsilon/2$. So for every $k > p$ and $l > 0$, we have

$$|r_{m_k n_k} - r_{m_{k+l} n_{k+l}}| \leqq |r_{m_k n_k} - r_{m_{k+1} n_{k+1}}| + |r_{m_{k+1} n_{k+1}} - r_{m_{k+2} n_{k+2}}| + \cdots + |r_{m_{k+l-1} n_{k+l-1}} - r_{m_{k+l} n_{k+l}}| < 2\epsilon_k + 2\epsilon_{k+1} + \cdots + 2\epsilon_{k+l-1} < \epsilon$$

This shows that $\{r_{m_p n_p}\}$ is a fundamental sequence.

Proof of (2). Let $\epsilon > 0$. There is a p such that, for every $l > 0$,

$$\sum_{k=p}^{p+l} \epsilon_k < \frac{\epsilon}{4}.$$

Let $m > m_p$. Consider the fundamental sequence $r_{m1}, r_{m2}, \cdots$. There is an N such that if $\mu, \nu > N$ then $|r_{m\mu} - r_{m\nu}| < \epsilon/4$. There is a $\mu > N$ such that $|r_{m\mu} - r_{m_p n_p}| < 2\epsilon_p$. For every $\nu > \max(p, N)$, we have

$$|r_{m_\nu n_\nu} - r_{m\nu}| \leqq |r_{m_\nu n_\nu} - r_{m_p n_p}| + |r_{m_p n_p} - r_{m\mu}| + |r_{m\mu} - r_{m\nu}| < \frac{\epsilon}{4} + \frac{2\epsilon}{4} + \frac{\epsilon}{4} = \epsilon.$$

This proves (2).

Proposition 19 is complemented by the following proposition.

PROPOSITION 20. If $\{r_{1n}\}, \{r_{2n}\}, \cdots$ is a fundamental sequence of fundamental sequences and $\{r_{1n}\} \sim \{s_{1n}\}, \{r_{2n}\} \sim \{s_{2n}\}, \cdots$ then $\{s_{1n}\}, \{s_{2n}\}, \cdots$ is a fundamental sequence of fundamental sequences, and if $\{r_n\}$ and $\{s_n\}$ are respectively their limits, then $\{r_n\} \sim \{s_n\}$.

The proof, which is a simple application of the definitions involved, is left as an exercise for the student.

Propositions 19 and 20 allow us to make the following definition.

DEFINITION 12. If $\rho_1, \rho_2, \cdots, \rho_n, \cdots$ is a fundamental sequence of equivalence classes, the limit is the equivalence class to which $\{r_n\}$ belongs, where $\{r_n\}$ is a limit of $\{r_{1n}\}, \{r_{2n}\}, \cdots$ and $\{r_{1n}\} \epsilon \rho_1, \{r_{2n}\} \epsilon \rho_2, \cdots$.

We may now state the following proposition.

PROPOSITION 21. Every fundamental sequence $\rho_1, \rho_2, \cdots, \rho_n, \cdots$ of equivalence classes of fundamental sequences of rational numbers has a limit ρ and the limit is unique.

7. *Real numbers*

Real numbers are equivalence classes of fundamental sequences of rational numbers. The following facts about real numbers are simply summary statements of results obtained in the preceding sections.

THEOREM 1. The real numbers are a field. This is a restatement of Proposition 13.

The identity with respect to addition is the zero class θ, i.e., the class to which the sequence $\{0, 0, \cdots, 0, \cdots\}$ belongs. The identity with respect to multiplication is the unit class e, i.e., the class to which the sequence $\{1, 1, \cdots, 1, \cdots\}$ belongs.

THEOREM 2. The real numbers are an ordered field.

THEOREM 3. The real-number system is archimedean, i.e., if $\rho > \sigma > \theta$ there is an n such that $n\sigma > \rho$.

The proof is left to the student.

DEFINITION 13. A number system R is complete if every fundamental sequence in R has a limit in R.

THEOREM 4. The real-number system is complete.

This is a restatement of Proposition 21.

Consider those equivalence classes which have members of the form $\{r, r, \cdots, r, \cdots\}$. This subset of the set of real numbers is in one-to-one correspondence with the set of rational numbers in such a way that sums and products of corresponding elements are corresponding elements: i.e., it is isomorphic with the rationals. We shall simply call this subset of the reals the rationals. We state the further theorem.

THEOREM 5. There is a rational number between every two real numbers.

The proof is left to the student.

8. *The Dedekind method*

The method of obtaining the real numbers from the rational numbers which has been elaborated here is due to G. Cantor. Another method which proceeds along rather different lines but yields the same results is the method of R. Dedekind. The Dedekind method rests upon the so-called Dedekind cut in the rational number system.

DEFINITION 14. A Dedekind cut (L, U) is a subdivision of the rational numbers into two nonempty disjoint sets L and U such that L has no largest element and if $x \in L, y \in U$, then $x < y$.

Every rational number r determines a unique Dedekind cut (L, U) if L consists of all $x < r$ and U of all $x \geqq r$. Conversely, if for a Dedekind cut (L, U), the set U has a smallest element r, we shall say that the cut (L, U) determines the rational number r.

The defect in the rational number system as envisaged by Dedekind is that there are cuts (L, U) which determine no rational number.

For example: Let L consist of all the nonpositive rational numbers and the positive rational numbers whose squares are less than 2 and U consist of the positive rational numbers whose squares are greater than or equal to 2. (L, U) is a Dedekind cut, but U has no smallest element.

We shall use the following property of Dedekind cuts.

PROPOSITION 22. If (L, U) is a Dedekind cut, for every $\epsilon > 0$ there is an $x \in L$ and a $y \in U$ such that $y - x < \epsilon$.

Proof. Since L and U are nonempty, there are rationals $r \in L$ and $s \in U$. There is a positive integer n such that $s - r < n\epsilon$. Consider the rational numbers

$$r, r + \frac{1}{n}(s - r), r + \frac{2}{n}(s - r), \cdots, s.$$

Among the numbers in this sequence which are in L there is a largest $r + (j/n)(s - r)$. Then $r + [(j + 1)/n](s - r) \in U$. But

$$r + \frac{j+1}{n}(s - r) - \left[r + \frac{j}{n}(s - r)\right] = \frac{1}{n}(s - r).$$

This proves the proposition.

We define sum, product, and order for Dedekind cuts.

DEFINITION 15. If (L_1, U_1) and (L_2, U_2) are Dedekind cuts, their sum (L, U) is the Dedekind cut for which L is the set of all $x + y$ where $x \in L_1$, $y \in L_2$, and where U is the set of all other rational numbers.

PROPOSITION 23. The (L, U) of Definition 15 is a Dedekind cut.

Proof. Since L_1 and L_2 are not empty there are $x \in L_1, y \in L_2$. Thus $x + y \in L$ so that L is not empty. By Proposition 22, there are $x \in L_1, y \in L_2$, such that $x + 1/2 \in U_1, y + 1/2 \in U_2$. Now $x + y + 1 \in U$. For if $x + y + 1 \in L$, then $x + y + 1 = z + w$ where $z \in L_1$ and $w \in L_2$. But since $z \in L_1$, $z < x + 1/2$; and since $w \in L_2$, $w < y + 1/2$; so that $z + w < x + y + 1$, in contradiction. Hence U is not empty.

Next we show that L has no largest element. Let $z \in L$. Then $z = x + y$ where $x \in L_1, y \in L_2$. But L_1 has no largest element, so that there is a $w \in L_1$ such that $w > x$. Now $w + y \in L$ and $w + y > z$. Finally we show that for every $z \in L$, $w \in U$, we have $w > z$. If $z > w$ then $z = w + k$ where $k > 0$. Now since $z \in L$, $z = x + y$ where $x \in L_1, y \in L_2$. But $x - k \in L_1$ and $w = z - k = x + y - k = (x - k) + y$, so that $w \in L$, contrary to $w \in U$ and $U \cap L = \phi$.

The product of Dedekind cuts may also be defined. In order to do this we must first distinguish between positive and negative cuts. A cut (L, U) is called positive if $0 \in L$. Since, by definition, L has no largest number, a cut is positive if and only if L contains positive numbers. A cut (L, U) is negative if U contains negative numbers. The addition inverse $-(L, U)$ of the cut (L, U) is the cut with the property $(L, U) + (-(L, U)) = \theta$, where θ is the cut which determines the rational number 0. The proof that every Dedekind cut has an addition inverse is left for the student.

DEFINITION 16. If (L_1, U_1) and (L_2, U_2) are positive Dedekind cuts, their product (L, U) is the cut for which L is the set of all negative numbers and all products xy, where $x \in L_1$, $y \in L_2$, and $x \geqq 0$, $y \geqq 0$.

If (L_1, U_1) and (L_2, U_2) are both negative, their product is the product of their addition inverses.

If (L_1, U_1) is positive and (L_2, U_2) is negative, their product is the addition inverse of the product of (L_1, U_1) and the addition inverse of (L_2, U_2).

If one or more of the factors (L_1, U_1) and (L_2, U_2) is θ the product is θ.

PROPOSITION 24. The product, as given by Definition 16, is a Dedekind cut.

Proof. It will suffice to prove the assertion for the case where (L_1, U_1) and (L_2, U_2) are both positive. Since L contains all negative rationals, it is not empty. By Proposition 22, there are $x \in L_1$ and $y \in L_2$ such that $x > 0$, $y > 0$ and $x + 1 \in U_1$ and $y + 1 \in U_2$. Now $xy + x + y + 1 \in U$. For if $xy + x + y + 1 \in L$ then $xy + x + y + 1 = zw$, where $z > 0$, $w > 0$, and $z \in L_1$, $w \in L_2$. But since $z \in L_1$, $z < x + 1$, and since $w \in L_2$, $w < y + 1$. Hence $zw < xy + x + y + 1$, in contradiction. Thus U is not empty.

Next we show that L has no largest element. Let $z \in L$, $z > 0$. Then $z = xy$ where $x \in L_1$, $y \in L_2$, and $x > 0$, $y > 0$. But L_1 has no largest element, so there is a $w \in L_1$ such that $w > x$. Now $wy \in L$ and $wy > z$. Finally, for every $z \in L$, $w \in U$, we have $w > z$. If $z > w$ then $z = w \cdot k$ where $k > 1$. Now since $z \in L$, $z = xy$ where $x \in L_1, y \in L_2$. But $x/k \in L_1$ and $w = z/k = xy/k = (x/k)y$ so that $w \in L$, contrary to $w \in U$ and $L \cap U = \phi$.

We also define an order relation for the set of Dedekind cuts.

DEFINITION 17. $(L_1, U_1) > (L_2, U_2)$ if there is an $x \in L_1 - L_2$.

Our next step is to establish a one-to-one correspondence between the equivalence classes of fundamental sequences of rational numbers and the Dedekind cuts.

Let $r_1, r_2, \cdots, r_n, \cdots$ be a fundamental sequence of rational numbers. Let L consist of all rational numbers which are less than all but a finite number of terms of the sequence $\{r_n\}$, except for the largest such number if there should be one, and let U consist of all other rational numbers. (L, U) is a Dedekind cut. For, by Proposition 10, there is an $M > 0$ such that $|r_n| < M$ for every n. Then $-M - 1 \in L$ and $M \in U$ so that neither L nor U is empty. Let $x \in L$ and $y \in U$. If $y < x$ then, since x is less than all but a finite number of terms of $\{r_n\}$, so is y. Thus $y \in L$, contrary to $y \in U$ and $L \cap U = \phi$, so that $y > x$. Hence (L, U) is a Dedekind cut.

Suppose $\{r_n\}$ and $\{s_n\}$ are equivalent fundamental sequences of rational numbers and that (L, U) and (L', U') correspond, respectively, to $\{r_n\}$ and $\{s_n\}$ by the above association. We show that $L = L'$.

Let $x \in L$. Then there is a $y \in L$ such that $x < y$. There is an N_1 such that for every $n > N_1$, $r_n > y$. Since $\{r_n\} \sim \{s_n\}$, there is an N_2 such that for every $n > N_2$, $s_n > r_n - (y - x)/2$. Let $N = \max(N_1, N_2)$. For every $n > N$,

$$x + \frac{y-x}{2} = y - \frac{y-x}{2} < r_n - \frac{y-x}{2} < s_n.$$

Hence there is a number greater than x which is less than all but a finite number of terms of the sequence $\{s_n\}$. Hence $x \in L'$. It follows that $L' \subset L$. Similarly, $L \subset L'$.

Accordingly, our correspondence may be considered as being between equivalence classes of fundamental sequences and Dedekind cuts. In order to complete the proof that the correspondence is one-to-one, we must show that fundamental sequences which are not equivalent are associated with different Dedekind cuts, and that every Dedekind cut is associated with some fundamental sequence. We leave the proof of these details to the student.

We designate the above correspondence by

$$(L, U) = f(\rho).$$

We show that this mapping has the following properties:

1. $f(\rho + \sigma) = f(\rho) + f(\sigma)$,
2. $f(\rho\sigma) = f(\rho)f(\sigma)$, and,
3. if $\rho > \sigma$, then $f(\rho) > f(\sigma)$.

Proof of (1). Let $(L_1, U_1) = f(\rho)$, $(L_2, U_2) = f(\sigma)$, and $(L, U) = f(\rho + \sigma)$. We must show that the Dedekind cut (L, U) is the sum of the cuts (L_1, U_1) and (L_2, U_2).

Let $\{r_n\} \in \rho$ and $\{s_n\} \in \sigma$. We show that if $x \in L_1$ and $y \in L_2$ then $x + y \in L$, and if $z \in L$ then there are $x \in L_1, y \in L_2$ such that $x + y = z$, thereby accomplishing the proof. First, suppose $x \in L_1, y \in L_2$. There is an $x' \in L_1$ such that $x' > x$. Now x' is less than all but a finite number of terms of $\{r_n\}$ and y is less than all but a finite number of terms of $\{s_n\}$. Hence $x + y$ is less than all but a finite number of terms of $\{r_n + s_n\}$ and is not the largest such rational number. Thus $x + y \in L$. Next suppose $z \in L$. There is a $z' > z$ such that $z' \in L$. $z' = x' + y'$ where x' is less than all but a finite number of terms of $\{r_n\}$ and y' is less than all but a finite number of terms of $\{s_n\}$. Let $x = x' - (z' - z)/2$, $y = y' - (z' - z)/2$. Then $x \in L_1$, $y \in L_2$ and $z = x + y$.

It follows that the Dedekind cut $f(\rho + \sigma)$ is the sum of the Dedekind cuts $f(\rho)$ and $f(\sigma)$.

Proof of (2). The proof, which is very much like that of (1), is left to the student.

Proof of (3). Suppose $\rho > \sigma$. Let $\{r_n\} \in \rho$, and $\{s_n\} \in \sigma$, and let $(L_1, U_1) = f(\rho)$, $(L_2, U_2) = f(\sigma)$. After a certain finite number of terms, $r_n > s_n$ for every n. Hence if x is less than all but a finite number of the s_n it is less than all but a finite number of the r_n. This shows that $L_1 \supset L_2$; hence

$f(\rho) \geqq f(\sigma)$. We leave it for the student to show that there is an $x \in L_1 - L_2$ so that $f(\rho) > f(\sigma)$.

What we have shown leads to the following proposition.

PROPOSITION 25. The Dedekind cuts form an ordered field which is isomorphic with the ordered field of equivalence classes of fundamental sequences of rational numbers.

Fundamental sequences of Dedekind cuts and limits of such sequences will now be defined.

DEFINITION 18. A sequence (L_1, U_1), (L_2, U_2), $\cdots$ of Dedekind cuts is called a fundamental sequence if there are two equivalent fundamental sequences $\{l_n\}$ and $\{u_n\}$ such that for every n, $l_n \in L_n$ and $u_n \in U_n$.

DEFINITION 19. If $\{(L_n, U_n)\}$ is a fundamental sequence of Dedekind cuts the limit of the sequence is the Dedekind cut $(L, U) = f(\rho)$ where ρ is the equivalence class to which $\{l_n\}$ belongs.

We finally state the following proposition without proof.

PROPOSITION 26. If $\rho_1, \rho_2, \cdots, \rho_n, \cdots$ is a sequence of equivalence classes and $(L_n, U_n) = f(\rho_n)$ for every positive integer n, then $\{\rho_n\}$ is a fundamental sequence if and only if $\{(L_n, U_n)\}$ is a fundamental sequence, and ρ is the limit of the sequence $\{\rho_n\}$ if and only if $(L, U) = f(\rho)$ is the limit of $\{(L_n, U_n)\}$.

This proposition shows the complete equivalence of the two approaches to real numbers.

Exercises

1.1 (a) Show that every ring R has a unique element θ such that $a + \theta = \theta + a = a$ for every $a \in R$.

(b) Show that $\theta \cdot a = a \cdot \theta = \theta$ for every $a \in R$.

1.2 Show that every field F has a unique element e such that for every $a \in F$, $ae = ea = a$.

1.3 Show that there is a field which has exactly five elements but that there is no field which has exactly ten elements.

1.4 Show that for every positive integer n there is a ring which has exactly n elements.

1.5 Show that in an ordered field F for every $x \neq \theta$, $xx > \theta$.

1.6 Give the details of the proof that if e is the identity element of an ordered field F then the mapping

$$f\left(\frac{n}{m}\right) = \frac{ne}{me}$$

produces an isomorphism between the rational field R and a subfield of F.

1.7 Show that there is no rational number whose square is 2 but that for every rational number $\epsilon > 0$ there are two rational numbers r and s such that $r^2 < 2 < s^2 < r^2 + \epsilon$.

2.1 Show that for every pair of rational numbers a and b, $|a + b| \leqq |a| + |b|$ and $|ab| = |a||b|$.

2.2 Show that if a sequence of rational numbers has a limit it is a fundamental sequence.

2.3 Show that every subsequence of a fundamental sequence of rational numbers is fundamental.

2.4 Show that the relation for fundamental sequences of rational numbers —$\{r_n\} \sim \{s_n\}$ if for every $\epsilon > 0$ there is an N such that if $n > N$ then $|r_n - s_n| < \epsilon$—satisfies the conditions for an equivalence relation given in Theorem 2, Chapter 1.

2.5 Show, for every rational number r, that $\{r^n/n!\}$ is a fundamental sequence.

3.1 Define the difference $\rho - \sigma$ between equivalence classes of fundamental sequences of rational numbers.

4.1 Prove the distributive law $\rho(\sigma + \tau) = \rho\sigma + \rho\tau$ for equivalence classes of fundamental sequences.

4.2 Show that if ρ and σ are equivalence classes of fundamental sequences of rational numbers such that ρ is not the zero class and $\{r_n\} \in \rho$, $\{r_n'\} \in \rho$, where $r_n \neq 0$, $r_n' \neq 0$, for every n, and $\{s_n\} \in \sigma$, $\{s_n'\} \in \sigma$, then $\{s_n/r_n\} \sim \{s_n'/r_n'\}$.

4.3 Define ρ^σ. Assuming the laws of exponents for rational numbers, show that they hold for equivalence classes of fundamental sequences.

5.1 Prove that for every ρ and σ, if $\rho \neq \sigma$ then (a) either $\rho > \sigma$ or $\rho < \sigma$, (b) if $\rho > \sigma$ then it is not true that $\sigma > \rho$, and (c) if $\rho > \sigma$ and $\sigma > \tau$ then $\rho > \tau$.

6.1 Show that every equivalence class, $\rho > \theta$, of fundamental sequences has a member of the form

$$\left\{r_n = k + \frac{k_1}{10} + \cdots + \frac{k_n}{10^n}\right\},$$

where $k, k_1, \cdots, k_n, \cdots$ are integers and $0 \leqq k_n \leqq 9$ for every n.

6.2 Generalize Exercise 6.1.

6.3 If $\{r_{1n}\}, \{r_{2n}\}, \cdots$ is a fundamental sequence of fundamental sequences, let r_{mn_m} be such that if $n > n_m$ then $|r_{mn_m} - r_{mn}| < 1/m$ for every m. Is $\{r_{mn_m}\}$ a fundamental sequence? Is it a limit of $\{r_{1n}\}, \{r_{2n}\}, \cdots$? Either prove or give a counterexample.

6.4 If $\{r_{1n}\}, \{r_{2n}\}, \cdots$ is a fundamental sequence of fundamental sequences and $\{r_{1n}\} \sim \{s_{1n}\}, \{r_{2n}\} \sim \{s_{2n}\}, \cdots$ show that $\{s_{1n}\}, \{s_{2n}\}, \cdots$ is a fundamental sequence, and if $\{r_n\}$ and $\{s_n\}$ are the respective sequence limits then $\{r_n\} \sim \{s_n\}$.

7.1 Show that a real number is rational if and only if its decimal expansion is repeating.

7.2 Find out what a continued fraction is and show that a continued fraction is terminating if and only if the real number it represents is rational.

7.3 Show that the real-number system is archimedean.

7.4 Show that the rational numbers are dense in the real numbers: i.e., if ρ and σ are real numbers and $\rho < \sigma$, then there is a rational number τ such that $\rho < \tau < \sigma$.

8.1 For every fundamental sequence of rational numbers $\{r_n\}$ let L consist of all rational numbers which are less than all but a finite number of terms of $\{r_n\}$ with the exception of the largest such number if there is one, and let U be all other rational numbers. This associates a Dedekind cut with every fundamental sequence. Show that if $\{r_n\}$ and $\{s_n\}$ are not equivalent then the corresponding Dedekind cuts are different.

8.2 Show that every Dedekind cut corresponds to some fundamental sequence in the correspondence given in Exercise 8.1.

8.3 Prove that every Dedekind cut in the rationals has an addition inverse.

8.4 Prove that every Dedekind cut in the rationals, except the cut which determines 0, has a multiplication inverse.

8.5 Prove that $f(\rho\sigma) = f(\rho)f(\sigma)$ where $f(\rho)$ is the mapping of equivalence classes onto Dedekind cuts defined in §8.

8.6 Prove Proposition 26.

8.7 Show that in the real-number system every Dedekind cut determines a real number, thus showing that the real numbers do not have the defect with respect to Dedekind cuts that the rationals have.

References

L. M. Graves, *Theory of Functions of a Real Variable*, New York, 1946, Chap. 2.

E. W. Hobson, *The Theory of Functions of a Real Variable*, Cambridge, 1927, Chap. 1.

K. Knopp, *Theory and Application of Infinite Series*, London, 1928, Chaps. 1, 2.

E. Landau, *Grundlagen der Analysis*, New York, 1946.

O. Perron, *Irrationalzahlen*, New York, 1948, Chap. 1.

B. L. van der Waerden, *Modern Algebra*, New York, 1950, Chap. 9.

4

Limit Theorems

1. *Introduction*

In the preceding chapter, we introduced the real-number system and showed that it is an ordered field which is complete and has a dense denumerable set, the rational numbers. The completeness property refers to the fact that every fundamental sequence of real numbers has a limit, and the density property refers to the fact that there is a rational number between every two real numbers.

Our purpose now is to derive a number of new properties of the real-number system from the ones we already have. It is indeed true that certain of the properties we shall obtain do not belong only to the real-number system but remain valid for a wide class of systems. Indications will be given of such possible generalizations.

2. *Least upper bound and greatest lower bound of a set*

If S is any set of real numbers and if there is an $x \in S$ such that $y \leqq x$ for every $y \in S$, then S is said to have a maximum. It is easy to show that every finite set of real numbers has a maximum. However, there are infinite sets of real numbers, such as the set of positive integers, which have no maxima.

DEFINITION 1. A number ξ is said to be an *upper bound* of S if $\xi \geqq x$ for every $x \in S$; a number η is said to be a *lower bound* of S if $\eta \leqq x$ for every $x \in S$.

If S has an upper bound and a lower bound then S is said to be bounded.

There are bounded sets of real numbers, such as the set $-1, -1/2, \cdots, -1/n, \cdots$, which have no maxima.

DEFINITION 2. A number u is said to be a *least upper bound* of S if (1) u is an upper bound of S, and (2) if ξ is an upper bound of S, then $\xi \geqq u$. A number l is said to be a *greatest lower bound* of S if (1) l is a lower bound of S and (2) if η is a lower bound of S, then $\eta \leqq l$.

The least upper bound of a set S is designated as *sup* S and the greatest lower bound as *inf* S.

PROPOSITION 1. A number u is a least upper bound of S if and only if (1) for every $\xi \in S$, $u \geqq \xi$ and (2) for every $\epsilon > 0$ there is a $\xi \in S$ such that $\xi > u - \epsilon$.

Proof. Property (1) is a restatement of the fact that u is an upper bound. For (2), suppose there is a $k > 0$ such that for every $\xi \in S$, $\xi \leqq u - k$. Then $u - k < u$ is an upper bound of S, so that u is not the least upper bound. The converse is also easy to prove.

A similar result holds for the greatest lower bound.

PROPOSITION 2. A set S can have at most one least upper bound.

Proof. If u_1 and u_2 are both least upper bounds of S then they are both upper bounds, so that $u_1 \leq u_2$ and $u_2 \leq u_1$. Hence, $u_1 = u_2$.

A similar result holds for the greatest lower bound.

Not every set has a least upper bound. Indeed, not every set has an upper bound. For example, the set of positive integers does not have an upper bound. However, in contrast with the above remark that there are bounded sets which have no maxima, we have the following theorem.

THEOREM 1. If a set S is nonempty and has an upper bound it has a least upper bound.

Proof. There are two real numbers u_1 and x_1 such that $u_1 - x_1 = 1$, where u_1 is an upper bound of S and x_1 is not an upper bound of S. Let m_2 be the midpoint of (x_1, u_1). If m_2 is an upper bound of S, let $x_2 = x_1$ and $u_2 = m_2$. If m_2 is not an upper bound of S, let $x_2 = m_2$ and $u_2 = u_1$. In either case, u_2 is an upper bound of S, x_2 is not an upper bound of S, and $u_2 - x_2 = 1/2$. Suppose, for a positive integer p, if we have the upper bounds $u_1, u_2, \cdots, u_p$ and the numbers $x_1, x_2, \cdots, x_p$, which are not upper bounds and are such that $u_1 - x_1 = 1$, $u_2 - x_2 = 1/2$, $\cdots$, $u_p - x_p = 1/2^{p-1}$, and such that $u_1 \geqq u_2 \geqq \cdots \geqq u_p$ and $x_1 \leqq x_2 \leqq \cdots \leqq x_p$, let m_{p+1} be the midpoint of (x_p, u_p). If m_{p+1} is an upper bound of S, let $x_{p+1} = x_p$ and $u_{p+1} = m_{p+1}$. If m_{p+1} is not an upper bound, let $x_{p+1} = m_{p+1}$ and $u_{p+1} = u_p$. In either case, $u_{p+1} - x_{p+1} = 1/2^p$. By finite induction, we have a nonincreasing sequence $u_1, u_2, \cdots, u_n, \cdots$. The sequence $\{u_n\}$ is a fundamental sequence. For let $\epsilon > 0$. There is an N such that $1/2^N + 1/2^{N+1} + \cdots < \epsilon$. Let p,

$q > N$ with $p < q$. Then

$$|u_p - u_q| \leqq |u_p - u_{p+1}| + |u_{p+1} - u_{p+2}| + \cdots + |u_{q-1} - u_q|$$
$$\leqq \frac{1}{2^p} + \cdots + \frac{1}{2^{q-1}} < \epsilon.$$

Hence $\{u_n\}$ has a limit u.

We show that u is the least upper bound of S. First, u is an upper bound. Let $x \in S$. For every $\epsilon > 0$, there is an n such that $u + \epsilon > u_n$. But $u_n > x$. Hence $u + \epsilon > x$. Since $\epsilon > 0$ is arbitrary, $u \geqq x$. Thus u is an upper bound of S. Next, we show that u is a least upper bound of S. For, suppose $\xi < u$. There is an n such that $u_n - x_n < u - \xi$. But $u - x_n \leqq u_n - x_n$. Hence $u - x_n < u - \xi$ so that $x_n > \xi$. But x_n is not an upper bound of S. Hence ξ is not an upper bound of S. Accordingly, we have u as the least upper bound of S.

We apply this result to sequences. As has been pointed out in Chapter 3, a sequence $\{a_n\}$ is not a set. But every sequence has an associated set, the set of values assumed by its terms.

A sequence is said to have an upper bound, to have a lower bound, and to be bounded, according as its set of values has an upper bound, has a lower bound, or is bounded.

DEFINITION 3. A sequence $\{a_n\}$ is said to be *nondecreasing* if $a_{n+1} \geqq a_n$ for every positive integer n. If $a_{n+1} \leqq a_n$ for every positive integer n, then $\{a_n\}$ is said to be *nonincreasing*.

THEOREM 2. If $\{a_n\}$ is a nondecreasing sequence which has an upper bound, then $\{a_n\}$ is convergent and its limit is the least upper bound.

Proof. Recall that a convergent sequence is simply a fundamental sequence. Since $\{a_n\}$ has an upper bound it has a least upper bound u. For every $\epsilon > 0$, there is an N such that $u \geqq a_N > u - \epsilon$. Since for every $n > N$, $a_n \geqq a_N$ and $u \geqq a_n$, we have $u \geqq a_n > u - \epsilon$. In other words, for every $n > N$, $|u - a_n| < \epsilon$. This proves the theorem.

A similar result holds for nonincreasing sequences.

3. *Nests of intervals*

The simplest kinds of sets of real numbers are intervals.

DEFINITION 4. A *closed interval* $I = [a, b]$ is the set of real numbers x such that $a \leqq x \leqq b$, $(a < b)$. An *open interval* $I = (a, b)$ is the set of real numbers x such that $a < x < b$.

We shall sometimes also be concerned with the intervals $I = [a, b)$ and $I = (a, b]$, which are respectively the sets of points x for which $a \leqq x < b$ and $a < x \leqq b$.

PROPOSITION 3. If $I_1, I_2, \cdots, I_n$ is a finite number of closed intervals, the set

$$I = \bigcap_{k=1}^{n} I_k$$

is either a closed interval, a single point, or is empty.

Proof. Let $I_k = [a_k, b_k]$ for every $k = 1, 2, \cdots, n$. Let $a = \max [a_1, a_2, \cdots, a_n]$ and $b = \min [b_1, b_2, \cdots, b_n]$. There is an i such that $a = a_i$ and a j such that $b = b_j$. There are three cases.

Case 1. $a_i = b_j = \xi$.

Then for every $k = 1, 2, \cdots, n$, $a_k \leqq a_i = \xi = b_j \leqq b_k$. It follows that $\xi \in I_k$ for every $k = 1, 2, \cdots, n$. Hence $\xi \in I = \bigcap_{k=1}^{n} I_k$. Suppose now that $\eta < \xi$. Then $\eta < a_i$ so that $\eta \notin I_i$ and, hence, $\eta \notin I = \bigcap_{k=1}^{n} I_k$. Moreover, if $\eta > \xi$, then $\eta > b_j$ so that $\eta \notin I_j$ and, hence, $\eta \notin I = \bigcap_{k=1}^{n} I_k$. Therefore, in this case, I is a single point.

Case 2. $a_i < b_j$.

Suppose $\xi \in [a_i, b_j]$. Then for every $k = 1, 2, \cdots, n$, $a_k \leqq a_i \leqq \xi \leqq b_j \leqq b_k$. It follows that $\xi \in I_k$ for every $k = 1, 2, \cdots, n$, so that $\xi \in I = \bigcap_{k=1}^{n} I_k$. Suppose $\xi < a_i$. Then $\xi \notin I_i$ so that $\xi \notin I = \bigcap_{k=1}^{n} I_k$. If $\xi > b_j$, then $\xi \notin I_j$, so that $\xi \notin I = \bigcap_{k=1}^{n} I_k$. Hence $I = \bigcap_{k=1}^{n} I_k = [a_i, b_j]$. Therefore, in this case, I is a closed interval.

Case 3. $a_i > b_j$.

If $\xi < a_i$ then $\xi \notin I_i$. If $\xi \geqq a_i$ then $\xi \geqq a_i > b_j$, so that $\xi \notin I_j$. In either case, $\xi \notin I = \bigcap_{k=1}^{n} I_k$. Hence, in this case, I is empty.

In contrast to this result, the following proposition holds for open intervals.

PROPOSITION 4. If $I_1, I_2, \cdots, I_n$ is a finite number of open intervals, the set

$$I = \bigcap_{k=1}^{n} I_k$$

is either an open interval or is empty.

Proof. Let $I_k = (a_k, b_k)$ for every $k = 1, 2, \cdots, n$. Let $a = \max [a_1, a_2, \cdots, a_n]$ and $b = \min [b_1, b_2, \cdots, b_n]$. There is an i such that $a = a_i$ and a j such that $b = b_j$. There are two cases:

Case 1. $a_i < b_j$.

If $\xi \in (a_i, b_j)$, then for every $k = 1, 2, \cdots, n$, $a_k \leqq a_i < \xi < b_j \leqq b_k$, so that $\xi \in I_k$. Hence $\xi \in I = \bigcap_{k=1}^{n} I_k$. If $\xi \notin (a_i, b_j)$, then either $\xi \leqq a_i$ or $\xi \geqq b_j$, so that either $\xi \notin (a_i, b_i)$ or $\xi \notin (a_j, b_j)$ and $\xi \notin I = \bigcap_{k=1}^{n} I_k$. Hence $I = \bigcap_{k=1}^{n} I_k = (a_i, b_j)$.

Case 2. $a_i \geqq b_j$.

If $\xi \leqq a_i$, then $\xi \notin (a_i, b_i) = I_i$. If $\xi > a_i$, then $\xi > a_i \geqq b_j$, so that $\xi \notin (a_j, b_j) = I_j$. Hence, for every ξ, $\xi \notin \bigcap_{k=1}^{n} I_k$, so that the set $I = \bigcap_{k=1}^{n} I_k$ is empty.

We now come to the case of a nonincreasing sequence of closed intervals.

THEOREM 3. If $I_1 = [a_1, b_1], \cdots, I_n = [a_n, b_n], \cdots$ is a nonincreasing sequence of closed intervals whose lengths converge to zero (i.e., $\lim_{n\to\infty} (b_n - a_n) = 0$), then $\bigcap_{k=1}^{\infty} I_k$ is a single point.

Proof. The sequence $\{a_n\}$ is nondecreasing and the sequence $\{b_n\}$ is nonincreasing. Now, $\{a_n\}$ has an upper bound. In particular, b_k is an upper bound for every k. Hence, by Theorem 2, the sequence $\{a_n\}$ is convergent. Let $\xi = \lim_{n\to\infty} a_n$. We show that $\xi \in I_k$, for every $k = 1, 2, \cdots$.

Suppose, on the contrary, that there is a k such that $\xi \notin I_k$. This means that either $\xi < a_k$ or $\xi > b_k$. Of course, since $\{a_k\}$ is nondecreasing it is not true that $\xi < a_k$. Hence $\xi > b_k$. Now, since b_k is an upper bound of $\{a_k\}$, it follows that ξ is not the least upper bound. This contradicts Theorem 2, according to which ξ is the least upper bound. Hence $\xi \in \bigcap_{k=1}^{\infty} I_k$.

Next, suppose $\eta \in \bigcap_{k=1}^{\infty} I_k$. Let $\epsilon > 0$. There is a positive integer n such that $b_n - a_n < \epsilon$. But $a_n \leqq \xi \leqq b_n$ and $a_n \leqq \eta \leqq b_n$ so that $|\xi - \eta| < \epsilon$. Since $\epsilon > 0$ is arbitrary, it follows that $\xi = \eta$.

We repeat here the application of Theorem 3 which was given in Chapter 2.

THEOREM 4. The set of all real numbers is nondenumerable.

Proof. The theorem is proved if we show that no sequence of distinct real numbers contains all the real numbers.

Let $\xi_1, \xi_2, \cdots, \xi_n, \cdots$ be a sequence of distinct real numbers. There is a closed interval I_1 of length less than 1 such that $\xi_1 \notin I_1$. There is a closed subinterval I_2 of I_1 of length less than $1/2$ such that $\xi_2 \notin I_2$. If we have the closed intervals

$$I_1 \supset I_2 \supset \cdots \supset I_{n-1}$$

such that the length of I_k is less than $1/k$ and $\xi_k \notin I_k$ for every $k = 1, 2, \cdots, n-1$, then there is a closed subinterval I_n of I_{n-1} whose length is less than $1/n$ such that $\xi_n \notin I_n$. By finite induction, we have a nonincreasing sequence of closed intervals

$$I_1 \supset I_2 \supset \cdots \supset I_n \supset \cdots$$

whose lengths converge to 0 such that for every n, $\xi_n \notin I_n$.

By Theorem 3, the set $\bigcap_{n=1}^{\infty} I_n$ consists of a single point ξ. Since for every n, $\xi \in I_n$ and $\xi_n \notin I_n$, we have $\xi \neq \xi_n$. This proves the theorem.

This theorem has an immediate generalization which is obtained by close examination of the proof. We shall see later that this generalization is of primary importance.

We shall need some further concepts before proving the generalization.

DEFINITION 5. A set S is said to be *nowhere dense* if for every open interval I there is an open subinterval $J \subset I$ such that no points of S are in J: i.e., $S \cap J = \phi$.

S is then nowhere dense if and only if for every closed interval I there is a closed interval $J \subset I$ such that no points of S are in J.

Examples:

1. Every finite set is nowhere dense.
2. There are denumerable sets which are not nowhere dense. The set of rational numbers is not nowhere dense.
3. We shall see later that there are infinite sets, indeed nondenumerable sets, which are nowhere dense.

DEFINITION 6. A set S is said to be of the first category if it is the union of a finite number or a denumerable number of nowhere-dense sets. If S is not of the first category it is said to be of the second category.

Example:

1. Every denumerable set is of the first category, since every set which consists of a single point is nowhere dense.

Moreover, as we shall see later, there are nondenumerable sets of the first category.

That there are sets which are of the second category is shown by the following theorem.

THEOREM 5. The set of all real numbers is of the second category.

The proof of this theorem is exactly that of Theorem 4.

Let S be a set of the first category. Then S is the union of a denumerable number of nowhere dense sets, i.e.,

$$S = S_1 \cup S_2 \cup \cdots \cup S_n \cup \cdots,$$

where the sets $S_1, S_2, \cdots, S_n, \cdots$ are all nowhere dense.

Let I be a closed interval. Since S_1 is nowhere dense, there is a closed interval $I_1 \subset I$ of length less than 1 such that $I_1 \cap S_1 = \phi$. Proceeding as in the proof of Theorem 4, we obtain a nonincreasing sequence of closed intervals

$$I_1 \supset I_2 \supset \cdots \supset I_n \supset \cdots$$

such that, for every n, the length of I_n is less than $1/n$ and $I_n \cap S_n = \phi$, the empty set. By Theorem 3, the set $\bigcap_{n=1}^{\infty} I_n$ consists of a single real number ξ. For every n, $\xi \in I_n$, but $I_n \cap S_n = \phi$, so that $\xi \notin S_n$. Hence $\xi \notin S$. We have shown that for every set S of the first category S does not contain all the real numbers. Hence the set of all real numbers is of the second category.

COROLLARY 1. Every interval is a set of the second category.

Since we have introduced the concept "set of the first category," this is a proper place to discuss some of its simple properties.

PROPOSITION 5. Every subset of a set of the first category is of the first category.

Proof. Let S be of the first category and $T \subset S$. Then $S = \bigcup_{n=1}^{\infty} S_n$ where the sets S_n are nowhere dense. By a direct application of the definition, we see that every subset of a nowhere dense set is nowhere dense. Thus the sets $T_n = T \cap S_n$ are nowhere dense. The proof that T is of the first category will be finished if we show that $T = \bigcup_{n=1}^{\infty} T_n$. Suppose $x \in \bigcup_{n=1}^{\infty} T_n$. There is an n such that $x \in T_n$. But $T_n = T \cap S_n$, so that $x \in T$. Hence $\bigcup_{n=1}^{\infty} T_n \subset T$. Suppose $x \in T$. Then since $T \subset S$, $x \in S$ so that, since $S = \bigcup_{n=1}^{\infty} S_n$, there is an n such that $x \in S_n$. But since $x \in T$ and $x \in S_n$, we have $x \in T_n = T \cap S_n$. Hence $x \in \bigcup_{n=1}^{\infty} T_n$ and $\bigcup_{n=1}^{\infty} T_n \supset T$. The two inclusions show that $T = \bigcup_{n=1}^{\infty} T_n$.

PROPOSITION 6. The union of a finite or denumerable number of sets of the first category is of the first category.

Proof. Let $S = \bigcup_{n=1}^{\infty} S_n$ where S_n is of the first category for every positive integer n. For each n,

$$S_n = \bigcup_{m=1}^{\infty} S_{nm},$$

where the sets S_{nm} are nowhere dense. Now $S = \bigcup_{n=1}^{\infty} \bigcup_{m=1}^{\infty} S_{nm}$, so that S is the union of a denumerable number of nowhere dense sets and is, accordingly, of the first category.

PROPOSITION 7. The complement of a set of the first category relative to an interval is of the second category.

Proof. Let I be an interval, open or closed, and $S \subset I$. Suppose S is of the first category. Let $C(S)$ be the complement of S relative to $I. I = S \cup C(S)$. If $C(S)$ were of the first category, then, by Proposition 6, I would be of the first category. But this contradicts the fact that I is of the second category. Hence $C(S)$ is of the second category.

That the complement of a set of the second category need not be of the first category is obvious.

4. *Metric space*

In obtaining the results of the last section, only certain properties of the real numbers were used. In fact, these results hold for any metric space.

A metric space is a set S and a distance $\delta(x, y)$ defined for all pairs $x \in S$, $y \in S$, subject to the following conditions:

1. $\delta(x, y)$ is a nonnegative real number for every $x \in S$, $y \in S$,
2. $\delta(x, y) = 0$ if and only if $x = y$,
3. $\delta(x, y) = \delta(y, x)$ for every $x \in S$, $y \in S$,
4. $\delta(x, y) + \delta(y, z) \geqq \delta(x, z)$ for every $x \in S$, $y \in S$, $z \in S$.

We give several examples of metric spaces.

1. The set of real numbers is a metric space if $\delta(x, y) = |x - y|$.
2. The set of rational numbers is a metric space if $\delta(x, y) = |x - y|$.
3. The set of n-tuples $x = (x_1, \cdots, x_n)$ of real numbers is a metric space if $\delta(x, y) = [\sum_{i=1}^{n} (x_i - y_i)^2]^{1/2}$.
4. The set of n-tuples $x = (x_1, \cdots, x_n)$ of real numbers is a metric space if
$$\delta(x, y) = \max [|x_i - y_i| \mid i = 1, \cdots, n],$$
where the notation $[|x_i - y_i| \mid i = 1, \cdots, n]$ means
$$[|x_1 - y_1|, |x_2 - y_2|, \cdots, |x_n - y_n|].$$
5. The set of those sequences $x = (x_1, x_2, \cdots, x_n, \cdots)$ of real numbers for which $\sum_{n=1}^{\infty} x_n^2 < \infty$ is a metric space if $\delta(x, y) = [\sum_{i=1}^{\infty} (x_i - y_i)^2]^{1/2}$.

It is necessary here to show that if $\sum_{i=1}^{\infty} x_i^2 < \infty$ and $\sum_{i=1}^{\infty} y_i^2 < \infty$ then $\sum_{i=1}^{\infty} (x_i - y_i)^2 < \infty$, as well as that the axioms of a metric space are satisfied.

This space is called Hilbert space.

Convergence and limit may be defined for any metric space.

DEFINITION 7. A sequence $x_1, x_2, \cdots, x_n, \cdots$ in a metric space S is said to be convergent if for every $\epsilon > 0$ there is an N such that if $m, n > N$ then $\delta(x_m, x_n) < \epsilon$.

DEFINITION 8. A point x is said to be the limit of a sequence $x_1, x_2, \cdots, x_n, \cdots$ in a metric space S if for every $\epsilon > 0$ there is an N such that if $n > N$ then $\delta(x, x_n) < \epsilon$.

For the spaces of real numbers and rational numbers these definitions specialize to the ones already given. We give a further definition.

DEFINITION 9. A metric space S is complete if every convergent sequence in S has a limit.

All the spaces given above as examples, with the exception of the space of rational numbers, are complete metric spaces. We leave this for the reader to prove for examples (3), (4), and (5).

To illustrate the extension of some of the theorems on real numbers to any metric space, we consider one or two examples. We first need another definition.

DEFINITION 10. In a metric space S, if $x \in S$ and $r > 0$, the open sphere $\sigma(x, r)$ is the set of all $y \in S$ such that $\delta(x, y) < r$, and the closed sphere $\bar{\sigma}(x, r)$ is the set of all $y \in S$ such that $\delta(x, y) \leqq r$.

In analogy with Theorem 3, we have:

PROPOSITION 8. If S is a complete metric space and $\bar{\sigma}(x_1, r_1) \supset \bar{\sigma}(x_2, r_2) \supset \cdots \supset \bar{\sigma}(x_n, r_n) \supset \cdots$ is a nonincreasing sequence of closed spheres in S for which $\lim_{n \to \infty} r_n = 0$, the set $\bigcap_{n=1}^{\infty} \bar{\sigma}(x_n, r_n)$ consists of a single point.

Proof. For every positive integer n, let $y_n \in \bar{\sigma}(x_n, r_n)$. Then $\{y_n\}$ is a convergent sequence in S. For let $\epsilon > 0$. There is an N such that $r_N < \epsilon/2$. For every $m, n > N$, $y_m \in \bar{\sigma}(x_N, r_N)$ and $y_n \in \bar{\sigma}(x_N, r_N)$. Hence $\delta(y_m, x_N) \leqq r_N < \epsilon/2$ and $\delta(y_n, x_N) \leqq r_N < \epsilon/2$. Accordingly, we have

$$\delta(y_m, y_n) \leqq \delta(y_m, x_N) + \delta(x_N, y_n) < \epsilon.$$

Since S is complete, the sequence $\{y_n\}$ has a limit y. We show that $y \in \bar{\sigma}(x_n, r_n)$ for every positive integer n. Let $\epsilon > 0$. There is an N such that for every $m > N$, $\delta(y, y_m) < \epsilon$. Pick $m > n$. Now $y_m \in \bar{\sigma}(x_m, r_m)$, so that $y_m \in \bar{\sigma}(x_n, r_n)$, and so $\delta(x_n, y_m) \leqq r_n$. It follows that

$$\delta(x_n, y) \leqq \delta(x_n, y_m) + \delta(y_m, y) < \epsilon + r_n.$$

Since this holds for every $\epsilon > 0$, $\delta(x_n, y) \leqq r_n$ and $y \in \bar{\sigma}(x_n, r_n)$. We have shown that $y \in \bigcap_{n=1}^{\infty} \bar{\sigma}(x_n, r_n)$.

Let $z \in \bigcap_{n=1}^{\infty} \bar{\sigma}(x_n, r_n)$. For every $\epsilon > 0$, there is an N such that $r_N < \epsilon/2$. Now $\delta(x_N, y) \leqq r_N < \epsilon/2$ and $\delta(x_N, z) \leqq r_N < \epsilon/2$, so that $\delta(y, z) \leqq \delta(y, x_N) + \delta(x_N, z) < \epsilon$. Since $\epsilon > 0$ is arbitrary, $\delta(y, z) = 0$, whence $y = z$. This completes the proof.

Our next proposition requires the following definition.

DEFINITION 11. A set T in a metric space S is nowhere dense if every sphere $\bar{\sigma}(x, r)$ has a subsphere $\bar{\sigma}(y, s) \subset \bar{\sigma}(x, r)$ such that $\bar{\sigma}(y, s) \cap T = \phi$. A set T is of the first category if it is the union of a finite or denumerable number of nowhere-dense sets. If T is not of the first category, it is of the second category.

PROPOSITION 9. Every complete metric space S is of the second category.

Proof. Let $T \subset S$ be of the first category. We show that there is an $x \in S - T$. Since T is of the first category, $T = \bigcup_{n=1}^{\infty} T_n$, where the sets T_n are nowhere dense.

There is a closed sphere $\bar{\sigma}(x_1, r_1)$, with $r_1 < 1$, such that $\bar{\sigma}(x_1, r_1) \cap T_1 = \phi$. There is a closed sphere $\bar{\sigma}(x_2, r_2) \subset \bar{\sigma}(x_1, r_1)$, with $r_2 < 1/2$, such that $\bar{\sigma}(x_2, r_2) \cap T_2 = \phi$. Proceeding as in the proof of Theorem 4, we obtain a nonincreasing sequence of closed spheres

$$\bar{\sigma}(x_1, r_1) \supset \bar{\sigma}(x_2, r_2) \supset \cdots \supset \bar{\sigma}(x_n, r_n) \supset \cdots,$$

with $r_n < 1/n$ such that $\bar{\sigma}(x_n, r_n) \cap T_n = \phi$ for every positive integer n.

By Proposition 8, $\bigcap_{n=1}^{\infty} \bar{\sigma}(x_n, r_n)$ consists of a single point x. As in the proof of Theorem 5, $x \notin T$.

5. *Limit points of a set*

We now return to the real-number system. Every set S of real numbers has associated with it a set of limit points, which will be defined in this section. While the same word is used for *limit point of a set* and *limit of a convergent sequence*, we must be clear at the start that the two ideas are different. We have already pointed out, in particular, that a sequence is not a set.

DEFINITION 12. If I is an open interval and ξ is a real number, I is said to be a *neighborhood* of ξ if $\xi \in I$.

DEFINITION 13a. A point ξ is said to be a *limit point* of a set S if every neighborhood of ξ contains an infinite number of points of S.

DEFINITION 13b. A point ξ is said to be a limit point of a set S if every neighborhood of ξ contains a point of S which is different from ξ.

PROPOSITION 10. The two definitions of limit point are equivalent.

Proof. This means that ξ is a limit point of S according to the first definition if and only if it is a limit point of S according to the second definition.

The proof is left to the student.

A set S may have no limit points, it may have one limit point, or it may have more than one limit point. A limit point of S may be in S or it may not be in S. For example:

1. If S is the set of rational numbers, every real number is a limit point of S.
2. If S is the open interval $(0, 1)$, then every point in the closed interval $[0, 1]$ is a limit point of S.
3. If S is the set of points $1/2, 1/3, \cdots, 1/n, \cdots$ then S has one limit point, 0. In this case, no point in S is a limit point of S. However, S does have a limit point.
4. If S is the set of points $1, 2, 3, \cdots, n, \cdots$ then S has no limit points. This is an example of an infinite set having no limit points. It should be noted that this set does not have an upper bound.

In contrast with this example we have the following theorem, known as the Bolzano-Weierstrass Theorem.

THEOREM 6. Every bounded infinite set S has at least one limit point.

Proof. Since S is bounded, there is a closed interval I such that $S \subset I$. The midpoint of I divides I into two closed subintervals. (These subintervals are disjoint except for a single point, but all that matters here is that their lengths are half that of I.) At least one of these subintervals contains an infinite number of points of S; for otherwise S, as the union of two finite sets, would be finite, contrary to the hypothesis. Let I_1 be such an interval. The midpoint of I_1 divides I_1 into two closed subintervals one of which, call it I_2, contains an infinite number of points of S. We then obtain a nonincreasing sequence of closed intervals $I \supset I_1 \supset I_2 \supset \cdots \supset I_n \supset \cdots$, each of which is half as long as its predecessor and contains an infinite number of points of S. By Theorem 3, the set $\bigcap_{n=1}^{\infty} I_n$ consists of a single point ξ.

We show that ξ is a limit point of S. Let $\mathcal{J} = (\alpha, \beta)$ be any open interval such that $\xi \in \mathcal{J}$, i.e., $\alpha < \xi < \beta$. Let $k = \min [\xi - \alpha, \beta - \xi]$. Then $k > 0$. There is an I_n whose length is less than k. Hence $I_n \subset \mathcal{J}$. But I_n contains an infinite number of points of S. Accordingly, $\mathcal{J}$ contains an infinite number of points of S. Since $\mathcal{J}$ is an arbitrary neighborhood of ξ, we have shown that ξ is a limit point of S. This proves the theorem.

We are also ready to prove the important Borel Covering Theorem. This theorem says that if a closed interval I is completely covered by a set $\mathbf{J}$ of open intervals, where in general $\mathbf{J}$ is an infinite set, it may be possible to leave out some of the open intervals and still have all of I covered. Indeed, a certain finite number of the intervals in J will cover I. The significance of this theorem as a tool will only be appreciated after it is used several times.

THEOREM 7. If I is a closed interval and J is a set of open intervals which covers I, i.e., for every $x \in I$ there is a $\mathcal{J} \in$ J such that $x \in \mathcal{J}$, then there is a finite set of intervals in J, say $\mathcal{J}_1, \mathcal{J}_2, \cdots, \mathcal{J}_n$, such that for every $x \in I$ there is a k, with $1 \leq k \leq n$, such that $x \in \mathcal{J}_k$.

Proof. Suppose the theorem false. Then no finite number of intervals of J covers I. The midpoint of I divides I into two closed intervals at least one of which, call it I_1, is covered by no finite number of intervals of J. Proceding in the usual way we obtain a nonincreasing sequence of closed intervals

$$I \supset I_1 \supset I_2 \supset \cdots \supset I_n \supset \cdots,$$

each member of which is half as long as its predecessor; every closed interval I_n of the sequence is such that no finite number of intervals of J covers it. Now, by Theorem 3, $\bigcap_{n=1}^{\infty} I_n$ consists of a single point ξ. $\xi \in I$. Hence there is a $\mathcal{J} \in$ J such that $\xi \in \mathcal{J}$. Let $\mathcal{J} = (\alpha, \beta)$. There is an n such that the length of I_n is less than min $[\xi - \alpha, \beta - \xi]$, so that $I_n \subset \mathcal{J}$. In other words, I_n is covered by a finite number, one, of elements of J. This contradicts the assumption that the theorem is false.

6. *Bolzano-Weierstrass Theorem in metric space*

In §4, we generalized certain facts about real numbers to metric spaces. The Bolzano-Weierstrass Theorem admits such an extension, but the form of the theorem must first be changed.

The concepts which appear in the statement of the theorem must first be given their equivalents for an arbitrary metric space.

DEFINITION 14. A set T in a metric space S in said to be bounded if there is an $M > 0$ such that, for every $x \in T, y \in T, \delta(x, y) < M$.

DEFINITION 15. A neighborhood of a point ξ in a metric space S is an open sphere $\sigma(x, r)$ such that $\xi \in \sigma(x, r)$.

DEFINITION 16. In a metric space S, a point ξ is a limit point of a set T if every neighborhood of ξ contains an infinite number of points of T.

There are bounded infinite sets T in certain metric spaces which have no limit points. An example is the space of rational numbers. The set whose members are .01, .01001, $\cdots$ is bounded and has no limit point. The reason, here, is that the space is not complete.

A second example is Hilbert space H. The set T whose members are $\xi_1 = (1, 0, \cdots)$, $\xi_2 = (0, 1, 0, \cdots)$, $\cdots$ is bounded, since $\delta(x, y) = \sqrt{2}$

for every $x \in T$, $y \in T$. However, T has no limit point. For let $x = (x_1, x_2, \cdots, x_n, \cdots)$ be any element of H. Suppose $\delta(x, \xi_m) < 1/2$ for some m. Then $x_m > 1/2$. Hence, for any $k \neq m$, $\delta(x, \xi_k) > 1/2$. It follows that x is not a limit point of T.

It appears accordingly that the consequences of boundedness in an arbitrary metric space are not the same as in the space of real numbers.

We introduce a notion of total boundedness which in the space of real numbers is equivalent to boundedness.

DEFINITION 17. In a metric space S, a set T is totally bounded if for every $\epsilon > 0$ there is a finite set $x_1, x_2, \cdots, x_n$ in S such that for every $x \in T$ there is at least one x_k, $k = 1, \cdots, n$ such that $\delta(x, x_k) < \epsilon$.

PROPOSITION 11. A set S of real numbers is bounded if and only if it is totally bounded.

The proof is left to the student.

Indeed, a perusal of the proof of Theorem 6 will indicate that what is used is the total boundedness character of boundedness.

PROPOSITION 12. A subset of a totally bounded set is totally bounded.

The proof is left for the student.

We now prove:

THEOREM 8. If S is a complete metric space, every totally bounded infinite set T in S has at least one limit point.

Proof. For every $\epsilon > 0$ there is a finite set $x_1, x_2, \cdots, x_n$ in S such that for every $x \in T$, $\delta(x, x_k) < \epsilon$ for at least one $k = 1, 2, \cdots, n$. In other words, every $x \in T$ is in at least one of the closed spheres $\bar{\sigma}(x_k, \epsilon)$, $k = 1, 2, \cdots, n$. Let $\epsilon_1 = 1/2$. There is a finite number of spheres of diameters less than $1/2$ such that every point of T is in at least one of them. There is, accordingly, a closed sphere $\bar{\sigma}(x_1, 1/2)$ which contains an infinite subset $T_1 \subset T$. Let $\epsilon_2 = 1/4$. By the same argument, there is a closed sphere $\bar{\sigma}(x_2, 1/4)$ which contains an infinite subset $T_2 \subset T_1$. Since $T_2 \subset \bar{\sigma}(x_1, 1/2) \cap \bar{\sigma}(x_2, 1/4)$, the set $\bar{\sigma}(x_1, 1/2) \cap \bar{\sigma}(x_2, 1/4)$ is nonempty. We obtain in this way a sequence of closed spheres

$$\bar{\sigma}(x_1, \tfrac{1}{2}), \quad \bar{\sigma}(x_2, \tfrac{1}{4}), \quad \cdots, \quad \bar{\sigma}\left(x_n, \frac{1}{2^n}\right), \quad \cdots$$

such that $\bar{\sigma}(x_n, 1/2^n) \cap \bar{\sigma}(x_{n+1}, 1/2^{n+1})$ is nonempty and $T_n = T \cap \bar{\sigma}(x_n, 1/2^n)$ is infinite for every positive integer n.

The sequence $x_1, x_2, \cdots, x_n, \cdots$ is convergent. For if $\epsilon > 0$ there is a N such that $\sum_{n=N}^{\infty} 1/2^n < \epsilon$. Let $n, m > N$, with $m > n$. For every k, there is a

$$y_k \in \bar{\sigma}\left(x_k, \frac{1}{2^k}\right) \cap \bar{\sigma}\left(x_{k+1}, \frac{1}{2^{k+1}}\right).$$

Thus,

$$\delta(x_n, x_m) \leqq \delta(x_n, y_n) + \delta(y_n, x_{n+1}) + \cdots + \delta(x_{m-1}, y_{m-1}) + \delta(y_{m-1}, x_m) < \epsilon.$$

Since S is complete, the sequence $\{x_m\}$ has a limit ξ.

We show that ξ is a limit point of T. Let $\sigma(x, r)$ be a neighborhood of ξ. Then $\delta(\xi, x) = \delta < r$. There is an N_1 such that for every $n > N_1$, $\delta(\xi, x_n) < (r - \delta)/2$. Let $N > N_1$ be such that $1/2^N < (r - \delta)/2$. For every $y \in \bar{\sigma}(x_N, 1/2^N)$,

$$\delta(x, y) \leqq \delta(x, \xi) + \delta(\xi, x_N) + \delta(x_N, y) < \delta + \frac{r - \delta}{2} + \frac{r - \delta}{2} = r.$$

Hence $\bar{\sigma}(x_N, 1/2^N) \subset \sigma(x, r)$, so that $\sigma(x, r)$ contains an infinite number of points of T. Therefore, ξ is a limit point of T.

Exercises

1.1 List all the properties that you can of the real number system.

2.1 Show that Propositions 1 and 2 hold for the rational number system as well as the real number system.

2.2 Show that for the rational number system a set S may have an upper bound without having a least upper bound.

2.3 Show that a nonincreasing sequence of real numbers which has a lower bound has a greatest lower bound.

2.4 Show that the set $1, 1/2, \cdots, 1/n, \cdots$ has no minimum but that 0 is its greatest lower bound.

2.5 Show that the set $2, 2.1, 2.11, \cdots$ has no maximum.

3.1 If $I_1, I_2, \cdots, I_n$ is a finite number of semiopen intervals which contain their left endpoints but not their right endpoints, what can be said about the set $I = \bigcap_{k=1}^{n} I_k$?

3.2 Show that if $I_1 = (a_1, b_1), \cdots, I_n = (a_n, b_n), \cdots$ is a nonincreasing sequence of open intervals whose lengths converge to 0 (i.e., $\lim_{n \to \infty} (b_n - a_n) = 0$) then $\bigcap_{k=1}^{\infty} I_k$ is either a single point or else is empty.

3.3 Give the conditions on the sequence of intervals $\{I_n\}$ of Exercise 3.2 under which $\bigcap_{k=1}^{\infty} I_k$ is empty and those under which it is a single point.

3.4 Show that in the Definition 5 of nowhere dense sets it does not matter whether open intervals or closed intervals are used.

3.5 Prove that the set of rational numbers is not nowhere dense. Prove that the set whose elements are $1/2, 1/3, \cdots, 1/n, \cdots$ is nowhere dense.

3.6 Show that the complement of a set of the second category may either be of the first category or of the second category.

4.1 Show that the set of n-tuples $x = (x_1, \cdots, x_n)$ of real numbers is a metric space if

$$\delta(x, y) = [\sum_{i=1}^{n} (x_i - y_i)^2]^{1/2}; \text{ if}$$

$$\delta(x, y) = \max [|x_i - y_i| \mid i = 1, \cdots, n].$$

4.2 Associate a number $\delta(x, y)$ with every pair of n-tuples of real numbers in two other ways than those given in Exercise 4.1 so that in each case the set of n-tuples is a metric space.

4.3 Show that Hilbert space is a metric space.

4.4 Prove that the metric space of n-tuples $x = (x_1, \cdots, x_n)$ of real numbers with

$$\delta(x, y) = [\sum_{i=1}^{n} (x_i - y_i)^2]^{1/2} \text{ is complete.}$$

4.5 Prove that Hilbert space is complete.

5.1 Prove that the two definitions of limit point of a set given in §5 are equivalent.

5.2 Show that every bounded sequence of real numbers has a convergent subsequence.

5.3 A point ξ is said to be a condensation point of a set S if every neighborhood of ξ contains a nondenumerable number of points of S. Show that every nondenumerable set of real numbers, whether bounded or not, has at least one condensation point.

6.1 For the real-number system, show that a set S is bounded if and only if it is totally bounded.

6.2 Show that every subset of a totally bounded set is totally bounded.

6.3 In any metric space S, the Borel Covering Theorem would assert that if a closed sphere is covered by a set of open spheres then a finite number of the open spheres cover the closed sphere. Show that this theorem does not hold in Hilbert space.

6.4 Show that the Borel Covering Theorem, as stated in Exercise 6.3, holds for the metric space of n-tuples $x = (x_1, \cdots, x_n)$ of real numbers with

$$\delta(x, y) = [\sum_{i=1}^{n} (x_i - y_i)^2]^{1/2}.$$

6.5 A metric space S is called separable if there is a denumerable set $T \subset S$ such that every sphere in S contains at least one point in T. Show that Hilbert space is separable.

6.6 Is it true for Hilbert space that every nondenumerable set has a condensation point?

6.7 Give an example of a metric space in which there is a nondenumerable set which has no condensation points.

6.8 Show that every totally bounded sequence in a metric space has a convergent subsequence.

6.9 The set of points $x = (x_1, \cdots, x_n, \cdots)$ in Hilbert space for which $|x_n| = 1/n$, $n = 1, 2, \cdots$ is called the Hilbert cube. Show that every infinite set in the Hilbert cube has a limit point. Show that the Hilbert cube is totally bounded.

6.10 Show that if a set S of real numbers is covered by a set I of open intervals then a finite or denumerable number of the intervals in I covers S.

References

E. Borel, "Sur quelques points de la théorie des fonctions," *Ann. Scient. de l'Éc. Normal* (3), 12 (1895).

C. Carathéodory, *Vorlesungen über reelle Funktionen*, Leipzig, 1927, Chaps. 1, 2.

L. M. Graves, *Theory of Functions of a Real Variable*, New York, 1946, Chap. 2.

F. Hausdorff, *Grundzüge der Mengenlehre*, New York, 1949, Chap. 8.

T. H. Hildebrandt, "The Borel Theorem and its Generalizations," *Bull. Amer. Math. Soc.* 32 (1926).

O. Perron, *Irrationalzahlen*, New York, 1948, Chap. 2.

5

Simple Properties of Sets

1. *Closed sets*

Many of the properties of closed and open intervals belong also to more general classes of sets, closed and open sets. Moreover, closed and open sets fit more naturally in the theory of real functions than do intervals. This will become apparent as the theory develops.

DEFINITION 1. A set S of real numbers is said to be *closed* if every limit point of S belongs to S.

Examples of sets which are closed and some which are not closed follow.

1. The closed intervals are closed sets.
2. Every finite set is closed since it has no limit points.
3. The set of all integers is a closed set since it has no limit points.
4. The set of all real numbers is a closed set.
5. The union of a finite number of closed intervals is a closed set.
6. The open intervals are not closed sets.
7. The set of rational numbers is not a closed set; for example, the point $\sqrt{2}$ is a limit point of the set which does not belong to the set.
8. The union of a denumerable number of closed intervals may or may not be a closed set. Thus, the union of the intervals

$$\left[\frac{1}{2}, 1\right], \left[\frac{3}{2}, 2\right], \cdots, \left[\frac{2n-1}{2}, n\right], \cdots$$

is a closed set. The union of the intervals

$$\left[\frac{1}{2}, 1\right], \left[\frac{1}{8}, \frac{1}{4}\right], \cdots, \left[\frac{1}{2^{2n-1}}, \frac{1}{2^{2n-2}}\right], \cdots$$

is not closed, for 0 is a limit point of the set which does not belong to it.

DEFINITION 2. The *derivative* of a set S of real numbers is the set of limit points of S.

The derivative of S is designated by S'.

We have the following propositions.

PROPOSITION 1. If $S \subset T$, then $S' \subset T'$.

Proof. Let x be a limit point of S. Then if I is any neighborhood of x, I contains an infinite number of points of S, hence of T. Hence x is a limit point of T.

PROPOSITION 2. If $S \subset T$ and $T - S$ is finite, then $S' = T'$.

The proof is left for the student.

PROPOSITION 3. If S is any set of real numbers then the derivative S' of S is closed.

Proof. We must show that every limit point of S' belongs to S'. Let x be a limit point of S'. Let I be any neighborhood of x. Then there is a $y \in I \cap S'$. Now I is a neighborhood of y and $y \in S'$. Hence I contains an infinite number of points of S. But I is an arbitrary neighborhood of x so that x is a limit point of S. Hence $x \in S'$.

Another set associated with a given set S is the closure of S.

DEFINITION 3. The *closure* $\bar{S}$ of a set S is the union of S and S'; i.e., $\bar{S} = S \cup S'$.

We give some examples of the derivative and closure of sets.

1. If S is the set of rational numbers, then S' is the set of all real numbers and $\bar{S}$ is the set of all real numbers.
2. If S is the set $\{1/2, 1/3, \cdots, 1/n, \cdots\}$, then S' is the set $\{0\}$ and $\bar{S}$ is the set $\{0, 1/2, 1/3, \cdots, 1/n, \cdots\}$.
3. If S is the open interval (a, b), then S' is the closed interval $[a, b]$ and $\bar{S}$ is the closed interval $[a, b]$.

(Proposition 3a follows Proposition 4; Propositions 3b and 3c follow Definition 5.)

PROPOSITION 4. $\bar{S}$ consists of those points every neighborhood of which contains at least one point of S.

The proof is left to the student.

PROPOSITION 3a. The closure $\bar{S}$ of an arbitrary set S is closed.

Proof. Let x be a limit point of $\bar{S}$. Let I be a neighborhood of x. Then I contains a point $y \in \bar{S}$. Thus I, as a neighborhood of y, contains at least one point of S. Since I is an arbitrary neighborhood of x, we have $x \in \bar{S}$.

Propositions 3 and 3a associate two closed sets $\bar{S}$ and S' with every set S. Many other closed sets may be associated with a given set S. We give some further illustrations.

DEFINITION 4. A point x is called a *condensation point* of a set S if every neighborhood of x contains a nondenumerable number of points of S.

DEFINITION 5. A point x is called a *point of the second category* of a set S if for every neighborhood I of x the set $I \cap S$ is of the second category.

PROPOSITION 3b. The set S_c of condensation points of any set S is closed.

Proof. Let x be a limit point of S_c. Let I be a neighborhood of x. Then I contains a point $y \in S_c$. Since I is also a neighborhood of y, I contains a nondenumerable number of points of S. Since I is an arbitrary neighborhood of x, the point $x \in S_c$.

PROPOSITION 3c. The set S_e of points of the second category of any set S is closed.

The proof is exactly the same as for the others.

PROPOSITION 5. $\bar{S} \supset S' \supset S_c \supset S_e$.

We leave the proof for the student.

The similarity of the proofs of Propositions 3, 3a, 3b, and 3c should suggest to the student the existence of a single theorem of which the above are all special cases. The discovery and proof of such a theorem will be left to the student.

2. *Further properties of closed sets*

It was pointed out at the beginning of this chapter that the union of a finite number of closed intervals is a closed set but that the union of a denumerable number of closed intervals need not be a closed set.

We prove that the union of a finite number of closed sets is closed. We first consider the case where there are two sets.

PROPOSITION 6. The union of two closed sets is closed.

Proof. Let F_1 and F_2 be closed sets and let $F = F_1 \cup F_2$. Suppose x is a limit point of F. We show that x is a limit point of either F_1 or F_2. Suppose x is not a limit point of F_1. Then there is a neighborhood J_1 of x which contains only a finite number of points of F_1. Suppose, moreover, that x is not a limit point of F_2. Then there is a neighborhood J_2 of x which contains only a finite number of points of F_2. The open interval $J = J_1 \cap J_2$ is a neighborhood of x which contains only a finite number of points of $F = F_1 \cup F_2$. But this shows that x is not a limit point of F, contrary to the assumption. Hence x is a limit point of either F_1 or F_2, and since these sets are closed, $x \in F_1$ or $x \in F_2$, so that $x \in F$.

COROLLARY 1. The union of a finite number of closed sets is closed.

The proof is by finite induction.

We have shown that the union of an infinite number of closed sets may not be closed. In contrast, we find that the intersection of any number of closed sets is a closed set.

PROPOSITION 7. The intersection of any number of closed sets is closed.

Proof. Let F_α, $\alpha \in \mathsf{A}$, be a set of closed sets and let $F = \bigcap_{\alpha \in \mathsf{A}} F_\alpha$. Suppose ξ is a limit point of F. If I is any neighborhood of ξ, then I contains an infinite number of points of F and so of F_α for every $\alpha \in \mathsf{A}$. Thus, for every $\alpha \in \mathsf{A}$, ξ is a limit point of F_α. But F_α is closed; hence $\xi \in F_\alpha$. Therefore, $\xi \in F = \bigcap_{\alpha \in \mathsf{A}} F_\alpha$.

The intersection of nonempty closed sets can be empty. Indeed the intersection of a nonincreasing sequence of closed sets can be empty. For example: if, for every n, F_n is the set of real numbers greater than or equal to n, each F_n is closed. But the set $\bigcap_{n=1}^{\infty} F_n$ is empty. For if ξ is any real number, there is an n such that $\xi < n$, so that $\xi \notin F_n$.

On the other hand, the following theorem holds, and is the generalization to closed sets of Theorem 3, Chapter 4, on closed intervals.

THEOREM 1a. The intersection of a nonincreasing sequence of nonempty bounded closed sets is a nonempty bounded closed set.

Proof. Let $\{F_n\}$ be a nonincreasing sequence of nonempty bounded closed sets. By Proposition 7, $F = \bigcap_{n=1}^{\infty} F_n$ is a closed set. Since $F \subset F_1$ and F_1 is bounded, F is bounded. We need only show that F is nonempty. Let $x_1 \in F_1$, $x_2 \in F_2$, $\cdots$, $x_n \in F_n$, $\cdots$. There are two possibilities; either the value set of the sequence $\{x_n\}$ is finite or it is infinite. If this value set is finite there is an N such that for all $n > N$ the x_n are the same, i.e., there is a ξ such that for every $n > N$, $x_n = \xi$. So $\xi \in F_n$ for every $n > N$. But since the sets F_n are nonincreasing, $\xi \in F_n$ for every $n \leqq N$. Hence $\xi \in F$. If the value set of the sequence $\{x_n\}$ is infinite, it is a denumerable set $D = \{x_1, x_{n_2}, \cdots, x_{n_k}, \cdots\}$, where $n_1 = 1 < n_2 < \cdots < n_k < \cdots$.

Since D is a subset of F_1 it is bounded and so, by the Bolzano-Weierstrass Theorem, it has a limit point ξ. But by Proposition 2 the set $D - \{x_1, x_n, \cdots, x_{n_k}\}$ has the same limit points as D, for every k. Hence, for every k, we have ξ as a limit point of $D - \{x_1, \cdots, x_{n_k}\}$. But $D - \{x_1, x_{n_2}, \cdots, x_{n_k}\}$ is a subset of F_{n_k}. Hence, by Proposition 1, ξ is a limit point of F_{n_k}. But F_{n_k} is closed. Accordingly, $\xi \in F_{n_k}$. But the sets F_n are nonincreasing and the n_k are increasing. It follows that $\xi \in F_n$ for every n. Therefore, $\xi \in F$ so that F is nonempty.

The Borel Covering Theorem also generalizes from closed intervals to bounded closed sets.

(Theorem 1b is in the next section.)

THEOREM 2a. If a bounded closed set F of real numbers is covered by a family I of open intervals, then there are a finite number of intervals $I_1, I_2, \cdots, I_n$ of the family I which cover F.

Proof. Suppose no finite number of intervals of I cover F. Since F is bounded, there is a finite number of closed intervals each of length less than 1 which covers F. Now there is at least one of these intervals, call it J_1, such that the part of F which is in J_1 is not covered by any finite number of intervals of I. For otherwise all of F would be covered by a finite number of intervals of I, contradicting our original assumption. Let $F_1 = F \cap J_1$. Since F_1 is bounded, there are a finite number of closed intervals, each of length less than $1/2$, which cover F_1. Now, for one of these intervals, call it J_2, no finite set of intervals in I covers that part of F_1 which is in J_2. Let $F_2 = F_1 \cap J_2$. In this way, we obtain a nonincreasing sequence of closed bounded sets

$$F_1 \supset F_2 \supset \cdots \supset F_n \supset \cdots$$

such that for every n, F_n is covered by a closed interval J_n of length less than $1/n$ and F_n is not covered by any finite number of intervals of I. By Theorem 1a, the set $\bigcap_{n=1}^{\infty} F_n$ is not empty. Let $\xi \in \bigcap_{n=1}^{\infty} F_n$. By the hypothesis of the theorem, there is an $I \in \mathsf{I}$ such that $\xi \in I$. Let $I = (a, b)$. There is an N such that $1/N < \min [\xi - a, b - \xi]$. But the length of J_N is less than $1/N$ and $\xi \in J_N$, so that $J_N \subset I$. Moreover, $F_N \subset J_N$. Hence $F_N \subset I$, and F_N is covered by a finite number of intervals in I; namely, one interval I. This contradicts our original assumption that F is not covered by any finite number of intervals of I, for a consequence of this assumption is that F_N is not covered by any finite set of intervals of I.

(Theorem 2b is in the next section.)

3. *Closed sets in metric space*

The definitions of limit point of a set, closed set, derivative of a set, etc., may be extended to any metric space. In a metric space S, a neighborhood of a point x is defined as an open sphere containing x. All other definitions given in this chapter may then be carried over to metric space.

We will consider possible extensions of Theorems 1a and 2a to metric space. We first observe that neither theorem in its present form holds for Hilbert space.

Regarding Theorem 1a, consider the denumerable set

$$\xi_1 = (1, 0, \cdots), \xi_2 = (0, 1, 0, \cdots), \cdots.$$

Let

$$F_1 = \{\xi_1, \xi_2, \cdots\}, F_2 = \{\xi_2, \xi_3, \cdots\}, \cdots, F_n = \{\xi_n, \xi_{n+1}, \cdots\}, \cdots.$$

For every n, the set F_n has no limit points, hence it is closed. Since for every k and m, $\delta(\xi_k, \xi_m) = \sqrt{2}$, every F_n is bounded. Moreover, $F_1 \supset F_2 \supset \cdots \supset F_n \supset \cdots$. On the other hand, the set $\bigcap_{n=1}^{\infty} F_n$ is empty, so that Theorem 1 does not hold.

Regarding Theorem 2a, consider the same denumerable set $F = \{\xi_1, \xi_2, \cdots\}$. F is closed and bounded. Consider the covering of F by the family of open spheres $\{\sigma(\xi_n, 1/2)\}$. No finite number of spheres belonging to this family covers F.

If total boundedness replaces boundedness then Theorems 1a and 2a are restored, not only to Hilbert space, but to any complete metric space.

THEOREM 1b. In any complete metric space S, the intersection of a nonincreasing sequence of nonempty totally bounded closed sets is a nonempty totally bounded closed set.

Proof. Let $\{F_n\}$ be a nonincreasing sequence of nonempty totally bounded closed sets. The method used in proving Proposition 7 shows that $F = \bigcap_{n=1}^{\infty} F_n$ is a closed set. Since $F \subset F_1$ and F_1 is totally bounded, F is totally bounded. We need only show that F is nonempty. The proof here may be made exactly as that for Theorem 1a. The details are left for the student.

THEOREM 2b. In a complete metric space S, if a closed totally bounded set F is covered by a family I of open spheres, then there is a finite set of open spheres in I which covers F.

The proof follows that for Theorem 2a.

4. *Perfect sets*

An important subclass of the closed sets is the class of perfect sets. In addition to being closed a perfect set is dense-in-itself, a concept which will be defined presently.

We again restrict our attention to the real-number case. Extension of our definitions to any metric space may be made by replacing open intervals as neighborhoods by open spheres as neighborhoods.

DEFINITION 6. If S and T are sets of real numbers, then S is said to be dense in T if every $x \in T$ is a limit point of S, i.e., if $T \subset S'$.

Applying this definition to the notion "nowhere dense" given in Chapter 4, we find that a set S is nowhere dense if and only if it is not dense in any open interval.

DEFINITION 7. A set S is said to be *everywhere dense* if it is dense in the set of all real numbers.

DEFINITION 8. A set S is said to be *dense-in-itself* if every $x \in S$ is a limit point of S, i.e., if $S \subset S'$.

Definition 8 is a special case of Definition 6 but has been repeated for emphasis.

Examples:

1. The set of rational numbers is everywhere dense, is dense-in-itself, and is dense in the set of irrational numbers.
2. Every closed interval is dense-in-itself.
3. Every open interval is dense-in-itself.
4. The set $\{0, 1/2, 1/3, \cdots, 1/n, \cdots\}$ is closed but is not dense-in-itself.

DEFINITION 9. A set S is called perfect if it is both closed and dense-in-itself.

Observe that S is closed if and only if $S' \subset S$ and S is dense-in-itself if and only if $S \subset S'$. We thus have the following proposition.

PROPOSITION 8. A set S is perfect if and only if $S' = S$.

Every perfect set is closed. On the other hand, as example (4) above shows, there are closed sets which are not perfect. However, the following theorem is true.

THEOREM 3. Every closed set is the union of a perfect set and a finite or denumerable set.

In order to prove this theorem we need the following proposition which is interesting in its own right.

PROPOSITION 9. If S is any set of real numbers then except for at most a denumerable subset of S every point of S is a condensation point of S.

Proof. Suppose $\xi \in S$ is not a condensation point of S. Then ξ has a neighborhood which contains only a finite or denumerable number of points of S. Clearly, this neighborhood may be taken so that its endpoints are rational numbers. The neighborhoods whose endpoints are rational numbers form a denumerable set. Hence the points of S not condensation points of S belong to one or more of a denumerable number of sets each of which is at most denumerable. But the union of a denumerable number of denumerable sets is denumerable. Hence the proposition is proved.

Proof of Theorem 3. Let S be any closed set and let S_c be the set of condensation points of S. We show three things: (1) $S_c \subset S$, (2) S_c is perfect, and (3) $S - S_c$ is finite or denumerable.

1. Every condensation point of S is of course a limit point of S, and since S is closed, S contains all its limit points. Hence $S_c \subset S$.

2. By Proposition 3c, the set S_c is closed. We must show that S_c is dense-in-itself. Let $\xi \in S_c$. Let I be a neighborhood of ξ. Then I contains a nondenumerable number of points of S. But, by Proposition 9, all but at most a de-

numerable number of these points are condensation points of S. Hence I contains points of S_c distinct from ξ. Therefore, ξ is a limit point of S_c and S_c is dense-in-itself. This completes the proof that S_c is perfect.

3. That $S - S_c$ is finite or denumerable is a restatement of Proposition 9.

This theorem holds in all the examples of metric spaces we have given. However, it is not true for all metric spaces. Perhaps the student can give an example for which it does not hold.

We shall find further properties of perfect sets, but first we shall introduce the open sets.

5. *Open sets*

In order to define open sets we first need the notion, "interior point of a set."

DEFINITION 10. A point x is an *interior point of a set* S if there is a neighborhood I of x such that $I \subset S$.

For example, for an open interval, every point is an interior point; for a closed interval, every point, except the endpoints, is an interior point, and the endpoints are not interior points; for the set of rational numbers, no point in the set is an interior point of the set.

DEFINITION 11. A set S is said to be open if every $x \in S$ is an interior point of S.

For example, an open interval is an open set; the union of any number of open intervals is an open set.

PROPOSITION 10. The union of any number of open sets is an open set.

Proof. Let G_α, $\alpha \in \mathsf{A}$, be a set of open sets and let $G = \bigcup_{\alpha \in \mathsf{A}} G_\alpha$. Let $\xi \in G$. Then $\xi \in G_\alpha$ for at least one $\alpha \in \mathsf{A}$. Since G_α is open there is a neighborhood I of ξ such that $I \subset G_\alpha$. But $G_\alpha \subset G$. Hence $I \subset G$ so that ξ is an interior point of G and G is open.

There is a one-to-one correspondence between the set of closed sets and the set of open sets as is shown by the next proposition.

PROPOSITION 11. The complement of every open set is closed and the complement of every closed set is open.

Proof. Let G be an open set and let $F = C(G)$. Let $\xi \in G$. There is a neighborhood I of ξ such that $I \subset G$; hence I contains no points of F, and ξ is not a limit point of F. Thus, F contains all its limit points and, accordingly, is a closed set.

Let F be a closed set and let $G = C(F)$. Let $\xi \in G$. Since F is closed, $\xi \notin F'$. But $\xi \notin F$. Hence $\xi \notin \bar{F}$. But this means that ξ has a neighborhood I such that $I \cap F = \phi$. Thus $I \subset G$ and G is open.

The mapping $F = C(G)$ accordingly establishes a one-to-one correspondence between the set of open sets and the set of closed sets.

This fact could have been used to prove Proposition 10 as follows:

$$G = \bigcup_{\alpha \in A} G_\alpha = C(\bigcap_{\alpha \in A} C(G_\alpha)).$$

$C(G_\alpha)$ is closed for every $\alpha \in A$ so that, by Proposition 7, $\bigcap_{\alpha \in A} C(G_\alpha)$ is closed whence $C(\bigcap_{\alpha \in A} C(G_\alpha))$ is open so that G is open.

We prove in addition that the intersection of a finite number of open sets $G_1, G_2, \cdots, G_n$ is open. Let

$$G = \bigcap_{k=1}^{n} G_k = C(\bigcup_{k=1}^{n} C(G_k)).$$

$C(G_k)$ is closed for every $k = 1, 2, \cdots, n$, so that, by Proposition 6, $\bigcup_{k=1}^{n} C(G_k)$ is closed, and by Proposition 11, $G = C(\bigcup_{k=1}^{n} C(G_k))$ is open.

Our next proposition is concerned with the cardinal number of the set of open sets.

PROPOSITION 12. The cardinal number of the set of open sets is c.

Proof. We first show that the cardinal number is at least c. For: consider the open intervals of length 1. There are c of them. Each one is an open set.

We now show that the cardinal number is at most c. In order to show this we first observe that there are exactly $\aleph_0$ open intervals with rational endpoints. This follows from the facts that there are $\aleph_0$ rational numbers, $\aleph_0 \cdot \aleph_0 = \aleph_0$, and Bernstein's Theorem. We call these the rational intervals. The rational intervals may be ordered as a sequence

$$R_1, R_2, \cdots, R_n, \cdots.$$

Now consider any open set G. Every $\xi \in G$ is in a rational interval $R_{n(\xi)}$ such that $R_{n(\xi)} \subset G$. Now if $\xi \in G$ then $\xi \in R_{n(\xi)} \subset \bigcup_{\xi \in G} R_{n(\xi)}$, so that $G \subset \bigcup_{\xi \in G} R_{n(\xi)}$. On the other hand, if $\eta \in \bigcup_{\xi \in G} R_{n(\xi)}$ there is a $\xi \in G$ such that $\eta \in R_{n(\xi)} \subset G$, so that $\bigcup_{\xi \in G} R_{n(\xi)} \subset G$. The $R_{n(\xi)}$, $\xi \in G$, form a subset of the set $R_1, R_2, \cdots, R_n, \cdots$ of rational intervals. The set of open sets may accordingly be put in one-to-one correspondence with a set of subsequences of the sequence of positive integers. Since the number of subsequences of any sequence is $2^{\aleph_0} = c$, it follows that there are at most c open sets.

Accordingly, there are exactly c open sets.

Since the open and closed sets are in one-to-one correspondence, we have also shown that there are c closed sets.

On the other hand, the total number of sets of real numbers, by Theorem 3, Chapter 2, is 2^c. This shows that there are sets which are neither open nor closed. Of course, such an elaborate argument is not needed to establish the last assertion, since, for example, the set of rational numbers is neither open nor closed.

We have already associated with every set S a closed set $\bar{S} \supset S$ called its *closure*. We now associate with S an open set $S_i \subset S$ called its *interior*.

DEFINITION 12. The set of interior points of a set S is called the *interior* of S and is designated by S_i.

Examples:

1. If S is open, then $S_i = S$.
2. If S is a closed interval $[a, b]$, then S_i is the open interval (a, b).
3. If S is the set of rational numbers, then S_i is empty.

PROPOSITION 13. For every set S the set S_i is open.

Proof. Let $\xi \in S_i$. Then there is a neighborhood I of ξ such that $I \subset S$. But every $x \in I$ is an interior point of S and so is in S_i. Hence $I \subset S_i$, so that S_i is open.

PROPOSITION 14. For every set S if F is a closed set such that $S \subset F$ then $\bar{S} \subset F$, and if G is an open set such that $G \subset S$ then $G \subset S_i$.

The proof is left to the student.

By Proposition 14, $\bar{S}$ is the smallest closed set containing S, and S_i is the largest open set contained in S.

6. *Structure of open sets*

Every open interval is an open set. Since the union of open sets is open, a set composed of a finite or denumerable number of disjoint open intervals is open. We show that these are the only open sets of real numbers.

THEOREM 4. If G is an open set of real numbers then G is the union of a finite or denumerable number of disjoint open intervals.

Proof. We associate with every $\xi \in G$ an open interval $I_\xi \subset G$ in the followir way:

Let I_ξ be the union of the set of all open intervals I_α, $\alpha \in \mathsf{A}$, such that $I_\alpha = (a_\alpha, b_\alpha) \subset G$ and $\xi \in I_\alpha$. If a and b are respectively the greatest lower bound of the a_α, $\alpha \in \mathsf{A}$, and the least upper bound of the b_α, $\alpha \in \mathsf{A}$, then $I_\xi = (a, b)$. For if $\eta \geqq b$ or $\eta \leqq a$ then $\eta \notin I_\alpha$ for any $\alpha \in \mathsf{A}$, so that $\eta \notin I_\xi$. On the other hand, if $\eta \in (a, b)$, then either $\eta = \xi$ so that $\eta \in I_\xi$, or $\xi < \eta < b$, or $a < \eta < \xi$. Suppose $\xi < \eta < b$. Since b is the least upper bound of the b_α, $\alpha \in A$, there is an α such that $\eta \in I_\alpha$. Hence $\eta \in I_\xi$. Similarly, if $a < \eta < \xi$ then $\eta \in I_\xi$. Therefore, I_ξ is an open interval.

We next show that if $\xi \in G$ and $\eta \in G$ then either $I_\xi = I_\eta$ or $I_\xi \cap I_\eta = \phi$. Suppose $x \in I_\xi \cap I_\eta$. Then $I_\xi \cup I_\eta$ is an open interval. Now $I_\xi \cup I_\eta$ contains ξ, so that $I_\xi \cup I_\eta \subset I_\xi$. Also, $I_\xi \cup I_\eta$ contains η, so that $I_\xi \cup I_\eta \subset I_\eta$. Accordingly, $I_\xi \cup I_\eta = I_\xi = I_\eta$.

Now, $G = \bigcup_{\xi \in G} I_\xi$ is the union of a set of disjoint open intervals.

Finally, any set of disjoint open intervals is finite or denumerable in number. For associate with each open interval of the set a rational number which is in the interval. Since disjoint open intervals are associated in this way with distinct rational numbers, the cardinal number of our set of open intervals does not exceed the cardinal number of the set of rational numbers, and so it is finite or denumerable.

The disjoint open intervals of Theorem 4 are called the *components* of G.

COROLLARY 2. Every closed set is the complement of a finite or denumerable number of disjoint open intervals.

DEFINITION 13. Two open intervals are said to be *abutting* if they have an endpoint in common. Otherwise, they are nonabutting.

COROLLARY 3. A set P is perfect if and only if it is the complement of a finite or denumerable number of disjoint open intervals, no two of which are abutting.

Proof. Suppose P is perfect. Then since P is closed the complement of P is the union of a finite or denumerable number of disjoint open intervals. Suppose two of these intervals are abutting and ξ is their common endpoint. Then $\xi \in P$, but evidently ξ is not a limit point of P. Hence P is not perfect, contrary to the assumption.

Suppose, on the other hand, P is the complement of a finite or denumerable number of disjoint open intervals no two of which are abutting. Then P is closed. Suppose $\xi \in P$ is not a limit point of P. Then ξ has a neighborhood which contains no other points of P. But this means that ξ is a point at which two intervals of $C(P)$ abut, in contradiction. Hence every $\xi \in P$ is a limit point of P, so that P is perfect.

7. *Open and closed sets relative to a set*

In most of our considerations, sets will be considered as subsets of a closed interval, or of an open interval, or of some other kind of set, rather than as subsets of the set of all real numbers. Accordingly, we shall define closed and open sets relative to a given set U.

DEFINITION 14. A set $F \subset U$ is closed relative to U if every limit point of F which is in U is in F.

DEFINITION 15. A set $G \subset U$ is open relative to U if every $\xi \in G$ has a neighborhood I such that $I \cap U \subset I \cap G$.

Examples:

1. If U is the closed interval $[0, 1]$ then the subsets of U which are closed relative to U are the same sets as the subsets of U which are closed relative to the set of all real numbers.
2. If U is the closed interval $[0, 1]$ then the subsets of U which are open relative to U consist of unions of finite or denumerable numbers of open intervals in U and intervals $[0, \xi)$, $(\eta, 1]$ and $[0, 1]$ where $0 < \xi \leqq 1$ and $0 \leqq \eta < 1$.

We prove just one proposition concerning these relative notions.

PROPOSITION 15. If F is closed relative to U, then the set $U - F$ is open relative to U; and if G is open relative to U, then the set $U - G$ is closed relative to U.

Proof. Let $\xi \in U - F$. Then ξ has a neighborhood I which contains no points of F, so that $I \cap U \subset I \cap (U - F)$ and $U - F$ is open relative to U.

Let $\xi \in G$. Then ξ has a neighborhood I such that $I \cap U \subset G$. Hence ξ is not a limit point of $U - G$. This means that every limit point of $U - G$ which is in U is in $U - G$. Hence $U - G$ is closed relative to U.

Exercises

1.1 In the real number system, show that
   (a) the set of irrational numbers is not closed.
   (b) for every real number r the set of numbers $s \geqq r$ is closed.
   (c) the intersection of a denumerable number of closed intervals is a closed set.

1.2 The statement that the derivative of a set S of real numbers is closed may be written $(S')' \subset S'$. Why? Using the notation $S^{(2)} = (S')'$, $S^{(n)} = (S^{(n-1)})'$, $n = 3, 4, \cdots$, give an example, for every positive integer n, of a set S for which $S^{(n)}$ is a proper subset of $S^{(n-1)}$.

1.3 Show that if $S \subset T$ and $T - S$ is finite then $S' = T'$.

1.4 Show that the closure $\bar{S}$ of S consists of those points every neighborhood of which contains at least one point of S.

1.5 Show, for every set S, that

$$\bar{S} \supset S' \supset S_c \supset S_e.$$

1.6 Find and prove a theorem which has Propositions 3, 3a, 3b, and 3c as special cases.

2.1 By the distance between two sets S and T we mean the number

$$\delta(S, T) = \inf [|x - y| \mid x \in S, y \in T].$$

Show that if S and T are disjoint bounded closed sets then $\delta(S, T) > 0$.

2.2 Show that if the restriction of boundedness is removed in Exercise 2.1 the conclusion no longer is valid.

2.3 Do the sets of real numbers, with the distance $\delta(S, T)$ of Exercise 2.1, form a metric space? Which metric space postulates are satisfied and which are not?

2.4 Show that for every unbounded closed set F there is a covering of F by means of open intervals such that no finite number of the intervals covers F.

3.1 Show that if S is a complete metric space and $F \subset S$ is closed, totally bounded, and is covered by a family I of open spheres, then there is a finite number of open spheres in I which covers F.

3.2 Is the assumption that S is complete in Exercise 3.1 an essential one? Explain.

3.3 Show that the interior of a set S is the complement of the closure of the complement of S.

3.4 Show that the closure of a set S is the complement of the interior of the complement of S.

3.5 Give an example of a set which is neither open nor closed and verify that its complement is neither open nor closed.

3.6 The boundary of a set S is the set $\bar{S} \cap \overline{C(S)}$. Show that the boundary of a closed set is nowhere dense.

3.7 A set is called *clairsemé* if it has no nonempty dense-in-itself subset. Show that every set is the union of a dense-in-itself set and a set which is clairsemé.

4.1 Show that the union of any number of sets each of which is dense-in-itself is dense-in-itself.

4.2 Is the intersection of a finite or denumerable number of sets each of which is dense-in-itself always dense-in-itself?

4.3 Give an example of a set which is neither nowhere dense nor everywhere dense.

4.4 Show that the union of a finite number of perfect sets is perfect.

4.5 Prove that for every set S of real numbers, except for a subset of S of the first category, every point of S is a point of second category of S.

4.6 Prove that the set S_e of points of the second category of any set S is perfect.

4.7 Prove that if S is a set of real numbers of the second category there is an interval every point of which is a point of the second category of S.

4.8 Show that if S is any metric space and $T \subset S$ is of the second category in S then there is a sphere every point of which is a point of the second category of T.

4.9 Give an example of a metric space in which there is a nondenumerable set which has no condensation points.

4.10 Generalize one of the proofs that the continuum is nondenumerable to show that every perfect set of real numbers is nondenumerable.

5.1 Define open and closed sets for any metric space.

5.2 Show that in any metric space the intersection of a finite number of open sets is an open set.

5.3 Show that the set of rational numbers is neither open nor closed.

5.4 Show, in any metric space S, that for every $T \subset S$ if $F \supset T$ and F is closed then $F \supset \bar{T}$ and if $G \subset T$ and G is open then $G \subset S_i$.

5.5 Show that in any metric space the complement of every open set is closed and the complement of every closed set is open.

6.1 In a metric space, an open set is called connected if it is not the union of two disjoint nonempty open sets. Show that the only connected open sets of real numbers are the open intervals.

6.2 Show that in the plane—i.e., the set $x = (x_1, x_2)$ of pairs of real numbers with $\delta(x, y) = [\sum_{i=1}^{2} (x_i - y_i)^2]^{1/2}$—every open set is the union of a finite or denumerable number of disjoint connected open sets.

6.3 Characterize the perfect sets in the plane in terms of their complements.

7.1 Show that every set is both open and closed relative to itself.

References

E. Borel, *Leçons sur les fonctions de variables rêeles*, Paris, 1928, Chap. 1.

C. Carathéodory, *Vorlesungen über reelle Funktionen*, Leipzig, 1927, Chap. 1.

F. Hausdorff, *Mengenlehre*, New York, 1944, Chap. 6.

E. W. Hobson, *The Theory of Functions of a Real Variable*, Cambridge, 1927, Chap. 2.

H. Kestelman, *Modern Theories of Integration*, Oxford, 1937, Chap. 1.

W. Sierpinski, *General Topology*, translated by C. C. Krieger, Toronto, 1934, Chap. 1.

6

The Cantor Ternary Set

Our object now is to introduce a special set whose features are indispensable to a full understanding of the concepts introduced in Chapter 5. Many students, even after having proved theorems using the formal definitions of "nowhere dense," "perfect," etc., retain false ideas regarding the kinds of sets which have these properties. The Cantor ternary set, first given by G. Cantor, should give the student a better insight into the material we are considering. The Cantor ternary set S is a subset of the closed interval $[0, 1]$. It is more convenient to define its complement, $C(S)$, relative to $[0, 1]$. $C(S)$ is the union of the following denumerable set of open intervals:

1. the open middle third, $(1/3, 2/3)$, of $[0, 1]$,
2. the open middle thirds, $(1/3^2, 2/3^2)$ and $(2/3 + 1/3^2, 2/3 + 2/3^2)$, of the two closed intervals in $[0, 1]$ which are complementary to $(1/3, 2/3)$,
3. the open middle thirds, $(1/3^3, 2/3^3)$, $(2/3^2 + 1/3^3, 2/3^2 + 2/3^3)$, $(2/3 + 1/3^3, 2/3 + 2/3^3)$, and $(2/3 + 2/3^2 + 1/3^3, 2/3 + 2/3^2 + 2/3^3)$, of the four closed intervals in $[0, 1]$ which are complementary to $(1/3^2, 2/3^2)$, $(1/3, 2/3)$, and $(2/3 + 1/3^2, 2/3 + 2/3^2)$; and so on, ad infinitum.

One might think at first that not much is left for S after all these intervals are put in $C(S)$. Actually, in some respects S is negligible, as compared with the whole interval; but in other respects it is not.

Our investigation of the character of S and of $C(S)$ is helped if the numbers in the interval $[0, 1]$ are expressed by their ternary expansions. It is an easy matter to show that every number in this interval has an expansion of the form

$$\frac{a_1}{3} + \frac{a_2}{3^2} + \cdots + \frac{a_n}{3^n} + \cdots,$$

where $a_n = 0$, 1, or 2 for every positive integer n, and every number has only one expansion except for the denumerable set of numbers which have terminating expansions. These have two expansions. It is convenient to simplify by using the notation

$$.a_1a_2 \cdots a_n \cdots$$

instead of

$$\frac{a_1}{3} + \frac{a_2}{3^2} + \cdots + \frac{a_n}{3^n} + \cdots.$$

It is easy to see that every number in $C(S)$ has at least one 1 appearing in its expansion. Accordingly, those numbers whose expansions are composed entirely of 0's and 2's belong to S. As the student may verify, the members of S whose expansions may contain 1's have terminating expansions. Hence S consists of all numbers whose ternary expansions are either composed entirely of 0's and 2's or which have terminating expansions.

Moreover, distinct expansions in 0's and 2's belong to distinct numbers, so that there is a one-to-one correspondence between such expansions and a subset of S. But, by the definition of $2^{\aleph_0}$, there are $2^{\aleph_0} = c$ such expansions. Therefore, the cardinal number of S is c.

PROPOSITION 1. The cardinal number of the Cantor ternary set is c.

We show next that the Cantor ternary set is nowhere dense. This is obtained as a special case of a more general proposition.

PROPOSITION 2. If a closed set F does not contain any interval, then F is nowhere dense.

Proof. Suppose F is not nowhere dense. Then there is an interval I such that every subinterval $J \subset I$ contains some points in F. Let $\xi \in I$. Then every neighborhood of ξ contains some points in F. Hence $\xi \in \bar{F}$ so that $I \subset \bar{F}$. But since F is closed, $\bar{F} \subset F$ so that $I \subset F$.

COROLLARY 1. The Cantor ternary set is nowhere dense.

Proof. The Cantor ternary set S is the complement relative to $[0, 1]$ of an open set $C(S)$. Hence S is closed. But, evidently, $C(S)$ is dense in $[0, 1]$, so that S contains no intervals. Therefore, S is nowhere dense.

This shows, incidentally, that there are nowhere-dense sets which are infinite; indeed, nondenumerable.

PROPOSITION 3. The Cantor ternary set is perfect.

Proof. S is closed. Every number in S is a limit point of numbers having terminating ternary expansions. The latter all belong to S. Hence S is dense-in-itself. Since S is closed and dense-in-itself, S is perfect.

Summarizing our results, we have in the Cantor ternary set a nowhere-dense, perfect set whose cardinal number is c.

Exercises

1.1 Show that if S is the Cantor ternary set then S consists of all numbers in $[0, 1]$ whose ternary expansions are composed entirely of 0's and 2's or which have terminating expansions.

1.2 A Cantor n-ary set may be defined for every $n > 2$ in an analogous way to that in which the Cantor ternary set is defined. Do this, and characterize the members of this set in terms of their n-ary expansions.

1.3 Show that the sum of the lengths of the component open intervals of $C(S)$ is 1, where S is the Cantor ternary set.

1.4 For every positive integer n find the sum of the lengths of the component open intervals of the complement of the Cantor n-ary set.

1.5 For every k such that $0 < k \leqq 1$ show that there is a nowhere-dense perfect set $S \subset [0, 1]$ such that the sum of the lengths of the component open intervals of the complement of S is equal to k.

1.6 By establishing a one-to-one correspondence between the set and the Cantor ternary set show that every nowhere-dense nonempty perfect set has cardinal number c.

References

C. Carathéodory, *Vorlesungen über reelle Funktionen*, Leipzig, 1927, p. 286.
L. M. Graves, *Theory of Functions of a Real Variable*, New York, 1946, Chap. 3.
F. Hausdorff, *Mengenlehre*, New York, 1944, Chap. 6.

7

Functions

1. *Definition*

Our main interest is in real functions of a real variable. Our functions will be defined on a set S, usually the set of all real numbers $(-\infty, \infty)$, but sometimes on the closed interval $[0, 1]$, the open interval $(0, 1)$, or some other set of real numbers. The set S is called the domain of the function. The function $f(x)$ associates with every $\xi \in S$ a real number $f(\xi)$. It will be convenient, in some considerations, to extend the real-number system by adjoining the symbols $+\infty$ and $-\infty$ and to say for some functions and some values of x that $f(x) = +\infty$ or $f(x) = -\infty$.

We now list some examples of the manner in which functions may be specified:

1. Let S be the set of all real numbers, except 0, and $f(x) = 1/x$ on S.
2. Let S be the set of all real numbers, and $f(x) = 1/x$ for $x \in S$, $x \neq 0$ and $f(0) = 0$.
3. Let S be the set of all real numbers, and $f(x) = 0$ for x irrational, $f(x) = 1$ for x rational.
4. Let S be the closed interval $[0, 1]$, $y = \sin 1/x$ for $x \in (0, 1]$ and $f(0) = 0$.

2. *Sets associated with a function*

Let $f(x)$ be a function defined on a set S. A number of sets may be associated with $f(x)$.

Let k be any real number. One set associated with $f(x)$ is the set of points $x \in S$ for which $f(x) < k$. Other subsets of S associated with $f(x)$ are those for which $f(x) > k$, $f(x) \leqq k$, $f(x) \geqq k$, $f(x) = k$, and if $k_1 < k_2$, the sets for which $k_1 < f(x) < k_2$, $k_1 \leqq f(x) \leqq k_2$, etc. These sets will be designated as $E[f(x) < k]$, $E[f(x) > k]$, $E[f(x) \leqq k]$, $E[k_1 \leqq f(x) \leqq k_2]$, etc.

The above sets are related to each other in various ways. For example, $E[f(x) < k]$ is the complement relative to S of $E[f(x) \geqq k]$. We prove one such relation.

PROPOSITION 1. For any real function $f(x)$, the following relation holds:

$$E[f(x) \geqq k] = \bigcap_{n=1}^{\infty} E\left[f(x) > k - \frac{1}{n}\right].$$

Proof. Suppose x is such that $f(x) \geqq k$. Then, for every positive n, $f(x) > k - 1/n$. On the other hand, if $f(x) > k - 1/n$ for every n, then $f(x) \geqq k$.

3. *Continuous functions*

Perhaps the most important class of functions are the continuous functions. We first consider functions defined on the set of all real numbers. We give the definition of continuity at a point in several forms.

DEFINITION 1a. If ξ is a real number, then $f(x)$ is said to be *continuous* at ξ if for every $\epsilon > 0$ there is a $\delta > 0$ such that if $|x - \xi| < \delta$ then $|f(x) - f(\xi)| < \epsilon$.

DEFINITION 1b. $f(x)$ is said to be continuous at ξ if for every convergent sequence $\{x_n\}$ whose limit is ξ the sequence $\{f(x_n)\}$ converges and $\lim_{n\to\infty} f(x_n) = f(\xi)$.

DEFINITION 1c. $f(x)$ is said to be continuous at ξ if for every $\epsilon > 0$ there is a neighborhood I of ξ such that for every $x \in I$, $|f(x) - f(\xi)| < \epsilon$.

DEFINITION 1d. $f(x)$ is said to be continuous at ξ if for every open set G containing $f(\xi)$ there is an open set H containing ξ such that for every $x \in H$, $f(x) \in G$.

These four definitions are equivalent. We prove only

PROPOSITION 2. Definitions 1a and 1b are equivalent.

Proof. Suppose that $f(x)$ is continuous at ξ, according to Definition 1a. Let $\{x_n\}$ be a convergent sequence whose limit is ξ. Let $\epsilon > 0$ and suppose $\delta > 0$ is such that if $|x - \xi| < \delta$ then $|f(x) - f(\xi)| < \epsilon$. There is an N such that if $n > N$ then $|x_n - \xi| < \delta$, and so $|f(x_n) - f(\xi)| < \epsilon$. Hence $\lim f(x_n) = f(\xi)$, and so $f(x)$ is continuous at ξ according to Definition 1b.

Suppose that $f(x)$ is not continuous at ξ according to Definition 1a. Then there is a $k > 0$ such that for every $\delta > 0$ there is an x with $|x - \xi| < \delta$ and $|f(x) - f(\xi)| > k$. Now there is an x_1 such that $|x_1 - \xi| < 1$ and $|f(x_1) - f(\xi)| > k$.

Then there is an x_2 such that $|x_2 - \xi| < \min[|x_1 - \xi|, 1/2]$ and $|f(x_2) - f(\xi)| > k$. Continuing in this way, we obtain a sequence $\{x_n\}$ which converges to ξ such that $|f(x_n) - f(\xi)| > k$ for every n. Hence, $f(x)$ is not continuous at ξ according to Definition 1b. It follows that if $f(x)$ is continuous at ξ according to Definition 1b then it is continuous at ξ according to Definition 1a.

The proof of the other equivalences is left to the student.

DEFINITION 2. $f(x)$ is said to be continuous on S if it is continuous at every point of S.

In much of the work which follows functions will be classified in accordance with the nature of their associated sets. For continuous functions, the associated sets are open and closed, as is proved in the following theorems.

THEOREM 1a. $f(x)$ is continuous on $(0, 1)$ if and only if for every k the sets $E[f(x) > k]$ and $E[f(x) < k]$ are open sets.

Proof. Suppose $f(x)$ is continuous on $(0, 1)$. Let $\xi \in (0, 1)$ be such that $f(\xi) > k$. There is an $\epsilon > 0$ such that $f(\xi) - \epsilon > k$. Since $f(x)$ is continuous at ξ, there is a $\delta > 0$ such that if $|x - \xi| < \delta$ then $|f(x) - f(\xi)| < \epsilon$. Hence, there is a neighborhood I of ξ such that for every $x \in I, f(x) > f(\xi) - \epsilon > k$. Thus, $E[f(x) > k]$ is open. Similarly, $E[f(x) < k]$ is open.

Suppose the sets $E[f(x) > k]$ and $E[f(x) < k]$ are open for every k. Let $\xi \in (0, 1)$ and let $\epsilon > 0$. Then, since $E[f(x) > f(\xi) - \epsilon]$ is open, there is a neighborhood I_1 of ξ such that for every $x \in I_1, f(x) > f(\xi) - \epsilon$. Moreover, since $E[f(x) < f(\xi) + \epsilon]$ is open there is a neighborhood I_2 of ξ such that for every $x \in I_2$, $f(x) < f(\xi) + \epsilon$. $I = I_1 \cap I_2$ is a neighborhood of ξ. For every $x \in I$, $|f(x) - f(\xi)| < \epsilon$, so that $f(x)$ is continuous at ξ.

THEOREM 1b. $f(x)$ is continuous on $[0, 1]$ if and only if, for every k, the sets $E[f(x) \geqq k]$ and $E[f(x) \leqq k]$ are closed.

The proof is left for the student.

The notion continuity relative to a set, which will now be introduced, shows that Theorems 1a and 1b are intimately connected.

DEFINITION 3. A function $f(x)$ defined on a set S is said to be continuous at a point $\xi \in S$ relative to a set $E \subset S$ if for every $\epsilon > 0$ there is a $\delta > 0$ such that if $x \in E$ and $|x - \xi| < \delta$ then $|f(x) - f(\xi)| < \epsilon$.

$f(x)$ is said to be continuous on S relative to E if it is continuous at every point of S relative to E.

We now have the following theorem, whose proof, although much like that of Theorem 1a, is given in order to illustrate the relative concepts involved.

THEOREM 2. A function $f(x)$, defined on a set S, is continuous on S relative to S if and only if, for every real number k, the sets $E[f(x) > k]$ and $E[f(x) < k]$ are open relative to S.

Proof. Suppose $f(x)$ is continuous on S relative to S. Let $\xi \in S$ be such that $f(\xi) > k$. There is an $\epsilon > 0$ such that $f(\xi) - \epsilon > k$. Since $f(x)$ is continuous at ξ relative to S, there is a $\delta > 0$ such that if $x \in S$ and $|x - \xi| < \delta$ then $|f(x) - f(\xi)| < \epsilon$. Hence there is a neighborhood I of ξ such that for every $x \in I \cap S$, $f(x) > f(\xi) - \epsilon > k$. Thus $E[f(x) > k]$ is open relative to S. Similarly, $E[f(x) < k]$ is open relative to S.

Suppose the sets $E[f(x) > k]$ and $E[f(x) < k]$ are open relative to S, for every k. Let $\xi \in S$, and let $\epsilon > 0$. Then since $E[f(x) > f(\xi) - \epsilon]$ is open relative to S, there is a neighborhood I_1 of ξ such that for every $x \in I_1 \cap S$, $f(x) > f(\xi) - \epsilon$. Moreover, since $E[f(x) < f(\xi) + \epsilon]$ is open relative to S, there is a neighborhood I_2 of ξ such that for every $x \in I_2 \cap S$, $f(x) < f(\xi) + \epsilon$. $I = I_1 \cap I_2$ is a neighborhood of ξ. For every $x \in I \cap S$, $|f(x) - f(\xi)| < \epsilon$, so that $f(x)$ is continuous at ξ relative to S.

COROLLARY 1. $f(x)$ is continuous on S relative to S if and only if for every k the sets $E[f(x) \geqq k]$ and $E[f(x) \leqq k]$ are closed relative to S.

Proof. The sets $E[f(x) \geq k]$ and $E[f(x) \leq k]$ are the complements relative to S of $E[f(x) < k]$ and $E[f(x) > k]$, respectively. Since the latter sets are open relative to S, the former are closed relative to S.

Theorems 1a and 1b are special cases of Theorem 2, since a subset of $(0, 1)$ is open relative to $(0, 1)$ if and only if it is open relative to the set of all real numbers, and a subset of $[0, 1]$ is closed relative to $[0, 1]$ if and only if it is closed relative to the set of all real numbers.

We now give some examples of continuous functions:

1. Let S be the interval $(0, 1)$ and $f(x) = 1/x$. Then $f(x)$ is continuous on $(0, 1)$.
2. Let S be any set and $f(x) = x$. Then $f(x)$ is continuous on S relative to S.
3. Let S be the set of all real numbers, $f(x) = 0$ if x is irrational, and $f(x) = 1$ if x is rational. Then $f(x)$ is not continuous anywhere. However, if E is the set of irrational numbers, then $f(x)$ is continuous on E relative to E.

4. *Properties of continuous functions*

In this section we show that the sum and product of continuous functions are continuous and that continuity relative to a set implies continuity relative to every subset.

PROPOSITION 3. If $f(x)$ and $g(x)$ are both continuous at ξ relative to a set S, then $f(x) + g(x)$ is continuous at ξ relative to S.

Proof. Let $\epsilon > 0$. There is a $\delta_1 > 0$ such that if $x \in S$ and $|x - \xi| < \delta_1$ then $|f(x) - f(\xi)| < \epsilon/2$, and a $\delta_2 > 0$ such that if $|x - \xi| < \delta_2$ then $|g(x) -$

$g(\xi)| < \epsilon/2$. If $\delta = \min[\delta_1, \delta_2]$ then if $x \in S$ and $|x - \xi| < \delta$,

$$|f(x) + g(x) - (f(\xi) + g(\xi))|$$
$$\leqq |f(x) - f(\xi)| + |g(x) - g(\xi)| < \frac{\epsilon}{2} + \frac{\epsilon}{2} = \epsilon.$$

PROPOSITION 4. If $f(x)$ and $g(x)$ are both continuous at ξ relative to a set S then $f(x) \cdot g(x)$ is continuous at ξ relative to S.

Proof. Let $\epsilon > 0$. There is a $\delta_1 > 0$ such that for every $x \in S$ such that $|x - \xi| < \delta_1$, $|f(x) - f(\xi)| < 1$, so that $|f(x)| < |f(\xi)| + 1$. Let $M = \max[|g(\xi)|, |f(\xi)| + 1]$. There is a $\delta_2 > 0$ such that if $x \in S$ and $|x - \xi| < \delta_2$ then $|f(x) - f(\xi)| < \epsilon/2M$, and a $\delta_3 > 0$ such that if $x \in S$ and $|x - \xi| < \delta_3$ then $|g(x) - g(\xi)| < \epsilon/2M$. Let $\delta = \min[\delta_1, \delta_2, \delta_3]$. Now for every x such that $|x - \xi| < \delta$ we have

$$|f(x)g(x) - f(\xi)g(\xi)| = |f(x)g(x) - f(x)g(\xi) + f(x)g(\xi) - f(\xi)g(\xi)|$$
$$\leqq |f(x)||g(x) - g(\xi)| + |g(\xi)||f(x) - f(\xi)| < M \cdot \frac{\epsilon}{2M} + M \cdot \frac{\epsilon}{2M} = \epsilon.$$

It is an easy matter to show that the set of functions continuous on a set S relative to S form a ring with $f(x) + g(x)$ and $f(x) \cdot g(x)$ as operations.

PROPOSITION 5. If $f(x)$ is continuous on S relative to S and $T \subset S$, then $f(x)$ is continuous on T relative to T.

Proof. Let $\xi \in T$. Then $\xi \in S$. Let $\epsilon > 0$. There is a $\delta > 0$ such that if $x \in S$ and $|x - \xi| < \delta$ then $|f(x) - f(\xi)| < \epsilon$. Since T is a subset of S, if $x \in T$ and $|x - \xi| < \delta$, then $|f(x) - f(\xi)| < \epsilon$. Hence $f(x)$ is continuous on T relative to T.

In addition to the above propositions, we shall prove the following theorem.

THEOREM 3. If $f(x)$ is continuous on a closed interval $[a, b]$, then for every η which is between $f(a)$ and $f(b)$ there is a $\xi \in [a, b]$ such that $f(\xi) = \eta$.

Proof. Let x_1 be the midpoint of $[a, b]$. Then, if $\eta \neq f(x_1)$, η either is between $f(a)$ and $f(x_1)$ or between $f(x_1)$ and $f(b)$. Hence there is an interval $[a_1, b_1] \subset [a, b]$ whose length is half that of $[a, b]$ such that η is between $f(a_1)$ and $f(b_1)$. Continuing this process, we obtain a nonincreasing sequence of closed intervals

$$[a, b] \supset [a_1, b_1] \supset \cdots \supset [a_n, b_n] \supset \cdots,$$

whose lengths converge to zero, such that η is between $f(a_n)$ and $f(b_n)$ for every n.

There is a unique ξ in the intersection of this sequence of intervals. We show that $\eta = f(\xi)$. Now, $f(x)$ is continuous at ξ. Let $\epsilon > 0$. There is a $\delta > 0$ such that if $|x - \xi| < \delta$ then $|f(x) - f(\xi)| < \epsilon$. There is an n such that $b_n - a_n < \delta$. Hence $|a_n - \xi| < \delta$ and $|b_n - \xi| < \delta$ so that $|f(a_n) -$

$f(\xi)| < \epsilon$ and $|f(b_n) - f(\xi)| < \epsilon$. Since η is between $f(a_n)$ and $f(b_n)$, it follows that $|\eta - f(\xi)| < \epsilon$. Since $\epsilon > 0$ is arbitrary, $f(\xi) = \eta$.

The property of Theorem 3 is not restricted to continuous functions. For example, the function $f(x) = \sin 1/x$, $x \in (0, 1]$ and $f(0) = 0$ has the property of Theorem 3 on every closed subinterval $[a, b]$ of $[0, 1]$ but is not continuous at $x = 0$.

5. *Uniform continuity*

A concept related to that of continuity, but, on the other hand, one which is distinctly different from continuity, is *uniform continuity*.

DEFINITION 4. A function $f(x)$ defined on a set S is said to be *uniformly continuous* on S if for every $\epsilon > 0$ there is a $\delta > 0$ such that if $x \in S$, $y \in S$, and $|x - y| < \delta$ then $|f(x) - f(y)| < \epsilon$.

If $f(x)$ is continuous on S, then for every $\xi \in S$, and $\epsilon > 0$, there is a $\delta = \delta(\epsilon, \xi) > 0$ such that if $x \in S$ and $|x - \xi| < \delta(\epsilon, \xi)$ then $|f(x) - f(\xi)| < \epsilon$. If there is a $\delta(\epsilon, \xi)$ with the above property such that the greatest lower bound, $\inf[\delta(\epsilon, \xi) \mid \xi \in S] = \delta(\epsilon) > 0$, for every $\epsilon > 0$, then $f(x)$ is uniformly continuous on S. The following examples illustrate the distinction between continuity and uniform continuity.

1. Let S be the open interval $(0, 1)$ and $f(x) = 1/x$ on S.
   (a) $f(x)$ is continuous on S. For let $\xi \in (0, 1)$ and let $\epsilon > 0$. If $\delta = \min[\xi^2\epsilon/2, \xi/2]$ then if $|x - \xi| < \delta$ it follows that

$$|f(x) - f(\xi)| = \left|\frac{1}{x} - \frac{1}{\xi}\right| = \frac{|x - \xi|}{x\xi} < \epsilon\frac{\xi^2/2}{\xi^2/2} = \epsilon.$$

   Observe that the choice of δ made here depends on both ϵ and ξ.
   (b) $f(x)$ is not uniformly continuous on S. For, suppose $\epsilon = 1$. Choose any $\delta > 0$. Of course $\delta < 1$, since $S = (0, 1)$. Now let $\xi = \delta/2$. Then

$$|f(\xi) - f(\xi + \delta)| = \left|\frac{1}{\xi} - \frac{1}{\xi + \delta}\right| = \frac{\delta}{\xi(\xi + \delta)} = \frac{4\delta}{3\delta^2} > 1.$$

   Hence, for every $\delta > 0$ there is an x_1 and an x_2 in $(0, 1)$ such that $|x_1 - x_2| = \delta$ and $|f(x_1) - f(x_2)| > 1$, so that $f(x)$ is not uniformly continuous on S.
2. In this example, we have a function $f(x) = x^2$ defined on $S = (0, 1)$ which is uniformly continuous on S. For if $\epsilon > 0$, let $\delta = \epsilon/2$; then if $|x_1 - x_2| < \delta$,

$$\begin{aligned}|f(x_1) - f(x_2)| &= |x_1^2 - x_2^2| = |x_1^2 - x_1x_2 + x_1x_2 - x_2^2| \\ &\leqq x_1|x_1 - x_2| + x_2|x_1 - x_2| < 2|x_1 - x_2| < 2\delta = \epsilon.\end{aligned}$$

In contrast, let $f(x) = x^2$ and $S = (-\infty, \infty)$. Suppose $\epsilon = 1$. Choose any $\delta > 0$. Let n be a positive integer such that $n > 1/2\delta$. We then have $|(n + \delta)^2 - n^2| = 2n\delta + \delta^2 > 1$. Hence x^2 is not uniformly continuous on $(-\infty, \infty)$.

3. As a third example, let S be the set of rational numbers. Let $f(x) = 0$ for $x \in S$ such that $x < \sqrt{2}$ and $f(x) = 1$ for $x \in S$ and $x > \sqrt{2}$.
   (a) $f(x)$ is continuous on S. For let $\xi \in S$. Then either $\xi > \sqrt{2}$ or $\xi < \sqrt{2}$. Suppose $\xi > \sqrt{2}$. There is a $\delta > 0$ such that if $|x - \xi| < \delta$ then $x > \sqrt{2}$. Hence if $|x - \xi| < \delta$, $|f(x) - f(\xi)| = 0$. Thus $f(x)$ is continuous at ξ. Similarly, if $\xi < \sqrt{2}$, $f(x)$ is continuous at ξ.
   (b) $f(x)$ is not uniformly continuous on S. For let $\epsilon = 1$. For every $\delta > 0$ there are $x_1 < \sqrt{2}$ and $x_2 > \sqrt{2}$ such that $|x_1 - x_2| < \delta$. But $|f(x_1) - f(x_2)| = 1$.
4. As a final example, let $S = (0, 1)$ and $f(x) = \sin 1/x$. In this case, $f(x)$ is again continuous but not uniformly continuous on S.
   (a) $f(x)$ is continuous on S. For let $\xi \in S$ and let $\epsilon > 0$. Let $\delta = \min [\xi/2, \xi^2\epsilon/2]$. If $|x - \xi| < \delta$ then

$$|f(x) - f(\xi)| = \left|\sin\frac{1}{x} - \sin\frac{1}{\xi}\right| = \left|2\cos\frac{x+\xi}{2x\xi}\sin\frac{x-\xi}{2x\xi}\right|$$

$$\leqq \frac{|x-\xi|}{x\xi} < \frac{2\delta}{\xi^2} \leqq \epsilon.$$

   Hence $f(x)$ is continuous on S.
   (b) $f(x)$ is not uniformly continuous on S. For let $\epsilon = 1$ and $\delta > 0$. There is an odd positive integer n such that $4/3\pi n < \delta$. So $|2/\pi n - 2/3\pi n| < \delta$ but $|\sin \pi n/2 - \sin 3\pi n/2| = 2$. This shows that $f(x)$ is not uniformly continuous on S.

   Now if $f(x)$ is uniformly continuous on S then $f(x)$ is continuous on S, but the converse does not hold, as has been amply illustrated by the above examples. However, it is an important fact that if the set S is closed and bounded, continuity and uniform continuity on S are equivalent notions. The proof of this theorem is our first application of the Borel Covering Theorem.

THEOREM 4. If S is a closed bounded set and if $f(x)$ is continuous on S relative to S, then $f(x)$ is uniformly continuous on S.

Proof. Let $\epsilon > 0$. For every $\xi \in S$ there is an open interval I_ξ such that $\xi \in I_\xi$ and, for every $x \in I_\xi$, such that $x \in S$, $|f(x) - f(\xi)| < \epsilon/4$. Now the open intervals I_ξ, $\xi \in S$, cover S, and S is closed and bounded, so that, by the Borel Covering Theorem, a finite number of them, $I_{\xi_1}, \cdots, I_{\xi_n}$, cover S. Consider the set E composed of the endpoints of this finite set of intervals and let $\delta > 0$ be half the shortest distance between the pairs of points of E. Suppose, now, that $x \in S$, $y \in S$ and $x < y$, $|x - y| < \delta$. In the first place, there can be at most one point z in E such that $x \leqq z \leqq y$. Thus either (1) x and y are in the same I_{ξ_k} or (2) $x \in I_{\xi_j}, y \in I_{\xi_k}$ and $I_{\xi_j} \cap I_{\xi_k} \neq \phi$. If (1) $x \in I_{\xi_k}, y \in I_{\xi_k}$ then $|f(x) - f(\xi_k)| < \epsilon/4$ and $|f(y) - f(\xi_k)| < \epsilon/4$, so that $|f(x) - f(y)| < \epsilon/2$. If (2) $x \in I_{\xi_j}, y \in I_{\xi_k}$ and $I_{\xi_j} \cap I_{\xi_k} \neq \phi$, there is a $z \in I_{\xi_j} \cap I_{\xi_k}$. So $|f(z) - f(\xi_j)| < \epsilon/4$, $|f(z) - f(\xi_k)| < \epsilon/4$, $|f(x) - f(\xi_j)| < \epsilon/4$, and $|f(y) - f(\xi_k)| < \epsilon/4$. It follows that

$$|f(y) - f(x)| \leqq |f(y) - f(\xi_k)| + |f(\xi_k) - f(z)| + |f(z) - f(\xi_j)| + |f(\xi_j) - f(x)| < \epsilon.$$

We have thus shown that for every $\epsilon > 0$ there is a $\delta > 0$ such that if $|x - y| < \delta$, $x \in S$, $y \in S$ then $|f(x) - f(y)| < \epsilon$, and so $f(x)$ is uniformly continuous on S.

This seems to be the appropriate place to make another, similar application of the Borel Covering Theorem. This requires some preliminary definitions.

DEFINITION 5. A function $f(x)$ is said to be *bounded on a set* S if there is an $M > 0$ such that for every $x \in S$, $|f(x)| < M$.

DEFINITION 6. A function $f(x)$ is said to be *bounded at a point* $\xi \in S$ relative to S if there is a neighborhood I of ξ and an $M > 0$ such that for every $x \in I \cap S$, $|f(x)| < M$.

PROPOSITION 6. If S is a closed bounded set and $f(x)$ is defined on S and bounded at every point of S relative to S then $f(x)$ is bounded on S.

Proof. For every ξ in S there is a neighborhood I_ξ of ξ and $M_\xi > 0$ such that, for every $x \in I_\xi \cap S$, $|f(x)| < M_\xi$. The open intervals I_ξ, $\xi \in S$, cover the closed bounded set S so that, by the Borel Covering Theorem, a finite number of them, say $I_{\xi_1}, I_{\xi_2}, \cdots, I_{\xi_n}$, cover S. Let $M = \max [M_{\xi_1}, M_{\xi_2}, \cdots, M_{\xi_n}]$. Every $x \in S$ is in I_{ξ_k} for some k so that $|f(x)| < M_{\xi_k} \leqq M$. It follows that $f(x)$ is bounded on S.

6. *Sets of points of discontinuity*

We shall first consider functions defined everywhere, i.e., on $(-\infty, \infty)$. It is possible for $f(x)$ to be discontinuous everywhere. For example, the function which is 0 on the irrationals and 1 on the rationals has this property. For let ξ be an irrational; then ξ is the limit of a sequence $\{\xi_n\}$ of rationals so that $\lim_{n\to\infty} \xi_n = \xi$, $\lim_{n\to\infty} f(\xi_n) = 1$, but $f(\xi) = 0$ so that $f(x)$ is not continuous at ξ. If ξ is a rational, then $f(x)$ is, by a similar argument not continuous at ξ.

For any function $f(x)$ we shall designate by $D(f)$ the set of values of x for which $f(x)$ is not continuous and by $C(f)$ the set of points for which $f(x)$ is continuous. The set $D(f)$ will be called the set of points of discontinuity of $f(x)$. We shall show that only for certain kinds of sets S is there a function $f(x)$ such that $S = D(f)$.

THEOREM 5. If $f(x)$ is any real function defined on $(-\infty, \infty)$, the set $D(f)$ of points of discontinuity of $f(x)$ is the union of a finite or denumerable number of closed sets.

Proof. We introduce the auxiliary sets $D_n(f)$, $n = 1, 2, \cdots$. Let $\xi \in D_n(f)$ if and only if for every neighborhood I of ξ there are $x \in I$, $y \in I$ such that $|f(x) - f(y)| \geqq 1/n$. The theorem will be proved if we show (1) $D(f) = \bigcup_{n=1}^{\infty} D_n(f)$, and (2) $D_n(f)$ is a closed set for every n.

Proof of (1). If $\xi \in \bigcup_{n=1}^{\infty} D_n(f)$ there is an n such that $\xi \in D_n(f)$. So for every $\delta > 0$ there is an x and a y such that $|x - \xi| < \delta$, $|y - \xi| < \delta$, and $|f(x) - f(y)| \geqq 1/n$, and so there is an x such that $|x - \xi| < \delta$ and $|f(x) - f(\xi)| > 1/3n$. Hence $f(x)$ is not continuous at ξ, so that $\xi \in D(f)$.

If $\xi \in D(f)$, there is an $\epsilon > 0$ such that for every $\delta > 0$ there is an x with $|x - \xi| < \delta$ and $|f(x) - f(\xi)| > \epsilon$. There is an n such that $\epsilon > 1/n$. Let I be any neighborhood ξ. There is then an $x \in I$ such that $|f(x) - f(\xi)| > \epsilon > 1/n$, so that $\xi \in D_n(f)$. Hence $\xi \in \bigcup_{n=1}^{\infty} D_n(f)$.

Proof of (2). Let n be a positive integer and let ξ be a limit point of $D_n(f)$. There is then a sequence $\{\xi_m\}$ where each $\xi_m \in D_n(f)$ and $\lim_{m\to\infty} \xi_m = \xi$. Let I be any neighborhood of ξ. There is an m such that $\xi_m \in I$, so that I is a neighborhood of ξ_m. Since $\xi_m \in D_n(f)$, there are $x \in I$, $y \in I$, such that $|f(x) - f(y)| \geqq 1/n$. Now, since I is an arbitrary neighborhood of ξ, it follows that $\xi \in D_n(f)$, so that $D_n(f)$ is closed.

DEFINITION 7. A set S will be said to be of *type* F_σ if it is the union of a finite number or a denumerable number of closed sets.

Theorem 5 may now be written as follows:

THEOREM 5′. If $f(x)$ is any real function defined on $(-\infty, \infty)$, the set of points of discontinuity of $f(x)$ is of type F_σ.

As a partial converse, we now show that every denumerable set S is the set of points of discontinuity of a function $f(x)$. The more general theorem that every set of type F_σ is the set $D(f)$ for some $f(x)$ also holds. The proof may be found in H. Hahn, *Reelle Funktionen*, p. 193.

Let $S = \{a_1, a_2, \cdots, a_n, \cdots\}$ be a denumerable set whose elements are $a_1, a_2, \cdots, a_n, \cdots$. Let $f(x) = 1/n$ for $x = a_n$ and $f(x) = 0$ for every $x \in C(S)$. Then $f(x)$ is not continuous at a_n, since $f(a_n) = 1/n$ and every neighborhood I of a_n contains a $\xi \in C(S)$, so that $|f(\xi) - f(a_n)| = 1/n$. If $\xi \in C(S)$, then $f(x)$ is continuous at ξ. For if $\epsilon > 0$, there is an n such that

$1/n < \epsilon$. Now there is a neighborhood I of ξ such that $a_1 \notin I$, $a_2 \notin I$, $\cdots$, $a_n \notin I$. Hence for every $x \in I$, $0 \leqq f(x) < 1/n < \epsilon$, so that $|f(x) - f(\xi)| < \epsilon$.

In particular, there are functions which are continuous at the irrational numbers and discontinuous at the rational numbers.

On the other hand, we shall now show that there are no functions which are continuous at the rational numbers and discontinuous at the irrational numbers. This follows from Theorem 5′ if we can show that the irrational numbers are not a set of type F_σ. The following propositions establish this fact. Our point of departure is Proposition 2, Chapter 6, which states that a closed set either is nowhere dense or contains an interval. A quick consequence of this proposition is the following one.

PROPOSITION 7. A set of type F_σ is either of the first category or contains an interval.

Proof. Let S be of type F_σ. Then $S = \bigcup_{n=1}^{\infty} S_n$, where the S_n are closed sets. If the sets S_n are all nowhere dense then S is of the first category. If one of the sets S_n, say S_m, is not nowhere dense, then S_m contains an interval, so that S contains an interval.

PROPOSITION 8. The set S of irrational numbers is not of type F_σ.

Proof. S does not contain an interval. Hence, by Proposition 7, if S were of type F_σ then S would be of the first category. But the set $C(S)$ of rational numbers is of the first category. This means that the set of all real numbers, as the union of two sets of the first category, is of the first category. This contradiction shows that the set S of all irrational numbers is not of type F_σ.

PROPOSITION 9. There is no function $f(x)$ which has the irrational numbers as its set of points of discontinuity.

Proof. By Theorem 5′ and Proposition 8.

7. *Semicontinuous functions*

An important generalization of continuity will now be obtained by dropping part of the demand imposed upon a function by the definition of continuity. We recall one of the definitions of continuity: $f(x)$ is continuous at ξ if, for every $\epsilon > 0$, there is a $\delta > 0$ such that if $|x - \xi| < \delta$ then

$$|f(x) - f(\xi)| < \epsilon.$$

The inequality $|f(x) - f(\xi)| < \epsilon$ may be replaced by the two inequalities

$$f(\xi) < f(x) + \epsilon$$

and

$$f(\xi) > f(x) - \epsilon.$$

Now, if we require only that $f(\xi) < f(x) + \epsilon$, we obtain the definition of lower-semicontinuity, and if we require that $f(\xi) > f(x) - \epsilon$, we obtain the definition of upper-semicontinuity.

DEFINITION 8. If $f(x)$ is defined on a set S, then $f(x)$ is *lower-semicontinuous* at $\xi \in S$ relative to S if for every $\epsilon > 0$ there is a $\delta > 0$ such that if $x \in S$ and $|x - \xi| < \delta$ then $f(\xi) < f(x) + \epsilon$. $f(x)$ is *upper-semicontinuous* at $\xi \in S$ relative to S if for every $\epsilon > 0$ there is a $\delta > 0$ such that if $x \in S$ and $|x - \xi| < \delta$ then $f(\xi) > f(x) - \epsilon$.

DEFINITION 9. $f(x)$ is said to be lower-semicontinuous (upper-semicontinuous) on S relative to S if it is lower-semicontinuous (upper-semicontinuous) at every $\xi \in S$ relative to S.

We shall now suppose that S is the set $(-\infty, \infty)$ of all real numbers. We then obtain the following theorem.

THEOREM 6a. $f(x)$ is lower-semicontinuous if and only if for every real number k the set $E[f(x) \leqq k]$ is closed. $f(x)$ is upper-semicontinuous if and only if, for every real number k, the set $E[f(x) \geqq k]$ is closed.

We prove only the first part of the theorem.

Proof. Suppose $f(x)$ is lower-semicontinuous. Let k be a real number and ξ a limit point of the set $E[f(x) \leqq k]$. Let $\epsilon > 0$. Then there is a $\delta > 0$ such that for every $\delta > 0$ there is an x such that $|x - \xi| < \delta$ and $f(\xi) \geqq f(x) + \alpha$. such that $|\eta - \xi| < \delta$. Hence $f(\xi) < f(\eta) + \epsilon \leqq k + \epsilon$. But $\epsilon > 0$ is arbitrary, so that $f(\xi) \leqq k$, $\xi \in E[f(x) \leqq k]$, and the set $E[f(x) \leqq k]$ is closed.

Suppose $f(x)$ is not lower-semicontinuous at ξ. There is an $\alpha > 0$ such that for ever $\delta > 0$ there is an x such that $|x - \xi| < \delta$ and $f(\xi) \geqq f(x) + \alpha$. There is accordingly a sequence $\{x_n\}$ such that $\lim_{n \to \infty} x_n = \xi$ and $f(x_n) \leqq f(\xi) - \alpha$ for every n. Hence the set $E[f(x) \leqq f(\xi) - \alpha]$ is not closed. This proves that if for every real number k the set $E[f(x) \leqq k]$ is closed then $f(x)$ is lower-semicontinuous.

With minor changes in details, we obtain a theorem such as Theorem 6a for all sets S.

THEOREM 6b. $f(x)$ is lower-semicontinuous on S relative to S if and only if for every real number k the set $E[f(x) \leqq k]$ is closed relative to S. The analogous statement holds for upper-semicontinuous functions.

The proof of this theorem and of the corollary which follows are left to the student.

COROLLARY 2. $f(x)$ is lower-semicontinuous on S relative to S if and only if for every real number k the set $E[f(x) > k]$ is open relative to S. The analogous statement holds for upper-semicontinuous functions.

Theorem 2 on continuous functions follows from Theorem 6b, since a continuous function is one which is at the same time lower-semicontinuous and upper-semicontinuous.

We have as yet had no evidence that there are semicontinuous functions that are not continuous. An example of such a function is the one given earlier in this chapter. Let S be any denumerable set whose elements are $a_1, a_2, \cdots, a_n, \cdots$. Let $f(a_n) = 1/n$, $n = 1, 2, \cdots$, and $f(x) = 0$ for $x \in C(S)$. It is easily verified that $f(x)$ is upper-semicontinuous everywhere but is discontinuous on S.

We shall show later that the set of points of discontinuity of a semicontinuous function must be of the first category. On the other hand, every F_σ-type set of the first category is the set of points of discontinuity for some semicontinuous function. The proof of this is left as an exercise for the student.

We now give a proposition on semicontinuous functions which indicates the part this concept plays in the theory of maxima and minima.

PROPOSITION 10. If $f(x)$ is lower-semicontinuous and bounded from below on $[a, b]$ then $f(x)$ has an absolute minimum on $[a, b]$.

Proof. There is an α such that $f(x) \geqq \alpha$ for every $x \in [a, b]$ and a β such that $f(x) < \beta$ for some $x \in [a, b]$. Let y_1 be the midpoint of $[\alpha, \beta]$. One of the two intervals $[\alpha, y_1]$, $[y_1, \beta]$, call it $[\alpha_1, \beta_1]$, has the property that $f(x) \geqq \alpha_1$ for every $x \in [a, b]$, and that $f(x) < \beta_1$ for some $x \in [a, b]$. In this way we obtain a nonincreasing sequence of closed intervals

$$[\alpha, \beta] \supset [\alpha_1, \beta_1] \supset \cdots \supset [\alpha_n, \beta_n] \supset \cdots$$

such that $\lim_{n\to\infty} (\beta_n - \alpha_n) = 0$, and $f(x) \geqq \alpha_n$ for every $x \in [a, b]$ and every n, and, for every n, there is an $x_n \in [a, b]$ such that $f(x_n) < \beta_n$. The intersection of these intervals is a unique point

$$\lim_{n\to\infty} \alpha_n = \lim_{n\to\infty} \beta_n = \eta.$$

The sequence $\{x_n\}$ has a convergent subsequence $\{x_{n_k}\}$, by Exercise 5.2, Chapter 4. Let $\xi = \lim_{k\to\infty} x_{n_k}$. Evidently, $\lim_{k\to\infty} f(x_{n_k}) = \eta$, since $\alpha_{n_k} \leqq f(x_{n_k}) < \beta_{n_k}$ for every k, and $\lim_{k\to\infty} \alpha_{n_k} = \lim_{k\to\infty} \beta_{n_k} = \eta$. Since $f(x)$ is lower-semicontinuous at ξ, $f(\xi) \leqq \eta$. But if $f(\xi) < \eta$ then $f(\xi) < \alpha_n$ for some n, contradicting $f(x) \geqq \alpha_n$ for every $x \in [a, b]$. Hence $f(\xi) = \eta$. But $f(x) \geqq \eta$ for every $x \in [a, b]$, since otherwise $f(x) < \alpha_n$, for some n. Accordingly, $f(x)$ has a minimum value η and it is attained at $x = \xi$.

8. *Interval functions*

Every function has several important semicontinuous functions associated with it. In order to obtain these associated functions we must introduce the notion, "interval function."

DEFINITION 10. An *interval function* $\phi(I)$ is a correspondence which associates a real number with every open interval.

(Closed intervals may be used too, but they are not needed here.)

DEFINITION 11. An interval function $\phi(I)$ is said to be *nonincreasing* if whenever $I \subset J$ then $\phi(I) \leqq \phi(J)$; *nondecreasing* if whenever $I \subset J$ then $\phi(I) \geqq \phi(J)$.

DEFINITION 12. An interval function $\phi(I)$ is said to be *bounded* if there is an $M > 0$ such that, for every I, $|\phi(I)| < M$.

We shall consider first only bounded interval functions. Every bounded interval function, $\phi(I)$, has two associated point functions $\bar{\phi}(x)$ and $\underline{\phi}(x)$ called the upper and lower derivatives of $\phi(I)$.

Before giving their definitions we explain a notation introduced in it. We shall use the abbreviations "sup" for *least upper bound* and "inf" for *greatest lower bound*, e.g.,

$$\sup\left[\phi(I) \mid \xi \in I,\, l(I) < \frac{1}{n}\right]$$

signifies the least upper bound of the set of values of $\phi(I)$ for all I which contain ξ and are of length less than $1/n$.

We proceed now to define $\bar{\phi}(x)$ and $\underline{\phi}(x)$. We first let

$$\bar{\phi}_n(x) = \sup\left[\phi(I) \mid x \in I,\, l(I) < \frac{1}{n}\right],$$

and

$$\underline{\phi}_n(x) = \inf\left[\phi(I) \mid x \in I,\, l(I) < \frac{1}{n}\right].$$

The sequence $\{\bar{\phi}_n(x)\}$ is a nonincreasing bounded sequence and so, by Theorem 2, Chapter 4, it has a limit. This limit is $\bar{\phi}(x)$. To show that $\{\bar{\phi}_n(x)\}$ is nonincreasing we note that the set of intervals containing x of length less than $1/(n+1)$ is a subset of those of length less than $1/n$ so that

$$\sup\left[\phi(I) \mid x \in I,\, l(I) < \frac{1}{n+1}\right] \leqq \sup\left[\phi(I) \mid x \in I,\, l(I) < \frac{1}{n}\right],$$

and $\bar{\phi}_{n+1}(x) \leqq \bar{\phi}_n(x)$. $\underline{\phi}(x)$ is defined similarly.

DEFINITION 13. If $\phi(I)$ is a bounded interval function its upper and lower derivatives are given respectively by

$$\bar{\phi}(x) = \lim_{n\to\infty}\left\{\sup\left[\phi(I) \mid x \in I,\, l(I) < \frac{1}{n}\right]\right\},$$

and

$$\underline{\phi}(x) = \lim_{n\to\infty}\left\{\inf\left[\phi(I) \mid x \in I,\, l(I) < \frac{1}{n}\right]\right\}.$$

DEFINITION 14. An interval function $\phi(I)$ is said to be *convergent* at x if $\bar{\phi}(x) = \underline{\phi}(x)$. If $\phi(I)$ is convergent at x then $\phi'(x) = \bar{\phi}(x) = \underline{\phi}(x)$ is called its derivative at x.

PROPOSITION 11. A bounded nonincreasing interval function $\phi(I)$ is convergent everywhere.

Proof. Let ξ be any point. For every $\epsilon > 0$, there is a neighborhood $I = (\alpha, \beta)$ of ξ such that $\phi(I) < \underline{\phi}(\xi) + \epsilon$. There is an N such that $1/N < \min [\xi - \alpha, \beta - \xi]$. Then, if $l(J) < 1/N$ and $\xi \in J$, it follows that $J \subset I$, so that $\phi(J) \leqq \phi(I) < \underline{\phi}(\xi) + \epsilon$. Thus $\bar{\phi}_N(\xi) \leqq \underline{\phi}(\xi) + \epsilon$. But the sequence $\{\bar{\phi}_n(\xi)\}$ is nonincreasing, so that its limit $\bar{\phi}(\xi) \leqq \underline{\phi}(\xi) + \epsilon$. But for any interval function $\phi(I)$, $\bar{\phi}(\xi) \geqq \underline{\phi}(\xi)$. It follows that $|\bar{\phi}(\xi) - \underline{\phi}(\xi)| \leqq \epsilon$. Since $\epsilon > 0$ is arbitrary, we have shown that $\phi(I)$ is convergent.

In the same way, a bounded nondecreasing interval function $\phi(I)$ is convergent everywhere.

We now prove the following theorem.

THEOREM 7. The derivative $\phi'(x)$ of a nonincreasing bounded interval function $\phi(I)$ is upper-semicontinuous.

Proof. Consider any ξ. Let $\epsilon > 0$. There is a neighborhood J of ξ such that $\phi(J) < \phi'(\xi) + \epsilon$. For every $x \in J$, $\phi'(x) \leqq \phi(J)$, since the interval function $\phi(I)$ is nonincreasing. Hence $\phi'(x) \leqq \phi(J) < \phi'(\xi) + \epsilon$, or $\phi'(\xi) > \phi'(x) - \epsilon$, so that $\phi'(x)$ is upper-semicontinuous at ξ.

In the same way, the derivative of a nondecreasing bounded interval function is lower-semicontinuous.

9. *Special semicontinuous functions*

We shall assume that $f(x)$ is a bounded real function defined on the set S of all real numbers. We associate the following interval functions with $f(x)$:

1. $u(I) = \sup [f(x) \mid x \in I]$. The function $u(I)$ is called the *upper bound of $f(x)$ in I.*
2. $l(I) = \inf [f(x) \mid x \in I]$. The function $l(I)$ is called the *lower bound of $f(x)$ in I.*
3. $\omega(I) = u(I) - l(I)$. The function $\omega(I)$ is called the *saltus of $f(x)$ in I.*

Now $u(I)$ is a nonincreasing interval function, for if $J \subset I$ then

$$\sup [f(x) \mid x \in J] \leqq \sup [f(x) \mid x \in I].$$

Similarly, $l(I)$ is a nondecreasing interval function.

$\omega(I) = u(I) - l(I)$ is a nonincreasing interval function. For let $J \subset I$. Then $u(J) \leqq u(I)$ and $l(J) \geqq l(I)$, so that $u(J) - l(J) \leqq u(I) - l(I)$.

By Theorem 7, it follows that the derivatives $u(x)$ and $\omega(x)$ of $u(I)$ and $\omega(I)$ exist and are upper-semicontinuous, and that the derivative $l(x)$ of $l(I)$ exists and is lower-semicontinuous.

DEFINITION 15. The functions $u(x)$ and $l(x)$ are respectively called the *upper and lower boundary functions of* $f(x)$, and $\omega(x)$ is called the *saltus of* $f(x)$.

We shall obtain some properties of these functions.

DEFINITION 16. If $f(x)$ and $g(x)$ are functions then $g(x)$ is said to be approached by $f(x)$ at ξ if for every $\epsilon > 0$, ξ is a limit point of the set

$$E[g(\xi) - \epsilon < f(x) < g(\xi) + \epsilon].$$

PROPOSITION 12. If $f(x)$ is a bounded function and $u(x)$ is its upper boundary, then $u(x) \geqq f(x)$ everywhere and $u(x)$ is approached by $f(x)$ everywhere, except at points of a finite or denumerable set which may be empty.

Proof. That $u(x) \geqq f(x)$ follows from the fact that $u(I) \geqq f(x)$ for every neighborhood I of x.

Let E be the set of points for which $u(x)$ is not approached by $f(x)$. Let $\xi \in E$. There is a $k > 0$ and a neighborhood I_1 of ξ such that if $x \in I_1$ and $x \neq \xi$ then $|f(x) - u(\xi)| > k$. But from the definition of $u(x)$ there is a neighborhood I_2 of ξ such that if $x \in I_2$ then $f(x) < u(\xi) + k$. Then for every $x \in I = I_1 \cap I_2$, $x \neq \xi$, $f(x) < u(\xi) - k$. Now there is a rational number r such that $u(\xi) - k < r < u(\xi)$, so that $u(\xi) > r$ and $f(x) < r$ for every $x \in I$, $x \neq \xi$. Also there is a positive integer n such that $1/n$ is less than the minimum distance of ξ from the endpoints of I.

Let us order the rational numbers as a sequence $r_1, r_2, \cdots, r_m, \cdots$, and let E_{nm} be the set of points ξ for which $u(\xi) > r_m$ and $f(x) < r_m$ for every $x \neq \xi$ such that $0 < |x - \xi| < 1/n$. We have shown above that

$$E = \bigcup_{m=1}^{\infty} \bigcup_{n=1}^{\infty} E_{nm}.$$

In order to show that E is finite or denumerable we have only to show that each E_{nm} is finite or denumerable. Fix n and m. Suppose $\xi \in E_{nm}$. We show that if $0 < |x - \xi| < 1/n$ then $x \notin E_{nm}$. Let x be such that $0 < |x - \xi| < 1/n$. Since for every y such that $|y - \xi| < 1/n$ and $y \neq \xi$, $f(y) < r_m$, it follows that there is a neighborhood J of x such that $u(J) \leqq r_m$. Hence $u(x) \leqq r_m$, so that $x \notin E_{nm}$. So E_{nm} is a string of real numbers such that the distance between any two of them is not less than $1/n$. Such a set is finite or denumerable.

This proposition shows that every function $f(x)$ can be approximated, in the sense described in the proposition, by a semicontinuous function $u(x)$.

PROPOSITION 13. If $\omega(x)$ is the saltus of a bounded function $f(x)$, then for every k the set $E = E[\omega(x) \geqq k]$ is closed.

Proof. $\omega(x)$ is upper-semicontinuous.

We now show that the saltus function $\omega(x)$ of $f(x)$ describes the continuity character of $f(x)$.

PROPOSITION 14. $f(x)$ is continuous at ξ if and only if $\omega(\xi) = 0$.

Proof. Suppose $\omega(\xi) = 0$. Let $\epsilon > 0$. There is a neighborhood I of ξ such that $\omega(I) < \epsilon$. For every $x \epsilon I$,

$$|f(x) - f(\xi)| < u(I) - l(I) = \omega(I) < \epsilon.$$

Hence $f(x)$ is continuous at ξ.

Suppose $\omega(\xi) = k > 0$. Then for every neighborhood I of ξ, $\omega(I) \geqq k$. So there are $x \epsilon I$, $y \epsilon I$, such that $|f(x) - f(y)| > k/2$, whence either $|f(x) - f(\xi)| > k/4$ or $|f(y) - f(\xi)| > k/4$. In other words, for every neighborhood I of ξ there is a $z \epsilon I$ such that $|f(z) - f(\xi)| > k/4$ and $f(x)$ is not continuous at ξ.

Since $\omega(x)$ is upper-semicontinuous, Proposition 13 provides an alternate proof that the set of points of discontinuity of $f(x)$ is of type F_σ. For the set $E[\omega(x) \geqq 1/n]$ is closed for every positive integer n. But $f(x)$ is discontinuous at ξ if and only if $\omega(\xi) \geqq 1/n$ for some n. Hence the set of points of discontinuity of $f(x)$ is

$$D = \bigcup_{n=1}^{\infty} E\left[\omega(x) \geqq \frac{1}{n}\right],$$

which is of type F_σ.

10. *Unbounded functions*

We have so far restricted our treatment of semicontinuous functions to the bounded case. The unbounded case may be handled in several ways. The way we choose is to extend the real number system by adding the symbols $+\infty$ and $-\infty$. We shall then consider the extension of the real functions to functions which assume either real values or the values $+\infty$, $-\infty$.

If $f(x)$ is any function of the above kind, we consider the associated function

$$\phi(x) = \frac{f(x)}{1 + |f(x)|}$$

if $f(x)$ is real, $\phi(x) = 1$ if $f(x) = +\infty$ and $\phi(x) = -1$ if $f(x) = -\infty$.

Our convention will be that $f(x)$ is lower- or upper-semicontinuous at ξ if and only if the bounded function $\phi(x)$ is lower- or upper-semicontinuous at ξ.

If $f(\xi) = +\infty$ then $\phi(\xi) = 1$ and $\phi(x)$ is upper-semicontinuous. Hence $f(x)$ is upper-semicontinuous at all points at which it is $+\infty$.

If $f(\xi) = -\infty$, it is easily seen that $f(x)$ is upper-semicontinuous at ξ if and only if for every $M > 0$ there is a $\delta > 0$ such that if $|x - \xi| < \delta$ then $f(x) < -M$.

If $f(\xi)$ is real, one sees that $f(x)$ is upper-semicontinuous at ξ if and only if $\phi(x)$ is upper-semicontinuous at ξ.

Similar statements apply to lower-semicontinuity. The proof of these statements is left to the student.

Exercises

2.1 Show for every $f(x)$ and k that

$$E[f(x) = k] = \bigcap_{n=1}^{\infty} E\left[k - \frac{1}{n} < f(x) < k + \frac{1}{n}\right]$$

3.1 Show that the four definitions of continuity at a point given in the text are equivalent.

3.2 Show that $f(x) = \tan x$ is continuous on $(0, \pi/2)$.

3.3 Show that $f(x) = e^x$ is continuous everywhere.

3.4 Show that if $f(x)$ is continuous on $(0, 1)$ then for every open set G the set of points for which $f(x) \in G$ is open.

3.5 Show that there is a continuous function $f(x)$ and an open set G such that the set of values of $f(x)$ for which $x \in G$ is not an open set.

3.6 If $f(x)$ is continuous on S relative to S and on T relative to T does it follow that $f(x)$ is continuous on $S \cup T$ relative to $S \cup T$? Explain.

3.7 Answer Exercise 3.6 for the case where S and T are disjoint closed sets. Prove.

4.1 If $f(x)$ and $g(x)$ are both continuous at ξ and $g(\xi) \neq 0$ show that $f(x)/g(x)$ is continuous at ξ.

4.2 If $f(x)$ and $g(x)$ and their domains are given discuss the function $f[g(x)]$. If $f(x)$ and $g(x)$ are both continuous, discuss the continuity of $f[g(x)]$.

4.3 Show that if $f(x)$ is continuous on a closed interval $[a, b]$ then it has a maximum and minimum on $[a, b]$.

5.1 Prove that every unbounded function on $(0, 1)$, even though it may be continuous, is not uniformly continuous.

5.2 Give an example, different from the one in the text, of a bounded continuous function which is not uniformly continuous.

The next three exercises apply to general metric space.

5.3 By a real function on a set T in a metric space we mean a real number $f(x)$ associated with every $x \in T$. Define continuity and uniform continuity for this case.

5.4 If S is a complete metric space and $T \subset S$ is closed and totally bounded, show that every real function which is continuous on T is uniformly continuous on T.

5.5 Show that if $f(x)$ is defined on S the set of points $F \subset S$ at which $f(x)$ is unbounded relative to is closed relative to S.

6.1 If F is an arbitrary closed nowhere-dense set, give an example of a function $f(x)$ whose set of points of discontinuity is the set F. Prove.

6.2 If S is any denumerable set, show that there is a nondecreasing function which has S as its set of points of discontinuity.

7.1 Give an alternate definition of semicontinuity and show that it is equivalent to the one given in the text.

7.2 Show that $f(x)$ is lower-semicontinuous on S relative to S if and only if, for every real number k, the set $E[f(x) \leqq k]$ is closed relative to S.

7.3 Let S be a denumerable set whose elements are $a_1, a_2, \cdots, a_n, \cdots$. Let $f(a_n) = 1/n$, $n = 1, 2, \cdots$, and $f(x) = 0$ for $x \in C(S)$. Show that $f(x)$ is upper-semicontinuous everywhere but is discontinuous on S.

7.4 Show that the sum and product of two lower-semicontinuous functions are lower-semicontinuous.

7.5 Show that for every set S of type F_σ and of the first category there is an upper-semicontinuous $f(x)$ which has S as its set of points of discontinuity.

7.6 Discuss the difference and quotient of semicontinuous functions.

8.1 Give an example of an interval function $\phi(I)$ such that for every x, $\bar{\phi}(x) \neq \underline{\phi}(x)$.

8.2 Give an example of a bounded interval function which is neither nonincreasing nor nondecreasing but which converges everywhere.

9.1 Show that the upper boundary $u(x)$ of any bounded function $f(x)$ is its own upper boundary.

9.2 Does a similar result hold for the saltus of a bounded function? Explain.

9.3 For any two bounded functions $f(x)$ and $g(x)$ show that the saltus of $f(x) + g(x)$ does not exceed the sum of the saltuses of $f(x)$ and $g(x)$ anywhere.

10.1 If $f(x)$ is allowed to assume the values $+\infty$ and $-\infty$ and upper-semicontinuity is defined in terms of the upper-semicontinuity of $\phi(x)$ as indicated in the text, show that if $f(\xi) = -\infty$ then $f(x)$ is upper-semicontinuous at ξ if and only if for every $M > 0$ there is a $\delta > 0$ such that if $|x - \xi| < \delta$ then $f(x) < -M$.

10.2 Show that if $f(x)$ is real it is upper-semicontinuous at ξ if and only if $\phi(x)$ is upper-semicontinuous at ξ.

References

E. Borel, *Leçons sur les fonctions de variables rêeles*, Paris, 1928, Chap. 2.

C. Carathéodory, *Vorlesungen über reelle Funktionen*, Leipzig, 1927, Chap. 3.

F. Hausdorff, *Mengenlehre*, New York, 1944, Chap. 9.

E. W. Hobson, *The Theory of Functions of a Real Variable*, Cambridge, 1927, Chap. 5.

S. Verblunsky, *An Introduction to the Theory of Functions of a Real Variable*, Oxford, 1939, Chaps. 4, 5.

8

Sequences of Functions

1. *Convergence and uniform convergence*

We base the discussion of convergence of sequences of functions on that of convergence of sequences of real numbers. A sequence $\{f_n(x)\}$ of functions is an association of a function $f_n(x)$ with every positive integer n, so that for any real number ξ the sequence $\{f_n(\xi)\}$ is simply a sequence of real numbers.

DEFINITION 1. The sequence $\{f_n(x)\}$ of functions is said to be convergent at ξ if the sequence $\{f_n(\xi)\}$ of numbers is convergent. The sequence $\{f_n(x)\}$ is said to converge on a set S if $\{f_n(\xi)\}$ converges for every $\xi \in S$.

In contrast with convergence is the notion of uniform convergence.

DEFINITION 2. The sequence $\{f_n(x)\}$ of functions is said to *converge uniformly* on a set S if for every $\epsilon > 0$ there is an N such that for every $m, n > N$ and for every $x \in S$,

$$|f_m(x) - f_n(x)| < \epsilon.$$

Convergence and uniform convergence are far from being the same thing. Examples which illustrate the distinction are the following:

1. Let S be the set of all real numbers and $\{f_n(x)\} = \{x/n\}$ a sequence of functions defined on S.
   (a) $\{f_n(x)\}$ converges on S. For suppose $\xi \in S$. Let $\epsilon > 0$ and $N > |\xi|/\epsilon$. For every $n, m > N$,

$$|f_n(\xi) - f_m(\xi)| = \left|\frac{\xi}{n} - \frac{\xi}{m}\right| < \frac{|\xi|}{N} < \epsilon.$$

   Hence $\{f_n(\xi)\}$ converges for every $\xi \in S$, so that $\{f_n(x)\}$ converges on S.

(b) $\{f_n(x)\}$ does not converge uniformly on S. For, let N be any positive integer. We show that there are a $\xi \in S$ and integers $n, m > N$ such that $|f_n(\xi) - f_m(\xi)| = 1$. Indeed, if $\xi = 6N$, $n = 2N$, and $m = 3N$, then

$$|f_n(\xi) - f_m(\xi)| = \left|\frac{6N}{2N} - \frac{6N}{3N}\right| = 1.$$

This shows that $\{f_n(x)\}$ does not converge uniformly on S.

2. Let S be the real numbers and $\{f_n(x)\} = \{1/(1 + nx^2)\}$ defined on S.

(a) $\{f_n(x)\}$ converges on S. For let $\xi \in S$. Let $\epsilon > 0$ and $N > 1/\xi^2\epsilon$. For every $n, m > N$,

$$|f_n(\xi) - f_m(\xi)| = \left|\frac{1}{1 + n\xi^2} - \frac{1}{1 + m\xi^2}\right| \leqq \frac{|m - n|}{mn\xi^2} < \frac{1}{N\xi^2} < \epsilon.$$

Hence, the sequence $\{f_n(\xi)\}$ converges for every $\xi \in S$, so that it converges on S.

(b) The convergence of $\{f_n(x)\}$ on S is not uniform. For, let $\epsilon = 1/12$ and N be arbitrary. If $\xi = 1/\sqrt{N}$, $n = 2N$ and $m = 3N$, then

$$|f_n(\xi) - f_m(\xi)| = \left|\frac{1}{1 + n\xi^2} - \frac{1}{1 + m\xi^2}\right|$$

$$= \frac{N\xi^2}{(1 + 2N\xi^2)(1 + 3N\xi^2)} = \frac{1}{12}.$$

Hence the sequence does not converge uniformly.

(c) However, the convergence is uniform on any closed interval which does not contain zero. Let $[a, b]$ be any closed interval with $a > 0$. Let $\epsilon > 0$ and let $N > 1/a^2\epsilon$. Then, for every $\xi \in [a, b]$ and $n, m > N$,

$$|f_n(\xi) - f_m(\xi)|$$

$$= \left|\frac{1}{1 + n\xi^2} - \frac{1}{1 + m\xi^2}\right| \leqq \frac{|m - n|}{mn\xi^2} < \frac{1}{N\xi^2} \leqq \frac{1}{Na^2} < \epsilon.$$

Hence the convergence of $\{f_n(x)\}$ on $[a, b]$ is uniform.

The distinction between convergence and uniform convergence should now be clear. For convergence of a sequence $\{f_n(x)\}$ on a set S all that is required is convergence at each point of S. For uniform convergence, more is required. The difference may be stated as follows:

If $\{f_n(x)\}$ converges at ξ, then for every $\epsilon > 0$ there is a smallest positive integer $N(\epsilon, \xi)$ such that if $n, m > N(\epsilon, \xi)$ then $|f_n(\xi) - f_m(\xi)| < \epsilon$. If for every $\epsilon > 0$ and every $\xi \in S$ there is such an $N(\epsilon, \xi)$ then $\{f_n(x)\}$ converges on S. The sequence converges uniformly if and only if for every $\epsilon > 0$ the set of integers $N(\epsilon, \xi)$, $\xi \in S$, may be chosen so that it has a maximum.

Another way of defining uniform convergence for sequences of functions bounded on a set S is in terms of a distance function on the set of all functions bounded on S.

For every pair $f(x)$, $g(x)$ of bounded functions, let

$$\delta(f, g) = \sup [|f(x) - g(x)| \mid x \in S].$$

With $\delta(f, g)$ as a distance, the set of bounded functions is a metric space. For

1. $\delta(f, g) \geqq 0$ and $\delta(f, g) = 0$ only if $f(x) = g(x)$,
2. $\delta(f, g) = \delta(g, f)$,
3. $\delta(f, g) + \delta(g, h) \geqq \delta(f, h)$.

The proof of (1), (2) and (3) is left to the student.

PROPOSITION 1. A sequence $\{f_n(x)\}$ defined on S converges uniformly on S if and only if for every $\epsilon > 0$ there is an N such that if $n, m > N$ then $\delta(f_n, f_m) < \epsilon$.

Proof. Suppose for every $\epsilon > 0$ there is an N such that if $n, m > N$ then $|f_n(x) - f_m(x)| < \epsilon/2$ for every $x \in S$. Since $|f_n(x) - f_m(x)| < \epsilon/2$ for every $x \in S$, it follows that

$$\delta(f_n, f_m) = \sup [|f_n(x) - f_m(x)| \mid x \in S] \leqq \epsilon.$$

Conversely, suppose for every $\epsilon > 0$ there is an N such that if $n, m > N$ then $\delta(f_n, f_m) < \epsilon$. But

$$\delta(f_n, f_m) = \sup [|f_n(x) - f_m(x)| \mid x \in S].$$

Hence $|f_n(x) - f_m(x)| < \epsilon$ for every $x \in S$, and $\{f_n(x)\}$ converges uniformly.

This interprets uniform convergence of a sequence of bounded functions as ordinary convergence of a sequence of elements in a certain metric space.

2. *Sequences of continuous functions*

We first show that continuity is preserved by uniform convergence.

THEOREM 1. If $\{f_n(x)\}$ is a sequence of functions defined on a set S and uniformly convergent on S, then if each $f_n(x)$ is continuous at $a \in S$ relative to S, it follows that $f(x) = \lim_{n \to \infty} f_n(x)$ is continuous at a relative to S.

Proof. Let $\epsilon > 0$. Since $\{f_n(x)\}$ is uniformly convergent, there is an N such that for every $n > N$, $|f(x) - f_n(x)| < \epsilon/3$ for every $x \in S$. Let $n > N$. Now since $f_n(x)$ is continuous at $x = a$, there is a $\delta > 0$ such that if $|\xi - a| < \delta$ and $\xi \in S$ then $|f_n(\xi) - f_n(a)| < \epsilon/3$. Now suppose $|\xi - a| < \delta$ and $\xi \in S$. Then

$$|f(\xi) - f(a)| \leqq |f(\xi) - f_n(\xi)| + |f_n(\xi) - f_n(a)| + |f_n(a) - f(a)| < \frac{\epsilon}{3} + \frac{\epsilon}{3} + \frac{\epsilon}{3} = \epsilon.$$

This shows that $f(x)$ is continuous at $x = a$ relative to S.

COROLLARY 1. If $\{f_n(x)\}$ is a sequence of functions continuous on S which converges uniformly on S to a function $f(x)$, then $f(x)$ is continuous on S.

In contrast, continuity is not necessarily preserved by ordinary convergence.

Example:

1. The sequence $\{f_n(x)\} = \{1/(1 + nx^2)\}$ illustrates this point. The functions in the sequence are continuous. Let us examine the limit $f(x)$. For $x = 0$, $1/(1 + nx^2) = 1$ for every n. Hence $\lim_{n\to\infty} f_n(0) = f(0) = 1$. For $x \neq 0$, let $\epsilon > 0$ and let $N > (1 - \epsilon)/x^2\epsilon$. Then for every $n > N$,

$$f_n(x) = \frac{1}{1 + nx^2} < \frac{1}{1 + Nx^2} < \epsilon.$$

This shows that $\lim_{n\to\infty} f_n(x) = f(x) = 0$. Hence $f(x) = 1$ if $x = 0$ and $f(x) = 0$ if $x \neq 0$. Thus $f(x)$ is not continuous at $x = 0$.

Indeed, every semicontinuous function is the limit of a sequence of continuous functions. We first prove a converse theorem which in turn needs a preliminary definition.

DEFINITION 3. A sequence $\{f_n(x)\}$ of functions is *uniformly bounded on a set S* if there is an $M > 0$ such that for every n and every $x \in S$, $|f_n(x)| < M$.

We shall suppose in the next few theorems that all functions are defined on the set of all real numbers.

THEOREM 2. The limit of a uniformly bounded nondecreasing sequence of continuous functions is lower-semicontinuous.

Proof. Let $\{f_n(x)\}$ be a sequence of continuous functions uniformly bounded on S and nondecreasing. For any ξ, $\{f_n(\xi)\}$ is bounded and nondecreasing, so that $f(\xi) = \lim_{n\to\infty} f_n(\xi)$ exists. We show that $f(x)$ is lower-semicontinuous at ξ. For let $\epsilon > 0$. There is an N such that $f_N(\xi) > f(\xi) - \epsilon/2$. Since $f_N(x)$ is continuous, there is a $\delta > 0$ such that if $|x - \xi| < \delta$ then $f_N(x) > f_N(\xi) - \epsilon/2$. So $f_N(x) > f(\xi) - \epsilon$. But since $\{f_n(x)\}$ is nondecreasing, $f(x) \geqq f_N(x)$, so that $f(x) > f(\xi) - \epsilon$. This shows that $f(x)$ is lower-semicontinuous at ξ.

The converse is more difficult.

THEOREM 3. Every bounded lower-semicontinuous function $f(x)$ is the limit of a nondecreasing sequence of continuous functions.

Proof. Since $f(x)$ is bounded, there is an $M > 0$ such that $|f(x)| < M$ for every x. For every positive integer n, let

$$g_n(x) = \inf\,[f(y) + n|x - y|],$$

where y varies over the set of all real numbers.

We now show that $g_n(x)$ is uniformly continuous. For any two numbers x_1 and x_2,

$$g_n(x_1) = \inf[f(y) + n|x_1 - y|] \leqq \inf[f(y) + n|x_1 - x_2| + n|x_2 - y|]$$
$$= g_n(x_2) + n|x_1 - x_2|.$$

By interchanging x_1 and x_2,

$$g_n(x_2) \leqq g_n(x_1) + n|x_1 - x_2|.$$

Hence

$$|g_n(x_1) - g_n(x_2)| \leqq n|x_1 - x_2|.$$

Let $\epsilon > 0$. There is a $\delta = \epsilon/n$ such that if $|x_1 - x_2| < \delta$ then $|g_n(x_1) - g_n(x_2)| < \epsilon$. This shows that the functions $g_n(x)$ are all uniformly continuous.

We next show that, for every n, $g_{n+1}(x) \geqq g_n(x)$:

$$g_{n+1}(x) = \inf[f(y) + n|x - y| + |x - y|] \geqq \inf[f(y) + n|x - y|] = g_n(x).$$

Finally we show that $\lim_{n\to\infty} g_n(x) = f(x)$. For every n, $g_n(x) = \inf[f(y) + n|x - y|] \leqq f(x)$. Hence $\lim_{n\to\infty} g_n(x) \leqq f(x)$.

To show that $\lim_{n\to\infty} g_n(x) \geqq f(x)$, let $k < f(x)$. Since $f(x)$ is lower-semi-continuous, there is a $\delta > 0$ such that if $|y - x| < \delta$ then $f(y) > k$. So $\inf[f(y) + n|x - y|] \geqq k$, where y is restricted to those numbers for which $|x - y| < \delta$. Suppose $|x - y| \geqq \delta$. Then $f(y) + n|x - y| > -M + n\delta$. There is an N such that if $n > N$ then $-M + n\delta > k$. We then have, for $n > N$, $g_n(x) = \inf[f(y) + n|x - y|] \geqq k$, where y is restricted to those numbers for which $|x - y| \geqq \delta$. In other words, for every $n > N$, $g_n(x) \geqq k$. Hence $\lim_{n\to\infty} g_n(x) \geqq k$ for every $k < f(x)$. Accordingly, $\lim_{n\to\infty} g_n(x) \geqq f(x)$.

We have thus proved the theorem by showing that $f(x) = \lim_{n\to\infty} g_n(x)$.

We now prove a theorem on the limit superior of a sequence of continuous functions. We need some related definitions.

DEFINITION 4. If F is a uniformly bounded set of functions, then $f(x) = \sup[g(x)|g(x) \in \text{F}]$ is the function such that for every ξ, $f(\xi) = \sup[g(\xi)|g(x) \in \text{F}]$.

DEFINITION 5. If $\{s_n\}$ is a bounded sequence of real numbers, the limit superior, $\overline{\lim_{n\to\infty}}\, s_n$, of $\{s_n\}$ is the largest number x such that for every $\epsilon > 0$ an infinite number of terms of the sequence are greater than $x - \epsilon$.

In other words, $\overline{\lim_{n\to\infty}}\, s_n$ is the unique number x with the property that for every $\epsilon > 0$ an infinite number of terms of the sequence $\{s_n\}$ are in the interval $(x - \epsilon, x + \epsilon)$ and only a finite number of terms of the sequence are greater than $x + \epsilon$.

DEFINITION 6. If $\{f_n(x)\}$ is a uniformly bounded sequence of functions, the limit superior, $f(x) = \overline{\lim_{n\to\infty}} f_n(x)$, of the sequence is the function such that for every ξ, $f(\xi) = \overline{\lim_{n\to\infty}} f_n(\xi)$.

PROPOSITION 2. If F is a uniformly bounded set of lower-semicontinuous functions, then $\sup [g(x)|g(x) \in \mathsf{F}]$ is lower-semicontinuous.

Proof. Consider any ξ. $f(\xi) = \sup [g(\xi)|g(x) \in \mathsf{F}]$. Let $\epsilon > 0$. There is a $g(x) \in \mathsf{F}$ such that $f(\xi) < g(\xi) + \epsilon/2$. Since $g(x)$ is lower-semicontinuous, there is a $\delta > 0$ such that if $|x - \xi| < \delta$ then $g(\xi) < g(x) + \epsilon/2$. But $g(x) \leqq f(x)$. It follows that

$$f(\xi) < g(\xi) + \frac{\epsilon}{2} < g(x) + \epsilon \leqq f(x) + \epsilon.$$

This shows that $f(x)$ is lower-semicontinuous at ξ.

PROPOSITION 3. If $\{s_n\}$ is a bounded sequence of numbers and $t_n = \sup \{s_n, s_{n+1}, \cdots\}$ for every positive integer n, then $\overline{\lim_{n\to\infty}}\ s_n = \lim_{n\to\infty} t_n$.

Proof. First, $\{t_n\}$ is a bounded sequence which is nonincreasing. Hence $\lim_{n\to\infty} t_n$ exists. Let $x = \lim_{n\to\infty} t_n$. For every $\epsilon > 0$ and every positive integer n, $t_n > x - \epsilon$. Since $t_n = \sup \{s_n, s_{n+1}, \cdots\}$, there is an $m \geqq n$ such that $s_m > x - \epsilon$. Hence there are an infinite number of terms of $\{s_n\}$ which exceed $x - \epsilon$. Let $y > x$. There is an $\epsilon > 0$ such that $y - \epsilon > x$. So there is an n such that $t_n < y - \epsilon$. Hence $s_n, s_{n+1}, \cdots$ are all less than $y - \epsilon$. We have shown that x is the largest number such that for every $\epsilon > 0$ an infinite number of terms of $\{s_n\}$ are greater than $x - \epsilon$. Accordingly, $x = \overline{\lim_{n\to\infty}}\ s_n$.

THEOREM 4. If $\{f_n(x)\}$ is a uniformly bounded sequence of continuous functions and $f(x) = \overline{\lim_{n\to\infty}} f_n(x)$, then there is a nonincreasing sequence $\{\phi_n(x)\}$ of lower-semicontinuous functions which converges and is such that $f(x) = \lim_{n\to\infty} \phi_n(x)$.

Proof. For every n, let

$$\phi_n(x) = \sup [f_n(x), f_{n+1}(x), \cdots].$$

By Proposition 2, $\phi_n(x)$ is lower-semicontinuous. The sequence $\{\phi_n(x)\}$ is clearly nonincreasing. By Proposition 3, $f(x) = \lim_{n\to\infty} \phi_n(x)$.

3. *Equicontinuity*

The sequence

$$\left\{\frac{1}{1+nx^2}\right\}$$

is uniformly bounded on $[0, 1]$ but is not uniformly convergent; nor is any subsequence uniformly convergent. Hence uniform boundedness and continuity are not enough conditions to assure uniform convergence of a sequence of functions, or of any of its subsequences.

We show that if a sequence of continuous functions converges uniformly, the functions must be uniformly bounded and must also obey a condition called *equicontinuity*. Conversely, we show that every uniformly bounded equicontinuous sequence of functions $\{f_n(x)\}$ on a closed interval has a uniformly convergent subsequence.

Suppose first that $\{f_n(x)\}$ is a sequence of continuous functions defined on $[0, 1]$ which converges uniformly. There is an N such that for every $n > N$ and every $x \in [0, 1]$, $|f_N(x) - f_n(x)| < 1$. As the student can readily verify, a continuous function on a closed interval is bounded. For every n, let M_n be such that $|f_n(x)| < M_n$ for every $x \in [0, 1]$. Let $M = \max [M_1, M_2, \cdots, M_N] + 1$. Then for every $x \in [0, 1]$ and every n, $|f_n(x)| < M$, so that $\{f_n(x)\}$ is uniformly bounded.

Let $\epsilon > 0$. There is an N such that for every $n > N$ and every $x \in [0, 1]$, $|f_n(x) - f_N(x)| < \epsilon/3$. For every n, there is a $\delta_n > 0$ such that if $|x - y| < \delta_n$ then $|f_n(x) - f_n(y)| < \epsilon/3$. Let $\delta = \min [\delta_1, \delta_2, \cdots, \delta_N]$. Then $\delta > 0$. For every $x, y \in [0, 1]$ such that $|x - y| < \delta$, if $n \leqq N$ then $|f_n(x) - f_n(y)| < \epsilon/3$, and if $n > N$, then

$$|f_n(x) - f_n(y)| \leqq |f_n(x) - f_N(x)| + |f_N(x) - f_N(y)| + |f_N(y) - f_n(y)| < \frac{\epsilon}{3} + \frac{\epsilon}{3} + \frac{\epsilon}{3} = \epsilon.$$

We introduce a definition.

DEFINITION 7. A sequence $\{f_n(x)\}$ defined on a closed interval $[a, b]$ is said to be *equicontinuous* if for every $\epsilon > 0$ there is a $\delta > 0$ such that if $|x - y| < \delta$ then $|f_n(x) - f_n(y)| < \epsilon$ for every n.

We have proved the following proposition.

PROPOSITION 4. If $\{f_n(x)\}$ is a uniformly convergent sequence of continuous functions it is equicontinuous.

The following important converse will now be proved.

THEOREM 5. Every uniformly bounded equicontinuous sequence of functions $\{f_n(x)\}$ on a closed interval $[a, b]$ has a uniformly convergent subsequence.

Proof. We first use only the uniform-boundedness restriction on the sequence: there is an $M > 0$ such that for every $x \in [a, b]$ and every n, $|f_n(x)| < M$.

Consider the rational numbers in $[a, b]$ ordered as a sequence $\{r_n\}$. The sequence $\{f_n(r_1)\}$, as a bounded sequence of real numbers, has a convergent subsequence

$f_{11}(r_1), f_{12}(r_1), \cdots$.

The sequence $\{f_{1n}(r_2)\}$ is bounded and so has a convergent subsequence

$f_{21}(r_2), f_{22}(r_2), \cdots$.

Having the sequences

$f_{11}(x), f_{12}(x), \cdots$

$f_{21}(x), f_{22}(x), \cdots$

$\cdots\cdots\cdots\cdots\cdots$

$f_{m-1,1}(x), f_{m-1,2}(x), \cdots,$

each of which is a subsequence of the preceding such that $\{f_{1n}(x)\}$ converges at $x = r_1$, $\{f_{2n}(x)\}$ converges at $x = r_2, \cdots, \{f_{m-1,n}(x)\}$ converges at r_{m-1}, there is a subsequence $\{f_{mn}(x)\}$ of $\{f_{m-1,n}(x)\}$ such that $\{f_{mn}(r_m)\}$ converges at $x = r_m$.

We thus have a sequence of sequences

$$\{f_{1n}(x)\},\ \{f_{2n}(x)\},\ \cdots,\ \{f_{mn}(x)\},\ \cdots$$

each of which is a subsequence of the preceding one such that for every m, $\{f_{mn}(r_m)\}$ converges. Consider the sequence

$$f_{11}(x), f_{22}(x), \cdots, f_{mm}(x), \cdots.$$

This sequence converges at all the rationals in $[a, b]$. For if n is any positive integer, then for $m > n$ the $f_{mm}(x)$ form a subsequence of

$$f_{nm}(x), f_{n,m+1}(x), \cdots, f_{n,m+p}(x), \cdots.$$

Hence the sequence $\{f_{mm}(r_n)\}$ converges.

We have thus shown that every uniformly bounded sequence of functions has a subsequence which is convergent on the set of rational numbers.

We now take advantage of the assumption that $\{f_n(x)\}$ is equicontinuous to show that the subsequence

$$f_{11}(x), f_{22}(x), \cdots$$

of $\{f_n(x)\}$ is uniformly convergent. Let $\epsilon > 0$. There is a $\delta > 0$ such that if $|x - y| < \delta$ then $|f_n(x) - f_n(y)| < \epsilon/3$ for every n. Consider a set $s_1, s_2, \cdots, s_k$ of rational numbers such that $a < s_1 < s_2 < \cdots < s_k < b$ and $\max [s_1 - a, s_2 - s_1, \cdots, s_k - s_{k-1}, b - s_k] < \delta$. There is an N such that for every $n, m > N$, $|f_{nn}(s_j) - f_{mm}(s_j)| < \epsilon/3$ for every $j = 1, 2, \cdots, k$. Now let $x \in [a, b]$. There is a j with $1 \leqq j \leqq k$ such that $|x - s_j| < \delta$. Hence for every $n, m > N$,

$$|f_{nn}(x) - f_{mm}(x)| \leqq |f_{nn}(x) - f_{nn}(s_j)| + |f_{nn}(s_j) - f_{mm}(s_j)| + |f_{mm}(s_j) - f_{mm}(x)| < \frac{\epsilon}{3} + \frac{\epsilon}{3} + \frac{\epsilon}{3} = \epsilon.$$

Hence the sequence $\{f_{mm}(x)\}$ converges uniformly.

This theorem plays an important role in such diverse fields as the calculus of variations, functions of a complex variable, differential equations, and topological groups.

4. *Limits of sequences of continuous functions*

We open the discussion by generalizing Theorem 1.

DEFINITION 8. A sequence $\{f_n(x)\}$ of functions is said to *converge uniformly at a point* ξ if for every $\epsilon > 0$ there is a $\delta > 0$ and an N such that if $n, m > N$ and $|x - \xi| < \delta$ then $|f_n(x) - f_m(x)| < \epsilon$.

We shall show that even though, as has been pointed out, convergence does not imply uniform convergence it does imply uniform convergence at certain points. First, we prove the following proposition.

PROPOSITION 5. If a convergent sequence $\{f_n(x)\}$ of continuous functions converges uniformly at a point ξ, then $f(x) = \lim_{n\to\infty} f_n(x)$ is continuous at ξ.

Proof. Let $\epsilon > 0$. There is a $\delta_1 > 0$ and an N such that if $|x - \xi| < \delta_1$ then $|f_N(x) - f(x)| < \epsilon/3$. But $f_N(x)$ is continuous at ξ, so that there is a $\delta_2 > 0$ such that if $|x - \xi| < \delta_2$ then $|f_N(x) - f_N(\xi)| < \epsilon/3$. Let $\delta = \min(\delta_1, \delta_2)$. If $|x - \xi| < \delta$ then

$$|f(x) - f(\xi)| \leqq |f(x) - f_N(x)| + |f_N(x) - f_N(\xi)| + |f_N(\xi) - f(\xi)| < \frac{\epsilon}{3} + \frac{\epsilon}{3} + \frac{\epsilon}{3} = \epsilon.$$

This shows that $f(x)$ is continuous at ξ.

As a companion to Proposition 5, we have:

PROPOSITION 6. If a sequence $\{f_n(x)\}$ of continuous functions converges to $f(x)$ on an open interval (a, b) it converges uniformly at some point $\xi \in (a, b)$.

Proof. We first show that for every $\epsilon > 0$ there is a closed subinterval $[a', b'] \subset (a, b)$ and an N such that if $n, m > N$ and $x \in [a', b']$ then $|f_n(x) - f_m(x)| \leqq \epsilon$. For if $x \in (a, b)$, there is an N such that for every n, $m > N$, $|f_n(x) - f_m(x)| \leqq \epsilon$. Let E_N be the set of points for which $|f_n(x) - f_m(x)| \leqq \epsilon$ for every $n, m > N$. Then

$$(a, b) = \bigcup_{N=1}^{\infty} E_N.$$

We show that each E_N is closed relative to (a, b). For every n, m the set E_{nm} of points for which $|f_n(x) - f_m(x)| \leqq \epsilon$ is closed relative to (a, b), since, as the student may readily verify, the function $|f_n(x) - f_m(x)|$ is continuous. Hence

$$E_N = \bigcap_{n=N+1}^{\infty} \bigcap_{m=N+1}^{\infty} E_{nm}$$

is a closed set, since the intersection of any number of closed sets is closed. But there is an N for which E_N is not nowhere dense. For, otherwise,

$$(a, b) = \bigcup_{N=1}^{\infty} E_N$$

would be of the first category. Since E_N is not nowhere dense it contains a closed interval. We have thus shown that for every $\epsilon > 0$ there is an N and a closed interval $[a', b'] \subset (a, b)$ such that for every $x \in [a', b']$ and n, $m > N$, $|f_n(x) - f_m(x)| \leqq \epsilon$.

Now there is an $[a_1, b_1] \subset (a, b)$ and an N_1 such that for $n, m > N_1$ and $x \in [a_1, b_1]$, $|f_n(x) - f_m(x)| \leqq 1$. There is an $[a_2, b_2] \subset (a_1, b_1)$ and an N_2 such that for every n, $m > N_2$ and $x \in [a_2, b_2]$, $|f_n(x) - f_m(x)| \leqq 1/2$. Proceeding in this way, we obtain a sequence of closed intervals, each of which is in the open interval obtained by suppressing the end points of its predecessor,

$$(a, b) \supset [a_1, b_1] \supset (a_1, b_1) \supset \cdots \supset [a_k, b_k] \supset (a_k, b_k) \supset [a_{k+1}, b_{k+1}] \supset \cdots,$$

and a sequence $N_1, N_2, \cdots, N_k, \cdots$ of positive integers such that, for every k, for every $x \in (a_k, b_k)$ and n, $m > N_k$, $|f_n(x) - f_m(x)| \leqq 1/k$.

But there is a $\xi \in \bigcap_{k=1}^{\infty} [a_k, b_k]$ so that $\xi \in \bigcap_{k=1}^{\infty} (a_k, b_k)$. The sequence $\{f_n(x)\}$ converges uniformly at ξ. For let $\epsilon > 0$. There is a k such that $1/k < \epsilon$, $\xi \in (a_k, b_k)$. For every $x \in (a_k, b_k)$ and n, $m > N_k$,

$$|f_n(x) - f_m(x)| \leqq \frac{1}{k} < \epsilon.$$

THEOREM 6. If $\{f_n(x)\}$ is a convergent sequence of continuous functions whose limit is $f(x)$, then $f(x)$ has a point of continuity in every interval.

Proof. Let (a, b) be an open interval. By Proposition 6 there is a $\xi \in (a, b)$ such that $\{f_n(x)\}$ converges uniformly at ξ, so that, by Proposition 5, $f(x)$ is continuous at ξ.

Now, Theorem 6 shows that the points of continuity of $f(x)$ are everywhere dense. On the other hand, the points of discontinuity of $f(x)$ form a set which is of type F_σ, and which, since its complement is everywhere dense, is of the first category. We have, accordingly, proved the following theorem.

THEOREM 7. The set of points of discontinuity of a function which is the limit of a convergent sequence of continuous functions is of the first category.

Since we have shown in Theorem 3 that every semicontinuous function is the limit of a sequence of continuous functions, we have a corollary to Theorem 7.

COROLLARY 2. Every semicontinuous function defined on an interval has points of continuity; indeed, its set of points of discontinuity is of the first category.

5. *Properties of uniform convergence*

Of course, a sequence $\{f_n(x)\}$ which converges on a set S_α for every $\alpha \in A$ converges on the union $S = \bigcup_{\alpha \in A} S_\alpha$. This is not always true for uniformly convergent sequences of functions.

PROPOSITION 7. If $S = \bigcup_{k=1}^{n} S_k$, and the sequence of functions $\{f_n(x)\}$ is defined on S and converges uniformly on each S_k, $k = 1, 2, \cdots, n$, then $\{f_n(x)\}$ converges uniformly on S.

Proof. Let $\epsilon > 0$. Then for every $k = 1, 2, \cdots, n$, there is an N_k such that for every $n, m > N_k$ and every $x \in S_k$, $|f_n(x) - f_m(x)| < \epsilon$. Let $N = \max [N_1, \cdots, N_n]$. Then for every $x \in S$ and $n, m > N$, $|f_n(x) - f_m(x)| < \epsilon$. This shows that $\{f_n(x)\}$ converges uniformly on S.

On the other hand, it is possible for a sequence $S_1, S_2, \cdots, S_n, \cdots$ of sets to be such that $\{f_n(x)\}$ is uniformly convergent on each set of the sequence but not on their union. For example, let S_n consist of the single number n. Let $f_m(n) = 1$ for every $n \leqq m$ and $f_m(n) = 0$ for every $n > m$. The sequence $\{f_m(x)\}$ of functions converges uniformly on each S_n. For since S_n consists of a single point n, we need only show that $\{f_m(n)\}$ converges. Let $N > n$. Then for every $\mu, \nu > N$, $|f_\mu(n) - f_\nu(n)| = 0$. However, the convergence on S is not uniform. For let N be any positive integer. Let $n > N$. Then $f_n(n) = 1$; but $f_{n+1}(n) = 0$, so that the convergence is not uniform.

This example shows that there are sequences of functions which converge on an infinite set but not uniformly on any infinite subset. We have, however, the following theorem of T. W. S. Youngs.

THEOREM 8. If S is nondenumerable and $\{f_n(x)\}$ converges on S, there is an infinite subset $E \subset S$ such that $\{f_n(x)\}$ converges uniformly on E.

Proof. For every positive integer n, let S_{1n} be the set of points of S such that if $\mu, \nu > n$ then $|f_\nu(x) - f_\mu(x)| < 1$. Clearly $S = \bigcup_{n=1}^{\infty} S_{1n}$, so that there is an N_1 such that S_{1N_1} is nondenumerable. For otherwise, S as the union of a sequence of denumerable sets would be denumerable. Using the notation $S_1 = S_{1N_1}$, we have for every $x \in S_1$ and $n, m > N_1$,

$$|f_n(x) - f_m(x)| < 1.$$

Choose any $x_1 \in S_1$. Since S_1 is nondenumerable, the above argument may be repeated so as to yield a positive integer N_2 and a nondenumerable subset $S_2 \subset S_1$ such that if $x \in S_2$ and $n, m > N_2$ then $|f_n(x) - f_m(x)| < 1/2$. Choose any $x_2 \in S_2$ such that $x_2 \neq x_1$.

Proceeding in this way, we obtain a nonincreasing sequence $S_1 \supset S_2 \supset \cdots \supset S_k \supset \cdots$ of sets, a sequence $N_1, N_2, \cdots, N_k, \cdots$ of positive integers, and a sequence of distinct numbers $x_1, x_2, \cdots, x_k, \cdots$ such that $x_k \in S_k$ for every k and such that for every $x \in S_k$ and $n, m > N_k$,

$$|f_n(x) - f_m(x)| < \frac{1}{k}.$$

Let $E = \{x_1, x_2, \cdots, x_k, \cdots\}$. We show that $\{f_n(x)\}$ converges uniformly on the infinite set E. For let $\epsilon > 0$. There is a k such that $\epsilon > 1/k$. Since $x_k \in S_k, x_{k+1} \in S_k, \cdots$, it follows that for every $n, m > N_k$, $|f_n(x_s) - f_m(x_s)| < 1/k < \epsilon$ for every $s \geqq k$. Since $x_1, x_2, \cdots, x_{k-1}$ is finite, there is an N' such that for every $n, m > N'$, $|f_n(x_s) - f_m(x_s)| < \epsilon$ for $s = 1, 2, \cdots, k - 1$. Let $N = \max(N_k, N')$. The above shows that for every $x \in E$ and $n, m > N$, $|f_n(x) - f_m(x)| < \epsilon$. This proves the theorem.

Exercises

1.1 If for every positive integer n, $f_n(x) = 1 - nx$ for $x \in [0, 1/n]$ and $f_n(x) = 0$ for $x \in [1/n, 1]$, show that $\{f_n(x)\}$ converges, but not uniformly, on $[0, 1]$.

1.2 Show that the sequence $\{f_n(x)\}$ of Exercise 1.1 converges uniformly on $[\epsilon, 1]$ for every $0 < \epsilon < 1$.

1.3 Give two more examples of sequences of functions which converge but not uniformly on their domains of definition.

1.4 Give an example of a sequence of functions which converges on $[0, 1]$ but does not converge uniformly on any interval $I \subset [0, 1]$.

1.5 Prove that the set of bounded functions on a set S forms a metric space if

$$\delta(f, g) = \sup [|f(x) - g(x)| \mid x \in S].$$

2.1 Show that if $\{f_n(x)\}$ is a sequence of functions, each lower-semicontinuous at $x = a$, which converges uniformly to a function $f(x)$ then $f(x)$ is lower-semicontinuous at $x = a$.

2.2 Give an example of a function $f(x)$ which is either upper-semicontinuous or lower-semicontinuous at every point but is not the limit of a sequence of continuous functions.

2.3 Show that the limit of a uniformly bounded nondecreasing sequence of lower-semicontinuous functions is lower-semicontinuous.

2.4 Prove Exercise 2.3 for the case where the functions involved are not necessarily bounded and may even assume the values $+\infty$ and $-\infty$.

2.5 Associate with every real number ξ the set S_ξ of points $x \leqq \xi$. For every bounded sequence $\{s_n\}$ show that the set associated with $\overline{\lim}\ s_n$ is $\overline{\lim}\ S_{s_n}$.

2.6 Associate with every real number ξ a set T_ξ in such a way that for every bounded sequence $\{s_n\}$ the set associated with $\underline{\lim}\ s_n$ is $\underline{\lim}\ T_n$.

2.7 Show that $\overline{\lim}\ (a_n + b_n) \leqq \overline{\lim}\ a_n + \overline{\lim}\ b_n$ for every two bounded sequences $\{a_n\}$ and $\{b_n\}$. Give an example for which the inequality holds.

2.8 Show that a sequence $\{a_n\}$ is fundamental if and only if $\overline{\lim}\ a_n = \underline{\lim}\ a_n$.

3.1 Show that the sequence of functions of Exercise 1.1 is not equicontinuous.

3.2 Show that a sequence $\{f_n(x)\}$ of functions on $[0, 1]$ is equicontinuous and uniformly bounded if and only if it is totally bounded in the space of continuous functions on $[0, 1]$ with

$$\delta(f, g) = \max\,[|f(x) - g(x)|\ |\ x \in [0, 1]].$$

3.3 Give a definition of equicontinuity for a set of functions which seems plausible to you.

3.4 Is the sequence $\{\sin nx/x\}$ uniformly bounded on the interval $(0, 1)$?

3.5 Is the sequence $\{\sin nx\}$ equicontinuous on $[0, 1]$? Prove.

4.1 Give an example of a sequence of functions which does not converge uniformly in any neighborhood of a certain point ξ but does converge uniformly at ξ.

4.2 Show that if $\{f_n(x)\}$ is a convergent sequence of continuous functions and if P is any perfect set then $\lim\limits_{n\to\infty} f_n(x)$ has a point of continuity on P relative to P.

4.3 If $\{f_n(x)\}$ is a convergent sequence of continuous functions on a set S, show that the set of points in S at which their limit is discontinuous relative to S is of the first category relative to S.

4.4 Show that if $T \subset S$ and R is of the first category relative to T then it is of the first category relative to S.

4.5 A series

$$\sum_{n=0}^{\infty} a_n x^n$$

is called a *power series*. Show that if a power series converges for $x = a \neq 0$ and if $0 < b < |a|$ then it converges uniformly to a continuous function on the interval $[-b, b]$.

References

R. Baire, *Leçons sur les fonctions discontinues*, Paris, 1905.

E. Borel, *Leçons sur les fonctions de variables réeles*, Paris, 1928, Chap. 3.

C. Carathéodory, *Vorlesungen über Reelle Funktionen*, Leipzig, 1927, Chap. 3.

Ch. J. de la Vallée Poussin, *Intégrales de Lebesgue, Fonctions d'ensembles, Classes de Baire*, Paris, 1934, Chap. 7.

T. W. S. Youngs, "On Uniform Convergence," *Amer. J. of Math.* 57 (1935), 549.

9

The Derivative of a Function

1. *The Dini derivates*

We consider real functions defined on the set $(-\infty, \infty)$ of all real numbers. We shall associate four functions, which are called the *Dini derivates* of $f(x)$, with every function $f(x)$. The Dini derivates may have either real values or the values $+\infty$ or $-\infty$.

If the four Dini derivates of $f(x)$ are equal and real (i.e., $\neq +\infty$ or $-\infty$) the derivative of $f(x)$ is said to exist. This is simply the derivative of a function, with which the student is familiar.

In order to be able to define the Dini derivates we shall first generalize our notions of "least upper bound" and "greatest lower bound" of sets, and "limit of a monotone sequence" so as to include the values $+\infty$ and $-\infty$.

For a set S of real numbers we shall write:

$$\begin{aligned}
&\text{Sup } S = \sup S && \text{if } S \text{ has an upper bound,}\\
&\text{Sup } S = +\infty && \text{if } S \text{ has no upper bound, and}\\
&\text{Inf } S = \inf S && \text{if } S \text{ has a lower bound,}\\
&\text{Inf } S = -\infty && \text{if } S \text{ has no lower bound.}
\end{aligned}$$

For a monotone sequence $\{s_n\}$ which can assume real values or $+\infty$, $-\infty$, we introduce the following notation:

If $\{s_n\}$ is nondecreasing,

$$\begin{aligned}
&\text{Lim } s_n = -\infty && \text{if } s_n = -\infty \text{ for every } n,\\
&\text{Lim } s_n = +\infty && \text{if } \{s_n\} \text{ has no upper bound,}\\
&\text{Lim } s_n = \lim s_n && \text{if } \{s_n\} \text{ has an upper bound and some } s_k \neq -\infty.
\end{aligned}$$

If $\{s_n\}$ is nonincreasing,

$$\begin{aligned}
&\text{Lim } s_n = +\infty && \text{if } s_n = +\infty \text{ for every } n,\\
&\text{Lim } s_n = -\infty && \text{if } \{s_n\} \text{ has no lower bound,}\\
&\text{Lim } s_n = \lim s_n && \text{if } \{s_n\} \text{ has a lower bound and some } s_k \neq +\infty.
\end{aligned}$$

We proceed now to the definition of the Dini derivates. We first introduce four sequences.

If $f(x)$ is a real function, ξ a point, then for every n, let

$$d_n^+(f;\xi) = \operatorname{Sup}\left[\frac{f(\xi)-f(x)}{\xi - x}\,\middle|\, 0 < x - \xi < \frac{1}{n}\right],$$

$$d_{n+}(f;\xi) = \operatorname{Inf}\left[\frac{f(\xi)-f(x)}{\xi - x}\,\middle|\, 0 < x - \xi < \frac{1}{n}\right],$$

$$d_n^-(f;\xi) = \operatorname{Sup}\left[\frac{f(\xi)-f(x)}{\xi - x}\,\middle|\, 0 < \xi - x < \frac{1}{n}\right],$$

$$d_{n-}(f;\xi) = \operatorname{Inf}\left[\frac{f(\xi)-f(x)}{\xi - x}\,\middle|\, 0 < \xi - x < \frac{1}{n}\right].$$

As the student can easily see, the sequences $\{d_n^+(f;\xi)\}$ and $\{d_n^-(f;\xi)\}$ are nonincreasing, and the sequences $\{d_{n+}(f;\xi)\}$ and $\{d_{n-}(f;\xi)\}$ are nondecreasing.

We consider the generalized limits of these sequences: $d^+(f;\xi) = \operatorname{Lim} d_n^+(f;\xi)$, $d_+(f;\xi) = \operatorname{Lim} d_{n+}(f;\xi)$, $d^-(f;\xi) = \operatorname{Lim} d_n^-(f;\xi)$, and $d_-(f;\xi) = \operatorname{Lim} d_{n-}(f;\xi)$.

DEFINITION 1. $d^+(f;\xi)$, $d_+(f;\xi)$, $d^-(f;\xi)$, and $d_-(f;\xi)$ are respectively called the *upper right*, *lower right*, *upper left*, and *lower left Dini derivates* of $f(x)$ at ξ.

The numbers $\bar{d}(f;\xi) = \max\,[d^+(f;\xi),\ d^-(f;\xi)]$ and $\underline{d}(f;\xi) = \min\,[d_-(f;\xi), d(f;\xi)]$ are called the *upper* and *lower derivatives* of $f(x)$ at ξ, respectively.

PROPOSITION 1. $d^+(f;\xi) \geqq d_+(f;\xi)$ and $d_-(f;\xi) \leqq d^-(f;\xi)$ for every $f(x)$ and ξ.

The proof is left to the student.

DEFINITION 2. If the four Dini derivates of $f(x)$ at ξ are equal but are different from $+\infty$ and $-\infty$, the derivative of $f(x)$ is said to exist at ξ and its value is that of the Dini derivates.

We now give another definition of the derivative in terms of sets of derivates. We again consider a function $f(x)$ and a point ξ. The set $D+(f;\xi)$ consists of all points η (including $\pm\infty$) such that there is a decreasing sequence $\{\xi_n\}$ converging to ξ such that

$$\operatorname{Lim} \frac{f(\xi) - f(\xi_n)}{\xi - \xi_n} = \eta.$$

$D+(f;\xi)$ is called the *set of right derivates* of $f(x)$ at ξ.

Similarly, the *set* $D-(f;\xi)$ *of left derivates* of $f(x)$ at ξ consists of all points η (including $\pm\infty$) such that there is an increasing sequence $\{\xi_n\}$ converging to ξ such that

$$\operatorname{Lim} \frac{f(\xi) - f(\xi_n)}{\xi - \xi_n} = \eta.$$

The set $D(f; \xi) = D+(f; \xi) \cup D-(f; \xi)$ is called the *set of derivates* of $f(x)$ at ξ.

PROPOSITION 2. The sets $D+(f; \xi)$, $D-(f; \xi)$, and $D(f; \xi)$ are all closed, contain $+\infty$ if they have no upper bound, and contain $-\infty$ if they have no lower bound.

The proof is left to the student.

PROPOSITION 3. $\operatorname{Sup} D(f; \xi) = \bar{d}(f; \xi)$, $\operatorname{Inf} D(f; \xi) = \underline{d}(f; \xi)$, $\operatorname{Sup} D+(f; \xi) = d^+(f; \xi)$, $\operatorname{Sup} D-(f; \xi) = d^-(f; \xi)$, $\operatorname{Inf} D+(f; \xi) = d_+(f; \xi)$, and $\operatorname{Inf} D-(f; \xi) = d_-(f; \xi)$.

The proof is left to the student.

2. *Simple properties of the derivative*

We first observe that a function $f(x)$ cannot have its derivative exist at ξ unless it is continuous at ξ. For if $f(x)$ is not continuous at ξ there is a $k > 0$ and a sequence $\{\xi_n\}$ converging to ξ such that either $f(\xi_n) > f(\xi) + k$ for every n or else $f(\xi_n) < f(\xi) - k$ for every n. Moreover the sequence $\{\xi_n\}$ may be taken so that all its terms are either to the left of ξ or to the right of ξ. Suppose for convenience that, for every n, $\xi_n > \xi$ and $f(\xi_n) > f(\xi) + k$. Then

$$\operatorname{Lim} \frac{f(\xi_n) - f(\xi)}{\xi_n - \xi} = +\infty,$$

so that the derivative of $f(x)$ at ξ does not exist.

It is not true, conversely, that if $f(x)$ is continuous its derivative exists. For example, the function $f(x) = x \sin 1/x$ for $x \neq 0$, $f(x) = 0$ for $x = 0$, is continuous at $x = 0$ but its derivative does not exist there.

Suppose now the derivative of $f(x)$ does exist everywhere. The derivative is then itself a function $f'(x)$. This function need not be continuous. For example, let $f(x) = x^2 \sin 1/x$ for $x \neq 0$ and $f(x) = 0$ for $x = 0$. Then $f'(x) = 2x \sin 1/x - \cos 1/x$ for $x \neq 0$ and $f'(x) = 0$ for $x = 0$. The function $f'(x)$ is discontinuous at $x = 0$. For if $\{\xi_n\}$ is any sequence of points converging to 0 for which $\cos 1/\xi_n = 1$ then $\lim_{n \to \infty} f'(\xi_n) = -1$.

Now every continuous function $f(x)$ has the property that for every a and b and for every η between $f(a)$ and $f(b)$ there is a ξ between a and b such that $f(\xi) = \eta$. It is an interesting fact that although the derivative of a function need not be continuous it does always have the above property.

We first prove Rolle's Theorem.

PROPOSITION 4. If $f(x)$ is continuous on $[a, b]$, $f(a) = f(b) = 0$ and $f'(x)$ exists on (a, b), there is a ξ such that $a < \xi < b$ and $f'(\xi) = 0$.

Proof. If $f(x)$ is identically 0, the proposition is obvious. Suppose there are points on (a, b) for which $f(x) \neq 0$. Then by Exercise 4.3, Chapter 7, $f(x)$ has a maximum and a minimum on $[a, b]$. At least one of these is different from zero. Suppose, for convenience, that

$$\max [f(x) \mid x \in [a, b]] > 0.$$

Then there is a $\xi \in (a, b)$ such that $f(\xi) = \max [f(x) \mid x \in [a, b]]$. Then $d^-(f; \xi) \geqq 0$ and $d_+(f; \xi) \leqq 0$. But since $f'(\xi)$ exists $d^-(f; \xi) = d_+(f; \xi) = 0$, so that $f'(\xi) = 0$. The proof for the case $\min [f(x) \mid x \in [a, b]] < 0$ is similar.

We now prove the theorem we have in mind.

THEOREM 1. If $f(x)$ is defined and $f'(x)$ exists on (a, b), if $[\alpha, \beta] \subset (a, b)$ and $f'(\alpha) < f'(\beta)$, then for every C such that $f'(\alpha) < C < f'(\beta)$ there is a γ such that $\alpha < \gamma < \beta$ and $f'(\gamma) = C$.

Proof. We first prove a special case, that for which $f'(\alpha) < 0 < f'(\beta)$. Then there is a ξ such that $\alpha < \xi < \beta$ and $f'(\xi) = 0$. For there is a ξ_1 such that $\alpha < \xi_1 < \beta$ and $f(\xi_1) < f(\alpha)$ and there is a ξ_2 such that $\alpha < \xi_2 < \beta$ and $f(\xi_2) < f(\beta)$. Hence $\min [f(x) \mid x \in [\alpha, \beta]]$ is attained at some $\xi \in (\alpha, \beta)$. Now obviously $d_-(f; \xi) \leqq 0$ and $d^+(f; \xi) \geqq 0$, so that, since $f'(\xi)$ exists, $f'(\xi) = 0$.

Now, to prove the theorem, let

$$F(x) = f(x) - Cx.$$

Then, since $f'(\alpha) < C < f'(\beta)$ by hypothesis, $f'(\alpha) - C < 0 < f'(\beta) - C$. But $F'(x) = f'(x) - C$, so that $F'(\alpha) < 0 < F'(\beta)$. So there is a γ with $\alpha < \gamma < \beta$ such that $F'(\gamma) = 0$. Then $F'(\gamma) = f'(\gamma) - C = 0$, so that $f'(\gamma) = C$.

Another property of the derivative is the following:

THEOREM 2. If the derivative $f'(x)$ of $f(x)$ exists, then $f'(x)$ is the limit of a sequence of continuous functions.

Proof. $f(x)$ is continuous. For every positive integer n the function

$$g_n(x) = n\left\{f\left(x + \frac{1}{n}\right) - f(x)\right\}$$

is continuous. But for every x,

$$f'(x) = \lim_{n \to \infty} g_n(x).$$

This proves the theorem.

3. *A theorem of G. C. Young*

The theorem we have in mind is concerned with the Dini derivates of an arbitrary function.

THEOREM 3. For every real function $f(x)$,

$$d^+(f;\xi) \geqq d_-(f;\xi) \text{ and } d^-(f;\xi) \geqq d_+(f;\xi),$$

except at a finite or denumerable set of values of ξ.

Proof. Let E be the set of points for which $d^+(f;\xi) < d_-(f;\xi)$. For every $\xi \in E$ there is a pair of rational numbers r_1 and r_2 such that $d^+(f;\xi) < r_1 < r_2 < d_-(f;\xi)$. Then there is a positive integer n such that if $0 < x - \xi < 1/n$ then $(f(x) - f(\xi))/(x - \xi) < r_1$ and if $0 < \xi - x < 1/n$ then $(f(x) - f(\xi))/(x - \xi) > r_2$.

Let $E_{r_1r_2n}$ be the set of points ξ for which $(f(x) - f(\xi))/(x - \xi) < r_1$ for every x such that $0 < x - \xi < 1/n$ and $(f(x) - f(\xi))/(x - \xi) > r_2$ for every x such that $0 < \xi - x < 1/n$. Then

$$E = \bigcup_{r_1<r_2} \bigcup_{n=1}^{\infty} E_{r_1r_2n},$$

where the union is with respect to all pairs of rational numbers $r_1 < r_2$.

We show that each set $E_{r_1r_2n}$ is denumerable, so that E is denumerable. Let $\xi \in E_{r_1r_2n}$. For every $\eta \in (\xi - 1/n, \xi)$, $(f(\eta) - f(\xi))/(\eta - \xi) > r_2$, so that $\eta \notin E_{r_1r_2n}$. Hence the set $E_{r_1r_2n}$ has the property that if $x \in E_{r_1r_2n}$, $y \in E_{r_1r_2n}$ then $|x - y| \geqq 1/n$. It follows that $E_{r_1r_2n}$ is denumerable.

4. *Continuous functions whose derivatives do not exist*

We showed above that there are continuous functions whose derivatives do not exist at certain places. We now show that there are continuous functions whose derivatives do not exist anywhere.

Our proof is an illustration of the way in which metric space methods find application to real variable theory.

Let C be the set of all periodic continuous functions on $(-\infty, \infty)$ of period 1. If $\delta(f, g) = \max|f(x) - g(x)|$ then C is a metric space. Moreover, C is complete. Hence, by Proposition 9, Chapter 4, C is of the second category.

We show that the set of functions in C which have a derivative somewhere is of the first category. Hence there are functions in C whose derivative exists nowhere. We show this by proving that the set F of functions in C whose upper and lower right derivates are finite somewhere is of the first category, thus establishing that the subset of F of functions whose derivative exists somewhere is of the first category. It is clear that $\mathsf{F} \subset \bigcup_{n=1}^{\infty} \mathsf{F}_n$, where F_n is the set of functions $f(x) \in \mathsf{C}$ for which there is a ξ and a positive integer n such that

$$\left|\frac{f(\xi + h) - f(\xi)}{h}\right| \leqq n$$

for every $h > 0$.

We now complete the proof of our theorem by showing that F_n is nowhere dense for every n. We first note that $\mathsf{C} - \mathsf{F}_n$ is everywhere dense in C. Let $\epsilon > 0$ and $f(x) \in \mathsf{C}$. As the student can readily show from the uniform continuity of $f(x)$, there is a function $g(x) \in \mathsf{C}$ whose graph is a broken line each of whose segments has slope either greater than n or less than $-n$, such that $|f(x) - g(x)| < \epsilon$ for every x. Then $g(x) \in \mathsf{C} - \mathsf{F}_n$ and $\delta(f, g) < \epsilon$, so that $\mathsf{C} - \mathsf{F}_n$ is everywhere dense in C.

We next show that F_n is a closed subset of C. For let $f(x)$ be a limit point of F_n. Then there is a sequence $\{f_m(x)\}$ in F_n such that $\lim_{m\to\infty} \delta(f_m, f) = 0$. For every m there is a ξ_m such that for every $h > 0$,

$$\left|\frac{f_m(\xi_m + h) - f_m(\xi_m)}{h}\right| \leqq n.$$

Since $f_m(x)$ is periodic of period 1, ξ_m may be taken to be in the interval $[0, 1]$. Moreover, we may assume without loss of generality that the sequence ξ_m is convergent. Let $\xi = \lim_{m\to\infty} \xi_m$. We show that for every $h > 0$,

$$\left|\frac{f(\xi + h) - f(\xi)}{h}\right| \leqq n.$$

For let $h > 0$ and $\epsilon > 0$. There is an N such that for every $m > N$ and every x, $|f(x) - f_m(x)| < \epsilon h/4$. But there is an $m > N$ such that $|f(\xi) - f(\xi_m)| < \epsilon h/4$ and $|f_m(\xi + h) - f_m(\xi_m + h)| < \epsilon h/4$. Then

$$\left|\frac{f(\xi + h) - f(\xi)}{h}\right| \leqq \left|\frac{f(\xi + h) - f(\xi_m + h)}{h}\right| + \left|\frac{f(\xi + h) - f_m(\xi + h)}{h}\right|$$
$$+ \left|\frac{f_m(\xi_m + h) - f_m(\xi_m)}{h}\right| + \left|\frac{f_m(\xi_m) - f(\xi_m)}{h}\right| + \left|\frac{f(\xi_m) - f(\xi)}{h}\right|$$
$$< \frac{\epsilon}{4} + \frac{\epsilon}{4} + n + \frac{\epsilon}{4} + \frac{\epsilon}{4} = n + \epsilon.$$

Since $\epsilon > 0$ is arbitrary, $f(x) \in \mathsf{F}_n$. Now F_n is a closed set whose complement is everywhere dense, so that F_n is nowhere dense.

We state this result in the form of a theorem.

THEOREM 4. There are functions which are continuous but whose derivative does not exist anywhere.

This theorem proves the existence of functions having the stated property but does not show how to construct such functions. The first example of a continuous function whose derivative does not exist anywhere was given by Weierstrass. Many examples of such functions have been constructed since then.

Exercises

1.1 Show that $\{d_n^+(f; \xi)\}$ is a nonincreasing sequence.

1.2 Show that $d^+(f; \xi) \geqq d_+(f; \xi)$ for every $f(x)$ and ξ.

1.3 Show that the sets $D+(f; \xi)$, $D-(f; \xi)$, and $D(f; \xi)$ are all closed, contain $+\infty$ if they have no upper bound, and contain $-\infty$ if they have no lower bound.

1.4 Show that $\text{Sup}\, D+(f; \xi) = d^+(f; \xi)$.

1.5 Show that $d^+(f+g; \xi) \leqq d^+(f; \xi) + d^+(g; \xi)$ if $d^+(f; \xi)$ and $d^+(g; \xi)$ are both finite.

2.1 If S is any denumerable set show that there is a continuous function $f(x)$ whose derivative does not exist at any point of S but does exist at every point of $C(S)$.

2.2 If S is any closed nowhere-dense set show that there is a function $f(x)$ whose derivative exists everywhere and has S as its set of points of discontinuity.

2.3 Show that if the derivative of $f(x)$ exists its set of points of discontinuity is of the first category; and that, conversely, for every set S of the first category there is a derivative which is discontinuous at every point of S.

3.1 (a) Show that if a set S has the property that for every $x \in S$ there is a neighborhood of x which contains no other points of S then S is finite or denumerable.

(b) Show that if a set S has the property that every point of S is the end point of an open interval which contains no points of S then S is finite or denumerable.

4.1 Show that if the upper and lower right derivates of $f(x)$ are finite somewhere, in $(0, 1)$, then there is an n and a $\xi \in (0, 1)$ such that

$$\left|\frac{f(\xi + h) - f(\xi)}{h}\right| \leqq n$$

for every $h > 0$, provided $f(x)$ is periodic with period 1.

4.2 Show that if $f(x)$ is continuous on $[0, 1]$ then for every $\epsilon > 0$ there is a function $g(x)$ whose graph is a broken line each of whose segments has slope either greater than n or less than $-n$ such that

$$|f(x) - g(x)| < \epsilon$$

for every $x \in [0, 1]$.

4.3 Using a construction similar to that of Exercise 4.2 to start from, construct a continuous function whose derivative does not exist anywhere.

4.4 Is it true that for every denumerable set S there is an $f(x)$ such that S is the set of points for which $d^+(f; \xi) < d_-(f; \xi)$? Prove or give a counterexample.

References

C. CARATHÉODORY, *Vorlesungen über reelle Funktionen*, Leipzig, 1927, Chap. 10.

E. W. HOBSON, *The Theory of Functions of a Real Variable*, Cambridge, 1928, Chap. 5.

E. J. MCSHANE, *Integration*, Princeton, 1944, Chap. 5.

10

Order Types and Ordinals

1. *Introduction*

This chapter is properly an immediate successor of Chapter 2. It has been withheld until now so that the student could have an earlier opportunity to deal with sets of real numbers and with real functions. However, we shall use ordinal numbers in the next two chapters in connection with further properties of sets and functions. In this chapter, we give a brief account of the essential properties of linear orders and of ordinal numbers.

DEFINITION 1. A *linear order* L consists of a set, also designated by L, and a relation "$<$" satisfying the following conditions:

1. for every $a \in L$, $b \in L$, such that $a \neq b$, either $a < b$ or $b < a$,
2. if $a < b$, then it is not true that $b < a$,
3. if $a < b$ and $b < c$, then $a < c$.

Some examples of linear orders are the following:

1. The positive integers ordered in their usual way.
2. The rational numbers ordered in their usual way.
3. The rational numbers ordered by means of a given one-to-one correspondence $\{r_n\}$ of the rational numbers with the positive integers, so that $r_n < r_m$ if $n < m$.
4. The points (x, y) in the plane ordered as follows: $(x_1, y_1) < (x_2, y_2)$ if $x_1 < x_2$ or if $x_1 = x_2, y_1 < y_2$.
5. The points $(x, y) = (r \cos \theta, r \sin \theta)$, $0 \leqq \theta < 2\pi$ ordered as follows: $(r_1 \cos \theta_1, r_1 \sin \theta_1) < (r_2 \cos \theta_2, r_2 \sin \theta_2)$ if $r_1 < r_2$ or if $r_1 = r_2, \theta_1 < \theta_2$.
6. The real polynomials $p(x)$ ordered as follows: $p(x) < q(x)$ if there is an x such that for every $\xi > x$, $p(\xi) < q(\xi)$.

2. *Special kinds of orders*

We shall characterize the rational numbers and the real numbers as orders. We shall need several concepts, discussed below, for the further expansion of the subject of order.

DEFINITION 2. If a linear order L has no first element and no last element it is said to be *unbounded;* i.e., L is unbounded if for every $x \in L$ there are $y \in L$ and $z \in L$ such that $y < x < z$.

DEFINITION 3. L is called *dense* if there is a $c \in L$ between every $a \in L$ and $b \in L$: i.e., if $a < b$, there is a c such that $a < c < b$.

DEFINITION 4. A dense linear order L is called *continuous* if for every decomposition of L into two sets A and B such that

1. $A \cap B = \phi$,
2. $A \cup B = L$,
3. A is nonempty, B is nonempty,
4. if $a \in A$ and $b \in B$ then $a < b$,

then either A has a last element or B a first element.

We give several examples of these concepts.

1. Every finite linear order is neither dense nor unbounded.
2. The linear order of integers in their usual order is unbounded but is not dense.
3. The linear order of rational numbers in their usual order is unbounded and dense but is not continuous.
4. The linear order of real numbers in their usual order is unbounded, dense, and continuous.

We now define an equivalence relation for the class of orders.

DEFINITION 5. Two linear orders L and L' are said to be *similar* if there is a one-to-one correspondence $a' = f(a)$ between them such that if $a < b$ then $f(a) < f(b)$.

PROPOSITION 1. The similarity relation for linear orders is an equivalence relation.

The proof is left for the student.

A class of similar linear orders is called an order type. We first characterize some of the most common order types.

THEOREM 1. If L and L' are unbounded, dense, denumerable linear orders then L and L' are similar.

Proof. Since L and L' are denumerable, their elements may be reordered as sequences

$a_1, a_2, \cdots, a_n, \cdots,$

$a_1', a_2', \cdots, a_n', \cdots.$

Call these orders A and A' respectively. A and L, as well as A' and L', are composed of the same elements but are different orders.

Mate $b_1 = a_1$ with $b_1' = a_1'$. Mate $b_2 = a_2$ with the first remaining element b_2' of A' which has the same order relation with b_1' in L' that b_2 has with b_1 in L. Then mate the first remaining element b_3' of A' with the first remaining element b_3 of A which has the same order relation with b_1, b_2 in L that b_3' has with b_1', b_2' in L'. Suppose, for a positive integer n, $b_1, b_2, \cdots, b_{n-1}$ have already been mated with $b_1', b_2', \cdots, b_{n-1}'$. If n is even, mate the first remaining element b_n of A with the first remaining element b_n' of A' which has the same order relation with $b_1', b_2', \cdots, b_{n-1}'$ in L' that b_n has with $b_1, b_2, \cdots, b_{n-1}$ in L. If n is odd, mate the first remaining element b_n' of A' with the first remaining element b_n of A which has the same order relation with $b_1, b_2, \cdots, b_{n-1}$ in L that b_n' has with $b_1', b_2', \cdots, b_{n-1}'$ in L'. By finite induction, there are $b_n \in L$ and $b_n' \in L'$ for every n. Let $b_n' = f(b_n)$. This mapping establishes a one-to-one order preserving correspondence between L and L', so that they are similar. We leave the details for the student.

The rational numbers and every open interval of rational numbers satisfy the above conditions. A closed interval of rational numbers does not satisfy them. It is thus possible that each of two orders is similar to a suborder of the other and that the two orders are not similar.

DEFINITION 6. The unbounded, dense, denumerable linear orders are called "of order type η."

A suborder L' of an order L is called dense in L if for every $a < b$, $a \in L$, $b \in L$, there is a $c \in L'$ such that $a < c < b$.

Before stating the next theorem, we need a remark on bounded sets in an order L. If $S \subset L$ then $x \in L$ is said to be an upper bound of S if for every $y \in S$ either $x > y$ or $x = y$. As a generalization of Theorem 1, Chapter 4, one may show that if L is a continuous linear order, then if non-empty $S \subset L$ has an upper bound it has a least upper bound which is designated by "sup S."

THEOREM 2. If L_1 and L_2 are continuous and unbounded and have denumerable suborders L_1' and L_2', dense in L_1 and L_2 respectively, then L_1 and L_2 are similar.

Proof. L_1' and L_2' are unbounded and dense themselves; hence, by Theorem 1, they are similar. Let $b = f(a)$ be a one-to-one order-preserving correspondence between L_1' and L_2'.

We extend this to a one-to-one order-preserving correspondence between L_1 and L_2 as follows: For every $a \in L_1$ let A be the set of all $x \in L_1'$, $x < a$.

Let $f(a) = \sup [f(x) \mid x \in A]$. The student may show that this correspondence is actually one-to-one and order-preserving between L_1 and L_2.

DEFINITION 7. The order type characterized by the properties given in Theorem 2 is called the λ order type.

The real numbers in their usual order are a λ order.

3. *Well-ordered sets*

The most important class of orders are the well-ordered sets.

DEFINITION 8. A linear order W is a *well-ordered set* if every suborder has a first element.

Examples of well-ordered sets are the following:

1. All finite linear orders.
2. The linear order $1, 2, \cdots, n, \cdots$ of positive integers.
3. The linear order $1, 2, \cdots, n, \cdots; 1', 2', \cdots$.

Examples of linear orders which are not well ordered are the following:

1. The linear order $\cdots, -3, -2, -1, 0, 1, 2, 3, \cdots$ of all integers.
2. The rational numbers in their usual order.

DEFINITION 9. The order type of a well-ordered set is called an *ordinal number*.

DEFINITION 10. The ordinal number of the order of positive integers is designated by ω.

The well-ordered set given in example (3) does not have the ordinal number ω. However, this order and the order of positive integers are both denumerable. This shows that well-ordered sets may have different ordinal numbers while they are sets having the same cardinal number. We shall see later that ω is the smallest infinite ordinal number.

Every denumerable set can be well-ordered so as to have the ordinal number ω. Such a well-ordering is established by any one-to-one correspondence between the set and the positive integers. We have already made much use of this by ordering the rational numbers as an ω order $r_1, r_2, \cdots, r_n, \cdots$.

One may ask whether nondenumerable sets, such as the real numbers, can be well-ordered. Of course, such sets cannot be well-ordered as ω orders. However, we have the general existence theorem due to Zermelo.

THEOREM 3. There exists a well-ordering for any set.

Proof. Let S be a set. Let there be a function $f(A)$ which associates an element $a \in S - A$ with every proper subset $A \subset S$, including the empty set.

The rudimentary idea of the proof is to let this function generate a well-ordering of S as follows: $a_1 = f(\phi)$, $a_2 = f(\{a_1\})$, $a_3 = f(\{a_1, a_2\})$, $\cdots$,

$a_\omega = f(\{a_1, a_2, \cdots, a_n, \cdots\})$, $\cdots$, etc., thus well-ordering the set. Of course, the set may not lend itself to being counted in this way; then subtler methods are needed. The idea of the proof becomes the following: we show that the function $f(A)$ establishes a one-to-one correspondence between S and a certain class C of subsets of S which is shown to be a well-ordered set with inclusion as the order relation. This shows that S may be well-ordered.

We first define the class C of subsets of S.

A system of subsets of S is called a *chain* if it has the following properties:

1. it contains the empty set ϕ,
2. if it contains a class of subsets of S, then it contains their union,
3. if it contains a proper subset $A \subset S$, then it contains the union of A and the element $f(A)$.

We are interested in the intersection C of all chains.

1. C contains the empty set, since it is the intersection of classes each of which contains the empty set.
2. If $A_\alpha \in \mathsf{C}$ for every $\alpha \in \mathsf{A}$, then $\bigcup_{\alpha\in\mathsf{A}} A_\alpha \in \mathsf{C}$. For A_α, $\alpha \in \mathsf{A}$ belongs to every chain, so that $\bigcup_{\alpha\in\mathsf{A}} A_\alpha$ belongs to every chain, whence $\bigcup_{\alpha\in\mathsf{A}} A_\alpha \in \mathsf{C}$.
3. If $A \in \mathsf{C}$, then $A \cup \{f(A)\} \in \mathsf{C}$. For A belongs to every chain, so that $A \cup \{f(A)\}$ belongs to every chain, so that $A \cup \{f(A)\} \in \mathsf{C}$.

We have shown that C itself is a chain.

Since C is the intersection of all chains, it follows that any subset of C which is a chain must be identical with C.

By $A \in \mathsf{C}$ *comparable* we mean that for every $X \in \mathsf{C}$ either $X \subset A$ or $A \subset X$.

We show that if A is comparable then for every $X \in \mathsf{C}$ either $X \subset A$ or $A \cup \{f(A)\} \subset X$. To show this we show that the sets $X \in \mathsf{C}$ which have this property form a chain.

1. $\phi \subset A$.

2. Given X_α, $\alpha \in \mathsf{A}$. If $X_\alpha \subset A$ for every $\alpha \in \mathsf{A}$, then $\bigcup_{\alpha\in\mathsf{A}} X_\alpha \subset A$. If $X_\alpha \supset A \cup \{f(A)\}$ for some $\alpha \in \mathsf{A}$ then $\bigcup_{\alpha\in\mathsf{A}} X_\alpha \supset A \cup \{f(A)\}$.

3. If $X \supset A \cup \{f(A)\}$, then $X \cup \{f(X)\} \supset A \cup \{f(A)\}$. If $X = A$, then $X \cup \{f(X)\} \supset A \cup \{f(A)\}$. If X is a proper subset of A then $X \cup \{f(X)\} \subset A$. For if $X \cup \{f(X)\}$ is not a subset of A it contains some element not in A; but X is a subset of A, so that this element does not belong to X. Since X is a proper subset of A there is an element in A not in X which belongs to $X \cup \{f(X)\}$, since A is comparable and so is a subset of $X \cup \{f(X)\}$. Hence $X \cup \{f(X)\}$ has at least two elements not belonging to X: an impossibility.

The property of comparable sets just obtained allows us to show that the sets $A \in \mathsf{C}$ which are comparable form a chain, so that all members of C are comparable.

1. ϕ is comparable.

2. Suppose A_α, $\alpha \in \mathsf{A}$, comparable. Let $X \in \mathsf{C}$. If $A_\alpha \subset X$ for all $\alpha \in \mathsf{A}$ then $\bigcup_{\alpha \in \mathsf{A}} A_\alpha \subset X$. If $A_\alpha \supset X$ for some $\alpha \in \mathsf{A}$ then $\bigcup_{\alpha \in \mathsf{A}} A_\alpha \supset X$. Hence $\bigcup_{\alpha \in \mathsf{A}} A_\alpha$ is comparable.

3. Suppose $A \in \mathsf{C}$ is comparable. Then for every $X \in \mathsf{C}$ either $X \subset A$ or $A \cup \{f(A)\} \subset X$, so that $A \cup \{f(A)\}$ is comparable.

We now know that for every $A \in \mathsf{C}$, $B \in \mathsf{C}$, either $A \subset B$ or $B \subset A$. Using "$\subset$" as the order relation, the members of C form a linear order.

We show that this linear order is a well-ordered set: Let A_α, $\alpha \in \mathsf{A}$, be any class of sets in C. Let $A = \bigcap_{\alpha \in \mathsf{A}} A_\alpha$. Consider all $B_\beta \in \mathsf{C}$, $\beta \in \mathsf{B}$ such that $B_\beta \subset A$. Then $B = \bigcup_{\beta \in \mathsf{B}} B_\beta \subset A$. If $B = A_\alpha$ for some $\alpha \in \mathsf{A}$ then B is the first member of this set. If B is not one of the A_α, then $B \cup \{f(B)\}$ is one and must be the first. In any case there is a $\beta \in \mathsf{A}$ such that $A_\beta \subset A_\alpha$ for every $\alpha \in \mathsf{A}$. Hence C, with "$\subset$" as order relation, is a well-ordered set.

Finally we show that there is a one-to-one correspondence between C and S. The function $a = f(A)$ yields the desired correspondence. For if $A \in \mathsf{C}$, $B \in \mathsf{C}$, and A is a proper subset of B, then $f(A) \in B$, so that $f(A) \neq f(B)$. Hence if $A \neq B$, then $f(A) \neq f(B)$. Next, for every $a \in S$ there is an $A \in \mathsf{C}$ such that $a = f(A)$. For let A be the union of all sets in C which do not contain a. If $a \neq f(A)$, then $a \notin A \cup \{f(A)\}$ in contradiction. Hence $a = f(A)$.

This one-to-one correspondence produces a well-ordering of S.

This proof is an existence proof; it does not show how to obtain a well-ordering of a set. For example, no one has exhibited an actual well-ordering of the real numbers.

4. *Comparability of well-ordered sets*

In this section we show that well-ordered sets are comparable. In order to do this we need the notion, "initial segment of a well-ordered set."

DEFINITION 11. By an *initial segment* W_a of a well-ordered set W we mean all $b \in W$ such that $b < a$.

We prove several simple propositions.

PROPOSITION 2. Every suborder of a well-ordered set is a well-ordered set.

The proof is left to the student.

PROPOSITION 3. Every element of a well-ordered set W, except the last if it has one, has an immediate successor.

Proof. Let $a \in W$, not the last. Let $W' \subset W$ consist of all elements of W which succeed a. W' has a first element a'; a' is the immediate successor of a.

PROPOSITION 4. If W is similar to W', $W' \subset W$, and $a_1 = f(a)$ is the function on W to W' which establishes the similarity, then for every $a \in W$ either $a = a_1$ or $a < a_1$ in W.

Proof. Suppose $a_1 < a$. Then $a_2 = f(a_1) < a_1$, $a_3 = f(a_2) < a_2$, $\cdots$. We then have a sequence $a, a_1, a_2, \cdots, a_n, \cdots$ in W such that $a_1 < a$, $a_2 < a_1$, $\cdots$. This sequence has no first element, contradicting the assumption that W is a well-ordered set.

PROPOSITION 5. A well-ordered set W is not similar to any of its initial segments.

Proof. Suppose W is similar to an initial segment W_a. The mate $a_1 = f(a)$ of a by the similarity mapping of W onto W_a must, by Proposition 4, be such that $a = a_1$ or $a < a_1$. But this is impossible, for no such a_1 exists in W_a, since W_a consists of all $a' < a$.

PROPOSITION 6. No two distinct initial segments of a well-ordered set W are similar.

Proof. One of them is an initial segment of the other. Hence, by Proposition 5, they are not similar.

We now prove the theorem of this section.

THEOREM 4. In the case of two well-ordered sets W and W', either

1. W and W' are similar,
2. W is similar to an initial segment of W',
3. W' is similar to an initial segment of W.

Proof. We mention first all the possibilities:

1. For every initial segment of W there is a similar initial segment of W' and conversely.
2. For every initial segment of W there is a similar initial segment of W' but not conversely.
3. For every initial segment of W' there is a similar initial segment of W but not conversely.
4. None of (1), (2), and (3) holds.

For every W_a there is at most one W_b' similar to W_a. For otherwise, two distinct initial segments of W' would be similar, contradicting Proposition 6. Suppose (1) holds. Then for every $a \in W$ there is a unique $b \in W'$ such that W_b' is similar to W_a. This establishes a mapping $b = f(a)$ of W into W'. The mapping $b = f(a)$ is of W onto W', since for every $b \in W'$, W_b' is similar to some W_a. This means that $b = f(a)$ is one-to-one between W and W'.

The mapping $b = f(a)$ is order-preserving. For suppose $a_1 \in W$, $a_2 \in W$, and $a_1 < a_2$. The similarity between W_{a_2} and an initial segment W_{b_2}' of W' also establishes a similarity between W_{a_1} and an initial segment W_{b_1}' of

W_{b_2}'. Thus, $b_1 = f(a_1)$, $b_2 = f(a_2)$, and $b_1 < b_2$. Hence if (1) holds then W and W' are similar.

Suppose (2) holds. Then there are initial segments W_b' of W' which are not similar to any initial segments of W. Let b_0 be the first element of W' with this property. Then every $b > b_0$ has this property; for otherwise, W_b' would be similar to some W_a, whence W_{b_0}', as an initial segment of W_b', would be similar to some initial segment of W_a. We thus have the following situation: Every initial segment of W is similar to an initial segment of W_{b_0}' and every initial segment of W_{b_0}' is similar to an initial segment of W. So, by (1), W is similar to W_{b_0}', an initial segment of W'.

If (3) holds, the same argument shows that W' is similar to an initial segment of W.

Finally, if (4) holds, there is a first $b_0 \in W'$ such that W_{b_0}' is not similar to any initial segment of W, and a first $a_0 \in W$ such that W_{a_0} is not similar to any initial segment of W'. But then every initial segment of W_{b_0}' is similar to an initial segment of W, hence of W_{a_0}; and every initial segment of W_{a_0} is similar to an initial segment of W_{b_0}'. It follows, by (1), that W_{a_0} is similar to W_{b_0}', contradicting the assertion that W_{a_0} is not similar to any initial segment of W'. Hence (4) cannot hold and the theorem is proved.

As we have mentioned previously, the order type of a class of similar well-ordered sets is called an ordinal number. Theorem 4 orders the ordinal numbers.

Let α and β be ordinals. Then $\alpha < \beta$ if the well-ordered sets of ordinal α are similar to initial segments of the well-ordered sets of ordinal β. It is easy to show that this relation satisfies the conditions of a linear order relation. Indeed, we have the following proposition.

PROPOSITION 7. Every set of ordinals is a well-ordered set.

Proof. Suppose the contrary holds. Then there is a sequence $\{\alpha_n\}$ of ordinals, with $\alpha_2 < \alpha_1$, $\alpha_3 < \alpha_2$, $\cdots$. Consider any well-ordered set W of ordinal α_1. Then, by Theorem 4, W has initial segments $W_{a_2}, W_{a_3}, \cdots, W_{a_n}, \cdots$ whose ordinal numbers are $\alpha_2, \alpha_3, \cdots, \alpha_n, \cdots$, respectively. Then $a_3 < a_2$, $a_4 < a_3$, $\cdots$, so that W has a subset which has no first element, thus contradicting the assumption that it is a well-ordered set.

5. *Comparability of cardinals*

We can now dispose of the open question regarding cardinal numbers which was left unfinished in Chapter 2.

Every ordinal number α has a cardinal number: the cardinal number of any set which may be well-ordered as an order whose ordinal number is α.

For every cardinal number $\aleph$ let $S(\aleph)$ be the set of ordinal numbers whose cardinal number is $\aleph$. Since every set of ordinals is a well-ordered set, the set of ordinals $S(\aleph)$ has a smallest ordinal $\alpha(\aleph)$. This is called the *initial ordinal* of the cardinal $\aleph$.

For example, ω is the initial ordinal of the cardinal $\aleph_0$. Other ordinals of cardinal $\aleph_0$ are the ordinal $\omega + 1$ of the well-ordered set $1, 2, \cdots, n, \cdots; 1'$ and $\omega + \omega$ of the well-ordered set $1, 2, \cdots, n, \cdots; 1', 2', \cdots, n', \cdots$. Thus every infinite cardinal has many ordinals among which there is a smallest, the initial ordinal of the cardinal.

Now, if a and b are two cardinal numbers, and $\alpha(a)$ and $\alpha(b)$ are the initial ordinal numbers of a and b, respectively, then if $W(a)$ and $W(b)$ are well-ordered sets whose ordinal numbers are $\alpha(a)$ and $\alpha(b)$ they are also sets whose cardinal numbers are a and b. But either one of $W(a)$ and $W(b)$ is similar to an initial segment of the other or else $W(a)$ and $W(b)$ are similar. Hence at least one of the sets $W(a)$ and $W(b)$ is equivalent to a subset of the other. Thus either $a = b$, $a < b$, or $b < a$, so that all cardinal numbers are comparable.

6. *The smallest nondenumerable ordinal number*

The ordinal number ω is the smallest infinite ordinal number. It has denumerable cardinal number. Suppose we consider the set of all ordinal numbers which have either finite or denumerable cardinal numbers. This set of ordinal numbers forms a well-ordered set. This well-ordered set W has an ordinal number which we designate by Ω.

We show that the cardinal number of Ω is nondenumerable and that Ω is the first nondenumerable ordinal number.

The proof follows from the next proposition.

PROPOSITION 8. For every infinite ordinal number α, the set of ordinal numbers less than α is a well-ordered set whose ordinal number is α.

Proof. Let W' be a well-ordered set whose ordinal number is α. Let $\beta < \alpha$ and let $W(\beta) = W_b$ be the initial segment of W' whose ordinal number is β. This establishes a one-to-one order-preserving correspondence between the ordinals less than α and the initial segments of W'. Moreover, if W' is infinite, there is a one-to-one order-preserving correspondence between its elements and its initial segments.

Now Ω is the well-ordered set of all finite or denumerable ordinals α. For every denumerable ordinal number α, Proposition 8 shows that the initial segment W_α of W has ordinal number α. Hence $\Omega > \alpha$, for every denumerable ordinal number α, so that Ω is nondenumerable.

If α is a nondenumerable ordinal number and W' a well-ordered set whose ordinal number is α then W' is not similar to any initial segment of W. Hence $\alpha \geqq \Omega$. This shows that Ω is the smallest nondenumerable ordinal number.

We have thus proved the following theorem.

THEOREM 5. The ordinal number Ω of the set of all ordinals of finite or denumerable cardinal is the first nondenumerable ordinal number.

The cardinal number of Ω is the smallest nonfinite cardinal number and is designated by $\aleph_1$.

We know that $2^{\aleph_0} > \aleph_0$. A basic question which has never been answered is the following: Is $2^{\aleph_0} = \aleph_1$?

This question is known as the *continuum problem*. The hypothesis that $2^{\aleph_0} = \aleph_1$ is known as the *continuum hypothesis*.

7. *Transfinite induction*

The method of finite induction for the positive integers is the following:

If a set S of positive integers is such that $1 \in S$ and if $n \in S$ implies $n + 1 \in S$, it follows that S is the set of all positive integers.

An equivalent form of the method for positive integers is the following:

If a set S of positive integers is such that $1 \in S$ and if all positive integers less than n are in S implies n is in S, it follows that S is the set of all positive integers.

While these two forms are equivalent for the positive integers only the second generalizes to any well-ordered set.

THEOREM 6. If S is the set of all ordinals less than a given ordinal α, and T is a subset of S such that

1. the first ordinal, 1, is in T,
2. for every ordinal $\beta < \alpha$, if all ordinals less than β are in T then β is also in T,

then $T = S$.

Proof. If $S - T$ is nonempty, then there is a first ordinal $\beta \in S - T$. By (1), $\beta \neq 1$. But all ordinals less than β are in T so that, by (2), $\beta \in T$. Hence, $S - T$ is empty.

Theorem 6 will be used a good deal in the next two chapters.

8. *Paradoxes*

Any treatment of transfinite numbers would be incomplete if attention were not called to the paradoxes that arise. We mention only the Burali-Forti paradox concerning the well-ordered set of all ordinal numbers. We first observe that for every infinite set W of ordinal numbers, there is an ordinal number which exceeds all the ordinal numbers in W. For let W' consist of all ordinal numbers which are either in W or are less than some ordinal number in W. Then W' is a well-ordered set. Its ordinal number α exceeds all the ordinals in W', by Proposition 8.

Now, consider the set of all ordinal numbers. By the above remarks, there is an ordinal number greater than any ordinal number in the set. However, since the set consists of all ordinal numbers, there can be no ordinal number greater than all the members of the set. This is the Burali-Forti paradox.

Although, in the last several decades, the paradoxes have been handled in ways which are acceptable to many mathematicians, these considerations are not within the scope of this book. We note, however, that in all our considerations the sets involved are all subsets of a given set and the ordinal numbers involved are always less than a given ordinal number. There are no known paradoxes in such cases.

Exercises

1.1 Give five more examples of linear orders.

1.2 Prove that the real polynomials $p(x)$, ordered by setting $p(x) < q(x)$ if there is an x such that for every $\xi > x$, $p(\xi) < q(\xi)$, form a linear order.

1.3 Rephrase the order relation of Exercise 1.2 in terms of the coefficients of the polynomials.

1.4 Why does the procedure of Exercise 1.2 not provide a linear order relation for the continuous functions?

A linear order L is said to be characterized if enough of its properties are given so that every linear order with these properties is similar to L. The next few exercises are concerned with characterizing orders.

2.1 Characterize the finite linear orders.

2.2 Characterize the positive integers as a linear order.

2.3 Characterize the integers as a linear order.

2.4 Characterize the linear order of example (4), §1. Are examples (4) and (5) similar orders?

2.5 Show that the similarity relation between linear orders satisfies the conditions for an equivalence relation given by Theorem 2, Chapter 1.

2.6 Show that the correspondence established in the proof of Theorem 2 is one-to-one and order-preserving.

2.7 Are the polynomials ordered as in example (6), §1, a dense order? Are they a continuous order?

4.1 Show that every suborder of a well-ordered set is a well-ordered set.

4.2 Show that if W and W' are similar well-ordered sets there is one and only one function $f(x)$ on W to W' which is one-to-one and order-preserving.

4.3 Show that the condition of Exercise 4.2 is satisfied by some orders which are not well-ordered sets.

5.1 Show that all initial ordinals of infinite cardinals are limiting ordinals, i.e., they have no immediate predecessor.

5.2 An ordinal α has property (*) if for every $\beta < \alpha$ every order of ordinals ξ_γ, $\gamma < \beta$ is such that

$$\sup [\xi_\gamma \mid \gamma < \beta] < \alpha.$$

Show that every initial ordinal of an infinite cardinal which has an immediate predecessor has property (*).

6.1 What is the cardinal number of the set of all ordinals of a given cardinal?

7.1 State a principle of transfinite induction for cardinal numbers.

7.2 Prove for every cardinal number $\aleph$ that $\aleph + \aleph = \aleph$.

7.3 Prove for every cardinal number $\aleph$ that $\aleph \cdot \aleph = \aleph$.

7.4 Show that if $\aleph = \sum_{n=1}^{\infty} \aleph_n$ where $\aleph_n < \aleph$ then $\aleph^{\aleph_0} > \aleph$. Hint: Use König's Theorem.

7.5 S is a partial order if there is an order relation $x < y$ such that if $x < y$ then it is not true that $y \leq x$, and if $x \leq y$ and $y \leq z$ then $x \leq z$. Show, as an application of the well-ordering theorem, that if S is a partial order in which every linear order L has a lower bound, then S has at least one minimal element: i.e., there is an $x \in S$ so that there is no $y \in S$ with $y < x$. (This is known as Zorn's Lemma.)

8.1 Show that for every set of ordinal numbers there is an ordinal number greater than all the members of the set.

References

A. Fraenkel, *Einleitung in die Mengenlehre*, Berlin, 1928, Chaps. 3–5.

K. Gödel, *The Consistency of the Continuum Hypothesis*, Princeton, 1940.

F. Hausdorff, *Mengenlehre*, New York, 1944, Chaps. 3, 4.

E. W. Hobson, *The Theory of Functions of a Real Variable*, Cambridge, 1927, Chap. 4.

W. Sierpinski, *Leçons sur les nombres transfinis*, Paris, 1928.

11

Borel Sets and Baire Functions

1. *Introduction*

The closed sets, open sets, and sets of type F_σ are special classes of sets belonging to a wider class of sets which are called the Borel sets. The continuous functions and limits of sequences of continuous functions belong to a class of functions called the Baire functions. In this chapter we give an account of some of the more basic properties of these classes of sets and functions.

2. *Borel sets*

The Borel sets are all the sets which may be obtained from the closed and open sets by repeatedly applying the operations of union and intersection to denumerable numbers of sets.

The closed sets are called "of type F_0." The unions of denumerable numbers of sets of type F_0 are called "of type F_1." The sets of type F_1 are those which we previously called "of type F_σ." The intersections of denumerable numbers of sets of type F_1 are called "of type F_2." We define sets of type F_α for every $\alpha < \Omega$. To do this we make the convention that if α is a limiting ordinal number, i.e., α has no immediate predecessor, then α is even. The first ordinal, 1, is odd. The immediate successors of odd and even ordinals are even and odd, respectively. This designates every ordinal $\alpha < \Omega$ as odd or even. If sets of type F_β have been defined for all $\beta < \alpha$, then the sets of type F_α are the unions or intersections of denumerable numbers of sets of types F_β, $\beta < \alpha$, according as α is odd or even. By transfinite induction, the sets of type F_α are thus defined for all $\alpha < \Omega$.

For $\alpha = \Omega$ no new sets are obtained, i.e., every set of type F_Ω is of type F_α

for some $\alpha < \Omega$. For if S is of type F_Ω then $S = \bigcap_{n=1}^{\infty} S_n$, S_n of type F_{α_n}, $\alpha_n < \Omega$. But each α_n is of denumerable cardinal, whence it readily follows that

$$\sup [\alpha_n \mid n = 1, 2, \cdots] = \beta$$

is of denumerable cardinal. Hence S is of type F_α, $\alpha = \beta + 1 < \Omega$.

A parallel class of sets starts with the open sets. The open sets are called "of type G_0." The intersection of a denumerable number of sets of type G_0 is said to be "of type G_1." If sets of type G_β have been defined for every $\beta < \alpha$, then the sets of type G_α are the intersections or unions of denumerable numbers of sets of type G_β, $\beta < \alpha$, according as α is odd or even. We obtain sets of type G_α for all $\alpha < \Omega$.

It can be shown that there are sets of type F_α and G_α for every $\alpha < \Omega$ which are not of type F_β or G_β for any $\beta < \alpha$, but the proof would take us too far afield.

The sets of types

$F_0, F_1, F_2, \cdots, F_\alpha, \cdots, \alpha < \Omega$

$G_0, G_1, G_2, \cdots, G_\alpha, \cdots, \alpha < \Omega$

are called the Borel sets.

A notation often used for the Borel sets of lower type is $F, F_\sigma, F_{\sigma\delta}, F_{\sigma\delta\sigma}, \cdots$ for sets of type $F_0, F_1, F_2, F_3, \cdots$, and $G, G_\delta, G_{\delta\sigma}, G_{\delta\sigma\delta}, \cdots$ for sets of type $G_0, G_1, G_2, G_3, \cdots$.

We prove some simple propositions.

PROPOSITION 1. The complement of every set of type F_α is of type G_α and the complement of every set of type G_α is of type F_α, for every $\alpha < \Omega$.

Proof. The proposition holds for $\alpha = 0$. Suppose it holds for every $\beta < \alpha$. Suppose α is even. Let S be any set of type F_α. Then $S = \bigcap_{n=1}^{\infty} S_n$, where S_n is of type F_{α_n}, $\alpha_n < \alpha$. By hypothesis each $C(S_n)$ is of type G_{α_n}. But $C(S) = \bigcup_{n=1}^{\infty} C(S_n)$, so that $C(S)$ is of type G_α. The proof for the case where α is odd is similar. Hence, by transfinite induction, for every $\alpha < \Omega$ the complement of every set of type F_α is a set of type G_α.

The proof that the complement of a set of type G_α is of type F_α is similar.

PROPOSITION 2. If $\alpha < \Omega$ is odd, the union of a denumerable number of sets of type F_α is of type F_α and the intersection of a denumerable number of sets of type G_α is of type G_α.

Proof. Let $S = \bigcup_{n=1}^{\infty} S_n$ where each S_n is of type F_α. Then

$$S_n = \bigcup_{m=1}^{\infty} S_{nm},$$

where each S_{nm} is of type $F_{\alpha_{nm}}$, $\alpha_{nm} < \alpha$. Accordingly,

$$S = \bigcup_{n=1}^{\infty} \bigcup_{m=1}^{\infty} S_{nm},$$

as the union of a denumerable number of sets of types $F_{\alpha_{nm}}$, $\alpha_{nm} < \alpha$, is of type F_α.

The proof for intersections of denumerable numbers of sets of type G_α is similar.

An analogous result holds for even ordinals. We leave it to the student to state and prove this proposition.

In addition to Proposition 2, the following proposition holds.

PROPOSITION 3. For every $\alpha < \Omega$, the union and intersection of any finite number of sets of type F_α (of type G_α) is of type F_α (of type G_α).

The proof is left for the student.

PROPOSITION 4. For every $\alpha < \Omega$ every set of type F_α is of type $G_{\alpha+1}$ and every set of type G_α is of type $F_{\alpha+1}$.

Proof. We first show that every set of type G_0 is of type F_1. If S is of type G_0, then S as an open set is the union of a finite or denumerable number of open intervals. But every open interval is the union of a denumerable number of closed intervals. It follows that S is the union of a denumerable number of closed intervals, so that S is of type F_1. Now let $\alpha < \Omega$ and suppose, for every $\beta < \alpha$, that every set of type G_β is of type $F_{\beta+1}$. Assume, for convenience, that α is odd (for every even ordinal the intersection operation has to be replaced by union). Let S be a set of type G_α. Then $S = \bigcap_{n=1}^{\infty} S_n$, where each S_n is of type G_{α_n}, $\alpha_n < \alpha$. By hypothesis each S_n is of type F_{α_n+1}, with $\alpha_n + 1 < \alpha + 1$. Since $\alpha + 1$ is even, $S = \bigcap_{n=1}^{\infty} S_n$ is of type $F_{\alpha+1}$. Accordingly, by transfinite induction, it follows that for every $\alpha < \Omega$ every set of type G_α is of type $F_{\alpha+1}$.

The proof that every set of type F_α is of type $G_{\alpha+1}$ is similar.

Proposition 4 shows that the class of all Borel sets is identical with the sets of types

$$F_0, F_1, \cdots, F_\alpha, \cdots, \alpha < \Omega,$$

as well as the sets of types

$$G_0, G_1, \cdots, G_\alpha, \cdots, \alpha < \Omega.$$

PROPOSITION 5. The Borel sets form the smallest system of sets such that

1. all closed sets are in the system,
2. the union of any denumerable number of sets in the system is in the system,

3. the intersection of any denumerable number of sets in the system is in the system.

Proof. Let S be any system of sets which satisfies (1), (2), and (3). Then every set of type F_0 is in S. The method of transfinite induction and properties (2) and (3) assure that, for every $\alpha < \Omega$, every set of type F_α is in S. The details are left for the student to provide. This shows that every Borel set is in S.

We note in passing that the sets of type F_α and of type G_α are unions and intersections of monotonic sequences of lower types.

Suppose that $\alpha < \Omega$ where α is odd. Then if S is of type F_α, $S = \bigcup_{n=1}^{\infty} S_n$, where the sets S_n are of lower type than F_α. Let $T_n = \bigcup_{k=1}^{n} S_k$. Then $S = \bigcup_{n=1}^{\infty} T_n$; the sets T_n are nondecreasing and of lower type than F_α.

Similarly if α is odd every set of type G_α is the intersection of a nonincreasing sequence of sets of lower type. If α is even every set of type F_α is the intersection of a nonincreasing sequence and every set of type G_α is the union of a nondecreasing sequence of sets of lower type.

3. *Baire functions*

The Baire functions are a class of functions analogous to the Borel sets. The continuous functions are said to be of type f_0 (Baire class 0). Functions which are limits of convergent sequences of continuous functions are of type f_1 (Baire class 1). For every $\alpha < \Omega$ if the functions of type f_β have been defined for every $\beta < \alpha$, then the functions of type f_α (Baire class α) are limits of convergent sequences of functions of types f_β, $\beta < \alpha$. By transfinite induction, this defines Baire functions of all classes $\alpha < \Omega$.

We prove a few simple properties of the Baire functions.

PROPOSITION 6. For every $\alpha < \Omega$, the sum and product of two functions of type f_α is of type f_α.

Proof. The proposition holds for $\alpha = 0$. Suppose $\alpha < \Omega$ and that the assertion holds for all $\beta < \alpha$. Let $f(x)$ and $g(x)$ be of type f_α. Then $f(x) = \lim_{n\to\infty} f_n(x)$ and $g(x) = \lim_{n\to\infty} g_n(x)$ where, for every n, $f_n(x)$ is of type f_{α_n}, $\alpha_n < \alpha$, and $g_n(x)$ is of type f_{β_n}, $\beta_n < \alpha$, so that $f_n(x) + g_n(x)$ and $f_n(x) \cdot g_n(x)$ are of type f_{γ_n}, $\gamma_n = \max(\alpha_n, \beta_n)$. Since $f(x) + g(x) = \lim_{n\to\infty} [f_n(x) + g_n(x)]$ and $f(x) \cdot g(x) = \lim_{n\to\infty} [f_n(x) g_n(x)]$, it follows that $f(x) + g(x)$ and $f(x) \cdot g(x)$ are of type f_α.

PROPOSITION 7. For every $\alpha < \Omega$, if $f(x)$ is of type f_α and $f(x)$ is never 0, then $1/f(x)$ is of type f_α and $-f(x)$ is of type f_α.

The proof is left for the student.

PROPOSITION 8. For every $\alpha < \Omega$, if $f(x)$ is of type f_α then $|f(x)|$ is of type f_α.

Proof. The proposition holds for functions of type f_0. Suppose for $\alpha < \Omega$, it holds for all functions of type f_β, $\beta < \alpha$. Let $f(x)$ be of type f_α. Then $f(x) = \lim_{n\to\infty} f_n(x)$, where each $f_n(x)$ is of a type f_{α_n}, $\alpha_n < \alpha$. But then each function $|f_n(x)|$ is of type f_{α_n}. Now $|f(x)| = \lim_{n\to\infty} |f_n(x)|$, so that $|f(x)|$ is of type f_α. The proof of the proposition is completed by transfinite induction.

PROPOSITION 9. For every $\alpha < \Omega$, if $f(x)$ and $g(x)$ are of type f_α, then $\max(f(x), g(x))$ and $\min(f(x), g(x))$ are of type f_α.

Proof. The functions $f(x) + g(x)$ and $|f(x) - g(x)|$ are of type f_α. Hence the functions $\max(f(x), g(x)) = \frac{1}{2}(f(x) + g(x)) + \frac{1}{2}|f(x) - g(x)|$ and $\min(f(x), g(x)) = \frac{1}{2}(f(x) + g(x)) - \frac{1}{2}|f(x) - g(x)|$ are of type f_α.

We now come to an important theorem.

THEOREM 1. For every $\alpha < \Omega$, the limit of a uniformly convergent sequence of functions of type f_α is of type f_α.

The proof of this theorem depends on the following lemma.

LEMMA 1. For every $\alpha < \Omega$, if $f(x)$ is of type f_α and for every x $|f(x)| \leqq k$ where $k > 0$, then $f(x) = \lim_{n\to\infty} f_n(x)$, where each $f_n(x)$ is of type f_{α_n}, $\alpha_n < \alpha$, and $|f_n(x)| \leqq k$ for every x.

Proof. Since $f(x)$ is of type f_α, there is a sequence $\{g_n(x)\}$ such that $\lim_{n\to\infty} g_n(x) = f(x)$, where $g_n(x)$ is of type f_{α_n}, $\alpha_n < \alpha$. Let $h_n(x) = \min[g_n(x), k]$ and $f_n(x) = \max[h_n(x), -k]$. By Proposition 9, $f_n(x)$ is of type f_{α_n}. Clearly $f(x) = \lim_{n\to\infty} f_n(x)$.

We now prove the theorem.

It holds for $\alpha = 0$. Suppose it holds for every $\beta < \alpha$. Let $\{f_n(x)\}$ be a uniformly convergent sequence of functions of type f_α and let $f(x) = \lim_{n\to\infty} f_n(x)$.

Now

$$f(x) = \sum_{n=1}^{\infty} (f_{n+1}(x) - f_n(x)) + f_1(x),$$

where the series converges uniformly to $f(x)$. Hence there is a convergent series $\sum_{n=1}^{\infty} k_n$ of positive numbers such that for every n and x, $|f_{n+1}(x) - f_n(x)| \leqq k_n$.

For every n the function $f_{n+1}(x) - f_n(x)$ is of type f_α. Hence there is a sequence $\{f_{nm}(x)\}$ of functions of lower type than f_α, which converges to

$f_{n+1}(x) - f_n(x)$, such that for every m and x, $|f_{nm}(x)| \leqq k_n$. Consider the sequence

$$g_1(x) = f_{11}(x), g_2(x) = f_{12}(x) + f_{22}(x), \cdots, g_m(x) = f_{1m}(x) + f_{2m}(x) + \cdots + f_{mm}(x), \cdots.$$

For every n, $g_n(x)$ is of lower type than f_α.

We show that $f(x) - f_1(x) = \lim_{m \to \infty} g_m(x)$, thus proving the theorem.

Let $\epsilon > 0$. There is an N such that $\sum_{n=N+1}^{\infty} k_n < \epsilon/3$. Hence, for every x,

$$|f(x) - f_1(x) - \sum_{n=1}^{N} (f_{n+1}(x) - f_n(x))| < \frac{\epsilon}{3}.$$

Fix x. There is an N' such that for every $n > N$ and $m > N'$,

$$|(f_{n+1}(x) - f_n(x)) - f_{nm}(x)| < \frac{\epsilon}{3N}.$$

Let $m > \max(N, N')$. Then

$$|f(x) - f_1(x) - g_m(x)| < |f(x) - f_1(x) - \sum_{n=1}^{N} (f_{n+1}(x) - f_n(x))| + \sum_{n=1}^{N} |(f_{n+1}(x) - f_n(x)) - f_{nm}(x)| + \sum_{n=N+1}^{m} |f_{nm}(x)| < \frac{\epsilon}{3} + N\frac{\epsilon}{3N} + \frac{\epsilon}{3} = \epsilon.$$

In Chapter 8, we showed that every function of type f_1 has a set of the first category as its set of points of discontinuity. Of course, this result does not hold for all Baire functions. For example, the function $f(x) = 1$, x rational, and $f(x) = 0$, x irrational, is discontinuous everywhere but is of type f_2. However, we have the following theorem.

THEOREM 2. For any $\alpha < \Omega$, if $f(x)$ is of class f_α there is a set S, whose complement is of the first category, such that $f(x)$ is continuous on S relative to S.

Proof. The theorem, of course, holds for $\alpha = 0$. Let $\alpha < \Omega$ and suppose it holds for every $\beta < \alpha$. Let $f(x)$ be of type f_α. Then $f(x) = \lim_{n \to \infty} f_n(x)$, where $f_n(x)$ is of type f_{α_n}, $\alpha_n < \alpha$. By assumption, for every n there is a set S_n, whose complement is of the first category, such that $f_n(x)$ is continuous on S_n relative to S_n. But the complement of $S = \bigcap_{n=1}^{\infty} S_n$ is of the first category and $f_n(x)$ is continuous on S relative to S for every n. By Exercise 4.3, Chapter 8, $f(x) = \lim_{n \to \infty} f_n(x)$ is continuous on a subset $T \subset S$ relative to T, where the complement of T relative to S is of the first category relative to S. By Exercise 4.4, Chapter 8, the set $S - T$ is of the first category relative to the set of all the real numbers. Thus the complement of T, as the union of two sets of the first category, is of the first category. By transfinite induction, the theorem holds for all $\alpha < \Omega$.

Now the number of all real functions is $c^c = 2^c > c$. We show, however, that the number of Baire functions is only c.

THEOREM 3. The Baire functions are c in number.

Proof. We observe first that there are c continuous functions. For, a continuous function is completely determined by its values at the rationals. Hence there are $c^{\aleph_0} = (2^{\aleph_0})^{\aleph_0} = 2^{\aleph_0} = c$ continuous functions. So the functions of type f_0 are c in number. Suppose $\alpha < \Omega$ and for every $\beta < \alpha$ there are c, or fewer, functions of type f_β. The class of all functions whose type is lower than f_α has cardinal number $c \cdot \aleph_0 = c$. But every function of type f_α is the limit of a sequence of functions of lower types so that the number of functions of type f_α is no more than $c^{\aleph_0} = c$. By transfinite induction, this holds for every $\alpha < \Omega$, so that there are no more than $c \cdot \aleph_1 = c$ Baire functions. But there are at least c Baire functions, since the functions $f(x) = a$ are Baire functions.

4. *Relation between Borel sets and Baire functions*

One might expect a connection to exist between the Borel sets and the Baire functions in view of the parallel way in which they have been defined. We restrict our discussion to the finite ordinals, and show that the sets associated with functions of finite Baire type are of finite Borel type, and conversely that if the sets associated with a function are all of the same finite Borel type then the function is of finite Baire type. Precisely, we show in Theorems 5 and 6 that a function $f(x)$ is of type f_α if and only if for every real number k the sets $E[f(x) > k]$ and $E[f(x) \geqq k]$ are of types G_α and F_α, respectively, if α is an even positive integer, and of types F_α and G_α, respectively, if α is an odd positive integer.

In order to carry out the work it is convenient to define sets of types A_α and B_α. For every $\alpha < \Omega$, a set S will be said to be of type A_α if there is a function $f(x)$ of type f_α and a real number k such that $S = E[f(x) > k]$, and a set S will be said to be of type B_α if there is a function $f(x)$ of type f_α and a real number k such that $S = E[f(x) \geqq k]$.

LEMMA 2. If $f(x) = \lim_{n \to \infty} f_n(x)$ then

$$E[f(x) > k] = \bigcup_{m=1}^{\infty} \bigcup_{r=1}^{\infty} \bigcap_{n=r}^{\infty} E\left[f_n(x) \geqq k + \frac{1}{m}\right].$$

Proof. Suppose $f(x) > k$. Then there is an m such that $f(x) > k + 1/m$. There is an r such that for every $n > r$, $f_n(x) \geqq k + 1/m$. Hence if

$x \in E[f(x) > k]$ then

$$x \in \bigcup_{m=1}^{\infty} \bigcup_{r=1}^{\infty} \bigcap_{n=r}^{\infty} E\left[f_n(x) \geqq k + \frac{1}{m}\right].$$

Suppose now that

$$x \in \bigcup_{m=1}^{\infty} \bigcup_{r=1}^{\infty} \bigcap_{n=r}^{\infty} E\left[f_n(x) \geqq k + \frac{1}{m}\right].$$

Then there is an m such that

$$x \in \bigcup_{r=1}^{\infty} \bigcap_{n=r}^{\infty} E\left[f_n(x) \geqq k + \frac{1}{m}\right].$$

Moreover, there is an r such that

$$x \in \bigcap_{n=r}^{\infty} E\left[f_n(x) \geqq k + \frac{1}{m}\right].$$

Thus

$$x \in E\left[f(x) \geqq k + \frac{1}{m}\right] \subset E\,[f(x) > k].$$

This shows that

$$\bigcup_{m=1}^{\infty} \bigcup_{r=1}^{\infty} \bigcap_{n=r}^{\infty} E\left[f_n(x) \geqq k + \frac{1}{m}\right] = E[f(x) > k].$$

PROPOSITION 10. For every finite ordinal α, every set of type A_α is of type G_α and every set of type B_α is of type F_α if α is even. Every set of type A_α is of type F_α and every set of type B_α is of type G_α if α is odd.

Proof. The proposition holds for $\alpha = 0$. Suppose it holds for every $\beta < \alpha$. Suppose first that α is odd. Let S be any set of type A_α. There is then a function $f(x)$ of type f_α and a real number k such that $S = E[f(x) > k]$. Now $f(x) = \lim_{n \to \infty} f_n(x)$, where the $f_n(x)$ are Baire functions of lower type than f_α. By Lemma 2,

$$S = \bigcup_{m=1}^{\infty} \bigcup_{r=1}^{\infty} \bigcap_{n=r}^{\infty} E\left[f_n(x) \geqq k + \frac{1}{m}\right].$$

But, by assumption, each $E[f_n(x) \geqq k + 1/m]$ is of type $F_{\alpha-1}$. Since $\alpha - 1$ is even, the intersection of a denumerable number of sets of type $F_{\alpha-1}$ is of type $F_{\alpha-1}$. Hence S is the union of a denumerable number of sets of type $F_{\alpha-1}$ and so is of type F_α.

Now suppose S is of type B_α. There is an $f(x)$ of type f_α and a real number k such that $S = E[f(x) \geqq k]$. But $S = E[-f(x) \leqq -k]$. $C(S) = E[-f(x) > -k]$, so that $C(S)$ is of type F_α, whence S is of type G_α. If α is a finite even ordinal the proof is quite similar. The proof is thus achieved by means of finite induction.

We shall prove the converse of Proposition 10. We first prove the following lemma.

LEMMA 3. For every finite ordinal α, if S is a set of type A_α or B_α, there is a function $f(x)$ of type $f_{\alpha+1}$ such that $f(x) = 1$ for every $x \in S$ and $f(x) = 0$ for every $x \in C(S)$.

Proof. Suppose S is of type A_α. Then there is a function $g(x)$ of type f_α such that $S = E[g(x) > 0]$. Let $h(x) = \max [g(x), 0]$. Then $h(x)$ is also of type f_α. For every positive integer n, let $f_n(x) = \min [nh(x), 1]$. The functions $f_n(x)$ are all of type f_α. The sequence $\{f_n(x)\}$ converges everywhere and $\lim_{n\to\infty} f_n(x)$ is 1 for $x \in S$ and 0 for $x \in C(S)$ and is of type $f_{\alpha+1}$.

Suppose S is of type B_α. Then $C(S)$ is of type A_α. Hence there is a function $f(x)$ of type $f_{\alpha+1}$ such that $f(x) = 1$ for $x \in C(S)$ and $f(x) = 0$ for $x \in S$. The function $1 - f(x)$ is of type $f_{\alpha+1}$ and is 1 on S and 0 on $C(S)$.

PROPOSITION 11. For every finite ordinal α, every set of type G_α is of type A_α and every set of type F_α is of type B_α if α is even. Every set of type F_α is of type A_α and every set of type G_α is of type B_α if α is odd.

Proof. The proposition holds for $\alpha = 0$. Suppose α is odd and the proposition holds for $\alpha - 1$. Let S be any set of type F_α. Then $S = \bigcup_{n=1}^{\infty} S_n$, where each S_n is of type $F_{\alpha-1}$ and the sequence $\{S_n\}$ is nondecreasing. Since, by assumption, every set of type $F_{\alpha-1}$ is of type $B_{\alpha-1}$, there is, by Lemma 3, a function $f_n(x)$ of type f_α, for every n, such that $f_n(x) = 1/2^n$ for every $x \in S_n$ and $f_n(x) = 0$ for every $x \in C(S_n)$. Now,

$$f(x) = \sum_{n=1}^{\infty} f_n(x)$$

is of type f_α, since the series converges uniformly. But $S = E[f(x) > 0]$, so that S is of type A_α. Similarly, every set of type G_α is of type B_α.

If α is even and the proposition holds for $\alpha - 1$, one shows in the same way that every set of type F_α is of type B_α and every set of type G_α is of type A_α.

The proposition then follows by finite induction.

Propositions 10 and 11 combine to give the following theorem.

THEOREM 4. For finite odd ordinals, a set is of type A_α if and only if it is of type F_α, and it is of type B_α if and only if it is of type G_α. For finite even ordinals a set is of type A_α if and only if it is of type G_α, and it is of type B_α if and only if it is of type F_α.

THEOREM 5. If $f(x)$ is any function of type f_α, where α is a finite ordinal, then for every real number k the sets $E[f(x) > k]$ and $E[f(x) \geqq k]$ are of type F_α and G_α respectively if α is odd and of type G_α and F_α respectively if α is even.

Proved by Theorem 4.

We need the following lemma for the proof of the converse of Theorem 5.

LEMMA 4. If α is a finite ordinal and S and T are disjoint sets of type B_α, there is a function $g(x)$ of type f_α such that $g(x) = 1$ on S, $g(x) = 0$ on T, and $0 < g(x) < 1$ elsewhere.

Proof. There is an $f_1(x)$ of type f_α such that $E[f_1(x) \leqq 0] = S$, and an $f_2(x)$ of type f_α such that $E[f_2(x) \leqq 0] = T$. Let $g_1(x) = \max[f_1(x), 0]$ and $g_2(x) = \max[f_2(x), 0]$. Then $g_1(x)$ and $g_2(x)$ are of type f_α, $g_1(x) = 0$ on S, $g_1(x) > 0$ on $C(S)$, $g_2(x) = 0$ on T, and $g_2(x) > 0$ on $C(T)$. The function $g_1(x) + g_2(x)$ is never 0. Let

$$g(x) = \frac{g_2(x)}{g_1(x) + g_2(x)} \cdot$$

Then $g(x) = 1$ for every $x \in S$ and $g(x) = 0$ for every $x \in T$, and $0 < g(x) < 1$ for every other x.

THEOREM 6. If α is a finite odd ordinal and $f(x)$ is such that for every real k the sets $E[f(x) > k]$ and $E[f(x) \geqq k]$ are of type F_α and G_α, respectively, then $f(x)$ is of type f_α. If α is even and the sets $E[f(x) > k]$ and $E[f(x) \geqq k]$ are of type G_α and F_α, respectively, then $f(x)$ is of type f_α.

Proof. By Theorem 4, the proof reduces to showing that if the sets $E[f(x) > k]$ and $E[f(x) \geqq k]$ are of type A_α and B_α, respectively, then $f(x)$ is of type f_α.

For every real k, suppose the sets $E[f(x) > k]$ and $E[f(x) \geqq k]$ are of type A_α and B_α. Then the sets $E[f(x) \leqq k]$, as complements of sets of type A_α, are of type B_α in view of Theorem 4.

Suppose, for convenience, that $0 < f(x) < 1$ for every x. Let n be a positive integer. For every $m = 0, 1, \cdots, n - 1$, the sets $E[f(x) \leqq m/n]$ and $E[f(x) \geqq (m + 1)/n]$ are of type B_α. Hence, by Lemma 4, there is a $g_m(x)$ of type f_α such that $g_m(x) = 0$ for $x \in E[f(x) \geqq (m + 1)/n]$, $g_m(x) = 1$ for $x \in E[f(x) \leqq m/n]$, and $0 < g_m(x) < 1$ for all other values of x. Let

$$g(x) = \frac{1}{n}[g_0(x) + g_1(x) + \cdots + g_{n-1}(x)].$$

Suppose $m/n \leqq f(x) < (m + 1)/n$. Then $g_0(x) = g_1(x) = \cdots = g_{m-1}(x) = 1$, $0 \leqq g_m(x) \leqq 1$, and $g_r(x) = 0$ for every $r > m$. Hence, $|f(x) - g(x)| < 1/n$ for every x. Moreover, $g(x)$, as the sum of a finite number of functions of type f_α, is itself of type f_α. It follows that $f(x)$, as the limit of a uniformly convergent sequence of functions of type f_α is of type f_α.

It was assumed that $0 < f(x) < 1$. We leave it for the student to reduce the general case to this one.

Exercises

2.1 Show that the union of a set of intervals, closed, open, or semiopen, is a Borel set.

2.2 Show that for every $\alpha < \Omega$ the complement of a set of type G_α is of type F_α.

2.3 Show that if $\alpha < \Omega$ is even the union of a denumerable number of sets of type G_α is of type G_α and the intersection of a denumerable number of sets of type F_α is of type F_α.

2.4 Show for every $\alpha < \Omega$ that the union and intersection of a finite number of sets of type F_α is of type F_α.

2.5 Prove that every set of type F_α is of type $G_{\alpha+1}$.

2.6 If $\alpha < \Omega$ is even, show that every set of type F_α is the intersection of a monotonically nonincreasing sequence of sets of lower type.

3.1 If $f(x)$ is of type f_α, $\alpha < \Omega$, and c is a real number, show that $cf(x)$ is of type f_α.

3.2 In the proof of Lemma 1, give the details showing that

$$f(x) = \lim_{n\to\infty} f_n(x).$$

3.3 Show that the function $f(x) = 1$, x rational; $f(x) = 0$, x irrational, is of type f_2.

3.4 Give a proof, different from the one in the text, that there are c continuous functions.

3.5 Show that if $f(x)$ is of Baire class α on S and $T \subset S$ then $f(x)$ is of Baire class α on T.

3.6 Show that the Dini derivates of a continuous function are functions of Baire class 2 at most.

3.7 Give an example of a continuous $f(x)$ for which $d^+(f; x)$ is not of Baire class 1.

4.1 Prove Proposition 10 for even finite ordinals.

4.2 Define Borel sets relative to a set S.

4.3 Show that if S is a Borel set relative to a Borel set $T \subset [0, 1]$ then S is a Borel set relative to $[0, 1]$.

4.4 Define Baire functions relative to a set S.

4.5 Show that if $f(x)$ is a Baire function relative to a Borel set S as well as relative to its complement $C(S)$ then $f(x)$ is a Baire function.

4.6 If $f(x)$ is continuous on a set $S \subset [0, 1]$ relative to S show that $f(x)$ may be extended on $[0, 1]$ to a Baire function.

4.7 If $f(x)$ is a Baire function on a set $S \subset [0, 1]$ relative to S show that $f(x)$ may be extended on $[0, 1]$ to a Baire function.

4.8 If S is a Borel set show that $S = (G - E_1) \cup E_2$, where G is open and E_1 and E_2 are of the first category.

References

H. HAHN, *Reelle Functionen*, New York, 1948.

F. HAUSDORFF, *Mengenlehre*, New York, 1944, Chaps. 7, 9.

C. KURATOWSKI, *Topologie I*, Warszawa-Lwow, 1933, Chap. 2, §26, 27; Chap. 3, §32, 33.

H. LEBESGUE, "Sur les fonctions représentables analytiquement," *Journal de Math.* (6), 1 (1905).

CH. J. DE LA VALLÉE POUSSIN, *Intégrales de Lebesgue, Fonctions d'ensembles, Classes de Baire*, Paris, 1934, Chap. 8.

W. SIERPINSKI, *General Topology*, translated by C. C. Krieger, Toronto, 1934, Chap. 7.

12

Applications of Well-Ordering

1. *Introduction*

The applications of the well-ordering theorem which will be given here are mainly of the following kind:

The continuum hypothesis will be assumed. This, together with the well-ordering theorem, allows any set whose cardinal number is c to be well-ordered as an order of ordinal number Ω. Transfinite induction may then be used in a manner analogous to that in which finite induction is used in the case of well-ordered sets whose ordinal number is ω.

An attempt will be made to indicate to the student the power of this method.

2. *Existence of a nondenumerable set whose intersection with every nowhere dense set is denumerable*

In order to show that there is such a set we first observe that every nowhere-dense set is a subset of a closed nowhere-dense set, its closure. Hence, we have only to show that there is a nondenumerable set whose intersection with every closed nowhere-dense set is finite or denumerable. Since there are c closed sets, there are at most c closed nowhere-dense sets. But there are at least c closed nowhere-dense sets, since every set consisting of a single point is one. Hence, there are exactly c closed nowhere-dense sets. They may be well-ordered as follows:

$$F_1, F_2, \cdots, F_\alpha, \cdots, \alpha < \Omega.$$

Since F_1 is nowhere dense, there is an $x_1 \notin F_1$. Since F_2 is nowhere dense it follows that $F_1 \cup F_2$ is nowhere dense, so that there is $x_2 \neq x_1$ such that

$x_2 \notin F_1 \cup F_2$. Suppose $\alpha < \Omega$ and that for every $\beta < \alpha$ there is an $x_\beta \notin \bigcup_{\gamma \leqq \beta} F_\gamma$. Then since the set of ordinals $\beta \leqq \alpha$ is denumerable the set $\bigcup_{\beta \leqq \alpha} F_\beta$ is of the first category. Accordingly,

$$\left(\bigcup_{\beta \leqq \alpha} F_\beta\right) \cup \left(\bigcup_{\beta < \alpha} \{x_\beta\}\right)$$

is of the first category, so that there is an $x_\alpha \neq x_\beta$ for every $\beta < \alpha$ such that $x_\alpha \notin \bigcup_{\beta \leqq \alpha} F_\beta$. We thus have, by transfinite induction, a set x_α, $\alpha < \Omega$ of distinct real numbers. This set is nondenumerable. Consider any closed nowhere-dense set. It is an F_α for some $\alpha < \Omega$. The only x_β, $\beta < \Omega$, which can be in F_α are those for which $\beta < \alpha$. Hence our set intersects every closed nowhere-dense set in a finite or denumerable set.

We have thus proved the following theorem.

THEOREM 1. There is a nondenumerable set whose intersection with every nowhere-dense set is finite or denumerable.

COROLLARY 1. There is a nondenumerable set whose intersection with every set of the first category is finite or denumerable.

Proof. The proof follows from Theorem 1 since every set of the first category is the union of a denumerable number of nowhere-dense sets.

COROLLARY 2. There is a set of the second category which contains no nondenumerable set of the first category.

The proof is left for the student.

3. *Existence of a function which is discontinuous on every nondenumerable set relative to the set*

In order to show that there is such a function we need some preliminary lemmas.

LEMMA 1. If $f(x)$ is continuous on a set S relative to S then $f(x)$ may be extended to a function $\phi(x)$ on the closure $\bar{S}$ of S such that $\phi(x)$ is upper-semicontinuous on $\bar{S}$ relative to $\bar{S}$ and $\phi(x) = f(x)$ on S.

Proof. For every interval I, let

$$\phi(f; I) = \sup\,[f(x) \mid x \in S \cap I]$$

if $S \cap I$ is not empty. $\phi(f; I)$ is undefined if $S \cap I = \phi$. For every $x \in \bar{S}$ let

$$\phi(x) = \lim_{n \to \infty} \left\{\sup\left[\phi(f; I) \mid x \in I,\, l(I) < \frac{1}{n}\right]\right\},$$

where $l(I)$ is the length of I.

We leave it for the student to show that $\phi(x)$ has the asserted properties.

LEMMA 2. If $f(x)$ is continuous on a set S relative to S then $f(x)$ may be extended to a Baire function $\phi(x)$ defined for all real numbers such that $\phi(x) = f(x)$ on S.

Proof. By Lemma 1, $f(x)$ may be extended to an upper-semicontinuous function $\psi(x)$ defined on $\bar{S}$ such that $\psi(x) = f(x)$ on S. Let $\phi(x) = \psi(x)$ on $\bar{S}$ and $\phi(x) = 0$ on $C(\bar{S})$. The student may readily verify that for every real k the set $E[\phi(x) \geqq k]$ is a Borel set. Hence by Theorem 6, Chapter 11, $\phi(x)$ is a Baire function.

Now Lemma 2 says that if $f(x)$ is continuous on a set S relative to S there is a Baire function defined everywhere which agrees with $f(x)$ on S. Our problem accordingly takes the following form: Show that there is a function $f(x)$ which does not agree with any Baire function on any nondenumerable set. Such a function $f(x)$ will not be continuous on any nondenumerable set relative to the set.

We showed in Chapter 11 that the Baire functions are c in number. They may be well-ordered as follows:

$$f_1(x), f_2(x), \cdots, f_\alpha(x), \cdots, \alpha < \Omega,$$

and the real numbers may be ordered as follows:

$$x_1, x_2, \cdots, x_\alpha, \cdots, \alpha < \Omega.$$

For every $\alpha < \Omega$, let

$$E_\alpha = [f_\beta(x_\alpha) \mid \beta \leqq \alpha].$$

Since $\alpha < \Omega$ has a finite or denumerable cardinal number, the set E_α is finite or denumerable. We may, accordingly, define a function $f(x)$ such that $f(x_\alpha) \notin E_\alpha$ for every $\alpha < \Omega$.

Now consider any $f_\beta(x)$, $\beta < \Omega$. If $\alpha > \beta$, then $f(x_\alpha) \neq f_\beta(x_\alpha)$. For $f(x_\alpha) \notin E_\alpha$, while $f_\beta(x_\alpha) \in E_\alpha$, since $\beta \leqq \alpha$. In other words, $f(x)$ and $f_\beta(x)$ agree on an at most denumerable set. This proves the theorem.

THEOREM 2. There is a function $f(x)$ which has a point of discontinuity on every nondenumerable set relative to the set.

This theorem has the following corollary.

COROLLARY 3. There is a function $f(x)$ whose points of continuity on any set relative to the set form a denumerable set.

Proof. Let $f(x)$ be the function of Theorem 2. If there were a set S such that the set $T \subset S$ of points of continuity of $f(x)$ relative to S were nondenumerable, then T would be a nondenumerable set with $f(x)$ continuous on T relative to T.

4. *Existence of a sequence of functions which converges on a nondenumerable set but converges uniformly on none of its nondenumerable subsets*

This result contrasts with the result of Youngs given in Chapter 8 that every sequence of functions which converges on a nondenumerable set converges uniformly on an infinite subset.

Let S be a nondenumerable set whose intersection with every nowhere-dense set is finite or denumerable. Theorem 1 shows the existence of such sets. The set $C(S)$ must be everywhere dense and, accordingly, it contains a denumerable subset $D = \{x_1, x_2, \cdots, x_n, \cdots\}$ which is everywhere dense. Define a function $f(x)$ as follows:

$$\begin{aligned} f(x) &= \frac{1}{n} \qquad x = x_n,\ n = 1, 2, \cdots \\ &= 0 \qquad x \in C(D). \end{aligned}$$

This function $f(x)$ is of Baire class 1. Let $\{f_n(x)\}$ be any sequence of continuous functions which converges to $f(x)$.

Moreover, if T is a nondenumerable subset of S then T is everywhere dense in some interval; for otherwise, S would contain a nondenumerable nowhere-dense set. Suppose $\{f_n(x)\}$ converges uniformly on a nondenumerable subset $T \subset S$. Then $\{f_n(x)\}$ converges uniformly on a set which is everywhere dense in some interval I. But, as in the proof of Theorem 5, Chapter 8, if a sequence of continuous functions converges uniformly on a set everywhere dense in an interval, then it converges uniformly on the interval. This proves that $f(x)$, as the limit of a uniformly convergent sequence of functions, is continuous on I. But $f(x)$ is discontinuous at every x_n and, since D is everywhere dense, there is an $x_n \in I$. We have thus proved our theorem.

THEOREM 3. There is a nondenumerable set S and a sequence $\{f_n(x)\}$ of continuous functions which converges on S but does not converge uniformly on any nondenumerable subset of S.

5. *Decomposition of the plane into a denumerable number of curves*

By a curve we shall understand, in this connection, either the points $(x, f(x))$ for a function $y = f(x)$ or the points $(f(y), y)$ for a function $x = f(y)$.

We may well-order the real numbers as follows:

$$x_1, x_2, \cdots, x_\alpha, \cdots, \alpha < \Omega.$$

The plane consists of all pairs (x_α, x_β), $\alpha < \Omega$, $\beta < \Omega$. Let

$$(x_\alpha, x_\beta) \in S \text{ if } \alpha \leqq \beta, \text{ and}$$

$$(x_\alpha, x_\beta) \in C(S) \text{ if } \beta < \alpha.$$

Then for every $\alpha < \Omega$ there are only a finite or denumerable number of points $(x_\alpha, x_\beta) \in C(S)$, and a finite or denumerable number of points $(x_\beta, x_\alpha) \in S$. In other words, for each x, the values of y for which $(x, y) \in C(S)$ may be ordered as a sequence $y_1, y_2, \cdots, y_n, \cdots$, where the sequence may be completed in an arbitrary way in case it is finite; and for every y, the values of y for which $(x, y) \in S$ may be ordered similarly as $x_1, x_2, \cdots, x_n, \cdots$. Let $f_n(x) = y_n$ and $\phi_n(y) = x_n$, $n = 1, 2, \cdots$. The curves $y = f_n(x)$ and $x = \phi_n(y)$, $n = 1, 2, \cdots$ cover the plane.

THEOREM 4. The plane may be covered by a denumerable number of curves.

6. *Existence of a function $f(x)$ such that $f(x + y) = f(x) + f(y)$ for every x and y but for which $f(x)$ is not of the form cx*

Of course, such a function will have to be discontinuous. To establish its existence, the continuum hypothesis will not be needed; only the well-ordering theorem will be used.

We first obtain a Hamel basis for the real numbers. By this we mean a set H of real numbers such that

1. every real number is a linear combination with rational coefficients of a finite number of elements of H: i.e., for every real number x there are numbers $x_1, \cdots, x_n$ in H and rational numbers $r_1, \cdots, r_n$ such that

$$x = r_1x_1 + \cdots + r_nx_n.$$

2. no proper subset of H has the property described by (1).

In order to obtain a Hamel basis, we well-order the real numbers:

$$x_1, x_2, \cdots, x_\alpha, \cdots \alpha < \Omega.$$

Let $x_1 \in H$ if $x_1 \neq 0$. Otherwise, let $x_2 \in H$. For a given α, suppose for every $\beta < \alpha$ that the decision has been made whether or not $x_\beta \in H$. Then $x_\alpha \in H$ if and only if x_α is not a linear combination with rational coefficients of any finite number of those x_β, $\beta < \alpha$, which are in H. By transfinite induction, the set H is defined.

We show that H is a Hamel basis. Consider any x_α. Either $x_\alpha \in H$ or else x_α is a linear combination with rational coefficients of a finite number of elements $x_{\alpha_1}, \cdots, x_{\alpha_n}$ in H where $\alpha_1 < \alpha, \cdots, \alpha_n < \alpha$. Hence H satisfies condition (1) for a Hamel basis. Next, let H' be a proper subset of H. There is then an $x_\alpha \in H - H'$. x_α is not a linear combination with rational coefficients of any finite number of elements of H'. For suppose $x_\alpha = r_1 x_{\alpha_1} + \cdots + r_n x_{\alpha_n}$, where $x_{\alpha_1} \in H', \cdots, x_{\alpha_n} \in H'$. If all $\alpha_k < \alpha$ then x_α would not be in H. If some $\alpha_k > \alpha$ then x_{α_k} as a linear combination of a finite number of members of H which precede it would not be in H.

We show next that every real number x has a unique representation

$$x = r_1 x_{\alpha_1} + \cdots + r_n x_{\alpha_n}$$

in terms of elements of H. For, suppose also that

$$x = s_1 x_{\beta_1} + \cdots + s_m x_{\beta_m}.$$

Then, by subtracting, we obtain

$$0 = t_1 x_{\gamma_1} + \cdots + t_k x_{\gamma_k}.$$

But $t_j = 0, j = 1, 2, \cdots, k$. For otherwise, one of the x_{γ_j} would be a linear combination of the others so that a proper subset of H would satisfy condition (1) for a basis. This shows that $n = m$ and $r_1 = s_1, \cdots r_n = s_n$; $\alpha_1 = \beta_1, \cdots, \alpha_n = \beta_n$.

We now observe that if $f(x)$ is defined arbitrarily on H and if for every x,

$$x = r_1 x_{\alpha_1} + \cdots + r_n x_{\alpha_n},$$

we define $f(x)$ by

$$f(x) = r_1 f(x_{\alpha_1}) + \cdots + r_n f(x_{\alpha_n}),$$

the function $f(x)$ has the property

$$f(x+y) = f(x) + f(y).$$

Now if $f(x_{\alpha_1}) = 1$ and $f(x_{\alpha_2}) = 0$, the function $f(x)$ cannot be of the form cx; but, as was just demonstrated, there is an $f(x)$ for which $f(x+y) = f(x) + f(y)$ for every x and y while $f(x_{\alpha_1}) = 1$ and $f(x_{\alpha_2}) = 0$.

Exercises

2.1 Show that every nondenumerable set may be decomposed into a nondenumerable number of disjoint nondenumerable sets.

2.2 Show that there is a set of the second category which contains no nondenumerable set of the first category.

3.1 Show that if $f(x)$ is continuous on S relative to S then if

$$\phi(f; I) = \sup [f(x) \mid x \in S \cap I]$$

if $S \cap I \neq \phi$,

$$\phi(x) = \lim_{n \to \infty} \left\{ \sup \left[\phi(f; I) \mid x \in I, l(I) < \frac{1}{n} \right] \right\}$$

is an upper-semicontinuous extension of $f(x)$ to the closed set $\bar{S}$.

3.2 Show that there is a function which is not a Baire function on any nondenumerable set relative to the set.

4.1 Show that if S is any set and $D = \{x_1, x_2, \cdots\}$ is a denumerable subset of S then $f(x) = 1/n$, $x \in D$, $f(x) = 0$, $x \in S - D$, is of Baire class 1 on S relative to S.

4.2 Show that if $\{f_n(x)\}$ is a sequence of continuous functions which converge uniformly on a set everywhere dense in an interval I then it converges uniformly on I.

5.1 Show that there is a nondenumerable set in the plane which has at most two points on any line.

6.1 Show that if $f(x)$ is continuous and such that $f(x + y) = f(x) + f(y)$ then $f(x)$ has the form cx.

6.2 Show that if for every $\alpha < \Omega$ there is a closed set F_α and if $\alpha < \beta < \Omega$ implies $F_\alpha \subset F_\beta$ then there is an $\alpha < \Omega$ such that $F_\beta = F_\alpha$ if $\alpha < \beta < \Omega$.

References

E. KAMKE, *Theory of Sets*, translated by F. Bagemihl, New York, 1950, Chap. 4, §12.

W. SIERPINSKI, *Hypothèse du continu*, Warszawa-Lwow, 1934.

13

Measure and Measurable Sets

1. *What is measure?*

Measure is a generalization of length. The measure of an interval, open, closed, or semiopen, is its length. In the preceding chapters we have been interested, however, in a variety of sets which are not intervals: open sets, closed sets, sets of type F_σ, Borel sets. It is natural to ask whether the notion of length (called *measure* for sets which are not intervals) can be extended to include such sets.

In this chapter we obtain such an extension, the *Lebesgue measure*. The Lebesgue measure applies to a wide class of sets, called the Lebesgue measurable sets. For example, every Borel set is a Lebesgue measurable set.

Now, there are certain conditions which any extension of length might be expected to obey. We shall enumerate such conditions. Later we shall show that the Lebesgue measure satisfies all of these conditions.

For convenience, measure will be defined only for subsets of the closed interval $U = [0, 1]$. When we speak of open sets, closed sets, sets of type F_σ, complements of sets, etc., we shall always mean "relative to U." Thus the semiopen intervals $[0, x)$ and $(x, 1]$ are open sets for every $0 < x < 1$.

Suppose now that we have a class M of sets, called the *measurable sets*, and for every set $S \in \mathsf{M}$ a number $\mu(S)$ called the *measure of* S. Conditions one might expect M and $\mu(S)$ to satisfy are the following:

1. For every $S \in \mathsf{M}$, $\mu(S) \geqq 0$.
2. If S is an interval, then $S \in \mathsf{M}$ and $\mu(S)$ is the length of S.
3. For every $S \in \mathsf{M}$ and $T \in \mathsf{M}$ such that $S \subset T$ we have $\mu(S) \leqq \mu(T)$.
4. For every $S \in \mathsf{M}$ we have $C(S) \in \mathsf{M}$ and $\mu(S) + \mu(C(S)) = 1$.
5. If $\{S_n\}$ is a sequence of sets such that $S_n \in \mathsf{M}$ for $n = 1, 2, \cdots$, and if $S = \bigcup_{n=1}^{\infty} S_n$, then $S \in \mathsf{M}$. Moreover, if the sets $S_1, S_2, \cdots, S_n, \cdots$ are

disjoint then

$$\mu(S) = \sum_{n=1}^{\infty} \mu(S_n).$$

6. If $S \in \mathsf{M}$ and $T = S + x = [y + x \mid y \in S]$, then $T \in \mathsf{M}$ and $\mu(T) = \mu(S)$. (Note: If $y \in S$ and $y + x > 1$, consider the number $y + x - 1$ instead of $y + x$.)

The properties listed above are not meant to be independent. Indeed, the student can readily verify that property 3 follows from the others.

By condition (1), $\mu(S)$ is a nonnegative set function. A set function which satisfies condition (5) is called *completely additive*, and one which satisfies condition (6) is called *invariant*, an invariant measure being one that is unchanged by translations.

2. *Definition of Lebesgue measure*

In defining the class of Lebesgue measurable sets and the Lebesgue measure of the sets in the class, it is convenient to start out by associating a nonnegative number, $m_e(S)$, with every set S. The number $m_e(S)$ will be called the *exterior measure of* S. In order to satisfy the conditions listed above, the set function $m_e(S)$ will then have to have its domain of definition restricted. The restricted domain of sets will be the Lebesgue measurable sets and the exterior measure $m_e(S)$ will be called the *Lebesgue measure* $m(S)$ for such sets. Lebesgue measure satisfies conditions 1–6. Exterior measure does not satisfy conditions (4) or (5).

In order to define exterior measure, we first associate a number, $L(G)$, with every open set G.

DEFINITION 1. For an open set G, the number $L(G)$ is the sum of the lengths of the component open intervals of G.

PROPOSITION 1. For every open set G, $L(G) \leqq 1$.

Proof. $G = \bigcup_{n=1}^{\infty} I_n$ where the intervals $I_1, I_2, \cdots, I_n, \cdots$ are disjoint and open. $L(G) = \sum_{n=1}^{\infty} l(I_n)$, where $l(I_n)$ is the length of I_n. But for every n, $\sum_{k=1}^{n} l(I_k) \leqq 1$, since $I_1, I_2, \cdots, I_n$ are disjoint intervals in $U = [0, 1]$. Hence, also, $L(G) \leqq 1$.

DEFINITION 2. For every set S, the number

$$m_e(S) = \inf [L(G) \mid G \supset S],$$

where G varies over all open sets containing S, is called the *exterior measure of* S.

PROPOSITION 2. Every set S has a unique exterior measure $m_e(S)$, and $0 \leqq m_e(S) \leqq 1$.

Proof. The uniqueness of the exterior measure and the fact that $0 \leqq m_e(S)$ are immediate consequences of the definition. Since $S \subset U$, U is open (recall that closed and open sets are defined relative to U), and $L(U) = 1$, $m_e(S) \leqq 1$.

PROPOSITION 3. If G is an open set, then $m_e(G) = L(G)$.

Proof. Let $H \supset G$ be an open set. Then every component of G is contained in a component of H. But $G \supset G$ is an open set. Hence, $\inf [L(H) \mid H \supset G] = L(G)$. Thus $m_e(G) = L(G)$.

We shall interchange the notations $L(G)$ and $m_e(G)$ according to expediency.

In order to define measurable sets we associate another number with every set S called the *interior measure of* S and designated by $m_i(S)$.

DEFINITION 3. For every set S the *interior measure of* S is the number

$$m_i(S) = 1 - m_e(C(S)).$$

DEFINITION 4. S is said to be *measurable* if $m_e(S) = m_i(S)$.

DEFINITION 5. If S is measurable, the number

$$m(S) = m_e(S) = m_i(S)$$

is called the *Lebesgue measure of* S.

We now obtain some simple properties of exterior measure and measure. We first state a lemma.

LEMMA 1. If $I_1, I_2, \cdots, I_n$ is a finite number of open intervals which cover U, the sum, $\sum_{k=1}^{n} l(I_k)$, of their lengths is not less than 1.

The proof is left to the student.

PROPOSITION 4. For every S, $m_e(S) + m_e(C(S)) \geqq 1$.

Proof. Let G and H be open sets such that $S \subset G$ and $C(S) \subset H$. Let $I_1, I_2, \cdots, I_n, \cdots$ be the components of G and $J_1, J_2, \cdots, J_n, \cdots$ the components of H. Since every $x \in U$ is either in S or in $C(S)$, the open intervals $I_1, I_2, \cdots, I_n, \cdots$ and $J_1, J_2, \cdots, J_n, \cdots$ cover U. But U is a bounded closed set. Hence, by the Borel Covering Theorem, a finite number of these intervals, say $I_{k_1}, I_{k_2}, \cdots, I_{k_m}$ and $J_{l_1}, J_{l_2}, \cdots, J_{l_n}$ cover U. By Lemma 1, the sum

$$\sum_{i=1}^{m} l(I_{k_i}) + \sum_{j=1}^{n} l(J_{l_j})$$

of the lengths of these intervals is not less than 1. But $L(G) \geqq \sum_{i=1}^{m} l(I_{k_i})$ and $L(H) \geqq \sum_{j=1}^{n} l(\mathcal{J}_{l_j})$. Hence $L(G) + L(H) \geqq 1$. We now have

$$\begin{aligned} m_e(S) + m_e(C(S)) &= \inf [L(G) \mid G \supset S] + \inf [L(H) \mid H \supset C(S)] \\ &= \inf [L(G) + L(H) \mid G \supset S, H \supset C(S)] \geqq 1. \end{aligned}$$

PROPOSITION 5. S is measurable if and only if $m_e(S) + m_e(C(S)) = 1$.

Proof. Suppose S is measurable. Then, since $m_e(S) = m_i(S)$ and $m_i(S) = 1 - m_e(C(S))$ it follows that $m_e(S) + m_e(C(S)) = 1$.

Suppose $m_e(S) + m_e(C(S)) = 1$. Then $m_e(S) = 1 - m_e(C(S)) = m_i(S)$, so that S is measurable.

COROLLARY 1. S is nonmeasurable if and only if $m_e(S) + m_e(C(S)) > 1$.

Proof. By Propositions 4 and 5.

Proposition 5 and its corollary show that exterior measure satisfies the condition (4) for a measure on the class of measurable sets and on no larger class of sets.

PROPOSITION 6. If S is measurable then $C(S)$ is measurable.

Proof. $C(C(S)) = S$. $m_e(C(S)) + m_e(C(C(S))) = m_e(C(S)) + m_e(S) = 1$, since S is measurable. Hence, by Proposition 5, $C(S)$ is measurable.

PROPOSITION 7. If $S \supset T$, then $m_e(S) \geqq m_e(T)$.

The proof is left to the student.

3. *Special measurable sets*

Before proving certain general theorems from which it follows that a large variety of sets are measurable, it will be instructive to prove directly from the definition that certain special sets are measurable. This includes the sets of exterior measure 0, denumerable sets, open sets, and closed sets.

PROPOSITION 8. If $m_e(S) = 0$, then S is measurable.

Proof. By Proposition 2, $m_e(C(S)) \leqq 1$. Hence $m_e(S) + m_e(C(S)) \leqq 1$, so that, by Proposition 4, $m_e(S) + m_e(C(S)) = 1$ and, by Proposition 5, S is measurable.

We have thus shown that the sets of exterior measure 0 are measurable and of measure 0.

Next we show that every denumerable set is of measure 0. We first obtain a lemma.

LEMMA 2. If $\mathcal{J}_1, \mathcal{J}_2, \cdots, \mathcal{J}_n, \cdots$ are open intervals and the open set $G = \bigcup_{n=1}^{\infty} \mathcal{J}_n$ has components $I_1, I_2, \cdots, I_n, \cdots$ then

$$\sum_{n=1}^{\infty} l(I_n) \leqq \sum_{n=1}^{\infty} l(\mathcal{J}_n).$$

The proof is left to the student.

PROPOSITION 9. Every denumerable set D is of measure 0.

Proof. Since D is denumerable, $D = \{a_1, a_2, \cdots, a_n, \cdots\}$. Let $\epsilon > 0$ and for every n let $\mathcal{J}_n$ be an open interval such that $a_n \in \mathcal{J}_n$ and $l(\mathcal{J}_n) < \epsilon/2^n$. Then

$$D \subset G_\epsilon = \bigcup_{n=1}^{\infty} \mathcal{J}_n.$$

Let $I_1, I_2, \cdots, I_n, \cdots$ be the components of G_ϵ. Then, by Lemma 2,

$$\sum_{n=1}^{\infty} l(I_n) \leqq \sum_{n=1}^{\infty} l(\mathcal{J}_n).$$

Hence

$$L(G_\epsilon) = \sum_{n=1}^{\infty} l(I_n) \leqq \sum_{n=1}^{\infty} l(\mathcal{J}_n) < \epsilon,$$

so that $m_e(D) = \inf [L(G) \mid D \subset G] < \epsilon$. Accordingly, $m_e(D) = 0$.

As a special case, the set of rational numbers is of measure 0. It is, accordingly, possible for a set of measure 0 to be everywhere dense.

PROPOSITION 10. Every open set G is measurable.

Proof. Let $I_1, I_2, \cdots, I_n, \cdots$ be the components of G. Since the series $\sum_{n=1}^{\infty} l(I_n)$ is convergent, for every $\epsilon > 0$ there is an $n = n(\epsilon)$ such that

$$\sum_{k=n+1}^{\infty} l(I_k) < \frac{\epsilon}{2}.$$

Then

$$\sum_{k=1}^{n} l(I_k) > L(G) - \frac{\epsilon}{2}.$$

Now let $\mathcal{J}_1, \mathcal{J}_2, \cdots, \mathcal{J}_m$ be the intervals in U complementary to $I_1, I_2, \cdots, I_n$. Moreover, let $\mathcal{J}_k'$, $k = 1, \cdots, m$ be an open interval concentric with $\mathcal{J}_k$ such that $l(\mathcal{J}_k') = l(\mathcal{J}_k) + \epsilon/2m$, and let $H = \bigcup_{k=1}^{m} \mathcal{J}_k'$. Then

$$L(H) \leqq \sum_{k=1}^{m} l(\mathcal{J}_k'),$$

and since

$$\sum_{k=1}^{m} l(\mathcal{J}_k) + \sum_{k=1}^{n} l(I_k) = 1,$$

it follows that

$$\sum_{k=1}^{m} l(\mathcal{J}_k') + \sum_{k=1}^{n} l(I_k) < 1 + \epsilon.$$

Thus $L(H) + L(G) < 1 + \epsilon$. But $C(G) \subset H$. Hence $m_e(G) + m_e(C(G)) < 1 + \epsilon$. Since $\epsilon > 0$ is arbitrary, $m_e(G) + m_e(C(G)) = 1$ and, by Proposition 5, G is measurable.

COROLLARY 2. Every closed set F is measurable.

Proof. F is the complement of an open set and so, by Proposition 6, it is measurable.

4. *The structure of a measurable set*

In this section, we show that the measurable sets are those which, in a certain sense, are approximated by a finite set of intervals. This structure of measurable sets allows us to visualize many of their properties. We first state two lemmas.

LEMMA 3. S is measurable if and only if, for every $\epsilon > 0$, there are open sets G and H such that $G \supset S$, $H \supset C(S)$, and $L(G) + L(H) < 1 + \epsilon$.

LEMMA 4. If U is covered by a sequence $I_1, I_2, \cdots, I_n, \cdots$ of open intervals, the sum of whose lengths is less than $1 + \epsilon$, $\epsilon > 0$, then

$$\sum_{i,j=1}^{\infty}{}' \, l(I_i \cap I_j) < \epsilon.$$

(The symbol "$\sum'$" signifies summation over all pairs $i, j = 1, 2, \cdots$, with $i \neq j$.)

The proof of these lemmas is left to the student.

We now state and prove the basic theorem on the structure of measurable sets.

THEOREM 1. S is measurable if and only if, for every $\epsilon > 0$, there is a positive integer $n = n(\epsilon)$ and there are disjoint intervals (open or closed) $I_1, I_2, \cdots, I_n$ such that

$$S = (\bigcup_{k=1}^{n} I_k \cup E_2) - E_1,$$

where E_1 and E_2 have exterior measures less than ϵ.

We prove the theorem for the case where the disjoint intervals are open. The case for which the intervals are closed follows, since a finite set is of measure 0.

Proof. Suppose S is measurable. Let $\epsilon > 0$. Then, by Lemma 3, there are open sets G and H whose components are respectively $I_1, I_2, \cdots, I_n, \cdots$ and

$\mathcal{J}_1, \mathcal{J}_2, \cdots, \mathcal{J}_n, \cdots$ such that $G \supset S$, $H \supset C(S)$, and $L(G) + L(H) < 1 + \epsilon$. By Lemma 4, since $I_1, I_2, \cdots, I_n, \cdots$ and $\mathcal{J}_1, \mathcal{J}_2, \cdots, \mathcal{J}_n, \cdots$ cover U and have length sum less than $1 + \epsilon$,

$$\sum_{i,j=1}^{\infty} l(I_i \cap \mathcal{J}_j) < \epsilon.$$

Since $\sum_{k=1}^{\infty} l(I_k)$ is a convergent series, there is an n such that $\sum_{k=n+1}^{\infty} l(I_k) < \epsilon$. Now

$$S = (\bigcup_{k=1}^{n} I_k \cup E_2) - E_1,$$

where $E_2 \subset \bigcup_{k=n+1}^{\infty} I_k$ and $E_1 \subset \bigcup_{i,j=1}^{\infty} (I_i \cap \mathcal{J}_j)$. That E_1 has exterior measure less than ϵ follows by Lemma 4, and that E_2 has exterior measure less than ϵ is obvious.

Suppose, conversely, that S is such that for every $\epsilon > 0$ there is an $n = n(\epsilon)$ and there are open intervals $I_1, I_2, \cdots, I_n$ and two sets E_1 and E_2 of exterior measure less than ϵ such that

$$S = (\bigcup_{k=1}^{n} I_k \cup E_2) - E_1.$$

Then $C(S) = (\bigcup_{k=1}^{m} \mathcal{J}_k \cup E_1') - E_2'$, where the $\mathcal{J}_k$ are the open intervals complementary to the I_k and E_1', E_2', differ respectively from E_1 and E_2 by finite sets. Now

$$m_e(S) < \sum_{k=1}^{n} l(I_k) + \epsilon$$

and

$$m_e(C(S)) < \sum_{k=1}^{m} l(\mathcal{J}_k) + \epsilon,$$

so that

$$m_e(S) + m_e(C(S)) < \sum_{k=1}^{n} l(I_k) + \sum_{k=1}^{m} l(\mathcal{J}_k) + 2\epsilon = 1 + 2\epsilon.$$

Since this holds for every $\epsilon > 0$, $m_e(S) + m_e(C(S)) = 1$ and so, by Proposition 5, S is measurable.

Another useful theorem which relates measurable sets to more familiar sets is the following one.

THEOREM 2. S is measurable if and only if for every $\epsilon > 0$ there is a closed set $F \subset S$ such that $m(F) > m_e(S) - \epsilon$.

Proof. Suppose S is measurable. Let $\epsilon > 0$. By Lemma 3, there are open sets G and H such that $G \supset S$, $H \supset C(S)$, and $L(G) + L(H) < 1 + \epsilon$. Let $F = C(H)$. Then F, as the complement of an open set, is a closed set. Obviously $F \subset S$. Moreover, $m(H) = L(H)$, $m(G) = L(G)$ and $m(F) + m(H) = 1$. Consequently,

$$m(F) = 1 - m(H) = 1 - L(H) > L(G) - \epsilon \geqq m_e(S) - \epsilon.$$

Suppose, conversely, that for every $\epsilon > 0$ there is a closed set $F \subset S$ such that $m(F) > m_e(S) - \epsilon$. Let $\epsilon > 0$. Then there is a closed set $F_\epsilon \subset S$ such that $m(F_\epsilon) > m_e(S) - \epsilon$. Let $G = C(F_\epsilon)$. Then $G \supset C(S)$. Let H be any open set such that $H \supset S$ and $L(H) < m_e(S) + \epsilon$. Now $m(F_\epsilon) + m(G) = 1$, so that

$$L(H) + L(G) < m_e(S) + m(G) + \epsilon < m(F_\epsilon) + m(G) + 2\epsilon = 1 + 2\epsilon.$$

Since $H \supset S$, $G \supset C(S)$, it follows that $m_e(S) + m_e(C(S)) = 1$ and, accordingly, that S is measurable.

The importance of Theorems 1 and 2 lies in their usefulness in obtaining the main properties of measurable sets. We give these properties in the next section.

5. *Properties of measurable sets*

We now show that the class of Lebesgue measurable sets and the Lebesgue measure $m(S)$ satisfy condition (5) of §1. We first prove two propositions on the exterior measure of sets.

PROPOSITION 11. If $S_1, S_2, \cdots, S_n, \cdots$ is a sequence of sets and $S = \bigcup_{n=1}^{\infty} S_n$ then

$$m_e(S) \leqq \sum_{n=1}^{\infty} m_e(S_n).$$

Proof. Let $\epsilon > 0$. For every n, let $G_n \supset S_n$ be an open set such that $L(G_n) < m_e(S_n) + \epsilon/2^n$. If $G = \bigcup_{n=1}^{\infty} G_n$, then G is an open set such that $G \supset S$ and, by a simple application of Lemma 2, $L(G) \leqq \sum_{n=1}^{\infty} L(G_n)$. Now

$$m_e(S) \leqq L(G) \leqq \sum_{n=1}^{\infty} L(G_n) < \sum_{n=1}^{\infty} m_e(S_n) + \epsilon,$$

for every $\epsilon > 0$, so that the proposition is proved.

LEMMA 5. If $G_1 \subset G_2 \subset \cdots \subset G_n \subset \cdots$ is a nondecreasing sequence of open sets and $G = \bigcup_{n=1}^{\infty} G_n$, then for every $\epsilon > 0$, there is an $n = n(\epsilon)$ such that $m(G) < m(G_n) + \epsilon$.

The proof, which is an exercise in double series of positive terms, is left to the student.

LEMMA 6. If $S \subset T$, $\epsilon_1 > \epsilon_2 > 0$, and there is an open set G such that $S \subset G$ and $L(G) < m_e(S) + \epsilon_2$, then there is an open set H such that $T \subset H$, $G \subset H$, and $L(H) < m_e(T) + \epsilon_1$.

The proof is left to the student.

PROPOSITION 12. If $S_1, S_2, \cdots, S_n, \cdots$ is a sequence of sets, $S = \bigcup_{n=1}^{\infty} S_n$, and $\epsilon > 0$, there is an $n = n(\epsilon)$ such that

$$m_e(S) < m_e(\bigcup_{k=1}^{n} S_k) + \epsilon.$$

Proof. Let $\epsilon_1, \epsilon_2, \cdots, \epsilon_n, \cdots$ be an increasing sequence of positive numbers whose limit is $\epsilon/2$. By repeated application of Lemma 6, there is a non-decreasing sequence $\{G_k\}$ of open sets such that

$$\bigcup_{n=1}^{k} S_n \subset G_k \text{ and } L(G_k) < m_e(\bigcup_{n=1}^{k} S_n) + \epsilon_k$$

for every $k = 1, 2, \cdots$. Let $G = \bigcup_{k=1}^{\infty} G_k$. By Lemma 5, there is an n such that $L(G) < L(G_n) + \epsilon/2$. Now $G \supset \bigcup_{k=1}^{\infty} S_k$. Hence

$$m_e(\bigcup_{k=1}^{\infty} S_k) \leqq L(G) < L(G_n) + \frac{\epsilon}{2} < m_e(\bigcup_{k=1}^{n} S_k) + \epsilon_n + \frac{\epsilon}{2} < m_e(\bigcup_{k=1}^{n} S_k) + \epsilon.$$

The remainder of this section pertains to measurable sets.

PROPOSITION 13. If S_1 and S_2 are measurable, then $S = S_1 \cup S_2$ is measurable.

Proof. Let $\epsilon > 0$. By Theorem 1, there are open intervals $I_1^{(1)}, \cdots, I_{n_1}^{(1)}$ and $I_1^{(2)}, \cdots, I_{n_2}^{(2)}$, and sets $E_1^{(1)}$, $E_2^{(1)}$, $E_1^{(2)}$, and $E_2^{(2)}$ of exterior measure less than $\epsilon/2$ such that

$$S_i = (\bigcup_{k=1}^{n_i} I_k^{(i)} \cup E_2^{(i)}) - E_1^{(i)}, \; i = 1, 2.$$

Then

$$S = ((\bigcup_{k=1}^{n_1} I_k^{(1)}) \cup (\bigcup_{k=1}^{n_2} I_k^{(2)}) \cup E_2) - E_1,$$

where $E_1 \subset E_1^{(1)} \cup E_1^{(2)}$ and $E_2 \subset E_2^{(1)} \cup E_2^{(2)}$. By Proposition 11, E_1 and E_2 are of exterior measure less than ϵ. Since $\epsilon > 0$ is arbitrary, Theorem 1 shows that S is measurable.

By finite induction, if $S_1, S_2, \cdots, S_n$ is a finite number of measurable sets, then $S = \bigcup_{k=1}^{n} S_k$ is measurable.

THEOREM 3. If $S_1, S_2, \cdots, S_n, \cdots$ is a denumerable number of measurable sets, then $S = \bigcup_{n=1}^{\infty} S_n$ is measurable.

Proof. Let $\epsilon > 0$. By Proposition 12, there is an n such that

$$m_e(S) < m_e\left(\bigcup_{k=1}^{n} S_k\right) + \frac{\epsilon}{2}.$$

By Proposition 13, the set $\bigcup_{k=1}^{n} S_k$ is measurable. Hence, by Theorem 2, there is a closed set $F \subset \bigcup_{k=1}^{n} S_k$ such that

$$m(F) > m\left(\bigcup_{k=1}^{n} S_k\right) - \frac{\epsilon}{2}.$$

Therefore, $m(F) > m_e(S) - \epsilon$ and, since $\epsilon > 0$ is arbitrary, Theorem 2 asserts that S is measurable.

We proceed to show that the measure of the union of a denumerable number of disjoint measurable sets is equal to the sum of their measures. We need several auxiliary propositions.

PROPOSITION 14. If S_1 and S_2 are disjoint sets such that the distance between them $\delta(S_1, S_2) > 0$, where

$$\delta(S_1, S_2) = \inf\,[|x - y| \mid x \in S_1, y \in S_2],$$

and if $S = S_1 \cup S_2$, then

$$m_e(S) = m_e(S_1) + m_e(S_2).$$

Proof. Let $\delta = \delta(S_1, S_2)$. Enclose each $x \in S_1$ in an open interval I_x of length less than $\delta/2$ and each point $y \in S_2$ in an open interval J_y of length less than $\delta/2$. Then $G_1 = \bigcup_{x \in S_1} I_x$ and $G_2 = \bigcup_{y \in S_2} J_y$ are open sets such that $S_1 \subset G_1$ and $S_2 \subset G_2$. Moreover, $G_1 \cap G_2 = \phi$. Now let $\epsilon > 0$, and let H be an open set such that $H \supset S$ and $L(H) < m_e(S) + \epsilon$. Let $H_1 = H \cap G_1$ and $H_2 = H \cap G_2$. Then $H_1 \supset S_1$ and $H_2 \supset S_2$. Now

$$m_e(S) > L(H) - \epsilon \geqq L(H_1) + L(H_2) - \epsilon \geqq m_e(S_1) + m_e(S_2) - \epsilon,$$

so that $m_e(S) \geqq m_e(S_1) + m_e(S_2)$. But, by Proposition 11, $m_e(S) \leqq m_e(S_1) + m_e(S_2)$, so that Proposition 14 is proved.

COROLLARY 3. If F_1 and F_2 are disjoint closed sets and if $F = F_1 \cup F_2$, then $m(F) = m(F_1) + m(F_2)$.

Proof. By Exercise 2.1, Chapter 5, $\delta(F_1, F_2) > 0$.

PROPOSITION 15. If S_1 and S_2 are disjoint measurable sets and if $S = S_1 \cup S_2$ then

$$m(S) = m(S_1) + m(S_2).$$

Proof. Let $\epsilon > 0$. By Theorem 2, there are closed sets F_1 and F_2 such that $F_1 \subset S_1$, $F_2 \subset S_2$ and $m(F_1) > m(S_1) - \epsilon/2$, $m(F_2) > m(S_2) - \epsilon/2$. But F_1 and F_2 are disjoint and $F = F_1 \cup F_2 \subset S$. Hence, by Corollary 3, we have

$$m(S_1) + m(S_2) < m(F) + \epsilon \leqq m(S) + \epsilon.$$

Since this holds for every $\epsilon > 0$, $m(S) \geqq m(S_1) + m(S_2)$. But, by Proposition 11, $m(S) \leqq m(S_1) + m(S_2)$, and the proposition is proved.

By finite induction, if $S_1, S_2, \cdots, S_n$ are disjoint measurable sets and $S = \bigcup_{k=1}^{n} S_k$, then

$$m(S) = \sum_{k=1}^{n} m(S_k).$$

We are now ready to prove the theorem.

THEOREM 4. If $S_1, S_2, \cdots, S_n, \cdots$ is a denumerable number of disjoint measurable sets and $S = \bigcup_{n=1}^{\infty} S_n$, then

$$m(S) = \sum_{n=1}^{\infty} m(S_n).$$

Proof, For every n, let $\phi_n = \sum_{k=1}^{n} m(S_k)$. By Proposition 15,

$$\phi_n = m(\bigcup_{k=1}^{n} S_k)$$

and $\bigcup_{k=1}^{n} S_k \subset U$, so that, by Proposition 7, $\phi_n \leqq 1$. But

$$\bigcup_{k=1}^{n+1} S_k \supset \bigcup_{k=1}^{n} S_k,$$

so that, again by Proposition 7, $\phi_{n+1} \geqq \phi_n$. The sequence $\{\phi_n\}$ is nondecreasing and bounded above so that it converges. Let $\phi = \lim_{n \to \infty} \phi_n$. Then $\phi \leqq 1$. Moreover, $\phi = \sum_{k=1}^{\infty} m(S_k)$.

Now, let $\epsilon > 0$. There is an $n = n(\epsilon)$ such that

$$\sum_{k=1}^{n} m(S_k) > \phi - \epsilon.$$

It follows that

$$m(S) \geqq m(\bigcup_{k=1}^{n} S_k) = \sum_{k=1}^{n} m(S_k) > \phi - \epsilon.$$

But $\epsilon > 0$ is arbitrary, so that

$$m(S) \geqq \phi = \sum_{n=1}^{\infty} m(S_n).$$

But, by Proposition 11,

$$m(S) \leqq \sum_{n=1}^{\infty} m(S_n).$$

Hence

$$m(S) = \sum_{n=1}^{\infty} m(S_n).$$

The above theorems on unions of measurable sets have their analogues in theorems on intersections of measurable sets.

THEOREM 5. If $S_1, S_2, \cdots, S_n, \cdots$ is a denumerable number of measurable sets and $S = \bigcap_{n=1}^{\infty} S_n$, then S is measurable.

THEOREM 6. If $S_1, S_2, \cdots, S_n, \cdots$ is a nonincreasing sequence of measurable sets and $S = \bigcap_{n=1}^{\infty} S_n$, then

$$m(S) = \lim_{n \to \infty} m(S_n).$$

Using the facts about complements of measurable sets, these theorems are simple consequences of Theorems 3 and 4.

THEOREM 7. All Borel sets are measurable.

Proof. The closed and open sets are measurable. Let $\alpha < \Omega$ and suppose for every $\beta < \alpha$ every set of type F_β and of type G_β is measurable. By Theorems 3 and 5 every set of type F_α and of type G_α is measurable. The theorem follows by transfinite induction.

Conversely, if sets of measure 0 are neglected, the Borel sets are all the measurable sets. Indeed, we have the following propositions.

PROPOSITION 16. If S is measurable, there is a set T of type F_1 such that $T \subset S$ and $m(T) = m(S)$.

Proof. Let T_n be a closed subset of S such that $m(T_n) > m(S) - 1/n$. The set

$$T = \bigcup_{n=1}^{\infty} T_n$$

has the desired properties.

PROPOSITION 17. If S is measurable, there is a set T of type G_1 such that $T \supset S$ and $m(T) = m(S)$.

The proof is left to the student.

6. *Nonmeasurable sets*

We now show that there are sets which are not measurable. We first prove this using the continuum hypothesis and well-ordering theorem.

We then give a second proof without using these methods. Even the second proof given is an existence proof—no example of a nonmeasurable set has ever been given.

We first prove a lemma.

LEMMA 7. If S is measurable then either S or $C(S)$ has a nonempty perfect subset.

Proof. Either S or $C(S)$ is of positive measure; say, $m(S) = k > 0$. There is a closed set $F \subset S$ such that $m(F) > k/2$. Now by Theorem 3, Chapter 5, $F = P \cup D$, where P is perfect and D is denumerable. By Proposition 9, $m(D) = 0$, so that $m(P) > k/2$. Hence $P \subset S$ is a nonempty perfect set.

PROPOSITION 18. There exist nonmeasurable sets.

Proof. This proof makes use of the well-ordering theorem and the continuum hypothesis. There are exactly c perfect sets. They may be well-ordered as follows:

$$P_1, P_2, \cdots, P_\alpha, \cdots, \alpha < \Omega.$$

We obtain a set S in the following way. Suppose $x_1 \in P_1$, $y_1 \in P_1$, $x_1 \neq y_1$. Put $x_1 \in S$, $y_1 \in C(S)$. Let $\alpha < \Omega$. Suppose for every $\beta < \alpha$ we already have chosen x_β, y_β. There are x_α, $y_\alpha \in P_\alpha$, $x_\alpha \neq y_\alpha$, such that $x_\alpha \neq x_\beta$, y_β and $y_\alpha \neq x_\beta, y_\beta$ for every $\beta < \alpha$. Put $x_\alpha \in S$, $y_\alpha \in C(S)$. By transfinite induction we obtain x_α, y_α, for every $\alpha < \Omega$. Let

$$S = [x_\alpha \mid \alpha < \Omega].$$

Every nonempty perfect set has at least one point in S and at least one point in $C(S)$. Hence, by Lemma 7, S is nonmeasurable.

The class of Lebesgue measurable sets, accordingly, does not include all sets.

Our second proof of the existence of nonmeasurable sets shows more. In fact, it shows that there is no set function defined for all sets which satisfies all the conditions of §1.

Let ξ be an irrational number. In terms of ξ, we obtain a subdivision of the interval $I = (0 \leqq x < 1)$ into a denumerable number of sets, each a translation of every other one. (In this discussion, every real number will be identified with the number of its residue class modulo 1 which is in I.)

Associate with every real number x the denumerable set

$$S_x = \{\cdots, x - 2\xi, x - \xi, x, x + \xi, x + 2\xi, \cdots\}.$$

We show first that for every x and y, S_x and S_y are either identical or disjoint. For suppose S_x and S_y are not disjoint. Then there is a $z \in S_x \cap S_y$. Let $w \in S_x$. Then $z = x + n\xi$, $z = y + m\xi$, and $w = x + l\xi$, where n, m, and l are integers. It follows that

$$w = x + l\xi = z + (l - n)\xi = y + (l - n + m)\xi,$$

so that $w \in S_y$. We accordingly have a decomposition of I into disjoint denumerable sets S_x.

We now define a set S consisting of one and only one element from each of the sets S_x. Moreover, for every integer m, let

$$S(m) = S + m\xi = [x + m\xi \mid x \in S].$$

The sets $S(m)$ are a denumerable number of translations of S.

We prove two things. First, that every z is in an $S(m)$, and then that it is in only one $S(m)$.

Now $z \in S_x$ for one and only one $x \in S$. Hence $z = x + m\xi$ for some m so that $z \in S(m)$.

Suppose $z \in S_n$. Then $z = y + n\xi$, $y \in S$. It follows that $x + m\xi = y + n\xi$. Hence $x - y = (n - m)\xi$. But this means that $y \in S_x$, so that $S_y = S_x$. Since S has only one element from each S_x, this shows that $y = x$. But then $(n - m)\xi = 0$, so that $n = m$.

We have now shown that the sets $S(m) = S_m$ are disjoint translations of S such that

$$I = \bigcup_{m=-\infty}^{\infty} S_m.$$

Suppose $\mu(T)$ is a measure, satisfying conditions 1–6 of §1, which is defined for all sets. What can the measure $\mu(S(0))$ of $S = S(0)$ be?

Suppose $\mu(S(0)) = 0$. Then by condition (6), $\mu(S(n)) = 0$ for every integer n. Since

$$I = \bigcup_{n=-\infty}^{\infty} S_n,$$

by condition (5), $\mu(I) = 0$, so that condition (2) is violated.

Suppose $\mu(S(0)) = k > 0$. Let $n > 1/k$. Then, by conditions (5) and (6),

$$\mu\left(\bigcup_{i=1}^{n} S_i\right) > 1.$$

But

$$\bigcup_{i=1}^{n} S_i \subset I$$

and, by conditions (2) and (3),

$$\mu\left(\bigcup_{i=1}^{n} S_i\right) \leqq 1,$$

in contradiction.

Hence $\mu(S(0))$ cannot be greater than 0, nor can it be equal to 0. Moreover, by condition (1), it cannot be less than 0. Hence any measure which satisfies conditions 1–6 cannot be defined for all subsets of I.

Exercises

1.1 Prove that condition (3) for a measure function follows from the other conditions.

1.2 A weaker property than condition (5) is the property of *finite additivity:*

5′: If $S_1, S_2, \cdots, S_n$ is a finite number of sets all in M and if $S = \bigcup_{k=1}^{n} S_k$ then $S \in \mathsf{M}$, and if the sets $S_1, S_2, \cdots, S_n$ are disjoint then

$$\mu(S) = \sum_{k=1}^{n} \mu(S_k).$$

Give an example of a set function which satisfies (1), (2), (3), (4), (5′), and (6), but not (5).

1.3 Show that there is no measure in Hilbert space having properties 1–6 for which all spheres have positive measure.

2.1 Show that every closed interval is measurable and that the measure is the length of the interval by direct use of the definition.

2.2 Show that every closed set is measurable by direct use of the definition.

2.3 Show that a set S is measurable if and only if, for every T,

$$m_e(T) = m_e(S \cap T) + m_e(C(S) \cap T).$$

2.4 Show that if $I_1, I_2, \cdots, I_n$ is a finite number of open intervals which cover U, the sum $\sum_{k=1}^{n} l(I_k)$ of their lengths is not less than 1.

2.5 Show that if $S \supset T$ then $m_e(S) \geqq m_e(T)$.

2.6 Show that if S and T are bounded sets of real numbers and if $S \oplus T$ is the set of all $x + y$, $x \in S$, $y \in T$ then $\inf S \oplus T = \inf S + \inf T$.

2.7 For S and T measurable, let $S \sim T$ if $(S - T) \cup (T - S)$ is of measure 0. Show that this is an equivalence relation.

2.8 If $\delta(S, T) = m((S - T) \cup (T - S))$ show that the equivalence classes of measurable sets in Exercise 2.7 form a metric space.

2.9 Show that $m_e(S) = \inf [m(T) \mid S \subset T]$ for all measurable sets containing S.

2.10 For every k, $0 < k < 1$, give an example of a nowhere-dense perfect set in $[0, 1]$ whose measure is k.

3.1 If $J_1, J_2, \cdots, J_n, \cdots$ are open intervals and the open set $G = \bigcup_{n=1}^{\infty} J_n$ has components $I_1, I_2, \cdots, I_n, \cdots$, show that

$$\sum_{n=1}^{\infty} l(I_n) \leqq \sum_{n=1}^{\infty} l(J_n).$$

4.1 Show that S is measurable if and only if, for every $\epsilon > 0$, there are open sets G and H such that $G \supset S$, $H \supset C(S)$, and $L(G) + L(H) < 1 + \epsilon$.

4.2 If U is covered by a sequence $I_1, I_2, \cdots, I_n, \cdots$ of open intervals, the sum of whose lengths is less than $1 + \epsilon$, $\epsilon > 0$, then

$$\sum_{i,j=1}^{\infty}{}' \, l(I_i \cap I_j) < \epsilon.$$

5.1 If $G_1 \subset G_2 \subset \cdots \subset G_n \subset \cdots$ is a nondecreasing sequence of open sets in $[0, 1]$ and $G = \bigcup_{n=1}^{\infty} G_n$, show that for every $\epsilon > 0$ there is an $n = n(\epsilon)$ such that $m(G) < m(G_n) + \epsilon$.

5.2 If $S_1, S_2, \cdots, S_n, \cdots$ are measurable, and $S = \bigcap_{n=1}^{\infty} S_n$, show that S is measurable.

5.3 If $S_1, S_2, \cdots, S_n, \cdots$ are measurable and nonincreasing and $S = \bigcap_{n=1}^{\infty} S_n$, show that $m(S) = \lim_{n \to \infty} m(S_n)$.

5.4 If S and T are measurable, show that $S - T$ is measurable.

5.5 Show that if S is measurable, there is a set T of type G_1 such that $T \supset S$ and $m(T) = m(S)$.

5.6 Show that Lebesgue measure is an invariant measure.

5.7 Show that Lebesgue measure is the only measure on the Borel sets which satisfies conditions 1–6 of §1.

5.8 Define Lebesgue measure for unbounded sets. Hint: as limit of measures of bounded sets.

5.9 Show that closed and open sets—bounded or unbounded—are measurable.

5.10 Show that every measurable set of finite measure satisfies the condition of Theorem 1.

5.11 Show that the converse of Exercise 5.10 holds.

5.12 Show that if $S_1, S_2, \cdots, S_n, \cdots$ is a sequence of disjoint measurable sets of finite measure, and $S = \bigcup_{n=1}^{\infty} S_n$, then if $\sum_{n=1}^{\infty} m(S_n)$ is a convergent series, S has finite measure and $m(S) = \sum_{n=1}^{\infty} m(S_n)$.

6.1 Using the continuum hypothesis, show that there is a set of positive exterior measure whose intersection with every set of measure 0 is finite or denumerable.

References

C. Carathéodory, *Vorlesungen über reelle Funktionen*, Leipzig, 1927, Chap. 5
H. Hahn and A. Rosenthal, *Set Functions*, Albuquerque, 1948, Chap. 2.
P. R. Halmos, *Measure Theory*, New York, 1950, Chap. 2.
H. Kestelman, *Modern Theories of Integration*, Oxford, 1937, Chap. 3.
Ch. J. de la Vallée Poussin, *Intégrales de Lebesgue, Fonctions d'ensembles, Classes de Baire*, Paris, 1934, Chap. 2.
G. Vitali and G. Sansone, *Moderna Teoria delle Funzioni di Variabile Reale*, Bologna, 1935, Chap. 2.

14

Metric Properties of Sets

1. *Introduction*

In this chapter we prove a covering theorem, the Vitali Covering Theorem, which plays a fundamental role in the theory of measure. We have already had one covering theorem, the Borel Covering Theorem, which asserts that every closed set (we again restrict ourselves to subsets of $U = [0, 1]$, so that all sets are bounded) which is covered by a set of open intervals is covered by a finite number of the open intervals in the set. In general, these open intervals will not be disjoint, while for the needs of measure theory it is desirable for them to be disjoint. The Vitali Covering Theorem achieves disjointness of the finite set of covering intervals at the price of further conditions on the initial arbitrary set of covering intervals. The Vitali Covering Theorem will then be used to obtain several important results in the theory of measure.

2. *The Vitali Covering Theorem*

We first define a *covering* in the sense of Vitali.

DEFINITION 1. If S is a measurable set and I is a set of closed intervals, then I is said to cover S in the Vitali sense if for every $x \in S$ and every $\epsilon > 0$ there is an $I \in \mathsf{I}$ such that $l(I) < \epsilon$ and $x \in I$.

Open intervals could be used as the covering intervals in this definition. However, it is more convenient for the applications to work with closed intervals.

THEOREM 1. (Vitali Covering Theorem). If S is a measurable set and I a set of closed intervals in U which covers S in the sense of Vitali, then for every $\epsilon > 0$ there is a finite number of disjoint intervals

$$I_1, I_2, \cdots, I_n$$

in I which covers all of S except for a set whose exterior measure is less than ϵ.

The proof we are giving is the one due to Banach. The bounded character of S will be needed in the proof.

Proof. Choose $I_1 \in \mathsf{I}$ such that, for every $\mathcal{J} \in \mathsf{I}$, $l(I_1) > \frac{1}{2}l(\mathcal{J})$. We have used only the fact that among a bounded set of positive numbers there is always one whose double exceeds all the others.

Choose $I_2 \in \mathsf{I}$ such that $I_1 \cap I_2 = \phi$ and such that for every $\mathcal{J} \in \mathsf{I}$ with $I_1 \cap \mathcal{J} = \phi$, $l(I_2) > \frac{1}{2}l(\mathcal{J})$.

Suppose $I_1, I_2, \cdots, I_{k-1}$ have already been chosen, are disjoint, and are such that for every $i = 1, 2, \cdots, k-1$, $l(I_i) > \frac{1}{2}l(\mathcal{J})$ for every $\mathcal{J} \in \mathsf{I}$ such that

$$\mathcal{J} \cap \left(\bigcup_{j=1}^{i-1} I_j\right) = \phi.$$

Then if there is an $x \in S - \bigcup_{j=1}^{k-1} I_j$, since x is in an arbitrarily small interval $\mathcal{J} \in \mathsf{I}$, there are intervals, $\mathcal{J} \in \mathsf{I}$, such that $\mathcal{J} \cap \left(\bigcup_{j=1}^{k-1} I_j\right) = \phi$. Among these intervals there is one twice whose length exceeds the length of any of the others.

Hence, by finite induction, either the theorem holds or there is a sequence

$$I_1, I_2, \cdots, I_n, \cdots$$

of disjoint intervals in I such that for every k, if $\mathcal{J} \in \mathsf{I}$ and $\mathcal{J} \cap \left(\bigcup_{j=1}^{k-1} I_j\right) = \phi$, then $l(I_k) > \frac{1}{2}l(\mathcal{J})$.

Since the intervals $I_1, I_2, \cdots, I_n, \cdots$ are disjoint and contained in $U = [0, 1]$, there is an n such that

$$\sum_{k=n+1}^{\infty} l(I_k) < \frac{\epsilon}{5}\cdot$$

For every $k = n + 1, n + 2, \cdots$ let $\mathcal{J}_k$ be the closed interval with the same midpoint as I_k such that $l(\mathcal{J}_k) = 5l(I_k)$. Let $G = \bigcup_{k=n+1}^{\infty} \mathcal{J}_k$. Then $m(G) < \epsilon$.

Now suppose $x \in S$ but $x \notin \bigcup_{k=1}^{n} I_k$. There is a $\mathcal{J} \in \mathsf{I}$ such that $x \in \mathcal{J}$ but $\mathcal{J} \cap \left(\bigcup_{k=1}^{n} I_k\right) = \phi$ But $\mathcal{J}$ is not disjoint with all the I_k, for $l(\mathcal{J}) > 2l(I_k)$ for some k. Let $m > n$ be the first positive integer such that $\mathcal{J} \cap I_m \neq \phi$. For the particular integer m, $l(\mathcal{J}) < 2l(I_m)$. For

$$\mathcal{J} \cap \left(\bigcup_{n=1}^{m-1} I_n\right) = \phi,$$

and if $l(\mathcal{J}) \geqq 2l(I_m)$ then I_m could not be chosen as a member of the sequence $I_1, I_2, \cdots, I_n, \cdots$. Now $m > n$ and $l(\mathcal{J}) < 2l(I_m)$, so that $\mathcal{J} \subset \mathcal{J}_m$. Hence

$$S - \bigcup_{k=1}^{n} I_k \subset \bigcup_{k=n+1}^{\infty} \mathcal{J}_k,$$

proving the theorem.

COROLLARY 1. For the S and I of the theorem, there is a finite or denumerable number of disjoint intervals $I_1, I_2, \cdots, I_n, \cdots$ in I which cover all of S except for a set of measure 0.

3. *Metric density*

We now define the metric density of a set S at a point x. We first must define the relative measure of a set S in an interval I. The student will notice the analogy between metric density of a set and derivative of a function. The interest in this concept lies chiefly in the Lebesgue Density Theorem (Theorem 2) which follows.

DEFINITION 2. If S is a measurable set and I an open interval, the *relative measure of S in I* is given by the number

$$\frac{m(S \cap I)}{l(I)}.$$

We observe at this time only that the relative measure is an interval function such that

$$0 \leqq \frac{m(S \cap I)}{l(I)} \leqq 1\,.$$

If the relative measure of S in I is designated by $\phi(I)$ then the associated point functions $\overline{\phi}(x)$ and $\underline{\phi}(x)$, as defined in Chapter 7, are respectively called the upper metric density and the lower metric density of S at x. If $\overline{\phi}(x) = \underline{\phi}(x)$ then the metric density of S is said to exist at x and the number $\phi(x) = \overline{\phi}(x) = \underline{\phi}(x)$ is called the metric density of S at x.

We give these definitions in detail. Let S be a measurable set and x a real number. For every positive integer n, let

$$\overline{\phi}_n(x) = \sup\left[\frac{m(S \cap I)}{l(I)}\,\middle|\, x \in I,\ l(I) < \frac{1}{n}\right], \text{ and}$$

$$\underline{\phi}_n(x) = \inf\left[\frac{m(S \cap I)}{l(I)}\,\middle|\, x \in I,\ l(I) < \frac{1}{n}\right];$$

and let

$$\bar{\phi}(x) = \lim_{n \to \infty} \bar{\phi}_n(x), \text{ and}$$

$$\underline{\phi}(x) = \lim_{n \to \infty} \underline{\phi}_n(x).$$

DEFINITION 3. The numbers $\bar{\phi}(x)$ and $\underline{\phi}(x)$ are called the *upper metric density* and the *lower metric density* of S at x, respectively.

DEFINITION 4. If $\bar{\phi}(x) = \underline{\phi}(x)$ the metric density of S is said to exist at x and the number $\phi(x) = \bar{\phi}(x) = \underline{\phi}(x)$ is called the *metric density* of S at x.

PROPOSITION 1. For every measurable set S and real number x,

$$0 \leqq \underline{\phi}(x) \leqq \bar{\phi}(x) \leqq 1.$$

The proof is left to the student.

PROPOSITION 2. For a measurable set S and real number x, if $\bar{\phi}(x) = 0$ the metric density of S exists and is equal to 0 at x, and if $\underline{\phi}(x) = 1$ the metric density of S exists and is equal to 1 at x.

We give some examples.

1. Let S be the closed interval $[1/2, 1]$. For every positive integer n, the relative measure of S in the interval $(1/2 - 1/n^2, 1/2 + 1/n)$ is $n/(n+1)$ and the relative measure of S in the interval $(1/2 - 1/n, 1/2 + 1/n^2)$ is $1/(n+1)$. It follows that the upper metric density of S at $1/2$ is 1 and the lower metric density of S at $1/2$ is 0, so that the metric density of S does not exist at $1/2$.
2. Let

$$S = \bigcup_{n=1}^{\infty} \left(\frac{1}{2} + \frac{1}{n}, \frac{1}{2} + \frac{1}{n} + \frac{1}{n^2}\right).$$

The relative measure of S is positive in every open interval containing the point $1/2$, but the metric density of S at $1/2$ exists and is 0, as the student may readily show.

PROPOSITION 3. If S is measurable and the metric density of S exists at x then the metric density of $C(S)$ exists at x and the sum of the two metric densities is equal to 1.

Proof. For every open interval I,

$$m(S \cap I) + m(C(S) \cap I) = l(I),$$

so that

$$\frac{m(S \cap I)}{l(I)} + \frac{m(C(S) \cap I)}{l(I)} = 1.$$

The proposition is now an immediate consequence of the definition.

PROPOSITION 4. If S is a measurable set and k a real number, then the set of points at which the lower metric density of S is less than k is measurable.

Proof. We first consider the set of points which are contained in open intervals of length less than $1/n$ in which the relative measure of S is less than $k - 1/m$. For all positive integers n and m this set G_{nm} is an open set. Now, the set of points at which the lower metric density of S is less than k is the set

$$\bigcup_{m=1}^{\infty} \bigcap_{n=1}^{\infty} G_{nm}.$$

But this is a Borel set of type G_2, and so it is measurable.

Similarly, the sets of points at which the lower metric density of S is greater than k and the upper metric density of S is greater than k or less than k are measurable.

We may now prove the main theorem on metric density of measurable sets. It is the Lebesgue Density Theorem:

THEOREM 2. If S is measurable, the metric density of S exists and is equal to 1 at every point of S except for a set of measure 0.

Proof. Suppose that the theorem is not true. Then there is a measurable set S such that the set of points of S at which the lower metric density of S is less than 1 has positive exterior measure. But then there is a positive integer n such that the set $T \subset S$ of points of S at which the lower metric density of S is less than $1 - 1/n$ has positive exterior measure. But T, as the intersection of two measurable sets (S and the set of all points at which the lower metric density of S is less than $1 - 1/n$), is measurable. So there is a positive integer n and a measurable subset $T \subset S$ such that the lower metric density of S is less than $1 - 1/n$ at every $x \in T$ and $m(T) = k > 0$. We shall show that this consequence of the assumption that the theorem is false leads to an impossibility.

Let $G \supset S$ be an open set which contains S such that $m(G) = m(S) + k/n$. For every $x \in T$ there is a sequence $\{I_{\nu x}\}$ of closed intervals containing x which are contained in G and have the property that

$$\lim_{\nu \to \infty} l(I_{\nu x}) = 0$$

and that

$$\frac{m(S \cap I_{\nu x})}{l(I_{\nu x})} < 1 - \frac{1}{n}$$

for every $\nu = 1, 2, \cdots$. The set of intervals

$$\mathsf{I} = [I_{\nu x} \mid x \in T, \nu = 1, 2, \cdots]$$

covers T in the Vitali sense. Hence all of T, except for a set of measure 0, is covered by a finite or denumerable number of disjoint intervals

$$I_1, I_2, \cdots, I_m, \cdots$$

in I. Let $H = \bigcup_{m=1}^{\infty} I_m$. Then $H \subset G$ and $m(H) \geqq k$.

Now, since

$$\frac{m(S \cap I_k)}{l(I_k)} < 1 - \frac{1}{n},$$

it follows that

$$\frac{m(C(S) \cap I_k)}{l(I_k)} > \frac{1}{n},$$

so that

$$m(C(S) \cap I_k) > \frac{1}{n} l(I_k).$$

Accordingly,

$$m(C(S) \cap H) = m(\bigcup_{k=1}^{\infty} (C(S) \cap I_k)) = \sum_{k=1}^{\infty} m(C(S) \cap I_k) > \sum_{k=1}^{\infty} \frac{1}{n} l(I_k)$$

$$= \frac{1}{n} m(H) \geqq \frac{k}{n}.$$

Since $G \supset H$, $m(C(S) \cap G) > k/n$.

On the other hand, $G = (S \cap G) \cup (C(S) \cap G)$, so that $m(G) = m(S \cap G) + m(C(S) \cap G)$. But $S \cap G = S$, so that $m(G) = m(S) + m(C(S) \cap G)$. But, from the definition of G, $m(G) = m(S) + k/n$. This shows that $m(C(S) \cap G) = k/n$. Hence the assumption that the theorem is false leads to a contradiction, so that the theorem is true.

This theorem may be stated in an alternate form.

THEOREM 3. If S is a measurable set, the metric density of S exists and is equal to 0 or 1 at every point, except for a set of measure 0.

Proof. By Theorem 2, $S = T_1 \cup Z_1$ where the metric density of S exists and is equal to 1 at every point of T_1 and Z_1 is of measure 0. Moreover, $C(S) = T_2 \cup Z_2$ where the metric density of $C(S)$ exists and is equal to 1 at every point of T_2 and Z_2 is of measure 0. By Proposition 3, the metric density of S exists and is 0 at every point of T_2. Hence the metric density of S exists and is 0 or 1 everywhere except at points of $Z = Z_1 \cup Z_2$. But Z, as the union of two sets of measure 0, is a set of measure 0.

4. *Converse of the Lebesgue Density Theorem*

The following converse of the Lebesgue Density Theorem holds.

THEOREM 4. If Z is any set of measure 0, there is a measurable set S such that the metric density of S does not exist at any points of Z.

Proof. Let $G_1 \supset G_2 \supset \cdots \supset G_n \supset \cdots$ be a sequence of open sets each covering Z. Since Z is of measure 0, the sets G_ν may be so chosen that for every n the relative measure of G_{n+1} is $1/n$ in each of the disjoint open intervals I_{np}, $p = 1, 2, \cdots$ whose union is G_n. Let

$$S = (G_1 - G_2) \cup (G_3 - G_4) \cup \cdots \cup (G_{2k-1} - G_{2k}) \cup \cdots.$$

S, as the union of a denumerable number of Borel sets, is a Borel set and so is measurable. Let z be any point in Z. For every n, there is a p_n such that z is in I_{np_n}, one of the disjoint open intervals constituting G_n. For odd values of n, the relative measure of S in I_{np_n} is not less than $1 - 1/n$. For then $S \supset G_n - G_{n+1}$, a set whose relative measure in I_{np_n} is exactly $1 - 1/n$. For even values of n, $S \cap I_{np_n} \subset G_{n+1}$, a set whose relative measure in I_{np_n} is $1/n$. Hence, in this case, the relative measure of S in I_{np_n} is not greater than $1/n$. But the length of I_{np_n} converges to 0 as n increases, both for odd and even values of n. The upper and lower metric densities of S at z are accordingly equal to 1 and 0, respectively, so that the metric density of S does not exist at any point of Z.

The next theorem is concerned with the set of points at which the metric density of a measurable set exists but is different from 0 or 1. This set is both of measure 0 and of the first category.

THEOREM 5. The set of points at which the metric density of a measurable set S exists but is not equal to 0 or 1 is of measure 0 and of the first category.

Proof. We are still assuming that all sets considered are contained in the closed interval $[0, 1]$. Let T be the set of points for which the metric density of S exists, U those points of T for which the metric density of S is 0 or 1, and $Z = T - U$. By the Density Theorem of Lebesgue, Z is of measure 0 and U is of measure 1. For every x, let $f_n(x)$, $n = 1, 2, \cdots$, be the relative measure of S in the interval $(x - 1/n, x + 1/n)$. For every n, the function $f_n(x)$ is a continuous function, as the student may readily verify, and so it is continuous on T relative to T. For every $x \in T$, the metric density of S exists, so that on T, $f(x) = \lim_{n \to \infty} f_n(x)$ exists, is equal to the metric density of S, and is a function of Baire class 1 on T relative to T. Its points of discontinuity must be a set of the first category relative to T. On the other hand, U, as a set of measure 1, is dense in T. Thus every interval containing a point of Z also contains points of U, that is, points for which $f(x)$ is either 0 or 1. Since for every x in Z, $f(x)$ is different from 0 or 1, Z is a subset of the set of points of discontinuity of $f(x)$. Z is, accordingly, of the first category relative to T and, therefore, relative to $[0, 1]$.

5. *Derivative of a monotone function*

As a further application of the Vitali Covering Theorem, we now show that the derivative of a nondecreasing function exists everywhere except possibly for points belonging to a set of measure 0.

DEFINITION 5. A function $f(x)$ is nondecreasing if whenever $y > x$ then $f(y) \geqq f(x)$.

We first show that certain sets associated with a nondecreasing function are measurable.

PROPOSITION 5. If $f(x)$ is bounded and nondecreasing the set of points of discontinuity of $f(x)$ is finite or denumerable.

Proof. Suppose $|f(x)| < M$, for every x, where M is a positive integer. Let S_n be the set of points for which the saltus of $f(x)$ exceeds $1/n$. Suppose S_n is infinite. Consider $2nM$ points in S_n. There are $2nM$ disjoint intervals in each of which the saltus of $f(x)$ exceeds $1/n$. In each of these intervals $I_j, j = 1, \cdots, 2nM$, there are x_j and y_j with $x_j < y_j$ such that $f(y_j) - f(x_j) > 1/n$. Then

$$f(1) - f(0) \geqq \sum_{j=1}^{2nM} (f(y_j) - f(x_j)) > 2nM \cdot \frac{1}{n} = 2M,$$

in contradiction. Hence S_n is finite, so that the set

$$S = \bigcup_{n=1}^{\infty} S_n$$

of points of discontinuity of $f(x)$ is finite or denumerable.

PROPOSITION 6. If $f(x)$ is bounded and nondecreasing the set of points for which the right upper derivate $d^+(f; \xi)$ is greater than k is measurable for every real number k.

Proof. Let n and m be positive integers, and let S_{nm} be the set of points for which $d_n^+(f; \xi) > k + 1/m$. Suppose $d_n^+(f; \xi) > k + 1/m$ and $f(x)$ is continuous at ξ. Then there is an $\eta > \xi$ such that

$$\eta - \xi < \frac{1}{n} \text{ and } \frac{f(\eta) - f(\xi)}{\eta - \xi} = k + \frac{1}{m} + \alpha$$

where $\alpha > 0$. Since $f(x)$ is continuous at ξ, there is a $\delta > 0$, $\delta < \eta - \xi$, such that if $\xi < \zeta < \xi + \delta$ then

$$f(\xi) \leqq f(\zeta) < f(\xi) + \alpha \cdot (\eta - \xi).$$

But for any such ζ,

$$\frac{f(\eta)-f(\zeta)}{\eta-\zeta} > \frac{f(\eta)-f(\zeta)}{\eta-\xi} = \frac{f(\eta)-f(\xi)-(f(\zeta)-f(\xi))}{\eta-\xi}$$
$$\geqq k+\frac{1}{m}+\alpha-\alpha = k+\frac{1}{m}.$$

Hence every point in S_{nm}, which is a point of continuity of $f(x)$, is the end-point of an interval contained in S_{nm}. Since the set of points of discontinuity of $f(x)$ is denumerable, the set S_{nm} is a Borel set. But

$$S = \bigcup_{m=1}^{\infty} \bigcap_{n=1}^{\infty} S_{nm}$$

is the set of points for which $d^+(f;\xi) > k$. Since the system of Borel sets is closed with respect to denumerable intersections and unions, S is a Borel set, and since every Borel set is measurable, S is measurable.

One may now show—and we omit the details—that if $f(x)$ is nondecreasing, the following sets are measurable:

$E[d^+(f;\xi) < k]$,

$E[d^+(f;\xi) \geqq k]$,

$E[d^+(f;\xi) \leqq k]$,

$E[d^+(f;\xi) < +\infty]$, and

$E[d^+(f;\xi) > -\infty]$,

as well as the sets associated in the same way with the other Dini derivates.

We now prove our theorem.

THEOREM 6. If $f(x)$ is bounded and nondecreasing then $f'(x)$ exists everywhere except for a set of measure 0.

Proof. We first show that the set T of points for which $d^+(f;\xi) = +\infty$ is of measure 0. Assume the contrary. Then T is measurable and $m(T) = \alpha > 0$. Let T_k be the set of points for which $d^+(f;\xi) > k$. Then T_k is measurable for every $k = 1, 2, \cdots$ and $T = \bigcap_{k-1}^{\infty} T_k$, so that $m(T_k) \geqq \alpha$ for every $k = 1, 2, \cdots$. Let k_0 be an integer such that

$$k_0 > 2\frac{f(1)-f(0)}{\alpha}.$$

Now every $x \in T_{k_0}$ is in a sequence $\{I_{nx}\}$ of closed intervals whose lengths converge to 0, on each of which the difference quotient of $f(x)$ exceeds k_0. The set

$$\mathsf{I} = [I_{nx} \mid x \in T_{k_0}, n = 1, 2, \cdots]$$

of closed intervals covers T_{k_0} in the Vitali sense. Hence a finite number of disjoint intervals

$$I_1 = [a_1, b_1], I_2 = [a_2, b_2], \cdots, I_m = [a_m, b_m]$$

in I has length sum greater than $\alpha/2$. Now

$$\frac{f(b_j) - f(a_j)}{b_j - a_j} > k_0, j = 1, 2, \cdots, m.$$

But

$$f(1) - f(0) \geqq \sum_{j=1}^{m} (f(b_j) - f(a_j)),$$

since $f(x)$ is a nondecreasing function. Hence

$$f(1) - f(0) \geqq \sum_{j=1}^{m} (f(b_j) - f(a_j)) > k_0 \sum_{j=1}^{m} (b_j - a_j) > k_0 \cdot \frac{\alpha}{2}$$
$$> 2\frac{f(1) - f(0)}{\alpha}\frac{\alpha}{2} = f(1) - f(0),$$

which is impossible. Hence $m(T_{k_0}) = 0$, so that $m(T) = 0$. Similarly, the set of points for which $d^-(f; \xi) = +\infty$ is of measure 0.

We observe that $d_+(f; \xi) \geqq 0$ and $d_-(f; \xi) \geqq 0$ everywhere since $f(x)$ is nondecreasing. Let S be the set of points for which $d^+(f; \xi)$ and $d^-(f; \xi)$ are both finite and one of them exceeds either $d_+(f; \xi)$ or $d_-(f; \xi)$. If $\xi \in S$ there are rational numbers r_1 and r_2 with $r_2 < r_1$ such that either $d_+(f; \xi)$ or $d_-(f; \xi)$ is less than r_2 and either $d^+(f; \xi)$ or $d^-(f; \xi)$ is greater than r_1. Designate the subset of S for which this holds for a certain $r_2 < r_1$ by $S_{r_1 r_2}$. Then $S = \cup S_{r_1 r_2}$ where the union is taken with respect to all r_1 and r_2 with $r_2 < r_1$.

We suppose now that $m(S) > 0$. Then there is a pair of rational numbers r_1 and r_2 with $r_2 < r_1$ such that $m(S_{r_1 r_2}) > 0$; for otherwise S, as the union of a denumerable number of sets of measure 0, would be of measure 0. For convenience, write $T = S_{r_1 r_2}$. By the Lebesgue Density Theorem T has points—let ξ be one of them—such that the metric density of T exists and is equal to 1 at ξ. There is an $\eta > \xi$ and a $\zeta > \xi$ such that the relative measures of T in $[\xi, \eta]$ and in $[\zeta, \xi]$ exceed r_2/r_1 and such that either

$$\frac{f(\eta) - f(\xi)}{\eta - \xi} < r_2$$

or

$$\frac{f(\xi) - f(\zeta)}{\xi - \zeta} < r_2.$$

Assume, for convenience, that

$$\frac{f(\eta) - f(\xi)}{\eta - \xi} < r_2.$$

Every $x \in T \cap (\xi, \eta)$ is in a sequence of closed intervals $\{I_{nx}\}$ all contained in (ξ, η), with lengths converging to 0, in each of which the difference quotient of $f(x)$ exceeds r_1. The intervals

$$\mathsf{I} = [I_{nx} \mid x \in T \cap (\xi, \eta), n = 1, 2, \cdots]$$

cover $T \cap (\xi, \eta)$ in the Vitali sense, so there is a finite number of them,

$$I_1 = [a_1, b_1], I_2 = [a_2, b_2], \cdots, I_m = [a_m, b_m],$$

which are disjoint and the sum of whose lengths exceeds $r_2/r_1 \cdot (\eta - \xi)$. Now

$$f(\eta) - f(\xi) \geqq \sum_{j=1}^{m} (f(b_j) - f(a_j)) > \sum_{j=1}^{m} r_1(b_j - a_j) > r_1 \frac{r_2}{r_1}(\eta - \xi) = r_2(\eta - \xi).$$

In other words,

$$\frac{f(\eta) - f(\xi)}{\eta - \xi} > r_2,$$

contradicting the fact that it is less then r_2. This proves the theorem.

Exercises

1.1 Give an example of a closed set $F \subset [0, 1]$ covered by a set I of open intervals such that every finite set of disjoint open intervals of I fails to cover a subset of F whose measure exceeds $1/4$.

2.1 Show that the Vitali Covering Theorem is true for unbounded measurable sets of finite measure.

2.2 Go through the steps of the proof of the Vitali Covering Theorem to show that open covering intervals may be used instead of closed intervals.

3.1 Define a concept for arbitrary sets which generalizes the concept of metric density for measurable sets. Hint: Use exterior measure instead of measure. This concept is called *exterior metric density*.

3.2 Show that if S is any set and k a real number then the set of points at which the lower exterior metric density of S is less than k is measurable. Hint: Every set S is a subset of a set T of type G_1 such that $m(T) = m_e(S)$.

3.3 Show that the Lebesgue Density Theorem holds for arbitrary sets if exterior metric density is used instead of metric density.

3.4 Give an example of a set S such that the exterior metric densities of S and of $C(S)$ are 1 everywhere.

3.5 Decompose the interval $[0, 1]$ into two disjoint sets S and T such that S is of measure 0 and T of the first category.

4.1 Give an example of a set S whose metric density exists and is equal to $1/2$ at a point ξ.

5.1 If $\mathcal{Z} \subset [0, 1]$ is any set of measure 0, show that there is a nondecreasing function $f(x)$ on $[0, 1]$ all of whose derivates are $+\infty$ at every point of $\mathcal{Z}$.

5.2 If $\mathcal{Z} \subset [0, 1]$ is any set of measure 0, show that there is a nondecreasing function $f(x)$ on $[0, 1]$, with bounded Dini derivates, whose derivative does not exist at any point of $\mathcal{Z}$.

References

C. Carathéodory, *Vorlesungen über reelle Funktionen*, Leipzig, 1927, note 1, p. 689.

H. Kestelman, *Modern Theories of Integration*, Oxford, 1937, Chap. 3.

E. J. McShane, *Integration*, Princeton, 1944, Chap. 10.

Ch. J. de la Vallée Poussin, *Intégrales de Lebesgue, Fonctions d'ensembles, Classes de Baire*, Paris, 1934, Chap. 4.

S. Saks, *Theory of the Integral*, translated by L. C. Young, Warszawa-Lwow, 1937, Chap. 4.

15

Measurable Functions

1. *Definition*

We have already had considerable experience with the sets associated with a function. A function is said to be measurable if its associated sets are measurable. Precisely, we may define measurable functions in the following way.

DEFINITION 1. A function $f(x)$ is said to be *measurable* if for every real number k the set $E = E[f(x) < k]$ is measurable.

There are several equivalent definitions. One such is the following: $f(x)$ is measurable if for every real number k the set $E = E[f(x) \leqq k]$ is measurable.

PROPOSITION 1. A function $f(x)$ is measurable if and only if for every real number k the set $E = E[f(x) \leqq k]$ is measurable.

Proof. Suppose $f(x)$ is measurable. Then for every positive integer n, the set $E = E[f(x) < k + 1/n]$ is measurable, so that

$$E = E[f(x) \leqq k] = \bigcap_{n=1}^{\infty} E\left[f(x) < k + \frac{1}{n}\right]$$

is measurable.

Conversely, suppose $E[f(x) \leqq k]$ is measurable for every k. Then $E[f(x) \leqq k - 1/n]$ is measurable for every positive integer n, so that

$$E[f(x) < k] = \bigcup_{n=1}^{\infty} E\left[f(x) \leqq k - \frac{1}{n}\right]$$

is measurable and $f(x)$ is a measurable function.

Other equivalent forms of the definition of measurable functions are the following:

A function $f(x)$ is measurable if and only if for every pair of real numbers k_1 and k_2 such that $k_1 < k_2$ the set $E = E[k_1 < f(x) < k_2]$ is measurable.

A function $f(x)$ is measurable if and only if for every pair of real numbers k_1 and k_2 with $k_1 < k_2$, the set $E = E[k_1 \leqq f(x) \leqq k_2]$ is measurable.

PROPOSITION 2. If $f(x)$ is measurable then for every real-number k the set $E = E[f(x) = k]$ is measurable.

Proof. Since $f(x)$ is measurable, for every positive integer n, the sets $E = E[f(x) \leqq k - 1/n]$ and $E = E[f(x) < k + 1/n]$ are measurable. The set $E = E[f(x) > k - 1/n]$, as the complement of a measurable set, is measurable. Moreover the set

$$E = E\left[k - \frac{1}{n} < f(x) < k + \frac{1}{n}\right]$$

is measurable, since it is the intersection of two measurable sets

$$E\left[f(x) < k + \frac{1}{n}\right] \quad \text{and} \quad E\left[f(x) > k - \frac{1}{n}\right].$$

But

$$E[f(x) = k] = \bigcap_{n=1}^{\infty} E\left[k - \frac{1}{n} < f(x) < k + \frac{1}{n}\right]$$

and so it is measurable.

The converse, however, is not true. For, let S be a nonmeasurable set. Consider one-to-one correspondences between S and a subset of the open interval $(0, 1)$, and between $C(S)$ and a subset of the open interval $(-1, 0)$. Define $f(x)$ by means of these correspondences. For every real number k, the set $E = E[f(x) = k]$ consists of at most one point, so it is measurable. On the other hand, the set $E[f(x) > 0] = S$, which is nonmeasurable, so that $f(x)$ is not a measurable function.

THEOREM 1. Every Baire function of finite type is measurable.

Proof. If $f(x)$ is a Baire function of finite type, then for every real number k the set $E = E[f(x) > k]$ is a Borel set and so is measurable.

2. *Simple properties of measurable functions*

We prove some simple propositions regarding measurable functions.

PROPOSITION 3. If $f(x)$ is measurable, then

1. $-f(x)$ is measurable,
2. $cf(x)$ is measurable for every real number c,

3. $f(x) + c$ is measurable for every real number c,
4. $[f(x)]^2$ is measurable.

Proof. 1. $E[-f(x) < k] = E[f(x) > -k]$ and so is measurable for every k.

2. $E[cf(x) < k] = E[f(x) < k/c]$ and so is measurable for every k if $c > 0$. If $c = 0$, $cf(x) = 0$ and is measurable. For $c < 0$, use (1).

3. $E[f(x) + c < k] = E[f(x) < k - c]$ and so is measurable for every k.

4. $E[[f(x)]^2 > k]$, $k \geqq 0$ is the union of $E[f(x) > \sqrt{k}]$ and $E[f(x) < -\sqrt{k}]$

and so, as the union of two measurable sets, is measurable.

PROPOSITION 4. If $f(x)$ is measurable then $|f(x)|$ is measurable.

Proof. For every real number $k \geqq 0$,

$$E[|f(x)| < k] = E[-k < f(x) < k]$$

is a measurable set. Hence $|f(x)|$ is measurable.

PROPOSITION 5. If $f(x)$ and $g(x)$ are measurable functions, then max $(f(x), g(x))$ and min $(f(x), g(x))$ are measurable.

Proof. Consider the function max $(f(x), g(x))$. For every real number k,

$$E[\max(f(x), g(x)) < k] = E[f(x) < k] \cap E[g(x) < k],$$

so that it is measurable.

On the other hand, it is possible for the function $\sup [f_\alpha(x) \mid \alpha \in \mathsf{A}]$ to be nonmeasurable even if each function $f_\alpha(x)$, $\alpha \in \mathsf{A}$, is measurable. For if S is a nonmeasurable set and for every $\xi \in S$ there is an $f_\xi(x) = 1$ at $x = \xi$ and $f_\xi(x) = 0$ elsewhere then $\sup [f_\xi(x) \mid \xi \in S]$ is 1 on S and 0 elsewhere and so it is nonmeasurable.

PROPOSITION 6. If $f(x)$ and $g(x)$ are measurable, then $E = E[f(x) > g(x)]$ is a measurable set.

Proof. $f(\xi) > g(\xi)$ if and only if there is a rational number r such that $f(\xi) > r > g(\xi)$. Order the rational numbers $r_1, r_2, \cdots, r_n, \cdots$ and let

$$E_n = E[f(x) > r_n > g(x)].$$

E_n is measurable, for

$$E_n = E[f(x) > r_n] \cap E[g(x) < r_n].$$

Hence

$$E[f(x) > g(x)] = \bigcup_{n=1}^{\infty} E_n$$

is measurable.

PROPOSITION 7. If $f(x)$ and $g(x)$ are measurable functions, then $f(x) + g(x)$ is a measurable function.

Proof. Let k be a real number. The set

$$E = E[f(x) + g(x) > k] = E[f(x) > k - g(x)].$$

But $k - g(x)$ is a measurable function so that, by Proposition 6, this set is measurable.

PROPOSITION 8. If $f(x)$ and $g(x)$ are measurable functions, then $f(x) \cdot g(x)$ is measurable.

Proof. $f(x) \cdot g(x) = \frac{1}{4}\{[f(x) + g(x)]^2 - [f(x) - g(x)]^2\}$.

PROPOSITION 9. If $\{f_n(x)\}$ is a sequence of measurable functions, then $\sup[f_n(x) \mid n = 1, 2, \cdots]$ and $\inf[f_n(x) \mid n = 1, 2, \cdots]$ are measurable if they exist.

Proof. Let k be a real number. Then, if $f(x) = \sup[f_n(x) \mid n = 1, 2, \cdots]$,

$$E[f(x) > k] = \bigcup_{n=1}^{\infty} E[f_n(x) > k]$$

is measurable, so that $\sup[f_n(x) \mid n = 1, 2, \cdots]$ is measurable. Similarly $\inf[f_n(x) \mid n = 1, 2, \cdots]$ is measurable.

PROPOSITION 10. If $\{f_n(x)\}$ is a sequence of measurable functions then $\limsup_{n\to\infty} f_n(x)$ and $\liminf_{n\to\infty} f_n(x)$ are measurable.

Proof. $E[\limsup f_n(x) < k] = \bigcup_{m=1}^{\infty} \bigcup_{n=1}^{\infty} E_{mn}$, where

$$E_{mn} = E\left[f_r(x) < k - \frac{1}{n}\middle| r = m, m + 1, \cdots\right].$$

But E_{mn} is measurable for every m, n so that $\bigcup_{m=1}^{\infty} \bigcup_{n=1}^{\infty} E_{mn}$ is measurable and $\limsup f_n(x)$ is measurable. Similarly $\liminf f_n(x)$ is measurable.

COROLLARY 1. If $\{f_n(x)\}$ is a convergent sequence of measurable functions and $f(x) = \lim_{n\to\infty} f_n(x)$ then $f(x)$ is measurable.

3. *Functions defined on measurable sets*

Instead of restricting the definition of measurable functions to functions on $[0, 1]$, we may just as well consider functions defined on an arbitrary measurable set S. A function $f(x)$ defined on S is called measurable if for every real number k the set $E[f(x) < k]$ is measurable. All the above propositions hold for this general case.

4. *Approximate uniform convergence*

We have shown that a convergent sequence of arbitrary functions may converge uniformly on no nondenumerable set. For convergent sequences of measurable functions, the facts are quite different. Indeed, we shall show that every convergent sequence of measurable functions is "approximately uniformly convergent" in an important sense.

DEFINITION 2. A sequence $\{f_n(x)\}$ defined on $[0, 1]$ is said to *converge approximately uniformly* if for every $\epsilon > 0$ there is an N and a measurable set S whose measure exceeds $1 - \epsilon$ such that for every $n, m > N$ and $x \in S$,

$$|f_n(x) - f_m(x)| < \epsilon.$$

The next proposition shows that the definition of approximate uniform convergence may be put in a seemingly stronger form.

PROPOSITION 11. A sequence $\{f_n(x)\}$ defined on $[0, 1]$ is approximately uniformly convergent if and only if, for every $\epsilon > 0$, there is a measurable set S whose measure exceeds $1 - \epsilon$ such that $\{f_n(x)\}$ converges uniformly on S.

Proof. Certainly a sequence of functions which satisfies the condition of the proposition is approximately uniformly convergent.

Suppose $\{f_n(x)\}$ converges and that for every $\epsilon > 0$ there is an N and a measurable set S whose measure exceeds $1 - \epsilon$ such that for every $n, m > N$ and $x \in S$,

$$|f_n(x) - f_m(x)| < \epsilon.$$

Let $\epsilon > 0$. For every positive integer n there is a measurable set S_n whose measure exceeds $1 - \epsilon/2^n$ and a positive integer $N(n)$ such that if μ, $\nu > N(n)$ and $x \in S_n$ then

$$|f_\nu(x) - f_\mu(x)| < \frac{\epsilon}{2^n}\cdot$$

Let $S = \bigcap_{n=1}^{\infty} S_n$. Then $\{f_n(x)\}$ converges uniformly on S. For let $\delta > 0$. There is an n such that $\epsilon/2^n < \delta$. For every $x \in S$, $x \in S_n$, so that if $\mu, \nu > N(n)$ then

$$|f_\mu(x) - f_\nu(x)| < \frac{\epsilon}{2^n} < \delta.$$

Finally, the measure of S exceeds $1 - \epsilon$. For the measure of $C(S) = \bigcup_{n=1}^{\infty} C(S_n)$ is less than $\sum_{n=1}^{\infty} \epsilon/2^n = \epsilon$.

We now show that for sequences of measurable functions convergence implies approximate uniform convergence. This is known as the Theorem of Egoroff.

THEOREM 2. If $\{f_n(x)\}$ is a convergent sequence of measurable functions, then $\{f_n(x)\}$ is approximately uniformly convergent.

Proof. For every $x \in [0, 1]$ and for every m there is an n such that if $\mu, \nu > n$ then $|f_\mu(x) - f_\nu(x)| < 1/m$. Let E_{mn} consist of those points ξ such that if $\mu, \nu > n$ then $|f_\mu(\xi) - f_\nu(\xi)| < 1/m$. Then $[0, 1] = \bigcup_{n=1}^{\infty} E_{mn}$ for every positive integer m. Moreover, for every m,

$$E_{m1} \subset E_{m2} \subset \cdots \subset E_{mn} \subset \cdots.$$

Furthermore, the sets E_{mn} are measurable. For the function $|f_\mu(x) - f_\nu(x)|$ is measurable for every μ and ν. Hence the set $E[|f_\mu(x) - f_\nu(x)| < 1/m]$ is measurable, so that the set

$$E_{mn} = \bigcap_{\mu,\nu=n+1}^{\infty} E\left[|f_\mu(x) - f_\nu(x)| < \frac{1}{m}\right]$$

is measurable. Let $\epsilon > 0$. There is an m such that $1/m < \epsilon$. Moreover, since the sets E_{mn}, $n = 1, 2, \cdots$ form a nondecreasing sequence whose union is $[0, 1]$, there is an n such that $m(E_{mn}) > 1 - \epsilon$. For every $\mu, \nu > n$ and every $x \in E_{mn}$, $|f_\mu(x) - f_\nu(x)| < 1/m < \epsilon$, so that the sequence $\{f_n(x)\}$ is approximately uniformly convergent.

Exercises

1.1 Show that $f(x)$ is measurable if and only if for every rational number r the set $E = E[f(x) < r]$ is measurable.

2.1 Show that if $f(x)$ and $g(x)$ are measurable and $g(x) \neq 0$ everywhere then $f(x)/g(x)$ is measurable.

2.2 If $f(x)$ is measurable show that $e^{f(x)}$ and $\sin f(x)$ are measurable.

2.3 Give an example of measurable functions $f(x)$ and $g(x)$ such that $f(g(x))$ is nonmeasurable.

3.1 Show that if $f(x)$ and $g(x)$ defined on a measurable set M are measurable then $f(x) + g(x)$ and $f(x) \cdot g(x)$ are measurable on M.

3.2 If $f(x)$ is monotonic and $g(x)$ is measurable, show that $f(g(x))$ is measurable.

4.1 Give an example of a sequence of measurable functions which converges on $[0, 1]$ but does not converge uniformly on any subset of measure 1.

References

C. Carathéodory, *Vorlesungen über reelle Funktionen*, Leipzig, 1927, Chap. 7.
H. Hahn and A. Rosenthal, *Set Functions*, Albuquerque, 1948, Chap. 3.
P. R. Halmos, *Measure Theory*, New York, 1950, Chap. 7.
H. Kestelman, *Modern Theories of Integration*, Oxford, 1937, Chap. 4.
Ch. J. de la Vallée Poussin, *Intégrales de Lebesgue, Fonctions d'ensembles, Classes de Baire*, Paris, 1934, Chap. 2.

16

Approximation of Measurable Functions

1. *Introduction*

In Chapter 13 various approximations of measurable sets were given in terms of simpler sets. This includes the approximation of a measurable set by a finite number of intervals, by a closed set, and by a set of type F_σ.

We now obtain analogous approximations of measurable functions by means of simpler functions. These approximations are known as the Theorems of Borel, Lusin, and Vitali-Carathéodory.

2. *Approximate continuity*

We first obtain an analogue for functions of the Lebesgue Density Theorem.

DEFINITION 1a. A measurable function $f(x)$ is said to be approximately continuous at ξ if for every pair of real numbers k_1 and k_2 such that $k_1 < f(\xi) < k_2$ the set $E[k_1 < f(x) < k_2]$ has metric density 1 at ξ.

We give two equivalent forms of this definition.

DEFINITION 1b. $f(x)$ is said to be approximately continuous at ξ if for every $\epsilon > 0$ the set $E[|f(x) - f(\xi)| < \epsilon]$ has metric density 1 at ξ.

DEFINITION 1c. $f(x)$ is said to be approximately continuous at ξ if for every pair of rational numbers r_1 and r_2 such that $r_1 < f(\xi) < r_2$ the set $E[r_1 < f(x) < r_2]$ has metric density 1 at ξ.

The proof that these definitions are equivalent is left to the student.

PROPOSITION 1. If $f(x)$ is continuous at ξ, then $f(x)$ is approximately continuous at ξ.

Proof. Let $\epsilon > 0$. The set $E[|f(x) - f(\xi)| < \epsilon]$ contains a neighborhood of ξ and accordingly has metric density 1 at ξ.

The converse is not true. For example, consider the function obtained as follows:

First, from each interval

$$\left(\frac{1}{n+1}, \frac{1}{n}\right), n = 1, 2, \cdots$$

remove a subinterval of length

$$\frac{1}{n}\left(\frac{1}{n} - \frac{1}{n+1}\right) = \frac{1}{n^2(n+1)}.$$

Let S denote the union of all the intervals so removed and let

$$\begin{aligned} f(x) &= 1, \ x \in S \\ &= 0, \ x \in C(S). \end{aligned}$$

Define the function by symmetry in the interval $[-1, 0]$. It is easy to show that this function is approximately continuous but not continuous at $x = 0$.

One may further show that, for any set S of the first category, there is a function $f(x)$ which is approximately continuous everywhere but is discontinuous at the points of S.

We now prove the analogue of the Lebesgue Density Theorem mentioned above.

THEOREM 1. If $f(x)$ is measurable then it is approximately continuous almost everywhere.

The term "almost everywhere" is commonly used to designate "except for a set whose measure is 0."

Proof. Let S be the set of points at which $f(x)$ is not approximately continuous. For every $\xi \in S$ there are rational numbers r_1 and r_2 such that $r_1 < f(\xi) < r_2$ and $E[r_1 < f(x) < r_2]$ has lower metric density less than 1 at ξ. For every pair of rational numbers r_1 and r_2 with $r_1 < r_2$ let $S_{r_1r_2}$ be the set of points in $E[r_1 < f(x) < r_2]$ for which $E[r_1 < f(x) < r_2]$ has lower metric density less than 1. Then

$$S = \cup S_{r_1r_2},$$

where the union is over all pairs r_1, r_2, of rational numbers such that $r_1 < r_2$. But each set $S_{r_1r_2}$ is of measure 0, by the Lebesgue Density Theorem, and the number of pairs r_1, r_2 is denumerable. Hence S is of measure 0.

3. *Approximation by continuous functions*

We first show that every measurable function may be approximated by a step function.

DEFINITION 2. A function $g(x)$ is called a *step function* if the closed interval $[0, 1]$ is the union of a finite number of intervals on each of which $g(x)$ is constant.

THEOREM 2. If $f(x)$ is a measurable function, then for every $\epsilon > 0$ there is a step function $g(x)$ such that $|f(x) - g(x)| < \epsilon$ on a set of measure greater than $1 - \epsilon$.

Proof. Let S be the set of points of approximate continuity of $f(x)$. For every $\xi \in S$, there is a sequence $\{I_{n\xi}\}$ of closed intervals containing ξ, whose lengths converge to 0, such that for every n the relative measure of the set

$$E[|f(\xi) - f(x)| < \epsilon]$$

exceeds $1 - \epsilon/2$. The set of intervals

$$\mathsf{I} = [I_{n\xi} \mid \xi \in S, n = 1, 2, \cdots]$$

covers S in the Vitali sense. But, by Theorem 1, $m(S) = 1$. Hence there are a finite number of disjoint intervals

$$I_{n_1\xi_1}, I_{n_2\xi_2}, \cdots, I_{n_k\xi_k}$$

in I, the sum of whose lengths exceeds $1 - \epsilon/2$. Define $g(x)$ as follows:

$$g(x) = f(\xi_j) \text{ for every } x \in I_{n_j\xi_j}, j = 1, 2, \cdots, k$$
$$= 0, \text{ elsewhere.}$$

The function $g(x)$ is a step function. Let E be the set of points for which $|f(x) - g(x)| < \epsilon$. The relative measure of E in $I_{n_j\xi_j}$ exceeds $1 - \epsilon/2$ for every $j = 1, 2, \cdots, k$. Hence

$$m(E) \geqq \sum_{j=1}^{k} \left(1 - \frac{\epsilon}{2}\right) l(I_{n_j\xi_j}) > \left(1 - \frac{\epsilon}{2}\right)^2 > 1 - \epsilon.$$

The following theorem is an immediate consequence of Theorem 2.

THEOREM 3. If $f(x)$ is a measurable function, then for every $\epsilon > 0$, there is a continuous function $g(x)$ such that $|f(x) - g(x)| < \epsilon$ on a set of measure greater than $1 - \epsilon$.

Proof. Let $g(x) = f(\xi_j)$ for $x \in I_{n_j\xi_j}, j = 1, 2, \cdots, k$, just as in the proof of Theorem 2, and let $g(x)$ be defined elsewhere so as to be continuous. Then $g(x)$ has the desired property.

This theorem is due to Borel.

4. *Approximation by Baire functions*

We first prove the following proposition.

PROPOSITION 2. If $f(x)$ is a measurable function, there is a sequence $\{g_n(x)\}$ of continuous functions which converges almost everywhere to $f(x)$.

Proof. By Theorem 3, for every positive integer n, there is a continuous function $g_n(x)$ such that $|f(x) - g_n(x)| < 1/2^n$ on a set S_n whose measure exceeds $1 - 1/2^n$. Let

$$S = \bigcup_{k=1}^{\infty} \bigcap_{n=k}^{\infty} S_n.$$

We show that $m(S) = 1$ and that $\{g_n(x)\}$ converges to $f(x)$ on S.

1. $m(\bigcap_{n=k}^{\infty} S_n) \geqq 1 - \sum_{n=k}^{\infty} m(C(S_n)) \geqq 1 - \sum_{n=k}^{\infty} 1/2^n = 1 - 1/2^{k-1}$. But $S \supset \bigcap_{n=k}^{\infty} S_n$ for every k. Hence $m(S) \geqq 1 - 1/2^{k-1}$ for every k, so that $m(S) = 1$.

2. Let $\xi \in S$. Then there is a positive integer k such that $\xi \in \bigcap_{n=k}^{\infty} S_n$. But then $\xi \in S_n$ for all $n \geqq k$. Choose $\epsilon > 0$. There is an $N > k$ such that $1/2^N < \epsilon$. But then for every $n > N$,

$$|g_n(\xi) - f(\xi)| < \frac{1}{2^n} < \frac{1}{2^N} < \epsilon.$$

COROLLARY 1. If $f(x)$ is measurable, then there is a set S of measure 1 such that $f(x)$ is of Baire class 1 on S relative to S.

Proof. The limit of the sequence $\{g_n(x)\}$ of functions each continuous on S and convergent on S is of Baire class 1 on S relative to S and is identical with $f(x)$.

One might suppose that it would follow that every measurable function is equal almost everywhere to a function of Baire class 1. This has not been proved in Proposition 2, since the sequence of continuous functions given there has not been shown to converge everywhere. Indeed the following considerations show that there are measurable functions which disagree with every function of Baire class 1 on a set of positive measure.

We start with a measurable set S such that both S and $C(S)$ have subsets of positive measure in every interval. The function.

$$\begin{aligned} f(x) &= 1, \ x \in S \\ &= 0, \ x \in C(S) \end{aligned}$$

is measurable. If $g(x)$ agrees with $f(x)$ almost everywhere, then there are sets T and V which have subsets of positive measure in every interval such that

$g(x) = 1$, $x \in T$, $g(x) = 0$, $x \in V$. But then $g(x)$ is discontinuous everywhere and is not of Baire class 1.

On the other hand, we have the following result, called the Theorem of Vitali-Carathéodory.

THEOREM 4a. If $f(x)$ is bounded and measurable, there is a function $g(x)$ which is the limit of a nonincreasing sequence of lower-semicontinuous functions such that $g(x) = f(x)$ almost everywhere.

Proof. Let $\{g_n(x)\}$ be the sequence of continuous functions defined in Proposition 2. Since $f(x)$ is bounded, the sequence $\{g_n(x)\}$ is uniformly bounded, so that its limit superior $g(x)$ is a real function. But, since $\{g_n(x)\}$ converges almost everywhere to $f(x)$, we have $f(x) = g(x)$ almost everywhere. Now if for every positive integer n, $h_n(x) = \sup [g_n(x), g_{n+1}(x), \cdots]$, the sequence $\{h_n(x)\}$ is a nonincreasing sequence of lower-semicontinuous functions such that

$$\lim_{n \to \infty} h_n(x) = \limsup_{n \to \infty} g_n(x).$$

This proves the theorem.

COROLLARY 2. If $f(x)$ is bounded and measurable, there is a function $g(x)$ of Baire class 2 such that $f(x) = g(x)$ almost everywhere.

We show that the corollary holds for the unbounded case.

Let $f(x)$ be any measurable function. The function

$$\phi(x) = \frac{f(x)}{1 + |f(x)|}$$

is measurable, and so there is a nonincreasing sequence $\{\phi_n(x)\}$ of lower-semicontinuous functions whose limit $\psi(x)$ is equal almost everywhere to $\phi(x)$. Now for every positive integer n let $\psi_n(x) = \min [\phi_n(x), 1 - 1/n]$. The functions $\psi_n(x)$ are of Baire class 1 and $\lim \psi_n(x) = \psi(x)$.

For every n, let

$$g_n(x) = \frac{\psi_n(x)}{1 - \psi_n(x)} \quad \text{if } \psi_n(x) \geqq 0$$

$$= \frac{\psi_n(x)}{1 + \psi_n(x)} \quad \text{if } \psi_n(x) \leqq 0.$$

Then $g_n(x)$ is of Baire class 1.

If

$$g(x) = \frac{\psi(x)}{1 - \psi(x)} \quad \text{if } \psi(x) \geqq 0$$

$$= \frac{\psi(x)}{1 + \psi(x)} \quad \text{if } \psi(x) \leqq 0$$

then $g(x) = \lim_{n\to\infty} g_n(x)$ and $g(x) = f(x)$ almost everywhere. The details are left for the student. We have accordingly obtained the following theorem.

THEOREM 4b. If $f(x)$ is measurable, there is a function $g(x)$ of Baire class 2 such that $f(x) = g(x)$ almost everywhere.

5. *Continuity of a measurable function*

We have shown in Chapter 12, using the continuum hypothesis, that there are functions which are discontinuous on every nondenumerable set relative to the set. The Theorem of Lusin which follows shows that the situation is quite different for measurable functions.

THEOREM 5. If $f(x)$ on $[0, 1]$ is measurable, then for every $\epsilon > 0$ there is a closed set F such that $m(F) > 1 - \epsilon$ and $f(x)$ is continuous on F relative to F.

Proof. Let S be the set of points of approximate continuity of $f(x)$. Then $m(S) = 1$. For every positive integer n every $\xi \in S$ is contained in a sequence $\{I_{\xi k}{}^{(n)}\}$, $k = 1, 2, \cdots$ of closed intervals, whose lengths converge to 0, such that the set $E_{\xi k}{}^{(n)}$ of points in $I_{\xi k}{}^{(n)}$ for which

$$|f(x) - f(\xi)| < \frac{\epsilon}{2^{n+1}}$$

has relative measure greater than $1 - \epsilon/2^{n+1}$ in $I_{\xi k}{}^{(n)}$. Let

$$\mathbf{I} = [I_{\xi k}{}^{(n)} \mid \xi \in S, k = 1, 2, \cdots].$$

By the Vitali Covering Theorem, $\mathbf{I}$ has a finite number of disjoint intervals

$$I_{\xi_1 k_1}{}^{(n)}, I_{\xi_2 k_2}{}^{(n)}, \cdots, I_{\xi_m k_m}{}^{(n)},$$

the sum of whose lengths exceeds $1 - \epsilon/2^{n+1}$. Let

$$E_n = \bigcup_{j=1}^{m} E_{\xi_j k_j}{}^{(n)}.$$

Then

$$m(E_n) = \sum_{j=1}^{m} m(E_{\xi_j k_j}{}^{(n)}) > \left(1 - \frac{\epsilon}{2^{n+1}}\right) \sum_{j=1}^{m} l(I_{\xi_j k_j}{}^{(n)}) > \left(1 - \frac{\epsilon}{2^{n+1}}\right)^2$$
$$> 1 - \frac{\epsilon}{2^n}.$$

Moreover, the saltus of $f(x)$ relative to E_n is less than $\epsilon/2^n$ at every point of E_n. Now let $E = \bigcap_{n=1}^{\infty} E_n$. We show that $m(E) > 1 - \epsilon$ and that $f(x)$ is continuous on E relative to E.

1. $C(E) = \bigcup_{n=1}^{\infty} C(E_n)$ so that

$$m(C(E)) \leqq \sum_{n=1}^{\infty} m(C(E_n)) < \sum_{n=1}^{\infty} \frac{\epsilon}{2^n} = \epsilon.$$

Hence $m(E) > 1 - \epsilon$.

2. Let $\xi \in E$. The saltus of $f(x)$ at ξ relative to E_n, hence relative to E, is less than $\epsilon/2^n$ for every n. It follows that the saltus of $f(x)$ at ξ relative to E is 0.

3. Let $F \subset E$ be a closed set such that $m(F) > 1 - \epsilon$. Then $f(x)$ is continuous on F relative to F.

This theorem may be given an alternate form if we make use of the following lemma.

LEMMA 1. If $f(x)$ is defined on a closed set $F \subset [0, 1]$ and is continuous, then $f(x)$ has an extension to a function $g(x)$ continuous on $[0, 1]$ such that $f(x) = g(x)$ on F.

The proof of this lemma is left to the student.

The lemma and Theorem 5 yield the following interesting theorem which strengthens Theorem 3.

THEOREM 6. If $f(x)$ is a measurable function, then for every $\epsilon > 0$ there is a continuous function $g(x)$ such that $f(x) = g(x)$ on a set of measure greater than $1 - \epsilon$.

Exercises

2.1 Define exterior approximate continuity for an arbitrary function by using the concept, "exterior metric density" (Exercise 3.1, Chapter 14).

2.2 Show that every function is exteriorly approximately continuous almost everywhere.

2.3 Give an example of a function which is approximately continuous everywhere but is discontinuous at $x = 0$.

2.4 Give an example of an approximately continuous function which is discontinuous at all rationals.

2.5 Show that the sum and product of two approximately continuous functions is approximately continuous.

2.6 Show that every approximately continuous function is of Baire class 1.

2.7 Show that if $f(x)$ is approximately continuous on $[a, b]$ it assumes all values between $f(a)$ and $f(b)$ on $[a, b]$.

3.1 Show that if $f(x)$, not necessarily measurable, is defined on $[0, 1]$ for every $\epsilon > 0$ there is a continuous $g(x)$ such that $|f(x) - g(x)| < \epsilon$ on a set of exterior measure greater than $1 - \epsilon$.

4.1 Show that there is a measurable set S such that both S and $C(S)$ have subsets of positive measure in every interval.

5.1 Prove that if $F \subset [0, 1]$ is closed and $f(x)$ is continuous on F then $f(x)$ may be extended to a $g(x)$ continuous on $[0, 1]$.

5.2 Give an example of a measurable function $f(x)$ defined on $[0, 1]$ such that $f(x)$ differs from every function of Baire class 1 on a set of positive measure.

References

L. W. Cohen, "A New Proof of Lusin's Theorem," *Fund. Math.* 9 (1927), 122.

H. Kestelman, *Modern Theories of Integration*, Oxford, 1937, Chap. 4.

E. J. McShane, *Integration*, Princeton, 1944, Chap. 6.

S. Saks, *Theory of the Integral*, translated by L. C. Young, Warszawá-Lwow, 1937, Chap. 3.

17

The Lebesgue Integral and the Riemann Integral

1. *Introduction*

In this chapter we introduce the definition of integration due to Lebesgue and compare it with the definition which had been given earlier by Riemann and Darboux. Although the latter definition is simple and appealing, it turns out to have certain limitations which make a more general concept of the integral desirable.

Its first defect is related to convergent sequences of functions. If $f_1(x)$, $f_2(x)$, $\cdots$ is a sequence of uniformly bounded functions which converges uniformly to a function $f(x)$, and if the functions $f_1(x)$, $f_2(x)$, $\cdots$ are all integrable in the Riemann sense, then $f(x)$ is also integrable in the Riemann sense and

$$R\int_0^1 f(x)dx = \lim_{n\to\infty} R\int_0^1 f_n(x)dx.$$

The defect appears if uniform convergence is replaced by ordinary convergence. Later in this chapter we shall give an example of a convergent sequence of uniformly bounded Riemann integrable functions whose limit is not integrable in the Riemann sense. The defect lies in the fact that not enough functions are integrable in the Riemann sense. The extension of the integral which was obtained by Lebesgue removes this defect.

The second defect is in reference to the fundamental theorem of the calculus. The situation here is rather complicated and a full discussion will be given in Chapter 19. In this chapter, we show that a defect exists by giving an example of a function $f(x)$ for which $f'(x)$ exists everywhere and is bounded but is not integrable in the Riemann sense.

The definition of the Riemann integral and details related to the defects mentioned above will be given later in this chapter.

Defects like the ones mentioned above impelled mathematicians to seek extensions of the integral concept. In 1902, H. Lebesgue obtained an extension which is quite adequate for the purposes of analysis.

Unless otherwise specified, all sets are subsets of $U = [0, 1]$ and complements of sets are relative to U.

2. *Definition of Lebesgue integral for bounded measurable simple functions*

We first define the Lebesgue integral for the characteristic function of a measurable set S.

DEFINITION 1. If S is any set, the *characteristic function* $f_S(x)$ of S is the function which is equal to 1 for every $x \in S$ and equal to 0 for every $x \in C(S)$.

DEFINITION 2. If S is measurable, the Lebesgue integral

$$\int_0^1 f_S(x)dx$$

of $f_S(x)$ is just the measure, $m(S)$, of S.

Note that if S is nonmeasurable, the Lebesgue integral of $f_S(x)$ is not defined. More generally, the Lebesgue integral is never defined for nonmeasurable functions.

We next extend the definition of the Lebesgue integral to the finitely simple measurable functions.

DEFINITION 3. A function $f(x)$ is finitely simple if its value set is finite, i.e., if the interval $U = [0, 1]$ may be decomposed into a finite number, $S_1, S_2, \cdots, S_n$, of disjoint sets such that $f(x)$ is a constant c_j on each S_j, $j = 1, 2, \cdots, n$.

We shall use the notation $[c_1, S_1; \cdots; c_n, S_n]$ for finitely simple functions.

DEFINITION 4. If $f(x) \equiv [c_1, S_1; \cdots; c_n, S_n]$ is a finitely simple measurable function, then

$$\int_0^1 f(x)dx = \sum_{j=1}^{n} c_j m(S_j).$$

The extension of the definition of the Lebesgue integral is readily made to include all bounded measurable simple functions.

DEFINITION 5. A function $f(x)$ is *simple* if its value set is finite or denumerable, i.e., if the interval $U = [0, 1]$ may be decomposed into a denumerable number, $S_1, S_2, \cdots$, of disjoint sets such that $f(x)$ is a constant, c_j, on each $S_j, j = 1, 2, \cdots$.

We shall use the notation $[c_i, S_i; i = 1, 2, \cdots]$ for simple functions. In some considerations the denumerable class of sets associated with a simple function appears more naturally in correspondence with all integers than with the positive integers. In such a case, the notation $f(x) \equiv [c_k, S_k; -\infty < k < +\infty]$ will be used to designate that U is decomposed into the sets $\cdots, S_{-2}, S_{-1}, S_0, S_1, S_2, \cdots$ and c_k is the value of $f(x)$ on S_k, for every integer k.

DEFINITION 6. If $f(x) \equiv [c_i, S_i; i = 1, 2, \cdots]$ is a bounded simple measurable function, then

$$\int_0^1 f(x)dx = \sum_{i=1}^{\infty} c_i m(S_i).$$

The consistency of this definition must be justified by showing that the value of

$$\int_0^1 f(x)dx$$

does not depend on the order of the terms of the series $\sum_{i=1}^{\infty} c_i m(S_i)$. This is equivalent to the assertion that the series $\sum_{i=1}^{\infty} c_i m(S_i)$ converges absolutely. The proof of this fact may be given as follows: Since $f(x)$ is bounded, there is an $M > 0$ such that $|c_i| < M$ for every $i = 1, 2, \cdots$. Accordingly,

$$\sum_{i=1}^{\infty} |c_i m(S_i)| = \sum_{i=1}^{\infty} |c_i| m(S_i) < M \sum_{i=1}^{\infty} m(S_i) = M.$$

3. *Unbounded measurable simple functions*

The definition of the Lebesgue integral for unbounded simple measurable functions is more delicate. Indeed, the Lebesgue integral may be defined only for certain of these functions, the so-called summable ones.

DEFINITION 7. If $f(x) \equiv [c_i, S_i; i = 1, 2, \cdots]$ is a measurable simple function, $f(x)$ is said to be *summable* if the series $\sum_{i=1}^{\infty} c_i m(S_i)$ converges absolutely.

DEFINITION 8. If $f(x) \equiv [c_i, S_i; i = 1, 2, \cdots]$ is a summable simple function, then

$$\int_0^1 f(x)dx = \sum_{i=1}^{\infty} c_i m(S_i).$$

Some examples will clarify the meaning of "summable function."

1. Decompose the interval $[0, 1/2)$ into a sequence of disjoint intervals whose lengths are respectively equal to $1/4, 1/8, \cdots, 1/2^n, \cdots$. Such

a decomposition is given by the intervals $[0, 1/4)$, $[1/4, 3/8)$, $\cdots$. Let $f(x) = n$ on the interval of the decomposition whose length is $1/2^n$. Decompose the interval $[1/2, 1)$ similarly, and let $f(x) = -n$ on the interval of the decomposition whose length is $1/2^n$. Finally, let $f(1) = 0$. Then $f(x)$ is a measurable simple function.
The series

$$\sum_{n=1}^{\infty} n \cdot \frac{1}{2^n} + \sum_{n=1}^{\infty} - n \cdot \frac{1}{2^n}$$

converges absolutely, so that the function $f(x)$ is summable. By properly grouping terms it is clear that

$$\int_0^1 f(x)dx = 0.$$

2. Using the same decomposition as in example 1, let $f(x) = 2^n$ on the interval of the decomposition of $[0, 1/2)$ whose length is $1/2^n$ and let $f(x) = -2^n$ on the interval of the decomposition of $[1/2, 1)$ whose length is $1/2^n$. Again, let $f(1) = 0$. The series

$$\sum_{n=1}^{\infty} 2^n \cdot \frac{1}{2^n} + \sum_{n=1}^{\infty} (-2^n)\frac{1}{2^n}$$

is conditionally convergent, so that $f(x)$ is not summable. The Lebesgue integral of $f(x)$ does not exist.
3. This time let $f(x) = 2^n$ on the interval of the decomposition of $[0, 1/2)$ whose length is $1/2^n$ and $f(x) = -1/2^n$ on the interval of the decomposition of $[1/2, 1)$ whose length is $1/2^n$. Let $f(1) = 0$. Now the series

$$\sum_{n=1}^{\infty} 2^n \cdot \frac{1}{2^n} + \sum_{n=1}^{\infty} \left(-\frac{1}{2^n}\right)\frac{1}{2^n}$$

is strictly divergent—the sum is $+\infty$ regardless of the order of terms. $f(x)$ is not summable but we may say that

$$\int_0^1 f(x)dx = +\infty.$$

Summarizing these examples, we note that an unbounded measurable simple function $f(x) \equiv [c_i, S_i; i = 1, \cdots]$ may be summable or it may be nonsummable. If it is nonsummable, and the series $\sum_{i=1}^{\infty} c_i m(S_i)$ is conditionally convergent, then

$$\int_0^1 f(x)dx$$

does not exist. If it is nonsummable, and the series $\sum_{i=1}^{\infty} c_i m(S_i)$ is strictly divergent, then

$$\int_0^1 f(x)dx = +\infty \quad \text{or} \quad -\infty$$

according as $\sum_{i=1}^{\infty} c_i m(S_i) = +\infty$ or $-\infty$.

4. *Summability of arbitrary measurable functions*

The notion of summability extends readily from measurable simple functions to arbitrary measurable functions. The concept of a net of points is useful in making this extension.

DEFINITION 9. A set $A = [a_k \mid -\infty < k < +\infty]$ will be called a *net* if it has the following properties:

1. $\cdots < a_{-2} < a_{-1} < a_0 = 0 < a_1 < a_2 < \cdots$,
2. $\lim_{k \to \infty} a_k = +\infty$ and $\lim_{k \to -\infty} a_k = -\infty$,
3. the norm, $N(A) = \sup [a_k - a_{k-1} \mid -\infty < k < +\infty]$, of A is finite.

It is convenient to order the nets.

DEFINITION 10. If $A = [a_k]$ and $B = [b_j]$ are two nets, then $B > A$ if for every k there is a j such that $a_k = b_j$, but there is at least one j such that $b_j \neq a_k$ for every k.

The nets do not form a linear order. For let $A \equiv [2k + 1 \mid -\infty < k < \infty]$ and $B \equiv [2k \mid -\infty < k < \infty]$. Then neither $A > B$ nor $B > A$. However, the order relation of Definition 10 does satisfy the conditions "if $A > B$ and $B > C$, then $A > C$" and "if $A > B$, then not $B > A$." A set with an order relation satisfying these conditions is called a *strict partial order*. The set of nets, ordered as by Definition 10, forms a strict partial order.

If $A = [a_k]$ and $B = [b_k]$ are nets, the net $C = [c_k]$ consisting of all points in A, all points in B, and one extra point satisfies the condition $C > A$ and $C > B$. Hence for every pair A, B of nets there is a net C such that $C > A$ and $C > B$.

We now prove some preliminary propositions leading to the definition of summability for arbitrary measurable functions.

Let $f(x)$ be measurable. For every net $A = [a_k]$ we shall consider the simple function

$$f_A(x) \equiv [a_k, S_k; \; -\infty < k < \infty],$$

where S_k is the set of points for which $a_k \leqq f(x) < a_{k+1}$. The sets S_k are clearly disjoint measurable sets whose union is the interval $U = [0, 1]$.

PROPOSITION 1. If $f(x)$ is measurable and $f_A(x)$ is summable for a net $A = [a_k]$ and if $B = [b_k]$ is a net, then $f_B(x)$ is summable and

$$\left| \int_0^1 f_A(x)dx - \int_0^1 f_B(x)dx \right| \leqq N(A) + N(B).$$

Proof. There is a net $C = [c_k]$ such that $C > A$ and $C > B$. We show first that $f_C(x)$ is summable and that

$$0 \leqq \int_0^1 f_C(x)dx - \int_0^1 f_A(x)dx \leqq N(A).$$

For every k, $-\infty < k < \infty$, let $c_{k1} < c_{k2} < \cdots < c_{km_k}$ be the members of the net C such that $a_k \leqq c_{kj} < a_{k+1}, j = 1, \cdots, m_k$. Let S_k be the set of points for which $a_k \leqq f(x) < a_{k+1}$ and S_{kj} the set of points for which $c_{kj} \leqq f(x) < c_{k,j+1}, j = 1, \cdots, m_k - 1$. Since $S_k = \bigcup_{j=1}^{m_k} S_{kj}$ and $0 \leqq c_{kj} - a_k < N(A)$ so that $-N(A) \leq |c_{kj}| - |a_k|$ for every $-\infty < k < \infty$, $j = 1, \cdots, m_k$, it follows that

$$-N(A) \leqq \sum_{k=-\infty}^{\infty} \sum_{j=1}^{m_k} |c_{kj}| m(S_{kj}) - \sum_{k=-\infty}^{\infty} |a_k| m(S_k) \leqq N(A).$$

Hence $f_C(x)$ is summable and, since

$$\sum_{k=-\infty}^{\infty} \sum_{j=1}^{m_k} c_{kj} m(S_{kj}) - \sum_{k=-\infty}^{\infty} a_k m(S_k) = \sum_{k=-\infty}^{\infty} \sum_{j=1}^{m_k} (c_{kj} - a_k) m(S_{kj})$$

$$\leqq \sum_{k=-\infty}^{\infty} \sum_{j=1}^{m_k} N(A) m(S_{kj}) = N(A),$$

we have

$$0 \leqq \int_0^1 f_C(x)dx - \int_0^1 f_A(x)dx \leqq N(A).$$

By proceeding in much the same way, we also obtain from the summability of $f_C(x)$ the conclusion that $f_B(x)$ is summable and that

$$0 \leqq \int_0^1 f_C(x)dx - \int_0^1 f_B(x)dx \leqq N(B).$$

The student may now verify from these two relations that

$$\left| \int_0^1 f_A(x)dx - \int_0^1 f_B(x)dx \right| \leqq N(A) + N(B).$$

As an immediate consequence of Proposition 1, we have:

PROPOSITION 2. If $f(x)$ is measurable, then $f_A(x)$ is summable either for all nets or for no nets.

Proposition 2 allows us to define summability for arbitrary measurable functions.

DEFINITION 11. A measurable function $f(x)$ is summable if the simple function $f_A(x)$ is summable for some net A.

COROLLARY 1. A measurable function $f(x)$ is summable if $f_A(x)$ is summable for all nets A.

Our next task is, of course, to define the Lebesgue integral for arbitrary summable functions. The groundwork for this definition is laid by the following two propositions.

PROPOSITION 3. If $f(x)$ is summable and $A_1, A_2, \cdots$ is a sequence of nets such that $\lim_{n\to\infty} N(A_n) = 0$, then the sequence

$$\int_0^1 f_{A_1}(x)dx, \int_0^1 f_{A_2}(x)dx, \cdots$$

is a convergent sequence of numbers.

Proof. Let $\epsilon > 0$. There is an N such that for every $n > N$, $N(A_n) < \epsilon/2$. By Proposition 1, for every $m, n > N$, it follows that

$$\left|\int_0^1 f_{A_m}(x)dx - \int_0^1 f_{A_n}(x)dx\right| \leqq N(A_m) + N(A_n) < \epsilon.$$

PROPOSITION 4. If $f(x)$ is summable and $A_1, A_2, \cdots$ and $B_1, B_2, \cdots$ are two sequences of nets such that $\lim_{n\to\infty} N(A_n) = \lim_{n\to\infty} N(B_n) = 0$, then

$$\lim_{n\to\infty} \int_0^1 f_{A_n}(x)dx = \lim_{n\to\infty} \int_0^1 f_{B_n}(x)dx.$$

Proof. Let $\epsilon > 0$. There is an m such that $N(A_m) < \epsilon/4$ and $N(B_m) < \epsilon/4$ and such that both

$$\left|\int_0^1 f_{A_m}(x)dx - \lim_{n\to\infty} \int_0^1 f_{A_n}(x)dx\right| < \frac{\epsilon}{4}$$

and

$$\left|\int_0^1 f_{B_m}(x)dx - \lim_{n\to\infty} \int_0^1 f_{B_n}(x)dx\right| < \frac{\epsilon}{4}.$$

By Proposition 1,

$$\left|\int_0^1 f_{A_m}(x)dx - \int_0^1 f_{B_m}(x)dx\right| \leqq N(A_m) + N(B_m) < \frac{\epsilon}{2}.$$

We then have

$$\left|\lim_{n\to\infty} \int_0^1 f_{A_n}(x)dx - \lim_{n\to\infty} \int_0^1 f_{B_n}(x)dx\right| \leqq \left|\lim_{n\to\infty} \int_0^1 f_{A_n}(x)dx - \int_0^1 f_{A_m}(x)dx\right|$$

$$+ \left|\int_0^1 f_{A_m}(x)dx - \int_0^1 f_{B_m}(x)dx\right| + \left|\int_0^1 f_{B_m}(x)dx - \lim_{n\to\infty} \int_0^1 f_{B_n}(x)dx\right| < \epsilon.$$

Propositions 3 and 4 allow us to define the Lebesgue integral for summable functions.

DEFINITION 12. If $f(x)$ is summable, the Lebesgue integral of $f(x)$ is given by

$$\int_0^1 f(x)dx = \lim_{n\to\infty} \int_0^1 f_{A_n}(x)dx,$$

where $A_1, A_2, \cdots$ is any sequence of nets such that $\lim_{n\to\infty} N(A_n) = 0$.

5. *The Riemann integral*

We now define the Riemann integral and then make a comparison between it and the Lebesgue integral.

DEFINITION 13. A *partition* is a finite set of numbers $a_0 = 0 < a_1 < a_2 < \cdots < a_n = 1$. The associated intervals $[a_0, a_1), [a_1, a_2), \cdots, [a_{n-1}, a_n]$ will also be called a partition.

We associate two numbers $\bar{\phi}_A(f)$ and $\underline{\phi}_A(f)$, defined as follows, with every bounded function $f(x)$ and every partition A:

$$\bar{\phi}_A(f) = \sum_{i=0}^{n-1} (a_{i+1} - a_i) \sup [f(x) \mid x \in [a_i, a_{i+1})]$$

$$\underline{\phi}_A(f) = \sum_{i=0}^{n-1} (a_{i+1} - a_i) \inf [f(x) \mid x \in [a_i, a_{i+1})].$$

The upper and lower Riemann integrals of $f(x)$ are defined in terms of the numbers $\bar{\phi}_A(f)$ and $\underline{\phi}_A(f)$.

DEFINITION 14. The upper and lower Riemann integrals of a bounded function $f(x)$ are respectively

$$R\overline{\int_0^1} f(x)dx = \inf \bar{\phi}_A(f), \text{ and}$$

$$R\underline{\int_0^1} f(x)dx = \sup \underline{\phi}_A(f)$$

for all partitions A.

DEFINITION 15. If

$$R\overline{\int_0^1} f(x)dx = R\underline{\int_0^1} f(x)dx$$

the Riemann integral of $f(x)$ is said to exist and the common value of the upper and lower integrals is designated as

$$R\int_0^1 f(x)dx.$$

If

$$R\overline{\int_0^1} f(x)dx \neq R\underline{\int_0^1} f(x)dx$$

the Riemann integral of $f(x)$ is said not to exist.

This definition of the Riemann integral suggests a possible definition of the Lebesgue integral along similar lines. We now give such a definition and show that for bounded functions it is equivalent to the one given previously for the Lebesgue integral. This definition involves a generalization of the notion of partition.

DEFINITION 16. A generalized partition $\mathsf{A} \equiv [A_1, \cdots, A_n]$ is a decomposition of the closed interval $U \equiv [0, 1]$ into a finite number of disjoint measurable sets $A_1, A_2, \cdots, A_n$.

If the partition A in Definition 13 is considered to be the intervals $[a_0, a_1), [a_1, a_2), \cdots, [a_{n-1}, a_n]$ instead of the numbers $a_0 = 0 < a_1 < \cdots < a_n = 1$, then it is clear that every partition is a generalized partition.

The upper and lower Lebesgue integrals of a function $f(x)$ will now be defined in precisely the same way as the upper and lower Riemann integrals, with the sole exception that generalized partitions will be used instead of partitions.

We associate with every function $f(x)$ and every generalized partition $\mathsf{A} \equiv [A_1, \cdots, A_n]$ the two numbers

$$\bar{\psi}_{\mathsf{A}}(f) = \sum_{i=1}^{n} m(A_i) \sup [f(x) \mid x \in A_i]$$

$$\underline{\psi}_{\mathsf{A}}(f) = \sum_{i=1}^{n} m(A_i) \inf [f(x) \mid x \in A_i].$$

Note that $\bar{\psi}_{\mathsf{A}}(f)$ and $\underline{\psi}_{\mathsf{A}}(f)$ are extensions of $\bar{\phi}_A(f)$ and $\underline{\phi}_A(f)$, respectively, i.e., if $\mathsf{A} \equiv A$ is a partition, then

$$\bar{\phi}_A(f) = \bar{\psi}_{\mathsf{A}}(f) \text{ and } \underline{\phi}_A(f) = \underline{\psi}_{\mathsf{A}}(f).$$

We now define the upper and lower Lebesgue integrals of a function.

DEFINITION 17. The *upper* and *lower Lebesgue integrals* of $f(x)$ are, respectively,

$$\overline{\int_0^1} f(x)dx = \inf \bar{\psi}_{\mathsf{A}}(f), \text{ and}$$

$$\underline{\int_0^1} f(x)dx = \sup \underline{\psi}_{\mathsf{A}}(f),$$

for all generalized partitions A.

Since every partition is also a generalized partition and since $\bar{\psi}_{\mathsf{A}}(f)$ and $\underline{\psi}_{\mathsf{A}}(f)$ are extensions of $\bar{\phi}_A(f)$ and $\underline{\phi}_A(f)$, the following proposition holds.

PROPOSITION 5. For every bounded function $f(x)$ the following inequalities hold:

$$R\overline{\int_0^1} f(x)dx \geqq \overline{\int_0^1} f(x)dx \geqq \underline{\int_0^1} f(x)dx \geqq R\underline{\int_0^1} f(x)dx.$$

An immediate consequence of this proposition is the following:

If the Riemann integral of $f(x)$ exists then the upper and lower Lebesgue integrals are equal to each other and to the Riemann integral. The following proposition establishes a connection between the Lebesgue integral, which was defined in one way, and the upper and lower Lebesgue integrals which were defined in quite a different way.

PROPOSITION 6. If $f(x)$ is bounded and measurable, then

$$\overline{\int_0^1} f(x)dx = \underline{\int_0^1} f(x)dx = \int_0^1 f(x)dx,$$

which is the Lebesgue integral of $f(x)$.

Proof. There is an $M > 0$ such that $|f(x)| < M$ for every $x \in [0, 1]$. Let $\epsilon > 0$ and let $A \equiv [a_k, -\infty < k < \infty]$ be a net such that $N(A) < \epsilon/2$. Let S_k be the set of points x for which $a_k \leqq f(x) < a_{k+1}$. Then $S \equiv [S_k]$ forms a generalized partition since the measurable sets S_k are empty for all but a finite number of values of k. Now,

$$\int_0^1 f_A(x)dx = \sum_{k=-\infty}^{\infty} a_k \cdot m(S_k),$$

and

$$0 \leqq \int_0^1 f(x)dx - \int_0^1 f_A(x)dx < \frac{\epsilon}{2}\cdot$$

On the other hand,

$$\overline{\int_0^1} f(x)dx \leqq \sum_{k=-\infty}^{\infty} m(S_k) \cdot \sup [f(x) \mid x \in S_k]$$

and

$$\underline{\int_0^1} f(x)dx \geqq \sum_{k=-\infty}^{\infty} m(S_k) \cdot \inf [f(x) \mid x \in S_k].$$

But, for every k,

$$\inf [f(x) \mid x \in S_k] \geqq a_k \qquad \text{and } \sup [f(x) \mid x \in S_k] < a_k + \frac{\epsilon}{2}\cdot$$

Hence

$$\underline{\int_0^1} f(x)dx \geqq \sum_{k=-\infty}^{\infty} m(S_k) \cdot \inf [f(x) \mid x \in S_k]$$

$$\geqq \sum_{k=-\infty}^{\infty} m(S_k) \cdot a_k = \int_0^1 f_A(x)dx \geqq \int_0^1 f(x)dx - \frac{\epsilon}{2},$$

and

$$\overline{\int_0^1} f(x)dx \leqq \sum_{k=-\infty}^{\infty} m(S_k) \cdot \sup [f(x) \mid x \in S_k] \leqq \sum_{k=-\infty}^{\infty} m(S_k) \left(a_k + \frac{\epsilon}{2}\right)$$

$$= \int_0^1 f_A(x)dx + \frac{\epsilon}{2} \leqq \int_0^1 f(x)dx + \frac{\epsilon}{2} \cdot$$

Moreover,

$$\overline{\int_0^1} f(x)dx \geqq \underline{\int_0^1} f(x)dx.$$

So,

$$\int_0^1 f(x)dx + \frac{\epsilon}{2} \geqq \overline{\int_0^1} f(x)dx \geqq \underline{\int_0^1} f(x)dx \geqq \int_0^1 f(x)dx - \frac{\epsilon}{2} \cdot$$

Since $\epsilon > 0$ is arbitrary, it follows that

$$\overline{\int_0^1} f(x)dx = \underline{\int_0^1} f(x)dx = \int_0^1 f(x)dx.$$

We note now that if $f(x)$ is unbounded its Riemann integral does not exist, for there will be intervals on which $\sup f(x)$ is infinite. All the above shows that the Lebesgue integral is more general than the Riemann integral, and is at least as general for bounded functions. That the Lebesgue integral is more general, even for the bounded case, is shown by the following example:

Let $f(x) = 0 \quad x$ irrational

$= 1 \quad x$ rational.

Since $f(x)$ is the characteristic function of the set R of rationals and $m(R) = 0$, the Lebesgue integral $\int_0^1 f(x)dx = 0$.

For the upper and lower Riemann integrals of $f(x)$, note that for every interval $[a, b)$, $\sup f(x) = 1$ and $\inf f(x) = 0$ for $x \in [a, b)$. It immediately follows that for every partition A, $\overline{\phi}_A(f) = 1$ and $\underline{\phi}_A(f) = 0$ so that

$$R\overline{\int_0^1} f(x)dx = 1 \text{ and } R\underline{\int_0^1} f(x)dx = 0.$$

Hence the Riemann integral of $f(x)$ does not exist.

6. *A condition for the existence of the Riemann integral*

The condition we are about to give ties Riemann integration to the Lebesgue theory of measure. It asserts that the Riemann integral of a bounded function $f(x)$ exists when and only when the set of discontinuities of $f(x)$ is of measure 0. This theorem will be useful later in our demonstration that the fundamental theorem of the calculus breaks down for the Riemann integral.

For we shall exhibit a function $f(x)$ whose derivative $f'(x)$ exists everywhere but has as its set of discontinuities a set of positive measure. Hence

$$R\int_0^1 f'(x)dx$$

does not exist.

Before proving our theorem we introduce an order relation for partitions analogous to the one given for nets.

DEFINITION 18. If $A \equiv [a_0, \cdots, a_n]$ and $B \equiv [b_0, \cdots, b_m]$ are two partitions, then $B > A$ if for every k, $0 \leqq k \leqq n$, there is a j, $0 \leqq j \leqq m$ such that $a_k = b_j$, but there is at least one $b_j \neq a_k$ for every $k = 0, 1, \cdots, n$.

The partitions have the property that for every pair A and B of partitions there is a partition C such that $C > A$ and $C > B$.

PROPOSITION 7. If $A \equiv [a_0, \cdots, a_n]$ and $B \equiv [b_0, \cdots, b_m]$ and $B > A$, then $\bar{\phi}_B(f) \leqq \bar{\phi}_A(f)$ and $\underline{\phi}_B(f) \geqq \underline{\phi}_A(f)$ for every function $f(x)$.

Proof. Let $b_{k1} = a_k < b_{k2} < \cdots < b_{kn_k} = a_{k+1}$ be those members b_{kj} of B such that $a_k \leqq b_{kj} \leqq a_{k+1}$. Now

$$\bar{\phi}_B(f) = \sum_{k=1}^{n} \sum_{j=2}^{nk} (b_{kj} - b_{k,\,j-1}) \cdot \sup [f(x) \mid x \in [b_{k,\,j-1}, b_{kj})]$$

$$\leqq \sum_{k=1}^{n} (a_{k+1} - a_k) \sup [f(x) \mid x \in [a_k, a_{k+1})] = \bar{\phi}_A(f).$$

Similarly, $\underline{\phi}_B(f) \geqq \underline{\phi}_A(f)$.

THEOREM 1. A necessary and sufficient condition that a bounded function $f(x)$ be Riemann-integrable is that the set of points for which $f(x)$ is discontinuous be of measure 0.

Proof. Suppose that the set E of discontinuities of $f(x)$ is not of measure 0. Since E is of type F_σ (Theorem 5′, Chapter 7), the set E is measurable. E is of positive measure. $E = \bigcup_{n=1}^{\infty} E_n$, where E_n is the set of points for which the saltus of $f(x)$ is at least equal to $1/n$. E_n is closed for every n, and for some n is of positive measure, say $\mu > 0$. So we have a set E_n such that $m(E_n) = \mu > 0$ and $\omega(f;\ x) \geqq 1/n$ for every $x \in E_n$. Now, let $A \equiv [a_0, \cdots, a_n]$ be a partition. Those intervals I of the partition A which contain points of E_n are of length sum at least equal to μ. The saltus of $f(x)$ in each of these intervals is at least $1/n$. It follows that

$$\bar{\phi}_A(f) - \underline{\phi}_A(f) = \sum_{i=0}^{n-1} (a_{i+1} - a_i) \sup [f(x) \mid x \in [a_i, a_{i+1})]$$

$$- \sum_{i=0}^{n-1} (a_{i+1} - a_i) \inf [f(x) \mid x \in [a_i, a_{i+1})] \geqq \frac{\mu}{n}$$

for every partition A. We show, on the other hand, that if $f(x)$ is Riemann integrable then for every $\epsilon > 0$ there is a partition $A(\epsilon)$ such that $\bar{\phi}_{A(\epsilon)}(f) - \underline{\phi}_{A(\epsilon)}(f) < \epsilon$. For let A be such that

$$\bar{\phi}_A(f) < R\int_0^1 f(x)dx + \frac{\epsilon}{2}$$

and B such that

$$\underline{\phi}_B(f) > R\int_0^1 f(x)dx - \frac{\epsilon}{2}$$

There is a partition $A(\epsilon)$ such that $A(\epsilon) > A$, $A(\epsilon) > B$. By Proposition 7, $\bar{\phi}_{A(\epsilon)}(f) \leqq \bar{\phi}_A(f)$ and $\underline{\phi}_{A(\epsilon)}(f) \geqq \underline{\phi}_B(f)$. It follows that $\bar{\phi}_{A(\epsilon)}(f) - \underline{\phi}_{A(\epsilon)}(f) < \epsilon$. Hence our function $f(x)$ is not Riemann-integrable.

Suppose that the set E of points of discontinuity of $f(x)$ is of measure 0. Again $E = \bigcup_{n=1}^{\infty} E_n$, where E_n, the set of points x for which $\omega(f; x) \geqq 1/n$, is a closed set. Each E_n is of measure 0 and, accordingly, is nowhere dense. (For a closed set which is not nowhere dense contains an interval and so is not of measure 0.) Since $f(x)$ is bounded, there is an $M > 0$ such that $|f(x)| < M$ for every $x \in [0, 1]$. Let $\epsilon > 0$. There is an n such that $1/n < \epsilon/2$. Let $[a_1, b_1]$, $[a_2, b_2]$, $\cdots$, $[a_k, b_k]$ be disjoint closed intervals in the complement of E_n the sum of whose lengths exceeds $1 - \epsilon/4M$. Let A be the partition determined by the intervals $J_1, J_2, \cdots, J_{k+1}$ complementary to $[a_1, b_1]$, $\cdots$, $[a_k, b_k]$ and subintervals $I_1, I_2, \cdots, I_m$ of $[a_1, b_1]$, $\cdots$, $[a_k, b_k]$ in each of which the saltus of $f(x)$ is less than $\dfrac{\epsilon}{2}$. Then

$$\begin{aligned}\bar{\phi}_A(f) - \underline{\phi}_A(f) &= \sum_{i=1}^{k+1} l(J_i) \sup[f(x) \mid x \in J_i] \\ &+ \sum_{j=1}^{m} l(I_j) \sup[f(x) \mid x \in I_j] - \sum_{i=1}^{k+1} l(J_i) \inf[f(x) \mid x \in J_i] \\ &- \sum_{j=1}^{m} l(I_j) \inf[f(x) \mid x \in I_j] = \sum_{i=1}^{k+1} l(J_i)\omega(f, J_i) \\ &+ \sum_{j=1}^{m} l(I_j)\omega(f, I_j) \leqq \frac{\epsilon}{4M} \cdot 2M + \frac{\epsilon}{2} = \epsilon.\end{aligned}$$

But

$$\bar{\phi}_A(f) \geqq R\overline{\int_0^1} f(x)dx$$

and

$$\underline{\phi}_A(f) \leqq R\underline{\int_0^1} f(x)dx.$$

Hence

$$R\overline{\int_0^1} f(x)dx \leqq R\underline{\int_0^1} f(x)dx + \epsilon$$

for every $\epsilon > 0$, so that $f(x)$ is Riemann-integrable.

7. *First defect of the Riemann integral*

We now give an example of a uniformly bounded sequence of Riemann-integrable functions whose limit is not Riemann-integrable. Let $r_1, r_2, \cdots$ be the rational numbers in the closed interval $U = [0, 1]$. For every positive integer n, let

$$f_n(x) = 1, \; x \in r_k, \; k = 1, 2, \cdots, n,$$
$$= 0, \text{ elsewhere.}$$

The sequence $f_n(x)$ converges to the function

$$f(x) = 1, \; x \text{ rational},$$
$$= 0, \; x \text{ irrational}.$$

For every n, the function $f_n(x)$ is Riemann-integrable, by Theorem 1, since its set of points of discontinuity is finite, and so is of measure 0.

However, as we have already seen, or if we wish, by Theorem 1, the function $f(x)$, which is discontinuous everywhere, is not Riemann-integrable.

8. *Second defect of the Riemann integral*

We now give an example of a function $f(x)$ whose derivative $f'(x)$ is bounded but is discontinuous on a set of positive measure. Our set of positive measure will be the nowhere-dense closed set E of measure $2/3$ defined as follows: Let I_{11} be the middle open interval of $[0, 1]$ of length $1/4$. Consider I_{11} as removed. Let I_{21} and I_{22} be the middle open intervals of length sum $(1/4)^2$ of the remaining two closed intervals. Consider I_{21} and I_{22} as removed. Let I_{31}, I_{32}, I_{33}, and I_{34} be the middle open intervals of length sum $(1/4)^3$ of the remaining four closed intervals. Consider I_{31}, I_{32}, I_{33}, and I_{34} as removed. Continue this process ad infinitum in the obviously suggested manner. Let

$$G = \bigcup_{n=1}^{\infty} \bigcup_{m=1}^{2^{n-1}} I_{nm},$$

and let $E = C(G)$. Now E is a closed nowhere-dense set. The sum of the lengths of the components of G is $1/3$, so that the measure of G is $1/3$. The measure of E is thus equal to $2/3$.

Let $f(x) = 0$ on E. We have yet to define $f(x)$ on each I_{nm}.

Let $I_{nm} = (a, b)$. Let $f(x) = (x - a)^2 \sin 1/(x - a)$ on $(a, \alpha]$, where α is any point to the left of $(a + b)/2$ at which the derivative of $(x - a)^2 \sin 1/(x - a)$ is 0. Let $f(x) = f(\alpha)$ for $x \in [\alpha, (a + b)/2]$. Define $f(x)$ on the right half of (a, b) by reflection about the line $x = (a + b)/2$. So $f(x)$ is defined on $[0, 1]$.

On (a, b), $|f(x)| \leqq (x-a)^2$ and $|f(x)| \leqq (x-b)^2$. The student can verify that $f'(x)$ exists on G, that it is bounded by 1, and that for every $I_{nm} = (a, b)$ there are sequences of points in I_{nm} converging to a and to b respectively on which $f'(x) = 1$ and $f'(x) = 0$.

We show, moreover, that $f'(x)$ exists and is equal to 0 on E. Let $\xi \in E$. Choose $\delta > 0$. Suppose $|x - \xi| < \delta$. Then if $x \in E$,

$$\left|\frac{f(x) - f(\xi)}{x - \xi}\right| = 0.$$

If $x \notin E$, then $x \in I_{nm} = (a, b)$ for some n, m. Suppose a is the endpoint of I_{nm} nearest to ξ. Then

$$\left|\frac{f(x) - f(\xi)}{x - \xi}\right| = \left|\frac{f(x)}{x - \xi}\right| < \left|\frac{f(x)}{x - a}\right| \leqq \left|\frac{(x-a)^2}{x - a}\right| < \delta.$$

Hence

$$|x - \xi| < \delta \text{ implies } \left|\frac{f(x) - f(\xi)}{x - \xi}\right| < \delta,$$

so that $f'(\xi) = 0$. The derivative $f'(x)$ exists everywhere and is bounded.

It is now an easy matter to show that $f'(x)$ is discontinuous on E. Since E is of positive measure, the Riemann integral of $f'(x)$ does not exist.

In subsequent chapters it will be shown that the above defects no longer appear in the theory of Lebesgue integration.

Exercises

2.1 Show that if an infinite series is absolutely convergent its sum does not depend upon the order of its terms.

2.2 Show that if an infinite series is conditionally convergent then for every ξ its terms may be rearranged so that the series will converge to ξ. Generalize.

2.3 Show that if the series $\sum_{n=1}^{\infty} a_n$ converges absolutely and if $\{b_n\}$ is a bounded sequence then $\sum_{n=1}^{\infty} a_n b_n$ converges absolutely.

4.1 Define summability for functions on $(-\infty, \infty)$.

4.2 Show that $f(x)$ is summable if and only if $f_1(x)$ and $f_2(x)$ are both summable, where $f_1(x) = f(x)$ if $f(x) > 0$, $f_1(x) = 0$ if $f(x) \leqq 0$ and $f_2(x) = f(x)$ if $f(x) < 0$, $f_2(x) = 0$ if $f(x) \geqq 0$.

4.3 Justify the following step in the proof of Proposition 1:

$$\sum_{k=-\infty}^{\infty} \sum_{j=1}^{m_k} c_{kj} m(S_{kj}) - \sum_{k=-\infty}^{\infty} a_k m(S_k) = \sum_{k=-\infty}^{\infty} \sum_{j=1}^{m_k} (c_{kj} - a_k) m(S_{kj}).$$

5.1 For every summable $f(x)$ on $[0, 1]$ and every $\epsilon > 0$ show that there is a bounded step function $g(x)$ such that

$$\int_0^1 |f(x) - g(x)|dx < \epsilon.$$

5.2 Show that if $f^2(x)$ is summable and periodic of period 1 then

$$\lim_{h\to 0} \int_0^1 (f(x+h) - f(x))^2 dx = 0.$$

5.3 Two functions $\phi(x)$ and $\psi(x)$ on $[a, b]$ are called *orthogonal* if

$$\int_a^b \phi(x)\psi(x)dx = 0.$$

If $\phi_1(x), \phi_2(x), \cdots, \phi_n(x)$ are orthogonal to each other and $f^2(x)$ is summable find the values of $a_1, a_2, \cdots, a_n$ for which

$$\int_a^b (f(x) - \sum_{i=1}^n a_i\phi_i(x))^2 dx$$

is a minimum.

5.4 If $\phi_1(x), \phi_2(x), \cdots, \phi_n(x)$ and $f(x)$ are as in Exercise 5.3 and $a_1, a_2, \cdots, a_n$ are those numbers for which

$$\int_a^b (f(x) - \sum_{i=1}^n a_i\phi_i(x))^2 dx$$

is a minimum, show that

$$\int_a^b f^2(x)dx \geqq \sum_{i=1}^n a_i^2.$$

5.5 Show, if $f^2(x)$ and $g^2(x)$ are summable on $[0, 1]$, that

$$\left[\int_0^1 f(x)g(x)dx\right]^2 \leqq \int_0^1 f^2(x)dx \int_0^1 g^2(x)dx.$$

This is known as *Schwartz's inequality*.

5.6 If $f(x)$ is summable on $[0, 2\pi]$, show that

$$\lim_{n\to\infty} \int_0^{2\pi} f(x) \sin nx\, dx = 0, \quad \lim_{n\to\infty} \int_0^{2\pi} f(x) \cos nx\, dx = 0.$$

Hint: First prove the statement for step functions.

5.7 If $f(x) \geqq 0$ and $g(x)$ are summable on $[0, 1]$ and $m \leqq g(x) \leqq M$ show that

$$m\int_0^1 f(x)dx \leqq \int_0^1 f(x)g(x)dx \leqq M\int_0^1 f(x)dx.$$

5.8 If $f(x)$ is summable and $g(x)$ is nondecreasing on $[0, 1]$ and if $\alpha \leqq \lim_{x\to 0} g(x)$ and $\beta \geqq \lim_{x\to 1} g(x)$, show that there is a $\xi \in [0, 1]$ such that

$$\int_0^1 f(x)g(x)dx = \alpha \int_0^\xi f(x)dx + \beta \int_\xi^1 f(x)dx.$$

5.9 Using the definition of Riemann integral show that

$$\int_0^\pi \sin x dx = 2.$$

5.10 Show that

$$\int_0^1 |f(x)|dx = 0$$

if and only if $f(x) = 0$ almost everywhere.

6.1 Give an example of a set of measure 0 such that no Riemann integrable function is discontinuous at all the points of S.

7.1 Give an example of a function on $[0, 1]$ which is differentiable but whose derivative is discontinuous at every point of a set of measure 1.

References

C. Carathéodory, *Vorlesungen über reelle Funktionen*, Leipzig, 1927, Chap. 8.

H. Kestelman, *Modern Theories of Integration*, Oxford, 1937, Chaps. 2, 5.

H. Lebesgue, *Leçons sur l'intégration et la recherche des fonctions primitives*, Paris, 1928, Chaps. 2, 5, 7.

E. J. McShane, *Integration*, Princeton, 1944, Chap. 2.

Ch. J. de la Vallée Poussin, *Intégrales de Lebesgue, Fonctions d'ensembles, Classes de Baire*, Paris, 1934, Chap. 3.

S. Saks, *Theory of the Integral*, translated by L. C. Young, Warszawa-Lwow, 1937, Chap. 1

18

The Lebesgue Integral as a Set Function

1. *Introduction*

The concepts of "summability" and "Lebesgue integral" which have been defined for functions on $U = [0, 1]$ may, with little change, be defined on any measurable set S of finite measure. Thus, for a measurable function $f(x)$ which is summable on U, it turns out that $f(x)$ is also summable on every measurable subset S of U and $f(x)$ has a Lebesgue integral

$$\int_S f(x)dx$$

on S. From this viewpoint the Lebesgue integral is a set function whose domain is the class of measurable subsets of U and whose range is the set of real numbers.

2. *Lebesgue integral on a measurable set*

Let S be any measurable set of positive measure. Summability and the Lebesgue integral will now be defined for functions on S in much the same way as for functions on U. If $f(x)$ is a measurable simple function on S—i.e., the value set of $f(x)$ is a finite or denumerable set $\{a_n\}$—and for every n the set S_n on which $f(x) = a_n$ is measurable, then $f(x)$ is summable if and only if the series $\sum_{n=1}^{\infty} a_n m(S_n)$ converges absolutely. If $f(x)$ is summable, then

$$\int_S f(x)dx = \sum_{n=1}^{\infty} a_n m(S_n).$$

For an arbitrary measurable function $f(x)$, defined on S, one proceeds in much the same way as for a function defined on U. In the first place, if A is a net, the function $f_A(x)$ is defined as before. It is again true that the simple functions $f_A(x)$ are summable either for all nets or for no nets. If the $f_A(x)$ are summable, then $f(x)$ is said to be summable. If $f(x)$ is summable and if A and B are nets, then

$$\left|\int_S f_A(x)dx - \int_S f_B(x)dx\right| < m(S) \cdot (\mathcal{N}(A) + \mathcal{N}(B)).$$

It then follows, as before, that if $f(x)$ is summable then

$$\int_S f(x)dx$$

may be defined as

$$\lim_{n\to\infty} \int_S f_{A_n}(x)dx,$$

where $\{A_n\}$ is any sequence of nets whose norms converge to 0.

The proof of these facts follows the lines of the proof for the case $S = U$. We state several propositions some of which will be useful later.

PROPOSITION 1. If $f(x) = c$ on S, then

$$\int_S f(x)dx = cm(S).$$

PROPOSITION 2. If $f(x)$ is summable on S, then $|f(x)|$ is summable on S and

$$\int_S |f(x)|dx \geqq \left|\int_S f(x)dx\right|.$$

PROPOSITION 3. If $f(x) \leqq g(x)$ on S and both $f(x)$ and $g(x)$ are summable on S, then

$$\int_S f(x)dx \leqq \int_S g(x)dx.$$

PROPOSITION 4. If $f(x)$ is summable on S and T is a measurable subset of S, then $f(x)$ is summable on T.

PROPOSITION 5. If $f(x)$ is summable on S and c is a real number, then $cf(x)$ and $f(x) + c$ are summable on S and

$$\int_S cf(x)dx = c\int_S f(x)dx, \quad \int_S (f(x) + c)dx = \int_S f(x)dx + c\cdot m(S).$$

PROPOSITION 6. If $f(x)$ and $g(x)$ are summable, if $h(x)$ is measurable and $f(x) \leqq h(x) \leqq g(x)$ then $h(x)$ is summable and

$$\int_S f(x)dx \leqq \int_S h(x)dx \leqq \int_S g(x)dx.$$

The proofs of these propositions follow readily from the definitions and are left to the student.

3. *Integral of a sum*

The object of this section is to prove that if $f(x)$ and $g(x)$ are summable on S, then $f(x) + g(x)$ is summable on S and

$$\int_S (f(x) + g(x))dx = \int_S f(x)dx + \int_S g(x)dx.$$

We first prove this for simple functions.

PROPOSITION 7. If $f(x)$ and $g(x)$ are summable simple functions on a measurable set S, then $f(x) + g(x)$ is a summable simple function on S and

$$\int_S (f(x) + g(x))dx = \int_S f(x)dx + \int_S g(x)dx.$$

Proof. Let $f(x) = [a_k, S_k; -\infty < k < \infty]$ and $g(x) = [b_k, T_k; -\infty < k < \infty]$. Then $f(x) + g(x)$ is the simple function given by $[(a_i + b_j), S_i \cap T_j; -\infty < i < \infty, -\infty < j < \infty]$. Now, the series

$$\sum_{i=-\infty}^{\infty} \sum_{j=-\infty}^{\infty} (a_i + b_j)m(S_i \cap T_j)$$

converges absolutely. For its absolute convergence is clear when the terms are rearranged as

$$\sum_{i=-\infty}^{\infty} \sum_{j=-\infty}^{\infty} a_i m(S_i \cap T_j) + \sum_{j=-\infty}^{\infty} \sum_{i=-\infty}^{\infty} b_j m(S_i \cap T_j)$$
$$= \sum_{i=-\infty}^{\infty} a_i m(S_i) + \sum_{j=-\infty}^{\infty} b_j m(T_j),$$

since the two summands are absolutely convergent in view of the summability of $f(x)$ and $g(x)$. We now have

$$\int_S (f(x) + g(x))dx = \sum_{i=-\infty}^{\infty} \sum_{j=-\infty}^{\infty} (a_i + b_j)m(S_i \cap T_j)$$
$$= \sum_{i=-\infty}^{\infty} a_i m(S_i) + \sum_{j=-\infty}^{\infty} b_j m(T_j) = \int_S f(x)dx + \int_S g(x)dx.$$

Before applying this proposition to obtain the theorem for the general case we need the following lemma.

LEMMA 1. If $f(x)$ and $g(x)$ are measurable on S, $f(x)$ is summable, and $|f(x) - g(x)| \leqq k$ for every $x \in S$, then $g(x)$ is also summable and

$$\left|\int_S f(x)dx - \int_S g(x)dx\right| \leqq k \cdot m(S).$$

Proof. For every $x \in S$,

$$f(x) - k \leqq g(x) \leqq f(x) + k$$

so that $g(x)$ is summable and

$$\left|\int_S f(x)dx - \int_S g(x)dx\right| \leqq k \cdot m(S),$$

by Propositions 5 and 6.

We are now ready to prove the theorem.

THEOREM 1. If $f(x)$ and $g(x)$ are summable functions on a measurable set S, then $f(x) + g(x)$ is summable and

$$\int_S (f(x) + g(x))dx = \int_S f(x)dx + \int_S g(x)dx.$$

Proof. Let $\{A_n\}$ be a sequence of nets such that $\lim_{n\to\infty} N(A_n) = 0$. Then, for every n,

$$0 \leqq f(x) - f_{A_n}(x) \leqq N(A_n),$$

and

$$0 \leqq g(x) - g_{A_n}(x) \leqq N(A_n),$$

so that

$$0 \leqq (f(x) + g(x)) - (f_{A_n}(x) + g_{A_n}(x)) \leqq 2N(A_n).$$

But $f_{A_n}(x)$ and $g_{A_n}(x)$ are summable simple functions. Hence $f_{A_n}(x) + g_{A_n}(x)$ is a summable simple function. By the lemma, $f(x) + g(x)$ is summable, and

$$\left|\int_S (f(x) + g(x))dx - \int_S (f_{A_n}(x) + g_{A_n}(x))dx\right| \leqq 2N(A_n) \cdot m(S).$$

Now, let $\epsilon > 0$. There is an n such that

$$\left|\int_S f(x)dx - \int_S f_{A_n}(x)dx\right| < \frac{\epsilon}{4}, \quad \left|\int_S g(x)dx - \int_S g_{A_n}(x)dx\right| < \frac{\epsilon}{4}$$

and $N(A_n) < \epsilon/4m(S)$. Then

$$\begin{aligned}
&\left|\int_S (f(x) + g(x))dx - \int_S f(x)dx - \int_S g(x)dx\right| \\
&\quad \leqq \left|\int_S (f(x) + g(x))dx - \int_S (f_{A_n}(x) + g_{A_n}(x))dx\right| \\
&\qquad + \left|\int_S f(x)dx - \int_S f_{A_n}(x)dx\right| + \left|\int_S g(x)dx - \int_S g_{A_n}(x)dx\right| \\
&\qquad < \frac{2\epsilon}{4m(S)} \cdot m(S) + \frac{\epsilon}{4} + \frac{\epsilon}{4} = \epsilon.
\end{aligned}$$

Since $\epsilon > 0$ is arbitrary,

$$\int_S (f(x) + g(x))dx = \int_S f(x)dx + \int_S g(x)dx.$$

4. *Absolute continuity*

We now come to the first important property of the Lebesgue integral as a set function: *absolute continuity*. For purposes of comparison we first define continuous set functions.

DEFINITION 1. A set function $\phi(S)$ defined on a class of measurable sets is said to be *continuous* if for every $\epsilon > 0$ there is a $\delta > 0$ such that if $m(S) < \delta$ then $|\phi(S)| < \epsilon$.

DEFINITION 2. A set function $\phi(S)$ defined on a class of measurable sets is said to be absolutely continuous if for every $\epsilon > 0$ there is a $\delta > 0$ such that if $S_1, S_2, \cdots, S_n$ is any finite number of disjoint sets for which

$$\sum_{k=1}^{n} m(S_k) < \delta$$

then

$$\sum_{k=1}^{n} |\phi(S_k)| < \epsilon.$$

PROPOSITION 8. A set function $\phi(S)$ defined on a class of measurable sets is absolutely continuous if and only if for every $\epsilon > 0$ there is a $\delta > 0$ such that if $S_1, S_2, \cdots, S_n, \cdots$ is any finite or denumerable number of disjoint sets for which

$$\sum_{n=1}^{\infty} m(S_n) < \delta$$

then

$$\sum_{n=1}^{\infty} |\phi(S_n)| < \epsilon.$$

The proof is left to the student.

PROPOSITION 9. If S_1 and S_2 are disjoint measurable sets on each of which $f(x)$ is summable, then $f(x)$ is summable on $S = S_1 \cup S_2$ and

$$\int_S f(x)dx = \int_{S_1} f(x)dx + \int_{S_2} f(x)dx.$$

Proof. Let
$$\begin{aligned} f_1(x) &= f(x) \quad x \in S_1 \\ &= 0 \quad\quad x \in S - S_1, \end{aligned}$$

and
$$\begin{aligned} f_2(x) &= f(x) \quad x \in S_2 \\ &= 0 \quad\quad x \in S - S_2. \end{aligned}$$

Then $f(x) = f_1(x) + f_2(x)$ for every $x \in S$. By Theorem 1,

$$\int_S f(x)dx = \int_S f_1(x)dx + \int_S f_2(x)dx.$$

But

$$\int_S f_1(x)dx = \int_{S_1} f(x)dx,$$

and

$$\int_S f_2(x)dx = \int_{S_2} f(x)dx.$$

COROLLARY 1. If $S_1, S_2, \cdots, S_n$ are disjoint measurable sets on each of which $f(x)$ is summable and $S = \bigcup_{k=1}^{n} S_k$, then $f(x)$ is summable on S and

$$\int_S f(x)dx = \sum_{k=1}^{n} \int_{S_k} f(x)dx.$$

Proof. By Proposition 9 and finite induction.

PROPOSITION 10. If $f(x)$ is summable on S, then for every $\epsilon > 0$ there is an $M > 0$ such that if T and R are the sets on which $f(x) > M$ and $f(x) < -M$, respectively, then

$$0 \leqq \int_T f(x)dx < \epsilon \text{ and } -\epsilon < \int_R f(x)dx \leqq 0.$$

Proof. Consider a net A such that $N(A) < \epsilon/2m(S)$. Then $f_A(x)$ is a summable simple function so that there is a $k > 0$ such that if T_1 is the set of points for which $f_A(x) > k$ then

$$\int_{T_1} f_A(x)dx < \frac{\epsilon}{2}\cdot$$

Let $M > k + N(A)$ and let T be the set of points for which $f(x) > M$. Then $T \subset T_1$ so that

$$\int_T f_A(x)dx < \frac{\epsilon}{2}\cdot$$

Now

$$\int_T f(x)dx \leqq \int_T f_A(x)dx + N(A) \cdot m(S) < \frac{\epsilon}{2} + \frac{\epsilon}{2m(S)} \cdot m(S) = \epsilon.$$

This proves half the proposition. The remainder of the proof can be supplied by the student.

We may now prove the theorem of this section.

THEOREM 2. If $f(x)$ is a summable function defined on a measurable set S then the Lebesgue integral of $f(x)$ is an absolutely continuous set function on the measurable subsets of S.

Proof. Let $\epsilon > 0$. There is an M such that if T and R are the sets on which $f(x) > M$ and $f(x) < -M$, respectively, then

$$0 \leqq \int_T f(x)dx < \frac{\epsilon}{3} \text{ and } -\frac{\epsilon}{3} < \int_R f(x)dx \leqq 0.$$

Let $\delta = \epsilon/3M$. Now, let $S_1, S_2, \cdots, S_n$ be disjoint measurable sets such that $\sum_{k=1}^{n} m(S_k) < \delta$. We show that

$$\sum_{k=1}^{n} \left| \int_{S_k} f(x)dx \right| < \epsilon,$$

thus establishing the absolute continuity.

Let $Q = \bigcup_{k=1}^{n} S_k$. Then

$$\sum_{k=1}^{n} \left| \int_{S_k} f(x)dx \right| \leqq \sum_{k=1}^{n} \int_{S_k} |f(x)|dx = \int_Q |f(x)|dx.$$

Let $Q_1 = Q - (T \cup R)$, $Q_2 = Q \cap T$, $Q_3 = Q \cap R$. Now

$$\int_Q |f(x)|dx = \int_{Q_1} |f(x)|dx + \int_{Q_2} f(x)dx - \int_{Q_3} f(x)dx.$$

But

$$0 \leqq \int_{Q_2} f(x)dx < \frac{\epsilon}{3} \text{ and } -\frac{\epsilon}{3} < \int_{Q_3} f(x)dx \leqq 0.$$

Moreover,

$$|f(x)| \leqq M \text{ on } Q_1 \text{ and } m(Q_1) \leqq m(Q) < \delta.$$

Hence,

$$\int_Q |f(x)|dx < M\delta + \frac{\epsilon}{3} + \frac{\epsilon}{3} = \epsilon.$$

Accordingly,

$$\sum_{k=1}^{n} \left| \int_{S_k} f(x)dx \right| < \epsilon.$$

5. *Complete additivity*

Another important property of the Lebesgue integral is that of complete additivity.

DEFINITION 3. A set function $\phi(S)$ defined on a class of sets is said to be *completely additive* if for any finite or denumerable number of disjoint sets

$S_1, S_2, \cdots, S_n, \cdots$ in the class their union $S = \bigcup_{n=1}^{\infty} S_n$ is in the class and

$$\phi(S) = \sum_{n=1}^{\infty} \phi(S_n).$$

We need two lemmas.

LEMMA 2. If $\phi(S)$ is completely additive, then $-\phi(S)$ is completely additive.

LEMMA 3. If $\phi(S)$ and $\psi(S)$ are completely additive, then $\phi(S) + \psi(S)$ is completely additive.

The proof of these lemmas is left to the student.

PROPOSITION 11. If S is a measurable set and $f(x)$ is a nonnegative summable function on S, then

$$\int_T f(x)dx$$

is a completely additive set function on the class of measurable subsets of S.

Proof. Let $T_1, T_2, \cdots, T_n, \cdots$ be disjoint subsets of S and let $T = \bigcup_{n=1}^{\infty} T_n$. Let $\epsilon > 0$. There is a $\delta > 0$ such that if $S_1, S_2, \cdots, S_n, \cdots$ is a sequence of disjoint sets such that $\sum_{n=1}^{\infty} m(S_n) < \delta$ then

$$\sum_{n=1}^{n} \int_{S_n} f(x)dx < \epsilon.$$

Now there is an N such that $m(T - \bigcup_{n=1}^{N} T_n) < \delta$. Hence

$$\int_{T-\bigcup_{n=1}^{N} T_n} f(x)dx < \epsilon.$$

Since

$$\int_T f(x)dx = \int_{T-\bigcup_{n=1}^{N} T_n} f(x)dx + \int_{\bigcup_{n=1}^{N} T_n} f(x)dx,$$

$$\sum_{n=1}^{N} \int_{T_n} f(x)dx = \int_{\bigcup_{n=1}^{N} T_n} f(x)dx > \int_T f(x)dx - \epsilon.$$

It follows that

$$\sum_{n=1}^{\infty} \int_{T_n} f(x)dx \geqq \int_T f(x)dx.$$

On the other hand, since for every N, $\bigcup_{n=1}^{N} T_n \subset T$,

$$\sum_{n=1}^{N} \int_{T_n} f(x)dx = \int_{\bigcup_{n=1}^{N} T_n} f(x)dx \leqq \int_T f(x)dx$$

so that

$$\sum_{n=1}^{\infty} \int_{T_n} f(x)dx \leqq \int_T f(x)dx.$$

We have accordingly shown that

$$\int_T f(x)dx = \sum_{n=1}^{\infty} \int_{T_n} f(x)dx.$$

THEOREM 3. If S is a measurable set and $f(x)$ is a summable function on S then

$$\int_T f(x)dx$$

is a completely additive set function on the class of measurable subsets of S.

Proof. Let
$$f_1(x) = f(x) \quad \text{if } f(x) \geqq 0$$
$$= 0 \quad \text{if } f(x) < 0,$$

and
$$f_2(x) = f(x) \quad \text{if } f(x) \leqq 0$$
$$= 0 \quad \text{if } f(x) > 0.$$

Then $f(x) = f_1(x) + f_2(x)$. Now $f_1(x)$ is a nonnegative summable function and $-f_2(x)$ is a nonnegative summable function. Hence, by Proposition 11 and Lemma 2,

$$\int_T f_1(x)dx \text{ and } \int_T f_2(x)dx$$

are completely additive on the measurable subsets of S. By Lemma 3,

$$\int_T f(x)dx$$

is completely additive.

We state one more proposition.

PROPOSITION 12. If $S_1, S_2, \cdots, S_n, \cdots$ are disjoint sets on each of which $f(x)$ is summable and the series

$$\sum_{n=1}^{\infty} \int_{S_n} |f(x)|dx$$

converges then $f(x)$ is summable on $S = \bigcup_{n=1}^{\infty} S_n$ and

$$\int_S f(x)dx = \sum_{n=1}^{\infty} \int_{S_n} f(x)dx.$$

The proof is left to the student.

6. *Limits of convergent sequences of integrable functions (uniformly bounded case)*

We now address ourselves to the behavior of the Lebesgue integral with respect to the limit operation. We observed that the Riemann integral is inadequate in this connection since certain uniformly bounded convergent sequences of Riemann integrable functions have limits which are not integrable in the Riemann sense.

THEOREM 4. If S is a measurable set and $\{f_n(x)\}$ is a uniformly bounded convergent sequence of measurable functions defined on S whose limit is $f(x)$ then

$$\lim_{n\to\infty} \int_S f_n(x)dx = \int_S f(x)dx,$$

where integration is taken in the Lebesgue sense.

Proof. $f(x)$, as the limit of a convergent sequence of measurable functions, is a measurable function. All functions involved are bounded and measurable, hence summable.

There is an $M > 0$ such that for every n and every $x \in S$, $|f_n(x)| < M$. Then also, for every $x \in S$, $|f(x)| \leqq M$. Now, let $\epsilon > 0$. By the Theorem of Egoroff, there is a measurable set $T \subset S$ such that $m(S - T) < \epsilon/4M$ and $\{f_n(x)\}$ converges uniformly on T to $f(x)$. There is an N such that for every $n > N$ and $x \in T$, $|f(x) - f_n(x)| < \epsilon/2m(T)$. Hence, for every $n > N$,

$$\begin{aligned}
&\left|\int_S f(x)dx - \int_S f_n(x)dx\right| \\
&\quad = \left|\int_T f(x)dx + \int_{S-T} f(x)dx - \int_T f_n(x)dx - \int_{S-T} f_n(x)dx\right| \\
&\quad \leqq \left|\int_T (f(x)dx - f_n(x))dx\right| + \left|\int_{S-T} (f(x) - f_n(x))dx\right| \\
&\quad < \frac{\epsilon}{2m(T)} \cdot m(T) + \frac{\epsilon}{4M} \cdot 2M = \epsilon.
\end{aligned}$$

Hence, for every $n > N$,

$$\left|\int_S f(x)dx - \int_S f_n(x)dx\right| < \epsilon.$$

7. *Limits of sequences of nonnegative integrable functions*

Before stating the next theorem we need a convention regarding functions which may have the values $+\infty$ and $-\infty$. First we shall consider limits in the extended sense; so that if $\{y_n\}$ is a nondecreasing unbounded sequence $\lim_{n\to\infty} y_n = +\infty$. If $f(x)$ is defined on S and the set of points $T \subset S$ at which $f(x) = +\infty$ or $-\infty$ is of positive measure, then $f(x)$ is not summable on S. If the set $T \subset S$ for which $f(x)$ is $+\infty$, $-\infty$, or is undefined, is of measure 0, then $f(x)$ is summable if and only if it is summable on $S - T$ and

$$\int_S f(x)dx = \int_{S-T} f(x)dx.$$

THEOREM 5. If $\{f_n(x)\}$ is a nondecreasing sequence of nonnegative summable functions defined on a set S and $f(x) = \lim_{n\to\infty} f_n(x)$ is summable on S, then

$$\int_S f(x)dx = \lim_{n\to\infty} \int_S f_n(x)dx.$$

Proof. Let $\epsilon > 0$. Since

$$\int_T f(x)dx$$

is absolutely continuous there is a $\delta > 0$ such that if $T \subset S$ and $m(T) < \delta$ then

$$\left|\int_T f(x)dx\right| < \frac{\epsilon}{3}.$$

But

$$\left|\int_T f_n(x)dx\right| \leqq \left|\int_T f(x)dx\right|$$

for every n. Hence, there is a $\delta > 0$ such that if $m(T) < \delta$ then

$$\left|\int_T f(x)dx\right| < \frac{\epsilon}{3} \text{ and } \left|\int_T f_n(x)dx\right| < \frac{\epsilon}{3}$$

for every n. By the Theorem of Egoroff there is a measurable set $R \subset S$ such that $\{f_n(x)\}$ converges uniformly to $f(x)$ on R and $m(S - R) < \delta$. Hence there is an N such that for every $n > N$ and every $x \in R$, $|f_n(x) - f(x)|$

$< \epsilon/3m(R)$. Now, if $n > N$, then

$$\left|\int_S f(x)dx - \int_S f_n(x)dx\right|$$

$$= \left|\int_R f(x)dx + \int_{S-R} f(x)dx - \int_R f_n(x)dx - \int_{S-R} f_n(x)dx\right|$$

$$\leqq \int_R |f(x) - f_n(x)|dx + \left|\int_{S-R} f(x)dx\right| + \left|\int_{S-R} f_n(x)dx\right|$$

$$< \frac{\epsilon}{3m(R)} \cdot m(R) + \frac{\epsilon}{3} + \frac{\epsilon}{3} = \epsilon$$

so, for every $\epsilon > 0$, there is an N such that if $n > N$ then

$$\left|\int_S f(x)dx - \int_S f_n(x)dx\right| < \epsilon.$$

This shows that

$$\int_S f(x)dx = \lim_{n\to\infty} \int_S f_n(x)dx.$$

As a companion to Theorem 5 we have the following proposition.

PROPOSITION 13. Under the conditions of Theorem 5, if $f(x)$ is not summable on S, then

$$\lim_{n\to\infty} \int_S f_n(x)dx = +\infty.$$

The proof of this proposition is left as an exercise for the student.

The next theorem is known as the Lemma of Fatou.

THEOREM 6. If $\{f(x)\}$ is a sequence of nonnegative summable functions, then

$$\int_S [\liminf_{n\to\infty} f_n(x)]dx \leqq \liminf_{n\to\infty} \int_S f_n(x)dx.$$

Proof. Let $g_n(x) = \inf[f_n(x), f_{n+1}(x), \cdots]$ for every positive integer n. Then $g_n(x)$ is measurable and since $0 \leqq g_n(x) \leqq f_n(x)$ and $f_n(x)$ is summable, $g_n(x)$ is summable. Now, the sequence $\{g_n(x)\}$ is nondecreasing and $\lim_{n\to\infty} g_n(x) = \liminf_{n\to\infty} f_n(x)$. Hence

$$\int_S [\liminf_{n\to\infty} f_n(x)]dx = \int_S [\lim_{n\to\infty} g_n(x)]dx = \lim_{n\to\infty} \int_S g_n(x)dx.$$

On the other hand, $g_n(x) \leqq f_n(x)$ for every $x \in S$, and every n so that

$$\int_S g_n(x)dx \leqq \int_S f_n(x)dx$$

for every n. Accordingly,

$$\lim_{n\to\infty}\int_S g_n(x)dx = \liminf_{n\to\infty}\int_S g_n(x)dx \leqq \liminf_{n\to\infty}\int_S f_n(x)dx.$$

Hence

$$\int_S [\liminf_{n\to\infty} f_n(x)]dx \leqq \liminf_{n\to\infty}\int_S f_n(x)dx.$$

COROLLARY 2. If $\{f_n(x)\}$ is a sequence of nonpositive summable, functions then

$$\int_S [\limsup_{n\to\infty} f_n(x)]dx \geqq \limsup_{n\to\infty}\int_S f_n(x)dx.$$

8. *Theorem of Lebesgue*

The Lemma of Fatou yields the following theorem.

THEOREM 7. If $\{f(x)\}$ is a sequence of functions summable on a measurable set S, and if there is a nonnegative summable function $g(x)$ such that $|f_n(x)| \leqq g(x)$ for every $x \in S$ and every n, then

1. $\displaystyle\int_S [\liminf_{n\to\infty} f_n(x)]dx \leqq \liminf_{n\to\infty}\int_S f_n(x)dx,$
2. $\displaystyle\int_S [\limsup_{n\to\infty} f_n(x)]dx \geqq \limsup_{n\to\infty}\int_S f_n(x)dx,$
3. if $\{f_n(x)\}$ converges, then $\displaystyle\lim_{n\to\infty}\int_S f_n(x)dx = \int_S \lim_{n\to\infty} f_n(x)dx.$

Proof. 1. The functions of the sequence $\{g(x) + f_n(x)\}$ are all nonnegative and summable. Hence, by the Lemma of Fatou,

$$\int_S [\liminf_{n\to\infty} (g(x) + f_n(x))]dx \leqq \liminf_{n\to\infty}\int_S (g(x) + f_n(x))dx.$$

But

$$\int_S [\liminf_{n\to\infty} (g(x) + f_n(x))]dx = \int_S [\liminf_{n\to\infty} f_n(x)]dx + \int_S g(x)dx,$$

and

$$\liminf_{n\to\infty}\int_S (g(x) + f_n(x))dx = \liminf_{n\to\infty}\int_S f_n(x)dx + \int_S g(x)dx.$$

We thus have

$$\int_S [\liminf_{n\to\infty} f_n(x)]dx \leqq \liminf_{n\to\infty}\int_S f_n(x)dx.$$

2. Apply the corollary to the Lemma of Fatou (Corollary 2) to the sequence $\{f_n(x) - g(x)\}$ of nonpositive summable functions.

3. From parts (1) and (2) and the definitions of limit inferior and limit superior,

$$\int_S [\limsup_{n\to\infty} f_n(x)]dx \geqq \limsup_{n\to\infty} \int_S f_n(x)dx$$
$$\geqq \liminf_{n\to\infty} \int_S f_n(x)dx \geqq \int_S [\liminf_{n\to\infty} f_n(x)]dx.$$

Now if $\{f_n(x)\}$ converges, then

$$\int_S [\limsup_{n\to\infty} f_n(x)]dx = \int_S [\liminf_{n\to\infty} f_n(x)]dx,$$

so that

$$\limsup_{n\to\infty} \int_S f_n(x)dx = \liminf_{n\to\infty} \int_S f_n(x)dx$$
$$= \int_S [\limsup_{n\to\infty} f_n(x)]dx = \int_S [\liminf_{n\to\infty} f_n(x)]dx.$$

In other words,

$$\int_S \lim_{n\to\infty} f_n(x)dx = \lim_{n\to\infty} \int_S f_n(x)dx.$$

This shows that the first defect given for the Riemann integral does not exist for the Lebesgue integral.

Exercises

2.1 Show that if $f(x)$ is summable on a set S of finite measure and if A and B are nets then

$$\left|\int_S f_A(x)dx - \int_S f_B(x)dx\right| < m(S)(\mathcal{N}(A) + \mathcal{N}(B)).$$

2.2 Under the conditions of Exercise 2.1 show that if $\{A_n\}$ and $\{B_n\}$ are two sequences of nets, and if $\lim_{n\to\infty} \mathcal{N}(A_n) = \lim_{n\to\infty} \mathcal{N}(B_n) = 0$, then $\lim_{n\to\infty} \int_S f_{A_n}(x)dx$ and $\lim_{n\to\infty} \int_S f_{B_n}(x)dx$ exist and are equal.

2.3 Show that if $f(x) = c$ on the measurable set S of finite measure then $\int_S f(x)dx = c\cdot m(S)$ and $\int_S (f(x) + c)dx = \int_S f(x)dx + c\cdot m(S)$.

2.4 If $f(x)$ is summable on S show that $|f(x)|$ is summable and $\int_S |f(x)|dx \geqq \left|\int_S f(x)dx\right|$.

2.5 If $f(x)$ and $g(x)$ are both summable on S and $f(x) \leqq g(x)$ then $\int_S f(x)dx \leqq \int_S g(x)dx$.

2.6 Show that if $f(x)$ is summable on S and $T \subset S$ is measurable then $f(x)$ is summable on T.

2.7 Prove Proposition 6.

4.1 Prove Proposition 8.

4.2 Show that for nonnegative additive set functions continuity implies absolute continuity.

5.1 If $\phi(S)$ is a completely additive set function show that $-\phi(S)$ is completely additive.

5.2 If $\phi(S)$ and $\psi(S)$ are completely additive show that $\phi(S) + \psi(S)$ is completely additive.

5.3 If $S_1, S_2, \cdots, S_n, \cdots$ are disjoint sets on each of which $f(x)$ is summable and the series

$$\sum_{n=1}^{\infty} \int_{S_n} |f(x)|dx$$

converges, show that $f(x)$ is summable on $S = \bigcup_{n=1}^{\infty} S_n$ and

$$\int_S f(x)dx = \sum_{n=1}^{\infty} \int_{S_n} f(x)dx.$$

5.4 If $f(x)$ is summable on S_1 and S_2, show that

$$\int_{S_1 \cup S_2} |f(x)|dx \leqq \int_{S_1} |f(x)|dx + \int_{S_2} |f(x)|dx.$$

6.1 If $\{f_n(x)\}$ is a nondecreasing sequence of nonnegative summable functions defined on a set S and $f(x) = \lim_{n\to\infty} f_n(x)$ is not summable on S, prove that

$$\lim_{n\to\infty} \int_S f_n(x)dx = +\infty.$$

References

C. Carathéodory, *Vorlesungen über reelle Funktionen*, Leipzig, 1927, Chap. 9.
H. Hahn and A. Rosenthal, *Set Functions*, Albuquerque, 1948, esp. Chap. 1.

H. LEBESGUE *Leçons sur l'intégration et la recherche des fonctions primitives*, Paris, 1928, Chap. 8.

E. J. MCSHANE, *Integration*, Princeton, 1944, Chap. 4.

CH. J. DE LA VALLÉE POUSSIN, *Intégrales de Lebesgue, Fonctions d'ensembles, Classes de Baire*, Paris, 1934, Chaps. 4–6.

S. SAKS, *Theory of the Integral*, translated by L .C. Young, Warszawa-Lwow, 1937, Chap. 1.

19

The Fundamental Theorem of the Calculus

1. *Introduction*

We return to real functions $f(x)$ defined on the closed interval $[0, 1]$. Every summable function $f(x)$ has the associated function

$$F(x) = \int_0^x f(\xi)d\xi.$$

Two formulas which the student has used in calculus are the following:

$$F'(x) = f(x),$$

and for a differentiable function,

$$f(x) - f(0) = \int_0^x f'(\xi)d\xi.$$

We have seen that the second formula is not always meaningful for Riemann integration. The purpose of this chapter is to discuss these two formulas for Lebesgue integration.

2. *The formula $F'(x) = f(x)$ for bounded simple functions*

We first point out that the case where $f(x)$ is the characteristic function of a measurable set S (i.e., $f(x) = 1$ for $x \in S$, $f(x) = 0$ for $x \in C(S)$) has already been considered. For in this case,

$$F(x) = \int_0^x f(\xi)d\xi = m(S \cap [0, x]),$$

from which it follows that

$$F(\xi) - F(x) = \int_x^\xi f(u)du = m(S \cap [x, \xi]).$$

But then

$$\frac{F(\xi) - F(x)}{\xi - x} = \frac{m(S \cap [x, \xi])}{\xi - x}.$$

In other words, the difference quotient of $F(x)$ and the relative measure of S are identical for every interval. It then follows from the definitions that the derivative of $F(x)$ exists wherever the metric density of S exists. But, the Lebesgue Density Theorem asserts that the metric density of S exists and is equal to 1 almost everywhere on S and is equal to 0 almost everywhere on $C(S)$. Hence, $F'(x)$ exists and $F'(x) = f(x)$ almost everywhere.

The proof for bounded simple functions, which we now give, follows along similar lines.

PROPOSITION 1. If $f(x)$ is a finitely simple measurable function, then

$$\frac{d}{dx}\int_0^x f(\xi)d\xi = f(x)$$

almost everywhere.

Proof. Since $f(x)$ is finitely simple, $f(x) = [c_1, S_1; \cdots; c_n, S_n]$, where $\bigcup_{k=1}^{n} S_k = [0, 1]$ and the sets $S_1, \cdots, S_n$ are measurable. Let $\max [1, |c_k| \mid k = 1, 2, \cdots, n] = M$ and, for every $k = 1, 2, \cdots, n$, let $R_k \subset S_k$ be the set of points in S_k at which the metric density of S_k is 1. Write $U_k = S_k - R_k$. Then $m(U_k) = 0$. Now let

$$F(x) = \int_0^x f(\xi)d\xi.$$

We show that for every $k = 1, 2, \cdots, n$, for every $x \in R_k$, $F'(x) = c_k$. For, since the metric density of S_k at x is 1, there is, for every $\epsilon > 0$, a positive integer m such that for every ξ for which either $0 < \xi - x < 1/m$ or $0 < x - \xi < 1/m$ the relative measure of S_k in $[x, \xi]$ or in $[\xi, x]$, as the case may be, exceeds $1 - \epsilon/2M$. Suppose, for convenience, that $0 < \xi - x < 1/m$. Then

$$\frac{F(\xi) - F(x)}{\xi - x} = \frac{\int_0^\xi f(u)du - \int_0^x f(u)du}{\xi - x} = \frac{1}{\xi - x}\left\{\int_{T_1} f(u)du + \int_{T_2} f(u)du\right\},$$

where $T_1 = S_k \cap [x, \xi]$ and $T_2 = C(S_k) \cap [x, \xi]$. Now

$$\int_{T_1} f(u)du = c_k \cdot m(S_k \cap [x, \xi]),$$

and since the relative measure of S_k in $[x, \xi]$ exceeds $1 - \epsilon/2M$,

$$\left(1 - \frac{\epsilon}{2M}\right)(\xi - x) < m(S_k \cap [x, \xi]) \leqq \xi - x.$$

Hence

$$\left(1 - \frac{\epsilon}{2M}\right)(\xi - x) \cdot c_k < \int_{T_1} f(u)du \leqq (\xi - x) \cdot c_k.$$

But, since the relative measure of $C(S_k)$ in $[x, \xi]$ is less than $\epsilon/2M$ and $|f(x)| < M$, everywhere, it follows that

$$-(\xi - x) \cdot M \cdot \frac{\epsilon}{2M} < \int_{T_2} f(u)du < (\xi - x) \cdot M \cdot \frac{\epsilon}{2M}.$$

If we add the two sets of inequalities and use the fact that $|c_k| \leqq M$, we obtain

$$(\xi - x)(c_k - \epsilon) < \int_x^\xi f(u)du < (\xi - x)\left(c_k + \frac{\epsilon}{2}\right),$$

or

$$c_k - \epsilon < \frac{F(\xi) - F(x)}{\xi - x} < c_k + \frac{\epsilon}{2}.$$

It follows that the derivative of $F(x)$ exists at x and is equal to $f(x) = c_k$. Since $m(\bigcup_{k=1}^{n} R_k) = 1$, we have shown that $F'(x)$ exists and is equal to $f(x)$ almost everywhere.

3. *The formula $F'(x) = f(x)$ for arbitrary summable functions*

We need some preliminary propositions.

PROPOSITION 2. If $f(x)$ is summable and

$$F(x) = \int_0^x f(\xi)d\xi$$

then $F'(x)$ exists almost everywhere.

Proof. Let S be the set of points at which $f(x) \geqq 0$, and T the set of points at which $f(x) \leqq 0$.

$$\begin{aligned} \text{If } f_1(x) &= f(x) && \text{for } x \in S \\ &= 0 && \text{for } x \in T, \text{ and} \\ f_2(x) &= -f(x) && \text{for } x \in T \\ &= 0 && \text{for } x \in S, \end{aligned}$$

then $f_1(x)$ and $f_2(x)$ are summable and $f(x) = f_1(x) - f_2(x)$. Moreover, if

$$F_1(x) = \int_0^x f_1(\xi)d\xi, \text{ and } F_2(x) = \int_0^x f_2(\xi)d\xi,$$

then $F(x) = F_1(x) - F_2(x)$. The functions $F_1(x)$ and $F_2(x)$ are nondecreasing. For if $\xi > x$, then

$$F_1(\xi) - F_1(x) = \int_x^\xi f_1(u)du \geqq 0,$$

since $f_1(x)$ is nonnegative. Similarly, $F_2(x)$ is nondecreasing. Hence the function $F(x)$ is the difference of two nondecreasing functions. But, we have already shown (Theorem 6, Chapter 14) that the derivative of a nondecreasing function exists almost everywhere. If Z_1 and Z_2 are the sets of points at which $F_1'(x)$ and $F_2'(x)$ do not exist, then $Z = Z_1 \cup Z_2$ contains the set of points at which $F'(x)$ does not exist. Since Z_1 and Z_2 are of measure 0, the set Z is of measure 0.

LEMMA 1. If $f(x) \geqq g(x)$ are both nonnegative and

$$F(x) = \int_0^x f(\xi)d\xi, \quad G(x) = \int_0^x g(\xi)d\xi,$$

then $F'(x) \geqq G'(x)$ wherever both derivatives exist.

The proof is left to the student.

LEMMA 2. If $F(x)$ is a nondecreasing function on $[0, 1]$ and if $[\alpha_k, \beta_k]$, $k = 1, 2, \cdots$ is a sequence of disjoint closed subintervals of $[0, 1]$, then $F(1) - F(0) \geqq \sum_{k=1}^{\infty} (F(\beta_k) - F(\alpha_k))$.

The proof is left to the student.

PROPOSITION 3. If $\{f_n(x)\}$ is a nondecreasing sequence of non-negative measurable functions which converges to a summable function $f(x)$, then

$$\frac{d}{dx}\int_0^x f(\xi)d\xi = \lim_{n\to\infty} \frac{d}{dx}\int_0^x f_n(\xi)d\xi$$

almost everywhere.

Proof. Let S be the set of points for which all the derivatives $f'(x)$ and $f_n'(x)$, $n = 1, 2, \cdots$ exist. The complement of S, as the union of a denumerable number of sets of measure 0, is of measure 0. Hence $m(S) = 1$.

Let

$$F(x) = \int_0^x f(\xi)d\xi \text{ and } F_n(x) = \int_0^x f_n(\xi)d\xi$$

for every $n = 1, 2, \cdots$. By Lemma 1, the sequence $\{F_n'(x)\}$ is nondecreasing on S and $\lim_{n\to\infty} F_n'(x) \leqq F'(x)$. Let $T \subset S$ be the set of points for which

$\lim_{n\to\infty} F_n'(x) < F'(x)$. Then $T = \bigcup_{m=1}^{\infty} T_m$, where T_m is the set on which $\lim_{n\to\infty} F_n'(x) < F'(x) - 1/m$. We show that for every m, T_m is of measure 0, so that T is of measure 0, proving the proposition.

Fix m, and let $\xi \in T_m$. Fix n. Since $F_n'(\xi) < F'(\xi) - 1/m$, ξ is the left endpoint of a sequence of closed intervals, whose lengths coverge to 0, on each of which the difference quotient of $F(x)$ exceeds that of $F_n(x)$ by more than $1/m$. By the Vitali Covering Theorem, there is a sequence

$$I_1 = [\alpha_1, \beta_1], \cdots, I_k = [\alpha_k, \beta_k], \cdots$$

of disjoint closed intervals such that

$$\sum_{k=1}^{\infty} (\beta_k - \alpha_k) \geqq m(T_m),$$

and for every $k = 1, 2 \cdots$,

$$\frac{F_n(\beta_k) - F_n(\alpha_k)}{\beta_k - \alpha_k} < \frac{F(\beta_k) - F(\alpha_k)}{\beta_k - \alpha_k} - \frac{1}{m},$$

or

$$(F(\beta_k) - F(\alpha_k)) - (F_n(\beta_k) - F_n(\alpha_k)) > \frac{(\beta_k - \alpha_k)}{m}.$$

But then

$$\sum_{k=1}^{\infty} (F(\beta_k) - F(\alpha_k)) - \sum_{k=1}^{\infty} (F_n(\beta_k) - F_n(\alpha_k)) > \frac{m(T_m)}{m}.$$

Moreover,

$$F(1) - F_n(1) = (F(1) - F_n(1)) - (F(0) - F_n(0)),$$

since $F(0) = F_n(0) = 0$. Since the function $F(x) - F_n(x)$ is nondecreasing, it follows from Lemma 2 that

$$F(1) - F_n(1) \geqq \sum_{k=1}^{\infty} \{(F(\beta_k) - F_n(\beta_k)) - (F(\alpha_k) - F_n(\alpha_k))\} > \frac{m(T_m)}{m}.$$

This being true for every n, we have

$$\lim_{n\to\infty} F_n(1) \leqq F(1) + \frac{m(T_m)}{m}.$$

On the other hand, $f(x) = \lim_{n\to\infty} f_n(x)$, so that by Theorem 5, Chapter 18, $\lim_{n\to\infty} F_n(1) = F(1)$. It follows that $m(T_m) = 0$ and the proposition is proved.

Propositions 1, 2, and 3 combine to yield the next proposition.

PROPOSITION 4. If $f(x)$ is nonnegative and summable, then

$$\frac{d}{dx}\int_0^x f(\xi)d\xi = f(x)$$

almost everywhere.

Proof. Let A_n be the net $A_n = \{1/2^n, 2/2^n, \cdots\}$, and let

$$\begin{aligned} f_n(x) &= f_{A_n}(x) \quad \text{if} \quad f(x) \leqq n, \\ &= 0 \qquad\quad\ \ \text{if} \quad f(x) > n. \end{aligned}$$

For every n, $f_n(x)$ is a finitely simple function and the sequence $\{f_n(x)\}$ is nondecreasing. It is easy to see that $\lim_{n\to\infty} f_n(x) = f(x)$. By Proposition 1, for every n,

$$\frac{d}{dx}\int_0^x f_n(\xi)d\xi = f_n(x)$$

everywhere except for a set Z_n of measure 0. By Proposition 3,

$$\frac{d}{dx}\int_0^x f(\xi)d\xi = \lim_{n\to\infty}\frac{d}{dx}\int_0^x f_n(\xi)d\xi$$

everywhere except for a set Z of measure 0. It follows that

$$\frac{d}{dx}\int_0^x f(\xi)d\xi = \lim_{n\to\infty} f_n(x)$$

almost everywhere. But $\lim_{n\to\infty} f_n(x) = f(x)$ almost everywhere. Hence

$$f(x) = \frac{d}{dx}\int_0^x f(\xi)d\xi$$

almost everywhere.

THEOREM 1. If $f(x)$ is summable, then

$$\frac{d}{dx}\int_0^x f(\xi)d\xi$$

exists and

$$f(x) = \frac{d}{dx}\int_0^x f(\xi)d\xi$$

almost everywhere.

Proof. $f(x) = f_1(x) - f_2(x)$ where $f_1(x)$ and $f_2(x)$ are nonnegative,

$$\frac{d}{dx}\int_0^x f(\xi)d\xi,\ \frac{d}{dx}\int_0^x f_1(\xi)d\xi, \text{ and } \frac{d}{dx}\int_0^x f_2(\xi)d\xi$$

all exist almost everywhere, by Proposition 2. Hence

$$\frac{d}{dx}\int_0^x f(\xi)d\xi = \frac{d}{dx}\int_0^x f_1(\xi)d\xi - \frac{d}{dx}\int_0^x f_2(\xi)d\xi = f_1(x) - f_2(x) = f(x)$$

everywhere except for a set of measure 0.

4. *Bounded variation and absolute continuity*

An adequate discussion of the second formula mentioned in §1 requires the notions of bounded variation and absolute continuity of a real function. We have already used absolutely continuous set functions. The relation between absolutely continuous functions of a real variable and absolutely continuous set functions will become clear in the text.

DEFINITION 1. A function $f(x)$ defined on $[0, 1]$ is said to be of *bounded variation* if there is an M such that for every partition $a_0 = 0 < a_1 < a_2 < \cdots < a_n = 1$ the number

$$\sum_{i=1}^{n} |f(a_i) - f(a_{i-1})| < M.$$

PROPOSITION 5. A function $f(x)$ defined on $[0, 1]$ is of bounded variation if and only if there is an M such that, for every partition $a_0 = 0 < a_1 < a_2 < \cdots < a_n = 1$, the sum of the saltuses

$$\sum_{i=1}^{n} \omega(f, [a_{i-1}, a_i]) < M.$$

The proof is left to the student.

PROPOSITION 6. If $f(x)$ is nonincreasing or nondecreasing and bounded, then it is of bounded variation.

The proof is left to the student.

It is clear from Proposition 6 that if $f(x)$ is the difference between two nondecreasing functions then it is of bounded variation. The converse, which is not so obvious, is also true.

PROPOSITION 7. $f(x)$ is of bounded variation if and only if $f(x) = f_1(x) - f_2(x)$ when $f_1(x)$ and $f_2(x)$ are nondecreasing.

Proof. We need only show that if $f(x)$ is of bounded variation then $f(x) = f_1(x) - f_2(x)$, where $f_1(x)$ and $f_2(x)$ are nondecreasing.

For every $x \in [0, 1]$ consider any partition $A_x = [a_0 = 0 < a_1 < \cdots < a_n = x]$. Some of the numbers $f(a_i) - f(a_{i-1})$ are positive and some are negative. Let $p(A_x; f)$ be the sum of the positive numbers among them, and

$n(A_x; f)$ the sum of the negative numbers. Now let

$$f_1(x) = \sup [p(A_x; f) \mid \text{all } A_x],$$

$$f_2(x) = \sup [-n(A_x; f) \mid \text{all } A_x].$$

The functions $f_1(x)$ and $f_2(x)$ are nondecreasing.

We show that $f(x) = f_1(x) - f_2(x) + f(0)$. Let $x \in [0, 1]$ and $\epsilon > 0$. There is a partition A_x such that $0 \leqq f_1(x) - p(A_x; f) < \epsilon/2$ and $0 \leqq n(A_x; f) + f_2(x) < \epsilon/2$, so that

$$-\frac{\epsilon}{2} \leqq f_1(x) - f_2(x) - (p(A_x; f) + n(A_x; f)) < \frac{\epsilon}{2}.$$

But obviously,

$$p(A_x; f) + n(A_x; f) = f(x) - f(0),$$

so that, $\epsilon > 0$ being arbitrary,

$$f(x) = f_1(x) - f_2(x) + f(0),$$

and $f(x)$ is the difference of two nondecreasing functions.

Examples of functions of bounded variation and not of bounded variation:

1. Every polynomial $p(x)$ on $[0, 1]$ is of bounded variation. For $p(x) = p_1(x) - p_2(x)$, where $p_1(x)$ is the sum of the terms of $p(x)$ with positive coefficients and $p_2(x)$ is the sum of the terms with negative coefficients with all the signs changed. Then $p_1(x)$ and $p_2(x)$ are nondecreasing functions.
2. The function $f(x) = x^2 \sin 1/x$ for $x \in (0, 1]$ and $f(0) = 0$ is of bounded variation in $[0, 1]$. (The proof is left to the student.)
3. The function $f(x) = x \sin 1/x$ for $x \in (0, 1]$ and $f(0) = 0$ is not of bounded variation in $[0, 1]$, but is of bounded variation in $[x, 1]$ for every x such that $0 < x < 1$. (The proof of this is left to the student.)

DEFINITION 2. A function $f(x)$ defined on $[0, 1]$ is said to be *absolutely continuous* if for every $\epsilon > 0$ there is a $\delta > 0$ such that if $I_1, I_2, \cdots, I_n$ is a finite number of disjoint or abutting closed intervals of length sum less than δ then

$$\sum_{k=1}^{n} \omega(I_k; f) < \epsilon.$$

PROPOSITION 8a. A function $f(x)$ defined on $[0, 1]$ is absolutely continuous if and only if for every $\epsilon > 0$ there is a $\delta > 0$ such that if $I_1, I_2, \cdots, I_n, \cdots$ is a finite or denumerable number of disjoint or abutting closed intervals of length sum less than δ, then

$$\sum_{n=1}^{\infty} \omega(I_n; f) < \epsilon.$$

PROPOSITION 8b. A function $f(x)$ defined on $[0, 1]$ is absolutely continuous if and only if for every $\epsilon > 0$ there is a $\delta > 0$ such that if $I_1 = [a_1, b_1], \cdots, I_n = [a_n, b_n]$ is a finite number of disjoint or abutting closed intervals of length sum less than δ, then

$$\sum_{k=1}^{n} |f(b_k) - f(a_k)| < \epsilon.$$

The proof is left to the student.

PROPOSITION 9. If $f(x)$ defined on $[0, 1]$ is absolutely continuous, then $f(x)$ is of bounded variation.

Proof. What we show is that if $f(x)$ is not of bounded variation then $f(x)$ is not absolutely continuous. Suppose $f(x)$ is not of bounded variation on $[0, 1]$. Let $\delta > 0$. Divide $[0, 1]$ into a finite number of abutting intervals each of length less than δ. An immediate consequence of the definition of bounded variation is that $f(x)$ is of unbounded variation in at least one of these intervals, $I = [a, b]$. There is then a partition $a_0 = a < a_1 < a_2 < \cdots < a_n = b$ such that $\sum_{i=1}^{n} |f(a_i) - f(a_{i-1})| > 1$. But $\sum_{i=1}^{n} |a_i - a_{i-1}| < \delta$. Since $\delta > 0$ is arbitrary, $f(x)$ is not absolutely continuous.

It is an important fact that the converse of this proposition is not true even if $f(x)$ is continuous. We now give an example of a nondecreasing continuous function which is not absolutely continuous.

Let S be the Cantor ternary set. Then $C(S)$ is an open set whose components are the intervals

$$\left(\frac{1}{3}, \frac{2}{3}\right), \left(\frac{1}{3^2}, \frac{2}{3^2}\right), \left(\frac{2}{3} + \frac{1}{3^2}, \frac{2}{3} + \frac{2}{3^2}\right), \left(\frac{1}{3^3}, \frac{2}{3^3}\right), \left(\frac{2}{3^2} + \frac{1}{3^3}, \frac{2}{3^2} + \frac{2}{3^3}\right),$$
$$\left(\frac{2}{3} + \frac{1}{3^3}, \frac{2}{3} + \frac{2}{3^3}\right), \left(\frac{2}{3} + \frac{2}{3^2} + \frac{1}{3^3}, \frac{2}{3} + \frac{2}{3^2} + \frac{2}{3^3}\right), \cdots.$$

For convenience we shall label these intervals, respectively,

$$I(1/2), I(1/4), I(3/4), I(1/8), I(3/8), I(5/8), I(7/8), \cdots.$$

The components of the complement $C(S)$ of the Cantor set all have labels of the form $I(m/2^n)$, and if $m/2^n > r/2^s$, then $I(m/2^n)$ is to the right of $I(r/2^s)$.

We now define our function $f(x)$ which is nondecreasing but not absolutely continuous. For every m and n, for every $x \in I(m/2^n)$, let $f(x) = m/2^n$. This defines $f(x)$ on $C(S)$ and, evidently, $f(x)$ is nondecreasing on $C(S)$.

Next we define $f(x)$ on S. Let $f(0) = 0$. Let $x \in S$, $x \neq 0$, and let

$$f(x) = \sup [f(\xi) \mid \xi \in C(S), \xi < x].$$

This defines $f(x)$ on all of $[0, 1]$.

1. $f(x)$ is nondecreasing. For suppose $x < y$. Then if $x \in C(S)$ and $y \in C(S)$, it is evident that $f(x) \leqq f(y)$, since $x \in I(m/2^n)$, $y \in I(r/2^s)$, and $m/2^n \leqq r/2^s$. If $x \in C(S)$ and $y \in S$, then also $f(x) \leqq f(y)$, since $f(y) = \sup [f(\xi) \mid \xi \in C(S), \xi < y] \geqq f(x)$. If $x \in S$ and $y \in C(S)$, then if $z < x$ and $z \in C(S)$, $f(z) < f(y)$. It follows that $f(y) \geqq \sup [f(z) \mid z \in C(S),\ z < x] = f(x)$. Finally, if $x \in S$ and $y \in S$, there is a $z \in C(S)$ such that $x < z < y$. But then $f(x) \leqq f(z)$ and $f(z) \leqq f(y)$ so that $f(x) \leqq f(y)$. This completes the proof that $f(x)$ is nondecreasing.

2. $f(x)$ is continuous. For let $\epsilon > 0$. There is an n such that $1/2^n < \epsilon/2$. For every $m < 2^n$ let $x_m \in I(m/2^n)$. Moreover, let $x_0 = 0$, $x_{2^n} = 1$. Then

$$f(x_0) = 0, f(x_1) = \frac{1}{2^n}, \cdots, f(x_{2^n-1}) = \frac{2^n - 1}{2^n}, f(x_{2^n}) = 1.$$

Let $\delta = \min [|x_i - x_{i-1}| \mid i = 0, 1, \cdots, 2^n]$. If $0 < y - x < \delta$ there is at most one x_i such that $x_{i-1} \leqq x \leqq x_i \leqq y \leqq x_{i+1}$. But then

$$0 \leqq f(y) - f(x) = f(y) - f(x_i) + f(x_i) - f(x) \leqq f(x_{i+1}) - f(x_i) + f(x_i) - f(x_{i-1}) = \frac{1}{2^n} + \frac{1}{2^n} < \epsilon.$$

Hence $f(x)$ is uniformly continuous on $[0, 1]$.

3. $f(x)$ is not absolutely continuous. For if $\delta > 0$ there is an n such that the sum of the lengths of all open intervals of the form $I(m/2^n)$ exceeds $1 - \delta$. Let

$$J_1 = [a_1, b_1], J_2 = [a_2, b_2], \cdots, J_s = [a_s, b_s]$$

be the closed intervals which are complementary to the $I(m/2^n)$. Now

$$\sum_{i=1}^{s} (b_i - a_i) < \delta.$$

But $s = 2^n$ and for every $k \leqq s$, $f(b_k) - f(a_k) = 1/2^n$. Hence

$$\sum_{i=1}^{s} (f(b_i) - f(a_i)) = 1.$$

Since $\delta > 0$ is arbitrary, $f(x)$ is not absolutely continuous.

5. $\int_0^x f'(\xi)d\xi$ *for nondecreasing functions*

We prove the following theorem.

THEOREM 2. If $f(x)$ is nondecreasing on $[0, 1]$, then $f'(x)$ is summable and for every $x \in [0, 1]$,

$$\int_0^x f'(\xi)d\xi \leqq f(x) - f(0).$$

Proof. Since $f(x)$ is nondecreasing, $f'(\xi)$ exists almost everywhere on $[0, 1]$. In line with our convention, the exceptional set of measure 0 on which $f'(x)$ might not be defined is inconsequential in considering the integral of $f'(x)$.

For every positive integer n, let $g_n(x) = \min[f'(x), n]$. Then $\{g_n(x)\}$ is a nondecreasing sequence of bounded nonnegative functions defined almost everywhere on $[0, 1]$. Each function $g_n(x)$ is summable. We show that

$$\int_0^x g_n(\xi)d\xi \leqq f(x) - f(0).$$

Let $\epsilon > 0$. Let S be the set of points in $[0, x]$ for which $g_n(\xi)$ is approximately continuous and $f'(\xi)$ exists. Then $m(S) = x$ and every $\xi \in S$ is the left endpoint of a sequence $\{I_{\xi m}\}$ of closed intervals in each $\{\xi, \alpha_m\}$ of which

$$g_n(\xi) \leqq f'(\xi) < \frac{f(\xi) - f(\alpha_m)}{\xi - \alpha_m} + \frac{\epsilon}{4},$$

and $|g_n(\xi) - g_n(u)| < \epsilon/4$ on a set whose relative measure in $I_{\xi m}$ exceeds $1 - \epsilon/4n$. By the Vitali Covering Theorem, there is a finite number of disjoint closed intervals

$$I_1 = (\xi_1, \eta_1), \cdots, I_k = (\xi_k, \eta_k)$$

in $[0, x]$ of length sum greater than $x(1 - \epsilon/4n)$ such that for every $j = 1, 2, \cdots, k$,

$$g_n(\xi_j) \leqq \frac{f(\xi_j) - (\eta_j)}{\xi_j - \eta_j} + \frac{\epsilon}{4},$$

and $|g_n(\xi_j) - g_n(u)| < \epsilon/4$ on a set E_j whose relative measure in I_j exceeds $1 - \epsilon/4n$.

Now, for every $j = 1, 2, \cdots, k$,

$$\begin{aligned}\int_{\xi_j}^{\eta_j} g_n(u)du &= \int_{E_j} g_n(u)du + \int_{I_j - E_j} g_n(u)du \\ &\leqq \int_{E_j}\left(\frac{f(\eta_j) - f(\xi_j)}{\eta_j - \xi_j} + \frac{\epsilon}{4} + \frac{\epsilon}{4}\right)du + \int_{I_j - E_j} ndu \\ &\leqq \left(\frac{f(\eta_j) - f(\xi_j)}{\eta_j - \xi_j} + \frac{\epsilon}{2}\right)(\eta_j - \xi_j) + n \cdot \frac{\epsilon}{4n} \cdot (\eta_j - \xi_j) \\ &= (f(\eta_j) - f(\xi_j)) + \frac{3\epsilon}{4}(\eta_j - \xi_j).\end{aligned}$$

It follows that

$$\begin{aligned}\int_0^x g_n(u)du &\leqq \sum_{j=1}^{k} \int_{\xi_j}^{\eta_j} g_n(u)du + n \cdot \frac{\epsilon}{4n} \cdot x \leqq \sum_{j=1}^{k} (f(\eta_j) - f(\xi_j)) \\ &\quad + \frac{3\epsilon}{4} \sum_{j=1}^{k} (\eta_j - \xi_j) + \frac{\epsilon}{4} \cdot x \leqq f(x) - f(0) + \epsilon.\end{aligned}$$

Accordingly, since $\epsilon > 0$ is arbitrary,

$$\int_0^x g_n(\xi)d\xi \leqq f(x) - f(0).$$

We now know that $f'(\xi) = \lim_{n\to\infty} g_n(\xi)$, that $\{g_n(\xi)\}$ is a nondecreasing sequence and that

$$\lim_{n\to\infty} \int_0^x g_n(\xi)d\xi \leqq f(x) - f(0).$$

Accordingly, by Proposition 11 and Theorem 5 of Chapter 18, $f'(\xi)$ is summable on $[0, x]$ and

$$\int_0^x f'(\xi)d\xi \leqq f(x) - f(0).$$

That the inequality cannot be omitted from this relation follows from the example given above of a continuous nondecreasing function which is not absolutely continuous. For if $f(x)$ is the function and S is the Cantor ternary set then $f'(x) = 0$ on $C(S)$ and $C(S)$ is of measure 1, so that

$$\int_0^1 f'(x) = 0.$$

On the other hand, $f(x)$ is continuous and nondecreasing, $f(0) = 0$, and $f(1) = 1$. Hence $f(1) - f(0) = 1$, so that

$$\int_0^1 f'(x)dx < f(1) - f(0).$$

6. $\int_0^x f'(\xi)d\xi$ *for absolutely continuous functions*

The next propositions show that we cannot expect the equality sign to hold for all x in the relation

$$\int_0^x f'(\xi)d\xi \leqq f(x) - f(0)$$

unless $f(x)$ is absolutely continuous.

PROPOSITION 10. If $f(x)$ is defined on $[0, 1]$ and is summable and

$$F(x) = \int_0^x f(\xi)d\xi,$$

then $F(x)$ is absolutely continuous.

Proof. By Theorem 2, Chapter 18,

$$\phi(S) = \int_S f(x)dx$$

is an absolutely continuous set function. So for every $\epsilon > 0$ there is a $\delta > 0$ such that if $S_1, S_2, \cdots, S_n$ are disjoint measurable sets for which $\sum_{k=1}^{n} m(S_k) < \delta$ then

$$\sum_{k=1}^{n} \left| \int_{S_k} f(x)dx \right| < \epsilon.$$

In particular, if $[a_1, b_1], \cdots, [a_n, b_n]$ are such that

$$\sum_{k=1}^{n} (b_k - a_k) < \delta,$$

then

$$\sum_{k=1}^{n} |F(b_k) - F(a_k)| = \sum_{k=1}^{n} \left| \int_{a_k}^{b_k} f(x)dx \right| < \epsilon,$$

whence the function $F(x)$ is absolutely continuous.

Now

$$\phi(x) = \int_0^x f'(\xi)d\xi$$

is absolutely continuous, but $f(x) - f(0)$ is absolutely continuous only when $f(x)$ is absolutely continuous. We accordingly have proved the following proposition.

PROPOSITION 11. If

$$\int_0^x f'(\xi)d\xi = f(x) - f(0)$$

for every $x \in [0, 1]$ then $f(x)$ is absolutely continuous.

We shall show, conversely, that if $f(x)$ is absolutely continuous, then

$$\int_0^x f'(\xi)d\xi = f(x) - f(0).$$

In other words, if $f(x)$ is the integral of any function at all, then $f(x) - f(0)$ is the integral of $f'(x)$.

The proof follows quickly from the next proposition.

PROPOSITION 12. If $f(x)$ is absolutely continuous and $f'(x) = 0$ almost everywhere, then $f(x)$ is a constant.

Proof. Let T be the set of points $x \in [0, 1]$ for which $f'(x) = 0$. Then $m(T) = 1$. Choose $\xi \in [0, 1]$ and $\epsilon > 0$. Since $f(x)$ is absolutely continuous, there is a $\delta > 0$ such that if $[a_1, b_1]$, $[a_2, b_2]$, $\cdots$, $[a_n, b_n]$ are disjoint and

$$\sum_{i=1}^{n} (b_i - a_i) < \delta$$

then

$$\sum_{i=1}^{n} |f(b_i) - f(a_i)| < \frac{\epsilon}{2}.$$

Now, every point in $[0, \xi]$ except for a set of measure 0 is the endpoint of a sequence of closed intervals whose lengths converge to 0, in each of which the difference quotient of $f(x)$ is less than $\epsilon/2$ in absolute value. By the Vitali Covering Theorem there is a finite number

$$[\alpha_1, \beta_1], [\alpha_2, \beta_2], \cdots, [\alpha_m, \beta_m]$$

of disjoint closed intervals such that

$$\sum_{i=1}^{m} (\beta_i - \alpha_i) > \xi - \delta$$

and

$$\left|\frac{f(\beta_i) - f(\alpha_i)}{\beta_i - \alpha_i}\right| < \frac{\epsilon}{2}, i = 1, 2, \cdots, m.$$

Thus $|f(\beta_i) - f(\alpha_i)| < \frac{\epsilon}{2} (\beta_i - \alpha_i)$, $i = 1, 2, \cdots, m$. Now

$$\begin{aligned} |f(\xi) - f(0)| &= |\sum_{i=1}^{m} (f(\beta_i) - f(\alpha_i)) + \sum_{i=0}^{m} f(\alpha_{i+1}) - f(\beta_i)| \\ &\leqq \sum_{i=1}^{m} |f(\beta_i) - f(\alpha_i)| + \sum_{i=0}^{m} |f(\alpha_{i+1}) - f(\beta_i)|, \end{aligned}$$

where $\beta_0 = 0$ and $\alpha_{m+1} = \xi$. But

$$\sum_{i=1}^{m} |f(\beta_i) - f(\alpha_i)| < \frac{\epsilon}{2} \sum_{i=1}^{m} (\beta_i - \alpha_i) \leqq \frac{\epsilon}{2} \xi \leqq \frac{\epsilon}{2},$$

and since

$$\sum_{i=0}^{m} (\alpha_{i+1} - \beta_i) < \delta, \sum_{i=0}^{m} |f(\alpha_{i+1}) - f(\beta_i)| < \frac{\epsilon}{2},$$

We thus have

$$|f(\xi) - f(0)| < \frac{\epsilon}{2} + \frac{\epsilon}{2} = \epsilon.$$

Since $\epsilon > 0$ is arbitrary, $f(\xi) = f(0)$.

COROLLARY 1. If $f(x)$ and $g(x)$ are absolutely continuous, if $f(0) = g(0)$ and $f'(x) = g'(x)$ almost everywhere on $[0, 1]$, then $f(x) = g(x)$ everywhere.

Proof. The function $f(x) - g(x)$ is absolutely continuous and its derivative is 0 almost everywhere, so that $f(x) - g(x) = 0$ everywhere.

THEOREM 3. If $f(x)$ is absolutely continuous, then

$$\int_0^x f'(\xi)d\xi = f(x) - f(0)$$

on $[0, 1]$.

Proof. Now $f(x)$ is of bounded variation. Hence $f'(x)$ exists almost everywhere and is summable. Let

$$g(x) = \int_0^x f'(\xi)d\xi + f(0).$$

Then

$$g'(x) = \frac{d}{dx}\left[\int_0^x f'(\xi)d\xi + f(0)\right] = f'(x)$$

almost everywhere, by Theorem 1. Moreover, $g(0) = f(0)$ and $g(x)$, as an integral, is absolutely continuous. The functions $f(x)$ and $g(x)$, accordingly, satisfy the conditions of the corollary, so that $f(x) = g(x)$ everywhere. But this simply says that

$$f(x) - f(0) = \int_0^x f'(\xi)d\xi.$$

We have restricted the discussion to the case where $f(x)$ is of bounded variation. If we remove this restriction, the function $f'(x)$ need not be summable, and the discussion involves a generalization of the integral concept which is outside the scope of this book. For a thorough treatment, the student may consult Saks, Theory of the Integral.

In the next few sections we give the application of the above concepts and theorems to the length of curves.

7. *Definition of length*

By a curve C we shall mean a pair of continuous functions $x = f(t)$, $y = g(t)$, where $0 \leqq t \leqq 1$. With every partition $A = [0 = t_0 < t_1 < \cdots < t_{n-1} < t_n = 1]$ we associate the number

$$L(C; A) = \sum_{i=1}^{n} [(f(t_i) - f(t_{i-1}))^2 + (g(t_i) - g(t_{i-1})^2]^{1/2}.$$

We define the length $L(C)$ of the curve C as sup $L(C; A)$, where A varies over all partitions. Evidently $L(C)$ can be any nonnegative real number or $+\infty$. If $L(C) < +\infty$ the curve is said to have finite length.

THEOREM 4. A curve C given by the functions $x = f(t)$, $y = g(t)$ has finite length if and only if $f(t)$ and $g(t)$ are of bounded variation.

Proof. Suppose $x = f(t)$ and $y = g(t)$ are of bounded variation. Then there are $M_1 > 0$, $M_2 > 0$, such that for every partition

$A = [0 = t_0 < t_1 < \cdots < t_{n-1} < t_n = 1]$,

$$\sum_{i=1}^{n} |f(t_i) - f(t_{i-1})| < M_1, \text{ and}$$

$$\sum_{i=1}^{n} |g(t_i) - g(t_{i-1})| < M_2.$$

Let $M = M_1 + M_2$. Then

$$L(C; A) = \sum_{i=1}^{n} [(f(t_i) - f(t_{i-1}))^2 + (g(t_i) - g(t_{i-1}))^2]^{1/2}$$
$$\leqq \sum_{i=1}^{n} |f(t_i) - f(t_{i-1})| + \sum_{i=1}^{n} |g(t_i) - g(t_{i+1})| < M$$

for every partition A. Thus $L(C) \leqq M$.

Conversely, suppose one of the two functions, say $f(t)$, is of unbounded variation. Then for every $M > 0$ there is a partition $A = [0 = t_0 < t_1 < \cdots < t_n = 1]$ such that

$$\sum_{i=1}^{n} |f(t_i) - f(t_{i-1})| > M.$$

But

$$L(C; A) = \sum_{i=1}^{n} [(f(t_i) - f(t_{i-1}))^2 + (g(t_i) - g(t_{i-1}))^2]^{1/2}$$
$$\geqq \sum_{i=1}^{n} |f(t_i) - f(t_{i-1})| > M.$$

Hence $L(C) = +\infty$.

8. *The formula* $\int_0^1 [(f'(t))^2 + (g'(t))^2]^{1/2}\, dt$

In elementary calculus the above formula is used for length of curve. It is interesting to see how the value given by this formula compares with the length as we defined it. We shall deal only with curves of finite length so that $f(t)$ and $g(t)$ will both be of bounded variation.

We need to consider the function $L(t)$, which is the length of that part of the curve C obtained for $0 \leqq \tau \leqq t$. Then $L(C) = L(1)$, $L(0) = 0$, and $L(t)$ is a nondecreasing function. Thus $L'(t)$ exists almost everywhere. We prove a lemma.

LEMMA 3. If $f(t)$ and $g(t)$ are of bounded variation, then $L'(t) = [(f'(t))^2 + (g'(t))^2]^{1/2}$ almost everywhere.

Proof. For every $t \in [0, 1]$ and every $h > 0$,

$$L(t + h) - L(t) \geqq [(f(t + h) - f(t))^2 + (g(t + h) - g(t))^2]^{1/2}.$$

Hence

$$\frac{L(t+h)-L(t)}{h} \geqq \left[\left(\frac{f(t+h)-f(t)}{h}\right)^2 + \left(\frac{g(t+h)-g(t)}{h}\right)^2\right]^{1/2},$$

so that $L'(t) \geqq [(f'(t))^2 + (g'(t))^2]^{1/2}$ wherever $L'(t), f'(t), g'(t)$ all exist, which is almost everywhere.

Moreover, we now show that $L'(t) \leqq [(f'(t))^2 + (g'(t))^2]^{1/2}$ almost everywhere. Let S be the set of points for which $L'(t), f'(t), g'(t)$ exist but $L'(t) > [(f'(t))^2 + (g'(t))^2]^{1/2}$. Then if S_n is the set of points $t \in S$ such that $\tau_1 \leqq t \leqq \tau_2$, $\tau_2 - \tau_1 < 1/n$ implies

$$\frac{L(\tau_2)-L(\tau_1)}{\tau_2-\tau_2} > \left[\left(\frac{f(\tau_2)-f(\tau_1)}{\tau_2-\tau_1}\right)^2 + \left(\frac{g(\tau_2)-g(\tau_1)}{\tau_2-\tau_1}\right)^2\right]^{1/2} + \frac{1}{n},$$

i.e., $[(f(\tau_2) - f(\tau_1))^2 + (g(\tau_2) - g(\tau_1))^2]^{1/2} < L(\tau_2) - L(\tau_1) - (\tau_2 - \tau_1)/n$, we have

$$S = \bigcup_{n=1}^{\infty} S_n.$$

We show that $m(S_n) = 0$ for every n, whence $m(S) = 0$. To do this let $\epsilon > 0$ and consider a partition $A = [0 = t_0 < t_1 < \cdots < t_m = 1]$ such that $\max [t_k - t_{k-1} < 1/n \mid k = 1, 2, \cdots, m]$ and $L(C) \leqq L(C; A) + \epsilon/n$.

$$L(C; A) = \sum_{i=1}^{n} [(f(t_i) - f(t_{i-1}))^2 + (g(t_i) - g(t_{i-1}))^2]^{1/2}$$
$$< \sum_{i=1}^{m} (L(t_i) - L(t_{i-1})) - \frac{m(S_n)}{n} = L(C) - \frac{m(S_n)}{n},$$

since in every interval of the partition A,

$$[(f(t_i) - f(t_{i-1}))^2 + (g(t_i) - g(t_{i-1})^2)]^{1/2} \leqq L(t_i) - L(t_{i-1}),$$

and in those intervals of the partition which contain points of S_n,

$$[(f(t_i) - f(t_{i-1}))^2 + (g(t_i) - g(t_{i-1}))^2]^{1/2} < L(t_i) - L(t_{i-1}) - \frac{1}{n}(t_i - t_{i-1}).$$

It follows that $m(S_n)/n < \epsilon/n$, and since $\epsilon > 0$ is arbitrary, that $m(S_n) = 0$.

LEMMA 4. The function $L(t)$ is absolutely continuous on $[0, 1]$ if and only if both $f(t)$ and $g(t)$ are absolutely continuous.

The proof is left to the student.

THEOREM 5. If C, given by $x = f(t)$, $y = g(t)$, is of finite length, then

$$L(C) \geqq \int_0^1 [(f'(t))^2 + (g'(t))^2]^{1/2}\, dt.$$

The equality holds if and only if $f(t)$ and $g(t)$ are both absolutely continuous.

Proof. $L(C) = L(1) - L(0)$. By Lemma 3, $[(f'(t))^2 + (g'(t))^2]^{1/2} = L'(t)$ almost everywhere. But, $L(t)$ is nondecreasing, so that

$$L(1) - L(0) \geqq \int_0^1 L'(t)dt$$

and the first part of the theorem holds. The second part follows from the statement of Lemma 4 that $L(t)$ is absolutely continuous if and only if $f(t)$ and $g(t)$ are absolutely continuous.

Exercises

3.1 Show that if $f(x) \geqq g(x)$ are both nonnegative and

$$F(x) = \int_0^x f(\xi)d\xi, \ G(x) = \int_0^x g(\xi)d\xi$$

then $F'(x) \geqq G'(x)$ wherever both derivatives exist.

3.2 Show that if $F(x)$ is a nondecreasing function on $[0, 1]$, and if $[\alpha_k, \beta_k]$, $k = 1, 2, \cdots$ is a sequence of disjoint closed subintervals of $[0, 1]$, then

$$F(1) - F(0) \geqq \sum_{k=1}^{\infty} (F(\beta_k) - F(\alpha_k)).$$

4.1 Show that the two definitions of bounded variation given in the text are equivalent.

4.2 Show that $f(x)$ nonincreasing and bounded is of bounded variation.

4.3 Show that $f(x) = x^2 \sin 1/x$ for $x \in [0, 1]$ and $f(0) = 0$ is of bounded variation in $[0, 1]$.

4.4 Show that $f(x) = x \sin 1/x$ for $x \in (0, 1]$ and $f(0) = 0$ is not of bounded variation in $[0, 1]$.

4.5 Prove Propositions 8a and 8b.

4.6 Show that if $f(x)$ is a nondecreasing function whose upper derivative exceeds $\beta > 0$ on a set S of measure $\alpha > 0$ then $f(1) - f(0) \geqq \alpha\beta$.

4.7 Show that if $f(x)$ is absolutely continuous and if Z is of measure 0 the set $E[y | f(x) = y, x \in Z]$ is also of measure 0.

4.8 Give an example of a continuous function $f(x)$ such that there is a measurable set S for which the set $f(S) = [y \mid y = f(x), x \in S]$ is non-measurable.

4.9 Can an absolutely continuous function have this property? Prove.

4.10 Show that the sum and product of two absolutely continuous functions is absolutely continuous.

4.11 Show that the sum and product of two functions of bounded variation is of bounded variation.

4.12 Give an example of a continuous function which is not of bounded variation in any interval.

4.13 Show that if $f(x)$ is not of bounded variation in the closed interval $[0, 1]$ there is a $\xi \in [0, 1]$ such that $f(x)$ is not of bounded variation in any open interval which contains ξ.

4.14 Discuss the conditions under which the following equation holds:

$$\int_a^b f(x)g'(x)dx = f(b)g(b) - f(a)g(a) - \int_a^b g(x)f'(x)dx.$$

8.1 Show that $L(t)$ is absolutely continuous if and only if $f(t)$ and $g(t)$ are both absolutely continuous.

References

C. Carathéodory, *Vorlesungen über reelle Funktionen*, Leipzig, 1927, Chap. 10.
H. Hahn and A. Rosenthal, *Set Functions*, Albuquerque, 1948, Chap. 4.
H. Kestelman, *Modern Theories of Integration*, Oxford, 1937, Chap. 7.
H. Lebesgue, *Leçons sur l'intégration et la recherche des fonctions primitives*, Paris, 1928, Chap. 9.
E. J. McShane, *Integration*, Princeton, 1944, Chap. 5.
S. Saks, *Theory of the Integral*, translated by L. C. Young, Warszawa-Lwow, 1937, Chap. 4.

20

Planar Measure and Double Integration

1. *Introduction*

We shall define measure for planar sets. For convenience, we consider subsets of the closed square $0 \leqq x \leqq 1$, $0 \leqq y \leqq 1$, which will be the universal set. The concepts of measurable function, $f(x, y)$, and summable function, as well as

$$\int_0^1 \int_0^1 f(x, y) dx\, dy$$

for a summable function, follow from this definition in much the same way as for the linear case. We show that if $f(x, y)$ is a summable function then the function $\phi_y(x) = f(x, y)$ is summable for almost every y, the function $\psi_x(y) = f(x, y)$ is summable for almost every x, and

$$\int_0^1 \int_0^1 f(x, y) dx\, dy = \int_0^1 \left[\int_0^1 f(x, y) dx \right] dy = \int_0^1 \left[\int_0^1 (fx, y) dy \right] dx.$$

This is known as the Theorem of Fubini.

2. *Definition of measure*

Let I be the unit square $0 \leqq x \leqq 1$, $0 \leqq y \leqq 1$, and let $S \subset I$. Using the notation $l(J)$ for the area of any square J, the exterior measure of S will be defined by the number

$$m_e(S) = \inf \sum_{n=1}^{\infty} l(I_n),$$

where $I_1, I_2, \cdots, I_n, \cdots$ is any sequence of squares whose sides are parallel to the co-ordinate axes which cover S. The interior measure of S is defined by the number

$$m_i(S) = 1 - m_e(C(S)).$$

S is said to be measurable if $m_e(S) = m_i(S)$, and if S is measurable, the measure of S is the number $m(S) = m_e(S) = m_i(S)$.

In defining measure, circles or rectangles may be used as the covering elements instead of squares without changing the value of the exterior measure—hence, measurability and measure—of any set.

The following proposition holds here, the proof being quite similar to that already given for the linear case.

PROPOSITION 1. A planar set S is measurable if and only if, for every $\epsilon > 0$,

$$S = ((\bigcup_{k=1}^{n} I_k) \cup E_1) - E_2,$$

where $I_1, I_2, \cdots, I_n$ are disjoint closed squares with sides parallel to the co-ordinate axes and E_1 and E_2 have exterior measure less than ϵ.

We now state several further properties of planar measurable sets. Again, the proofs, which are different only in minor details from the linear case, are not given.

A planar set G is open if every $x \in G$ is inside a square I such that $I \subset G$; it is closed if it contains all its limit points. It is an easy matter to show that open and closed sets are measurable and that unions and intersections of denumerable numbers of measurable sets are measurable. It follows that all planar Borel sets are measurable and that, just as in the linear case, if sets of measure 0 are neglected they are the only measurable sets. Indeed, if S is measurable, there is a set T of type G_1 and a set R of type F_1 such that $S \subset T$, $R \subset S$, and $m_e(T - S) = 0$, $m_e(S - R) = 0$; and, for every $\epsilon > 0$, there is an open set G and a closed set F such that $S \subset G$, $F \subset S$, and $m_e(G - S) < \epsilon$, $m_e(S - F) < \epsilon$. The proof of these somewhat routine matters is left to the student.

3. *Relation between planar measure and linear measure*

With every planar set S in the unit square we associate a class of linear sets. For every $y \in [0, 1]$ let S_y be the set of values x for which $(x, y) \in S$, and for every $x \in [0; 1]$ let S_x be the set of values of y for which $(x, y) \in S$. We shall show that if S is measurable then S_y is measurable for almost every y and S_x is measurable for almost every x. We then show that the functions $m(S_y)$ and $m(S_x)$ are measurable functions of y and x respectively, and that

$$m(S) = \int_0^1 m(S_y)dy = \int_0^1 m(S_x)dx.$$

On the other hand, using the continuum hypothesis, we show that either S_y can be measurable for every y or S_x measurable for every x but S may still be nonmeasurable.

We need some simple lemmas.

LEMMA 1. If S is a planar set and $m_e(S) < k^2$, then the set of values of y for which $m_e(S_y) > k$ is of exterior measure less than or equal to k.

Proof. $S \subset T$ where T is the union of a finite or denumerable number of closed squares with sides parallel to the co-ordinate axes the sum of whose areas is k^2. The student may show that the set of values of y for which $m(T_y) > k$ is of exterior measure less than k. The lemma follows immediately.

LEMMA 2. If S is a measurable planar set, then, for every $\epsilon > 0$,

$$S_y = ((\bigcup_{k=1}^{n(y)} I_{y,k}) \cup E_y) - E_y',$$

where the $I_{y,k}$ are disjoint closed intervals and $m_e(E_y) < \epsilon$, $m_e(E_y') < \epsilon$ everywhere, except for sets of values of y whose exterior measure is less than ϵ.

Proof. By Proposition 1,

$$S = ((\bigcup_{k=1}^{n} I_k) \cup E) \cup E',$$

where $I_1, I_2, \cdots, I_n$ are disjoint squares and $m(E) < \epsilon^2$, $m(E') < \epsilon^2$. Let

$$\bigcup_{k=1}^{n(y)} I_{y,k} = \bigcup_{k=1}^{n} I_{k,y}$$

for every y. Application of Lemma 1 to the sets E and E' yields Lemma 2.

THEOREM 1. If S is a planar measurable set in the closed square $0 \leqq x \leqq 1$, $0 \leqq y \leqq 1$, then the sets S_y are measurable for almost every y, the sets S_x are measurable for almost every x, the functions $m(S_y)$ and $m(S_x)$ are measurable, and

$$m(S) = \int_0^1 m(S_y)dy = \int_0^1 m(S_x)dx.$$

Proof. By Lemma 2, for every positive integer n there is a set T_n of values of y such that $m_e(C(T_n)) < 1/2^n$ and for every $y \in T_n$,

$$S_y = ((\bigcup_{k=1}^{n(y)} I_k) \cup E_y) - E_y',$$

where the I_k are closed intervals and $m_e(E_y) < 1/n$, $m_e(E_y') < 1/n$. Clearly S_y is measurable if

$$y \in \bigcup_{k=1}^{\infty} \bigcap_{n=k}^{\infty} T_n = T,$$

for then S_y satisfies the condition of Theorem 1, Chapter 13. We show that $m(T) = 1$, thus proving the first part of the theorem.

$$m(T) \geqq m(\bigcap_{n=k}^{\infty} T_n) \geqq 1 - \sum_{n=k}^{\infty} m(C(T_n)) \geqq 1 - \sum_{n=k}^{\infty} \frac{1}{2^n} = 1 - \frac{1}{2^{k-1}}.$$

Since this holds for every k, $m(T) = 1$.

To prove the second part of the theorem we first observe that it holds for the special case where S is the union of a finite number of disjoint squares. We leave this for the student to verify. Now let S be an arbitrary planar measurable set, let $\epsilon > 0$, and let T be the union of a finite number of disjoint squares with sides parallel to the coordinate axes such that $S = (T \cup E) - E'$ where $m(E) < \epsilon$, $m(E') < \epsilon$. Then, by Lemma 2, on a set of values of y of measure greater than $1 - \sqrt{\epsilon}$, $S_y = (T_y \cup E_y) - E_y'$, where $m(E_y) < \sqrt{\epsilon}$, $m(E_y') < \sqrt{\epsilon}$. Then

$$\underline{\int_0^1} m(S_y)dy > \int_0^1 (1 - \sqrt{\epsilon})m(T_y)dy - \sqrt{\epsilon}$$
$$> \int_0^1 m(T_y)dy - 2\sqrt{\epsilon} = m(T) - 2\sqrt{\epsilon},$$

and

$$\overline{\int_0^1} m(S_y)dy < \int_0^1 (1 + \sqrt{\epsilon})m(T_y)dy$$
$$+ \sqrt{\epsilon} < \int_0^1 m(T_y)dy + 2\sqrt{\epsilon} = m(T) + 2\sqrt{\epsilon}.$$

Hence

$$m(T) - 2\sqrt{\epsilon} < \underline{\int_0^1} m(S_y)dy \leqq \overline{\int_0^1} m(S_y)dy < m(T) + 2\sqrt{\epsilon}.$$

On the other hand, $m(T) - \epsilon < m(S) < m(T) + \epsilon$.
It follows that

$$m(S) - \epsilon - 2\sqrt{\epsilon} < \underline{\int_0^1} m(S_y)dy \leqq \overline{\int_0^1} m(S_y)dy < m(S) + \epsilon + 2\sqrt{\epsilon}.$$

Since $\epsilon > 0$ is arbitrary, we have shown that

$$m(S) = \underline{\int_0^1} m(S_y)dy = \overline{\int_0^1} m(S_y)dy.$$

Similarly,

$$m(S) = \underline{\int_0^1} m(S_x)dx = \overline{\int_0^1} m(S_x)dx.$$

We now give a proof of the existence of a nonmeasurable planar set S which contains at most one point on every line parallel to the x-axis or on every line parallel to the y-axis so that either S_y is measurable for every y or S_x for every x.

The proof given in Chapter 12 of the existence of a decomposition of the plane into $\aleph_0$ curves shows this, for the set of points composing one of these curves must be nonmeasurable. For if all were measurable, they would be of measure 0, by Theorem 1. Then the entire plane would be of measure 0.

4. *Measurable and summable functions of two variables*

We consider functions $f(x, y)$ defined on the closed square $0 \leqq x \leqq 1$, $0 \leqq y \leqq 1$. Such a function is said to be measurable if for every real number k the set $E[f(x, y) > k]$ of points for which $f(x, y) > k$ is measurable. In order to define summable functions, we again must define summability first for simple functions. We sketch the procedure. A simple measurable function, $f(x, y) = [a_k, S_k; k = 1, 2, \cdots]$ is summable if the series $\sum_{k=1}^{\infty} a_k \cdot m(S_k)$ converges absolutely. If it does, then

$$\int_0^1 \int_0^1 f(x, y)dx\, dy = \sum_{k=1}^{\infty} a_k m(S_k).$$

For an arbitrary measurable function, $f(x, y)$, associate $f_A(x, y)$ with every net A and the function $f(x, y)$. Again, we have either $f_A(x, y)$ summable for all nets or for no nets so that $f(x, y)$ is said to be summable if $f_A(x, y)$ is summable. For two nets A and B,

$$\left| \int_0^1 \int_0^1 f_A(x, y)dx\, dy - \int_0^1 \int_0^1 f_B(x, y)dx\, dy \right| \leqq N(A) + N(B),$$

so we may define

$$\int_0^1 \int_0^1 f(x, y)dx\, dy = \lim_{n \to \infty} \int_0^1 \int_0^1 f_{A_n}(x, y)dx\, dy,$$

where $\lim_{n \to \infty} N(A_n) = 0$.

5. *Theorem of Fubini*

We are now ready to generalize the theorem of §3 to the integral of summable functions. If $f(x, y)$ is any function defined on $0 \leqq x \leqq 1$, $0 \leqq y \leqq 1$, then for every $y \in [0, 1]$ we have $\phi_y(x) = f(x, y)$ is a function of x; and for every $x \in [0, 1]$, we have $\psi_x(y) = f(x, y)$ is a function of y.

THEOREM 2. If $f(x, y)$ is summable, then $\phi_y(x)$ is summable for almost every y and $\psi_x(y)$ is summable for almost every x. The functions

$$\Phi(y) = \int_0^1 \phi_y(x)dx \quad \text{and} \quad \Psi(x) = \int_0^1 \psi_x(y)dy$$

are then summable functions of y and x, respectively, and

$$\int_0^1\int_0^1 f(x, y)dx\,dy = \int_0^1 \Phi(y)dy = \int_0^1 \Psi(x)dx.$$

Proof. We prove the theorem for nonnegative simple functions first. The theorem, for the case where $f(x, y)$ is the characteristic function of a measurable set S, is merely a restatement of Theorem 1. For then

$$\int_0^1\int_0^1 f(x, y)dx\,dy = m(S), \quad \Phi(y) = \int_0^1 \phi_y(x)dx = m(S_y),$$

and

$$\Psi(x) = \int_0^x \psi_x(y)dy = m(S_x).$$

Now, if $f(x, y)$ is finitely simple, then $f(x, y) = [a_k, S_k; k = 1, 2, \cdots, n]$ and

$$\int_0^1\int_0^1 f(x, y)dx\,dy = \sum_{k=1}^{n} a_k m(S_k) = \sum_{k=1}^{n} a_k \int_0^1 m(S_{k,y})dy$$

$$= \int_0^1 \sum_{k=1}^{n} a_k m(S_{k,y})dy = \int_0^1 dy\left[\int_0^1 \phi_y(x)dx\right],$$

the function $\phi_y(x)$ being summable for almost every y, since it is the sum of a finite number of functions each of which is summable for almost every y. Suppose now that $f(x, y) = [a_k, S_k; k = 1, 2, \cdots]$ is an arbitrary summable simple function. Consider the auxiliary functions $f_n(x, y) = [a_k, S_k; k = 1, 2, \cdots, n]$. Then

$$\int_0^1\int_0^1 f(x, y)dx\,dy = \lim_{n\to\infty} \int_0^1\int_0^1 f_n(x, y)dx\,dy.$$

Let $\phi_y^{(n)}(x) = f_n(x, y)$ for every $y \in [0, 1]$. Then

$$\Phi_n(y) = \int_0^1 \phi_y^{(n)}(x)dx < \infty$$

for almost all y, $\Phi_n(y)$ is a summable function, and

$$\int_0^1 \Phi_n(y)dy = \int_0^1\int_0^1 f_n(x, y)dx\,dy,$$

so that

$$\lim_{n\to\infty} \int_0^1 \Phi_n(y)dy = \int_0^1\int_0^1 f(x, y)dx\,dy.$$

Since

$$\int_0^1\int_0^1 f_n(x, y)dx\,dy \leqq \int_0^1\int_0^1 f(x, y)dx\,dy,$$

the sequence

$$\left\{\int_0^1 \Phi_n(y)dy\right\}$$

is bounded and nondecreasing, so that $\lim_{n\to\infty} \Phi_n(y)$ is summable. But $\phi_y(x) = \lim_{n\to\infty} \phi_y^{(n)}(x)$ for every y, so that

$$\Phi(y) = \int_0^1 \phi_y(x)dx = \lim_{n\to\infty} \int_0^1 \phi_y^{(n)}(x)dx = \lim_{n\to\infty} \Phi_n(y).$$

Hence $\Phi(y)$ is summable and

$$\int_0^1 \Phi(y)dy = \lim_{n\to\infty} \int_0^1 \Phi_n(y)dy = \int_0^1 \int_0^1 f(x, y)dx\, dy.$$

It is now an easy matter to prove the theorem for the arbitrary nonnegative summable function $f(x, y)$. For if A is any net, then since $f_A(x, y)$ is summable, the function $\phi_{y,A}(x) = f_A(x, y)$ is summable for almost every y and

$$\left|\int_0^1 \phi_y(x)dx - \int_0^1 \phi_{y,A}(x)dx\right| \leqq N(A).$$

Moreover,

$$\left|\int_0^1 \int_0^1 f(x, y)dx\, dy - \int_0^1 \int_0^1 f_A(x, y)dx\, dy\right| \leqq N(A).$$

But

$$\int_0^1 \int_0^1 f_A(x, y)dx\, dy = \int_0^1 \left[\int_0^1 \phi_{y,A}(x)dx\right]dy.$$

Hence

$$\left|\int_0^1 \int_0^1 f(x, y)dx\, dy - \int_0^1 \left[\int_0^1 \phi_y(x)dx\right]dy\right|$$

$$\leqq \left|\int_0^1 \int_0^1 f(x, y)dx\, dy - \int_0^1 \int_0^1 f_A(x, y)dx\, dy\right|$$

$$+ \left|\int_0^1 \int_0^1 f_A(x, y)dx\, dy - \int_0^1 \left[\int_0^1 \phi_{y,A}(x)dx\right]dy\right|$$

$$+ \int_0^1 \left[\int_0^1 |\phi_y(x) - \phi_{y,A}(x)|dx\right]dy \leqq 2N(A).$$

Since $N(A)$ can be arbitrarily near to zero, we have

$$\int_0^1 \int_0^1 f(x, y)dx\, dy = \int_0^1 \left[\int_0^1 \phi_y(x)dx\right]dy.$$

It now follows easily from the fact that every summable function is the difference between two nonnegative summable functions that the theorem holds for all summable functions. We leave the proof of this to the student.

The proof that

$$\int_0^1 \int_0^1 f(x, y)dx\, dy = \int_0^1 \left[\int_0^1 \psi_x(y)dy\right]dx$$

is quite similar.

Exercises

2.1 Show that the exterior measure of every planar set is the same if circles are used as the covering elements instead of squares.

2.2 Show that a planar set S is measurable if and only if for every $\epsilon > 0$,

$$S = \left(\bigcup_{k=1}^{n} I_k\right) \cup E_1 - E_2,$$

where $I_1, I_2, \cdots, I_n$ are closed squares with sides parallel to the co-ordinate axes and E_1 and E_2 have exterior measure less than ϵ.

2.3 Show that every planar closed set is measurable.

2.4 Show that S is measurable if and only if there is a set $T \subset S$ of type F_1 such that $m_e(S - T) = 0$.

3.1 If T is the union of a denumerable number of closed squares whose sides are parallel to the co-ordinate axes, show that T_y is measurable for every y and

$$m(T) = \int_0^1 m(T_y)dy.$$

3.2 For the set T of Exercise 3.1, show that if $m(T) < k^2$ then the set of values of y for which $m(T_y) > k$ is of exterior measure less than k.

4.1 Define measure for unbounded planar sets.

4.2 Define summability and the Lebesgue integral for functions on an unbounded planar set of finite or infinite measure.

4.3 For a nonnegative function $f(x)$ defined on $[0, 1]$ consider the ordinate set $E = E[(x, y) \mid x \in [0, 1], y \leq f(x)]$. Show that $f(x)$ is summable if and only if E is measurable and of finite measure, and if $f(x)$ is summable, that

$$\int_0^1 f(x)dx = m(E).$$

4.4 Define summability for a nonnegative function defined on the whole (x, y)-plane.

4.5 Show that $f(x, y) = e^{-(x^2+y^2)}$ is summable.

4.6 Show that if $|f(x, y)|$ is summable, then $f(x, y)$ is a summable function of x for almost every y, and

$$\int_{-\infty}^{\infty}\int_{-\infty}^{\infty} f(x, y)dx\, dy = \int_{-\infty}^{\infty} dy \int_{-\infty}^{\infty} f(x, y)dx.$$

Show that this means that order of integration may be interchanged.

4.7 Show that the unit square $(0 \leqq x \leqq 1, 0 \leqq y \leqq 1)$ may be mapped into the unit line segment $0 \leqq x \leqq y$ in such a way that measurable sets are taken into measurable sets and measure is preserved.

References

C. Carathéodory, *Vorlesungen über reelle Funktionen*, Leipzig, 1927, Chap. 11.
H. Hahn and A. Rosenthal, *Set Functions*, Albuquerque, 1948, Chap. 4.
P. R. Halmos, *Measure Theory*, New York, 1950, Chap. 7.
E. J. McShane, *Integration*, Princeton, 1944, Chap. 10.
S. Saks, *Theory of the Integral*, translated by L. C. Young, Warszawa-Lwow, 1937, Chap. 3.

Index

359

306 7 2411